Budgeting and Financial Management for Nonprofit Organizations

Second Edition

Budgeting and Financial Management for Nonprofit Organizations

Using Money to Drive Mission Success

Second Edition

Lynne A. Weikart
James Madison University

Greg G. Chen
Baruch College

Long Grove, Illinois

For information about this book, contact:
Waveland Press, Inc.
4180 IL Route 83, Suite 101
Long Grove, IL 60047-9580
(847) 634-0081
info@waveland.com
www.waveland.com

Copyright © 2022 by Lynne A. Weikart and Greg G. Chen

10-digit ISBN 1-4786-4619-5
13-digit ISBN 978-1-4786-4619-8

All rights reserved. No part of this book may be reproduced, stored in a retrieval system, or transmitted in any form or by any means without permission in writing from the publisher.

Printed in the United States of America

7   6   5   4   3   2   1

Contents

Preface xv
About the Authors xviii

PART I
Introduction

1 *An Introduction to Nonprofits: Mission and Money* 3
Definition of a Nonprofit 4
Nonprofit Origins and Growth 5
   The Modern Nonprofit Structure 5
   The Identification of Nonprofits as the Third Sector 6
Size and Scope of the Nonprofit World 7
   Nonprofit Structure 8
   Differences between the Business and Nonprofit Worlds 10
Setting Financial Policies 11
The Link between Mission and Money 12
The Push for Accountability:
  Watchdog Organizations and Their Standards 13
   The Tension between Serving Clients and Protecting the Nonprofit 15
Conclusion 15
KEY TERMS 16 ■ DISCUSSION QUESTIONS 16 ■
SUGGESTED READINGS 16 ■ ASSIGNMENTS 17 ■ NOTES 18

Part II
Planning and Budgeting

2 Budgeting as Part of the Planning Process   21

    Budgeting Vocabulary   22
    The Link between Mission and Budgeting   22
    Roles of the Board, Executive Director, and Staff   23
    The Tools of Budgeting   24
        Budgeting as a Planning Tool   24
        Budgeting as a Management Tool   26
        Budgeting as a Communications Tool   27
    Operating and Capital Budgets   28
        Two Sides of a Coin: Revenues and Expenses   28
        Link between Operating and Capital Budgets   30
    Formatting Budgets: Line-Item Budgets,
      Program Budgets, and Performance Budgets   30
        Line-Item Budgets   31
        Program Budgets   31
        Performance Budgeting or Results-Based Budgeting   32
        Cutbacks and Performance-Based Budgeting   34
    The Budget Process as a Cycle   34
        The Preparation Stage   35
        The Approval Stage   38
        The Execution Stage   39
        Ending the Fiscal Year:
          The Auditing and Reporting Stage   43
        Periodic Budget Reviews and Revisions   44
    Applying Indirect Costs for a New Program   45
    Cutback Budgeting   46
    Conclusion   47
    KEY TERMS 47 ■ DISCUSSION QUESTIONS 48
    SUGGESTED READINGS 48 ■ CASE STUDY 48
    ASSIGNMENTS 52 ■ NOTES 54

3 Liquidity and Managing Cash Flow   57

    Liquidity   58
        Timing of Cash Flows and Undercapitalization   59
        Restricted Monies   59
        Liquidity Targets   59

Cash and Cash-Flow Management 60
   Cash Budget 60
   Examples of Cash-Flow Management
     and Cash-Flow Budget 60
   Working through a Cash-Flow Analysis 63
   Cash-Flow Budgeting in Practice 65
   Updating the Cash Budget with Actuals 66
Cash-Flow Strategies 66
   What Do We Do When We Run Out of Cash? 68
   What Do We Do When We Have
     Too Much Short-Term Cash? 69
Conclusion 71
KEY TERMS 72 ■ DISCUSSION QUESTIONS 72
SUGGESTED READINGS 72 ■ CASE STUDY 72
ASSIGNMENTS 73 ■ NOTES 74

4 *Analyzing Costs*   75

Direct Costs and Indirect Costs 76
   Estimating Direct and Indirect Costs 77
Costing Services and Allocating Costs 78
   Direct Method to Allocate Costs 78
   Step-Down Method to Allocate Costs 79
   Working through the Step-Down Method 79
Fixed, Variable, and Step Costs 81
Average Costs and Marginal Costs 83
   Examples of Average and Marginal Costs 83
Opportunity Costs and Accounting Costs 85
   Opportunity Costs 85
   Accounting Costs 85
   A Short Study in Determining Program Costs 86
Relevant Costs in Financial Decision Making 86
   Extension of Existing Services: Marginal Analysis 87
   Potential New Programs or Services: Break-Even Analysis 87
Conclusion 88
KEY TERMS 88 ■ DISCUSSION QUESTIONS 89
SUGGESTED READINGS 89 ■ CASE STUDY 89
ASSIGNMENTS 90 ■ NOTES 91

Part III
Financial Analysis in Nonprofit Organizations

5 Basic Principles of Accounting and Reporting Requirements 95

Accounting Standards Structure 96
Principles of Accounting 97
   The Four Key Assumptions 98
   The Four Basic Principles 98
   The Four Basic Constraints 99
   Importance of Accounting Principles 100
Basis of Accounting 100
   Cash Accounting 101
   Accrual Accounting 101
   Modified Accrual Accounting Method 102
   Differences of Accounting Methods 102
Fund Accounting 102
   Unrestricted Net Assets 103
   Restricted Net Assets 103
   Rules Concerning Volunteers 104
Introduction to Financial Statements 104
   Balance Sheet or Statement of Financial Position 105
   Income Statement or Statement of Activities 106
   Statement of Cash Flow 106
   Connections among Financial Statements 107
   Statement of Functional Expenses 107
The Accounting Cycle 108
Reporting Requirements 109
   National-Level Requirements 109
   State-Level Requirements 111
The Task of Financial Responsibility 111
Conclusion 112
KEY TERMS 112 ■ DISCUSSION QUESTIONS 112
SUGGESTED READINGS 113 ■ CASE STUDY 113
ASSIGNMENTS 114 ■ NOTES 115

6 Understanding Financial Statements 117

The Statement of Financial Position (Balance Sheet) 118
Assets 120
   Current Assets 120
   Long-Term Assets 121

Liabilities 123
  Current Liabilities 123
  Long-Term Liabilities 124
Net Assets (Fund Balance) 124
  Unrestricted Net Assets 125
  Restricted Net Assets 125
Nonprofit Financial Statements:
  The Statement of Activities (Income Statement) 125
  Revenues 126
Relationship between the Statement of Financial Position
  and the Statement of Activities 128
Cash-Flow Statement 132
Statement of Functional Expenses 133
Conclusion 134
KEY TERMS 134 ■ DISCUSSION QUESTIONS 134
SUGGESTED READINGS 135 ■ ASSIGNMENTS 135 ■ NOTES 136

7 *Financial Analysis* 137

Financial Resources 138
  Liquidity 138
  Long-Term Solvency 138
  Efficiency 139
  Profitability 139
  Matching 139
  Revenue Diversification 140
Conducting Ratio Analysis 140
  Ratios and Liquidity 141
  Ratios and Long-Term Solvency 142
  Ratios and Efficiency 143
  Ratios and Profitability 146
Matching 147
Diversification 148
  Common Size Ratio 148
  Contributions Ratio 149
  Program Services Expense Ratio 150
Red Flags 150
Financial Health of the ABC Nonprofit Corporation 151
Ratios and Rating Agencies 151
Conclusion 152
KEY TERMS 152 ■ DISCUSSION QUESTIONS 152
SUGGESTED READINGS 153 ■ CASE STUDY 153
ASSIGNMENTS 155 ■ NOTES 155

Part IV
Financial Management

8 *Understanding Revenues*   **159**

Theoretical Development of
  Finance for Nonprofits: The Benefits Theory   160
  Types of Benefits   161
  Matching Benefits and Revenues   162
Existing Sources of Revenue   162
  Donations   163
  Government Grants and Payment of Fees
    for Services and Goods   166
  Earned Revenues   166
Nonprofit Revenue Strategies   167
  Funding Models of Large Nonprofits:
    The Benefits Theory in Practice   167
  Diversification: Revenue Strategies
    and Risk Management   171
  Advantages and Disadvantages of
    Different Funding Sources   171
Conclusion   173
KEY TERMS 173   ■   DISCUSSION QUESTIONS 174
SUGGESTED READINGS 174   ■   CASE STUDY 174
ASSIGNMENTS 175   ■   NOTES 176

9 *Performance Measurement in Financial Management*   **177**

Purpose of Performance Measurement   178
  Planning Programs and Securing Funding   178
  Linking Performance to Budgets   179
Key Elements in Performance Measurement Systems   179
  Outcomes as Compared to Outputs   181
  Efficiency as Compared to Effectiveness   181
  Application of Performance Measurement   182
Development of Performance Measurement Systems   182
  The Urban Institute's Steps to Develop a
    Performance Measurement System   183
  The Balanced Scorecard System   184
  The Challenges of Selecting
    Performance Measures/Indicators   185

Data Collection 186
   Relationship between Performance Measurement
     and Program Evaluation 186

Conclusion 188

KEY TERMS 188 ■ DISCUSSION QUESTIONS 188
SUGGESTED READINGS 189 ■ CASE STUDY 189
ASSIGNMENTS 190 ■ NOTES 191

10 *Time Value of Money and Cost-Benefit Analysis* 193

The Time Value of Money 194
   Calculating Future Value 195
   Calculating Present Value 197
   Net Present Value: A Decision Criterion 202

Introduction to Cost-Benefit Analysis 204
   Conceptual Framework of Cost-Benefit Analysis 204
   Steps in Conducting Cost-Benefit Analysis 205

Conclusion 209

KEY TERMS 209 ■ DISCUSSION QUESTIONS 210
SUGGESTED READINGS 210 ■ CASE STUDY 210
ASSIGNMENTS 211 ■ NOTES 212

11 *Capital Budgeting and Financing* 213

Capital Budgeting and Capital Assets 214

The Relationship between
  Capital Budgets and Operating Budgets 214
   Accepting or Not Accepting a
     Donated Capital Asset: An Example 215

Capital Budgeting Process 216
   Life-Cycle Costing 216

Capital Financing: Pay-as-You-Go and Debt Financing 219

Debt Financing: Bank Loans and Bond Issuance 220
   Securing a Bank Loan 220
   Issuing Bonds 221

Payment Schedules 223
   Level Debt Service Payments 223
   Level Principal Payments 224

Capital Budget Policy and Debt Policy 226

Conclusion 228

KEY TERMS 228 ■ DISCUSSION QUESTIONS 228
SUGGESTED READINGS 229 ■ CASE STUDY 229
ASSIGNMENTS 230 ■ NOTES 230

12 *Investment Strategies*   231

Investment Policies and Guidelines   232
     Role and Responsibilities of the Board   232
     Investment Policy Statement   233

Short-Term Investment Strategy   233
     Issues in Short-Term Investment   234
     Investment Objectives: Safety, Liquidity, and Yield   234
     Default and Market Risks   234
     Key Short-Term Investment Vehicles   236

Long-Term Investment Strategy   239
     Key Issues in Endowment Investment:
       Spending Policy   239
     Key Issues in Endowment Investment:
       Investment Policy   242
     Other Key Investment Practices and Considerations   246
     Key Long-Term Investment Vehicles   247

Conclusion   249

KEY TERMS 250 ■ DISCUSSION QUESTIONS 250
SUGGESTED READINGS 250 ■ CASE STUDY 251
ASSIGNMENTS 251 ■ NOTES 252

13 *Internal Controls*   253

Defining Internal Controls   254

The Internal Control System   254
     Safeguarding Assets   255
     Controlling Personnel and Nonpersonnel Services   256
     Setting Audit Standards   257

Independent Sector and Accountability   258
     The Sarbanes–Oxley Act   261

Examples of Fraud   262
     Controlling Cash and Its Equivalents and
       Reconciliation of Bank Accounts   262
     Accessing Cash: Forging Signatures
       and Controlling Payroll   263
     Nonprofits as Victims   263
     Internal Control Issues   263

Conclusion   264

KEY TERMS 264 ■ DISCUSSION QUESTIONS 264
SUGGESTED READINGS 264 ■ ASSIGNMENTS 265 ■ NOTES 266

Part V
New Directions

14 *Adapting to Turbulent Times* 269

    The Effects of the 2008 Economic Crisis   270

    The Effects of the Covid-19 Pandemic   271

    Assessing Financial Risks   272
        Mitigating Risk: Increasing Revenues   273
        Mitigating Risk: Cutting Costs   273
        Mitigating Risk: Collaborations   274
        Mitigating Risk: Changing the Structure   275

    The Growth of Nonprofit Capital Intermediaries   277
        Venture Philanthropy   277
        Nonprofit Loan Funds   278

    The Role of Government in Promoting Innovation   278
        The Federal Level   279
        State Governments   279
        Local Governments   280
        Universities   281

    The Role of Foundations in Promoting Social Enterprise   281

    The Fourth Sector of Social Enterprise   282
        The Yunus Centre   283

    Program-Related Investments and the New L3Cs   283
        The Rise of the B Corporation   285

    Conclusion   286

    KEY TERMS 287   ■   DISCUSSION QUESTIONS 287
    SUGGESTED READINGS 287   ■   ASSIGNMENT 288   ■   NOTES 288

Appendix A: IRS Form 990,
  Return of Organization Exempt From Income Tax   291

Appendix B: Debits and Credits   305

Appendix C: A Sample Investment Policy Statement   309

Glossary   315

Index   323

Preface

When we got together with the idea to write *Budgeting and Financial Management for Nonprofits,* we considered our past experiences and current thinking and models. We have taught budgeting and financial management for decades and are highly experienced in the widely ranging field of nonprofit management, among us having worked as a nonprofit's executive director a and a nonprofit consultant. The real-life struggles and successes of nonprofit management that we have experienced, along with the long-range perspective we have gained from the study of nonprofits' history and our engagement in the most recent developments in nonprofit strategy and structure, led us to conclude that there was only one theme possible for this book: the link between nonprofit mission and money.

We have seen over the course of our careers that how effectively a nonprofit achieves its mission is intrinsically tied to its finances. Money drives mission. Donations fund programs that provide public services, aiding mission success. Well-managed budgets and investments can spur long-term growth and achievement. Alternatively, financial mismanagement can damage and even destroy nonprofit organizations. A board of directors making decisions based on data the members do not fully understand can create a host of debilitating problems. We feel that it is vitally important that students understand how to use the tools of budgeting and financial management to fulfill the missions of their nonprofits and how these tools can be used to drive decision making. The best way to do this is to present the tools to students in as practical and realistic a way as possible.

This volume is designed to prepare the next generation of nonprofit managers. It is intended to provide the financial grounding that a student will need to become a successful nonprofit manager. The organizational mission cannot be achieved unless the resources are available to fund the mission and the manager understands how to apply those resources. Our goal is to enable nonprofit managers to understand and use the financial tools available to create stable financial foundations for their nonprofits and to develop financial strategies that will allow them to weather economic storms and ultimately thrive in both expanding and contracting economies. In this book we provide the fundamentals of financial tools for nonprofit managers and describe the future of nonprofit strategies, encouraging managers to be flexible, creative, and innovative, inspired by the current and coming models of nonprofit organization and funding.

No company, profit or nonprofit, can thrive without sound financial strategy. Nonprofit managers come from a variety of backgrounds, and some tend to avoid the important issues of accounting and financial management out of fear. This book presents financial concepts in a straightforward, comprehensible format, grounded in real examples, readily accessible to students from any background.

Structure and Organization of the Book

Each chapter begins with a list of learning objectives and an introduction that lay out the chapter's goals. Abundant tables and figures throughout the chapters ensure that students gain familiarity with accounting data and financial statements. Examples are integrated where they are most illustrative of the discussion and most effective for students to learn important points in budgeting and financial management.

Case studies, discussion questions, and assignments at the end of the chapters allow students to test their knowledge of what they have read and to build their skills. The case studies provide detailed information on real or theoretical situations and ask students to participate—for instance, by examining a nonprofit's budget to determine revenues and program costs to make fiscal year comparisons, by generating appropriate data to aid decision makers in determining whether to launch a new program, by following the steps toward creating a balanced budget, or by completing a cost-benefit analysis. Assignments include activities such as developing a cash budget, applying the direct allocation method, recording transactions, and creating a statement of financial position.

Key terms appear in bold in the text and are listed at the end of the chapters, and lists of suggested readings refer students to sources for more information. Three appendixes provide complementary information, such as a sample Form 990, and the glossary defines all of the key terms.

The book is divided into five parts: a short introduction followed by sections on planning and budgeting, financial analysis, financial management, and new directions. The introduction links the mission of the nonprofit to its resources and provides the framework for the skill building that follows. It traces the growth of nonprofits and describes the current fiscal and governance structures. It explains the three sectors: government, business, and nonprofit. The difference between business and nonprofits is analyzed in terms of governing authority, funding, and structure.

The section on planning and budgeting begins with discussion of the foundations of budgeting and then addresses the importance of liquidity, managing cash flow, and analyzing costs. The chapters in this section are comprehensive and practical, explaining by example as well as by theory. Chapter 3, on liquidity and cash flow, is extremely important for nonprofit managers. The cost allocation discussed in Chapter 4, on analyzing costs, is key to developing sound budgets.

The third section, which addresses financial analysis in nonprofit organizations, provides a useful guide to nonprofit accounting that allows students to understand financial analysis. It ends with a practical explanation of financial tools every nonprofit manager needs to understand and use. The chapters in this section explain the unique accounting structure used by nonprofits and teach students how to apply ratio analysis to further their understanding of nonprofits. It is critical for nonfinancial managers to be able to use the power of accounting data to understand how a nonprofit's resources are being used. With this understanding, these decision makers will have powerful financial information to support the organization's mission.

The fourth section, on financial management, tackles the major topics of managing nonprofits through revenue diversification, performance measurement, cost-benefit analysis, capital budgeting, investment strategies, and internal controls. This section offers strategies for dealing with a constricting economic environment and reduced donor revenues. Each chapter tackles a pressing issue in nonprofit financial management. Chapter 12, on investment strategies, provides an important introduction to this topic, which may seem like a distant fantasy for the start-up nonprofit manager. An understanding of investment strategies should be part of the toolkit and vocabulary of the manager of every nonprofit with long-term mission goals and the intent to establish long-term fiscal stability to achieve those goals.

The final section describes the most current developments in nonprofit organization and strategy, focusing on the growth in entrepreneurial financial strategies that are propelling nonprofits into the "fourth sector." The fourth sector is a merging of the best of the business world with the nonprofit mission through the use of entrepreneurial skills. This merging allows nonprofits to keep their missions in the forefront while raising revenues in entrepreneurial organizational structures.

Acknowledgments

We have so many to acknowledge and appreciate. We would like to thank a host of people who have lent us their expertise and read drafts of parts of this book: Richard Buery, president and chief executive officer of the Children's Aid Society; Dall Forsythe, vice president of finance for Atlantic Philanthropies; Professor Jack Krauskopf of Baruch College School of Public Affairs; Professor Fred Lane, recently retired from Baruch College School of Public Affairs; Stan Schneider, president of Metis Associates; Donna Tapper, managing senior associate, research and evaluation, with Metis Associates; Lawrence Schweinhart, president of the HighScope Foundation; and Stacie H. Reid, my favorite CPA. We are indebted to Liz Gewirtzman for the many conversations we have had about ideas in this book. We are indebted to our students who suffered through drafts of this book and helped enrich and shape the book through their suggestions and criticisms. Lastly, we are indebted to Laura Gentile, Esq., for the many times she has provided direction and counsel.

About the Authors

Lynne A. Weikart retired as an associate professor at Baruch College School of Public Affairs. She has a PhD in political science from Columbia University, and she is currently a practitioner in residence at James Madison University, where she teaches budgeting and financial management. She has had extensive financial management experience in the governmental and nonprofit sectors. Before her academic career, she held several high-level government positions, including budget director of the Division of Special Education in New York City (NYC) public schools and executive deputy commissioner of the New York State Division of Human Rights. For several years, she also served as the executive director of a nonprofit, City Project, which was a progressive fiscal think tank that focused on reforming NYC's resource allocation patterns. Professor Weikart's current research focuses on resource allocation in urban areas as well as on urban finance, and she has published many articles on these subjects. In addition, she has published three books: she is coauthor of *Budget Tools: Financial Methods in the Public Sector*, Second Edition (CQ Press, 2015) and author of *Follow the Money: Who Controls New York City Mayors?* (State University of New York Press, 2009). Her new book, *Mayor Michael Bloomberg: Politics, Policy, and the Limits of Power*, is to be published in the summer of 2021 (Cornell University Press). She won the Luther Gulick Award for Outstanding Academic from the New York Metropolitan Chapter of the American Society for Public Administration in 2001.

Greg G. Chen, associate professor at Baruch College School of Public Affairs, has a PhD in public administration from the University of Victoria in British Columbia, Canada. He also has an MA in educational administration from the University of Victoria and an MEng degree in metallurgical engineering from the University of Science and Technology Beijing, China. He was a manager of the budgeting and financial reporting department in the Ministry of Finance, and budget manager and senior policy adviser for the Crown Agencies Secretariat, a central agency overseeing public authorities of the Premier's Office of British Columbia, Canada, before taking his professorship in the United States. He had previously been an associate dean in the College of WISCO in China. Professor Chen conducts research and publishes papers in the areas of budgeting and financial management for nonprofit organizations and governments, program evaluation and cost-benefit analysis of diverse public and nonprofit organizations and programs, and comparisons of the health care systems and finance in Canada, the United States, and China. His research led to the article "Do Meeting Standards Affect Charitable Giving?", which appeared in *Nonprofit Management and Leadership* (vol. 19, no. 3, 2009). He is coauthor of *Budget Tools: Financial Methods in the Public Sector* (CQ Press, 2009).

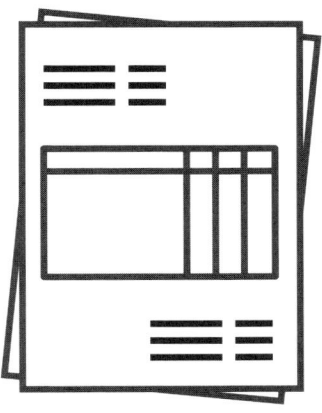

Part I

Introduction

An Introduction to Nonprofits
Mission and Money

> Sustaining the mission of an organization is the primary task of nonprofit leadership.
>
> —Allen J. Proctor[1]

LEARNING OBJECTIVES

The learning objectives for this chapter are as follows:
- Defining nonprofits
- Understanding the origins of nonprofits
- Learning about the size and scope of the nonprofit sector
- Distinguishing between for-profits and nonprofits
- Understanding the necessity for financial policies
- Recognizing the link between mission and money
- Understanding the role of watchdog organizations

*T*he financial world of nonprofits—the structure, process, policies, and practices of budgeting, financial analysis, and financial management—is intrinsically tied to the missions of those organizations. Decision makers in nonprofits must understand the finances of their organizations and how their resources can be used to fulfill the organizations' missions. This book is designed to help you, the student of the nonprofit sector who wishes to work in that sector, to develop the confidence to question and critique the work of a nonprofit's financial officer; it will also serve as a resource when you are stymied about next steps for your nonprofit. Should you expand? Cut back? Reduce every department by 10% or eliminate a program? This volume will enable you to develop the tools to answer those questions.

The twenty-first century has begun with great political and economic turmoil, and nonprofit organizations, as always, must navigate this turmoil and the resultant roadblocks on their paths to mission success. In many ways much of the twentieth century was an easier time for nonprofits, a time when they demonstrated enormous growth and enjoyed generous government resources for many social service programs. Now, they face a challenging and changing future. It is essential that the current and future nonprofit leadership gain the fundamental and advanced skills necessary to navigate the challenges and changes ahead.

Definition of a Nonprofit

A nonprofit is a corporation that is a legal entity separate from its owners. Like all corporations in the United States, a nonprofit registers in the state in which it does business. Although corporations, including nonprofit corporations, are creatures of state law, only the Internal Revenue Service (IRS) can confer the tax benefits of the federal tax code. Thus, it is to the IRS that we refer when distinguishing which corporations are nonprofits. The IRS distinguishes a **nonprofit corporation** from a for-profit corporation by the fact that a nonprofit may not distribute its income to those who control it. The income is to be used solely for the mission of the nonprofit. The IRS recognizes many kinds of nonprofits, and these organizations need not pay federal income tax. States may tax nonprofits, but most choose not to. The IRS identifies tax-exempt nonprofit organizations as 501(c)s, of which there are 27 different categories (for more information, see irs.gov/charities-and-nonprofits). Of these 27, only organizations in one of them—the 501(c)3s—are the traditional nonprofits most of us think of, organizations that include public charities and private foundations. Donors receive federal tax deductions for their contributions to only this particular type of 501(c). The IRS also requires that nonprofits not confer improper benefits on anyone and that they refrain from campaigning for or against political candidates. A small amount of lobbying is permitted. Another good source for information on the IRS rules concerning nonprofits is the Council on Foundations (cof.org), a nonprofit association of grant-making foundations and corporations.

Nonprofits can be divided into three groups: public charities, private foundations, and other nonprofit organizations. Public charities and private foundations are 501(c)3s. Other nonprofit organizations are classified as 501(c)1s through 501(c)27s. The 501(c)3 **public charities** are the bulk of the 1.6 million nonprofits operating in the United States and include charities related to the arts, education, health care, and other human services. A **private foundation** is different from a public charity. It is an individual, family, or corporation that is endowed (funded) as a nonprofit to provide support to public charities. Private foundations are subject to federal taxes. The "other" category includes thousands of social and recreational clubs, trade associations, labor unions, veterans' associations, and advocacy organizations. These other 501(c)s are tax exempt, but donors do not receive tax deductions for any contributions made to them. They represent organizations such as civic organizations and business leagues. Religious organizations are not required to register with the IRS, although many do.

The Council on Foundations provides clarification of the differences in tax treatment between public charities and other nonprofits. The National Football League (NFL) and a soup kitchen, for example, are both nonprofits and are exempted from federal income tax, but of the two, only the soup kitchen is a charity that can receive tax-deductible charitable contributions and also is exempt from property tax and sales tax. Trade associations, such as the NFL, and other noncharitable nonprofits, are unlikely to be exempt from either the property tax or the sales tax, and financial contributions to the NFL are not tax deductible.[2]

Nonprofit Origins and Growth

The kinds of nonprofits that exist in the United States today have a history more than 400 years old. The forerunner of today's U.S. nonprofit institutions was the Statute of Charitable Uses, which was created in England in 1602. Under this statute, for the first time in England, property could be set aside for charitable purposes. When English settlers came to America, they brought English law with them, and along came the charities. As in England, most early American towns had systems to aid the destitute, usually involving a combination of taxes and private charity. Also as in England, organizations rose up to help the poor, funded by public taxes and private contributions. For example, in the early 1800s, the New York State Legislature awarded $750 to the Society for the Relief of Poor Widows with Small Children.[3]

The Modern Nonprofit Structure

In the early nineteenth century, the U.S. Supreme Court established the right of private nonprofit organizations to be free of unreasonable influence from the political sector. In 1816, attorney Daniel Webster and Chief Justice John Marshall helped develop the modern nonprofit structure. Webster, relying on Article I, Section 10 of the U.S. Constitution (which prohibits states from interfering with the obligation of contracts), defended New Hampshire's Dartmouth College Board of Trustees' right to independence from the New Hampshire governor and state legislature, which had sought to replace the trustees with their own choices. Chief Justice Marshall agreed with Webster, explaining, "If charitable gifts and charitable institutions were subject to the perpetual threat of legislative interference, no sensible person would be willing to make donations for charitable, educational, or religious purposes."[4]

Although Marshall declared that states could not interfere with citizens forming voluntary associations, states retained the right to regulate nonprofits. In addition, the federal government maintained a powerful gatekeeping role in determining, through the IRS, which organizations could become charitable organizations. The IRS further required nonprofits to file annual financial statements. Often, federal statutes, such as antidiscrimination laws, applied to nonprofits as well.

Important to the growth of the modern nonprofit was the protection of trustees created by the "**prudent man rule**." In 1830, Massachusetts Supreme Court Justice Samuel Putnam, in *Harvard College v. Amory*, rejected an attempt to hold trustees personally responsible for the loss of investment capital in a stock (in the absence of mismanagement):[5]

> Trustees are justly and uniformly considered favorably, and it is of great importance to bereaved families and orphans, that they should not be held to make good, losses in the depreciation of stocks or the failure of the capital itself, which they held in trust, provided they conduct themselves honestly and discreetly and carefully, according to the existing circumstances, in the discharge of their trusts. If this were held otherwise, no prudent man would run the hazard of losses which might happen without any neglect or breach of good faith.[6]

Trustees had to exercise discretion, but they could not be held personally responsible for losses caused by fluctuations of the market. The so-called prudent man rule became the basis of the Uniform Prudent Investor Act (UPIA). In 1992, this act was created by the American Law Institute and was endorsed by the National Conference of Commissioners on Uniform State Laws in 1995 and supported by 44 states. Under the UPIA, personal immunity for the loss of investment capital was broadened to include the entire portfolio of stocks and not simply one or two stocks. This became known as the **prudent investor rule**.

The Identification of Nonprofits as the Third Sector

Nonprofits grew enormously in the twentieth century. The income tax imposed in the early part of the century (1913) created incentives for charitable donations as an income tax deduction, which was instituted a few years later (1917). The Great Depression, which began in 1929, proved too much for the world of private charities and local government. The federal government stepped in, and many people believed that the government's involvement in providing aid to the poor would end nonprofit work. As Friedman and McGarvie note, "Philanthropists and their organizations, especially the new foundations, resisted the expansion of federal authority."[7] But they need not have worried. Nonprofits grew in size and scope during the twentieth century and worked closely with federal and state governments.

In the 1950s and 1960s, the U.S. Congress sought more power over the growing nonprofit sector. The Revenue Act of 1950 imposed a tax on the unrelated business income of many charities. Congress passed the Tax Reform Act in 1969, which divided all nonprofit organizations categorized as 501(c)3s into public charities and private foundations, and then proceeded to impose a special tax on private foundations. In general, the Tax Reform Act of 1969 imposed more regulation on the nonprofit sector. According to Salamon and Flaherty:

> Because of a variety of perceived abuses among private foundations, however, for tax purposes the U.S. Congress established a separate definition of foundations and subjected them to payout and excise tax requirements as well as additional regulations and reporting requirements in order to ensure that their funds were indeed devoted to public, rather than private, purposes.[8]

The 1970s were a momentous time for the nonprofit sector. In 1973, John D. Rockefeller III initiated and funded the Commission on Private Philanthropy and Public Needs (1973–1977). Known as the Filer Commission for its chair, prominent businessman John H. Filer, it established "a new conceptual framework of American society, a framework that added a 'third sector' of voluntary giving and voluntary service alongside the first sector of government and the second sector of the private economic marketplace."[9] The commission produced five volumes of specialized studies by scholars and led to the creation of the first of many university centers devoted to the study of the nonprofit sector. The Filer Commission named the nonprofit world the **third sector**, and through its recommendations came greater interest in this new sector as research about it began in earnest. This was a major turning point for nonprofits. Now, in the twenty-first century, we face another turning point as the Covid-19 pandemic and subsequent governmental cutbacks have placed nonprofits in a perilous financial position.

Size and Scope of the Nonprofit World

The National Center for Charitable Statistics reports that 1.54 million nonprofit organizations were registered with the IRS in 2016. These organizations are diverse in purpose and the types of individuals that they serve. (See Table 1.1.) Of these, approximately 1.3 million are public charities, and almost 127,000 are private foundations. In addition, there are about 21,000 religion-related organizations, however, since many do not have to file with the IRS, their scope in the nonprofit sector is probably greater.[10]

Although over 1 million nonprofits are public charities, not all of them file with the IRS the yearly tax form called the **Form 990**. Small nonprofits, whose annual gross receipts are $50,000 or less, submit Form 990-N, also known as the e-Postcard. Slightly larger nonprofits, whose annual gross receipts are less than $200,000 and their assets are less than $500,000, file the two-page Form 990-EZ.

In 2016, the nonprofits that filed a Form 990 reported revenues totaling $2.62 trillion and total assets worth $5.99 trillion. Annually the nonprofit sector spends $2 trillion and employs more than 10% of the total private workforce in the United States, paying more than $826 billion on salaries, benefits, and payroll taxes. Although the public is most familiar with relatively large nonprofits, such as the

Table 1.1 Types and Numbers of Public Charities

Type of Charity	Number	% of Total
All Public Charities	318,015	100.0
Human Services	111,797	35.2
Education	54,632	17.2
Other Education	52,471	16.5
Health	38,853	12.2
Other Public and Social Benefit	38,071	12.0
Other Health Care	31,799	10.0
Arts	31,894	10.0
Religion Related	20,880	6.6
Environment and Animals	14,932	4.7
Hospitals and Primary Care Facilities	7,054	2.2
International	6,956	2.2
Higher Education	2,161	0.7

Source: National Center for Charitable Statistics (2020, June). *The Nonprofit Sector in Brief 2019* (nccs.urban.org/publication/nonprofit-sector-brief-2019#the-nonprofit-sector-in-brief-2019).

YMCA or the American Red Cross, only 2% of all charitable organizations have annual budgets of more than $10 million. Most nonprofits are small, with nearly 88% spending less than $500,000. However, it is the largest nonprofits, those with $10 million or more in expenses, that account for most of the sector's spending, over 88%.[11]

Nonprofit revenues come from a variety of sources (see Figure 1.1):

- 49% comes from payment for services and fees;
- 31.8% is derived from government grants;
- 12.5% comes from contributions;
- 1.5% is donation bequests; and
- 5.2% comes from other revenues, such as dues and special events.[12]

Health nonprofits and hospitals take in the most nonprofit revenue, comprising the largest resources of revenues for nonprofits (59.2% and 49.8%, respectively). (See Table 1.2.) Education and higher education also receive substantial revenues. The majority of these revenues come from payment for services and fees (e.g., college tuition or medical exams). Other nonprofits are less dependent on fees and more dependent on private contributions and government grants.

Nonprofit Structure

Nonprofits may file for corporation status in any of the 50 U.S. states. In order to seek corporate status, a nonprofit must create articles of incorporation and bylaws. The articles of incorporation, a legal document, is filed with the state, usu-

An Introduction to Nonprofits   9

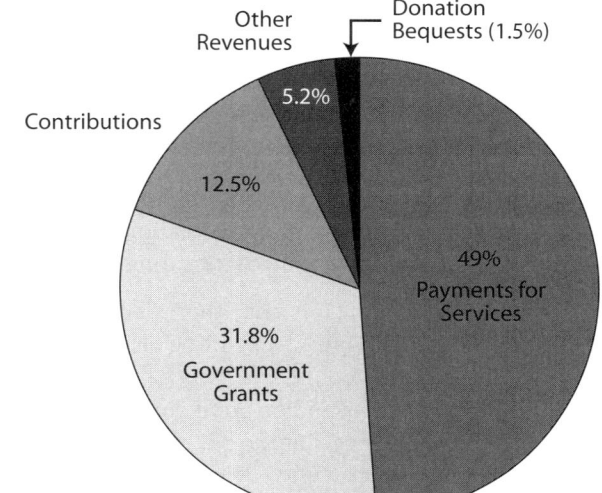

Figure 1.1 Sources of revenue for nonprofits.

Source: National Council of Nonprofits (2019). *Nonprofit Impact Matters: How America's Charitable Nonprofits Strengthen Communities and Improve Lives* (nonprofitimpactmatters.org/site/assets/files/1/nonprofit-impact-matters-sept-2019-1.pdf).

Table 1.2   Nonprofit Revenues by Type of Charity in 2016

Type of Charity	Revenues (in billions)	% of Total
All Public Charities	$ 2,041.5	100.0
Health	$ 1,208.5	59.2
Hospitals and Primary Care Facilities	$ 1,016.0	49.8
Education	$ 353.8	17.3
Human Services	$ 243.0	11.9
Higher Education	$ 226.4	11.1
Other Health Care	$ 192.5	9.4
Other Education	$ 127.4	6.2
Other Public and Social Benefits	$ 117.1	5.7
Arts	$ 40.2	2.0
International	$ 39.7	1.9
Environment and Animals	$ 19.8	1.0
Religion Related	$ 19.4	1.0

Source: National Center for Charitable Statistics (2020, June). *The Nonprofit Sector in Brief 2019* (nccs.urban.org/publication/nonprofit-sector-brief-2019#the-nonprofit-sector-in-brief-2019).

ally the state in which the nonprofit operates. This document contains the organization's basic information, such as name, address, composition of the board of directors, and a statement of purpose. Even though this is a state filing, it is best for a nonprofit to follow the IRS guidelines, because once the state has recognized the nonprofit as a corporation, the nonprofit can ask the IRS for tax-exempt status. When the IRS then examines the articles of incorporation, it expects to see a statement of purpose that is within its guidelines. It also expects to see in the articles of incorporation that no part of any profits will be distributed to officers or directors, and that the organization will undertake very little lobbying. Regardless of intention, a nonprofit does not have the federal tax benefits of nonprofit status until the IRS approves its application.

Bylaws are the nonprofit's organizational rules. They set the process under which the nonprofit will be governed. Specifically, they establish the number and process by which trustees are chosen, the size of the board and how it will function, the duties of the executive director, and the rules and procedures for holding meetings. They also spell out policies regarding conflicts of interest.

Board of Trustees. Usually the board of trustees will set up a committee structure within the board. Depending on its size, the board may have an executive committee, a finance committee, a personnel committee, a program committee, a fundraising committee, and an audit committee. These committees may invite staff to attend their meetings, but the board members run the committees. The board of trustees will hire an executive director, and that executive director will hire a staff. Depending on the size and resources of the nonprofit, the staff could consist of a finance officer and staff, a development officer and staff, and a program director and staff, as well as other administrative staff members.

The board of trustees carries the fiduciary responsibility to oversee the nonprofit. Regardless of the decisions of the executive director, it is the board members who are responsible for the financial decisions made in the nonprofit. Board members use board insurance to protect themselves against fraud and corruption, while the prudent investor rule protects the board of trustees against any negative consequences of good-faith errors in judgment.

The modern nonprofit structure in the United States has evolved to include a complex set of financial guidelines that are largely dependent on the state of incorporation. Some states require extensive annual filings, while others require nothing. The federal government requires an annual filing of the IRS Form 990.

Differences between the Business and Nonprofit Worlds

Traditionally, most writers explain the differences between businesses and nonprofits by focusing on the topic of **mission**. Businesses are about making money for their stockholders. Money is, in effect, their mission. In contrast, nonprofits are based on strong institutional belief systems centered on compelling public missions. Service, not money, is their objective. In the for-profit world, corporations charge for their services; in the nonprofit world, nonprofits often give away their services for free. Businesses raise funds from investors, sales, and loans, while nonprofits raise funds from government contracts and grants, foundations, fees, and donors. Businesses pay for all sorts of expertise, such as accounting, marketing, and legal advice; nonprofits often get such advice for free or at a reduced cost. (See Table 1.3.)

Although the distinction between businesses and nonprofits in their missions remains paramount, in the modern world, many nonprofits are now raising money

Table 1.3 Differences between Businesses and Nonprofits

Aspect	Business	Nonprofit
Organizational structure	Sole proprietor Partnership Corporation	Corporation
Policy decisions	Individual owner Board/shareholders	Board of trustees
Day-to-day management	Individual General partner Offices of corporation	Executive director and staff
Market	Customers who pay for services or items	Mixed; some clients rarely pay for services or items
Capital	Loans, owners' equity, sales, stocks, investors	Government contracts and grants, foundations, fees, contributions, donations of services
Competition	Other businesses	Mixed; some nonprofits are now involved in competitive businesses
Cash flow	Fluctuates depending on the market and economy	Fluctuates depending on the political and economic climate
Professional advice	Pays for accountants, marketing experts, lawyers, and other management experts	Often obtains pro bono services from lawyers, accountants, and management experts (or at least is charged reduced fees)

by operating businesses. While on the surface this might seem counter to IRS regulations, it is allowable in certain instances. A business operated by a nonprofit may be one recognized as contributing to the nonprofit and thus pays no taxes, or it may be a regular for-profit corporation intended to make profits that are taxable, and any profits are donated to the nonprofit. We discuss this topic further in Chapter 14.

Setting Financial Policies

The financial policies of a nonprofit are paramount in keeping the organization in good financial condition. Financial policies are guidelines for conducting the day-to-day operations of a nonprofit. They provide the foundation on which the organization runs its programs and operates to fulfill its mission. The most common financial policies are those concerning investments, cash control, check sign-off, and revenue collection. Nonprofit organizations and their staff members, by and large, are not financial experts; their focus and expertise are dedicated to their mission. Without proper attention to or understanding of the organization's finances, however, problems can occur. Mismanagement and corruption bring misery to nonprofit board members and staff and can seriously damage an organization's success.

Remember that much of what nonprofits do is outside the purview of government oversight. Some states have few or no requirements constraining nonprofit organizations. The IRS may give limited attention to them unless they are very large. Governments are reactive when it comes to nonprofit organizations, mostly in response to public perception of wrongdoing. If issues of mismanagement or corruption in a nonprofit hit the newspapers, then the state's attorney general is likely to act. Without such media coverage, however, it is rare that a nonprofit's mismanagement of its resources is noticed outside of those involved in its mission.

U.S. states do have some rules governing nonprofits. Almost all require registration and annual reporting, usually financial statements and the IRS Form 990. More than two-thirds require charities and other nonprofits to register, usually with the attorney general's office, prior to fundraising in the individual state.[13] Requiring the filing of annual 990s and financial statements, however, does not amount to monitoring nonprofits. Most states do not have sufficient staff to provide consistent or close monitoring. This lack of oversight at both the state and federal levels is another reason nonprofits need to establish clear financial policies. When an organization's leaders understand the financial landscape in which they work, they are equipped with important managerial tools for decision making.

Nonprofits can get help in developing first-rate financial policies. Independent Sector, a nonpartisan coalition of 550 nonprofits, has established the Principles for Good Governance and Ethical Practice Resource Center, where nonprofits can obtain very good advice about financial issues. The center's website also provides free publications about governance and ethics (independentsector.org/resource/principles). In effect, Independent Sector encourages nonprofits to monitor themselves and provides the information to help them do so.

The Link between Mission and Money

Those drawn to work in nonprofits are motivated by service and often do not hail from financial backgrounds. Without money, however, those working in nonprofits could not serve. Without savvy fiscal strategy, a nonprofit cannot flourish. A nonprofit's mission demands the resources needed to fulfill that mission, thus illustrating the link between mission and money. It is unwise for the leaders of a nonprofit to create a mission statement without understanding the size and depth of the resources they will need to carry out that mission. Some would argue that the mission statement is a dream, whereas the organization's stated goals and objectives represent more realistic, tempered thoughts about achieving that mission. We believe this is shortsighted. Too often nonprofits have wonderful missions, produce good programs, and yet are always teetering on the edge of "going under." Their problem is that they do not have enough money. If nonprofits are to survive a difficult economy, they must think beyond traditional resources, because traditional resources cannot fully fund their missions.

A nonprofit's strategic plan must broaden its definition of resources. Does the nonprofit charge for services? Why not? Has the nonprofit raised an endowment? Why not? Does the nonprofit sell its services for a profit? Why not? Does the nonprofit own a for-profit business from which it derives profits? Why not?

Imagine a nonprofit that operates an employment and training program. The staff has been very successful in graduating clients from the program to full employment. How could the organization gain more revenue for the program?

- The nonprofit could sell its expertise. Instead of serving only one group of people, it could sell its training opportunities to others for a profit. Both employed and unemployed individuals may be looking for new career opportunities in various industries that require specialized education or training.
- The nonprofit could sell a product. If the staff is training clients to be cooks, the program should be advertising its products for sale. This does not have to be as elaborate as running a restaurant. The staff may want to look into catering or setting up a small bakery.
- The nonprofit could create a for-profit business and donate those profits to the nonprofit.

In order for a nonprofit to consider these options, it must be open to augmenting its mission as it changes its methods. Under any one of these changes, the nonprofit is not simply stating a mission to provide a service; rather, it is stating a mission that sells its expertise in order to finance its mission. Part of the mission is to sell its uniqueness, its expertise.

Allen J. Proctor, a well-respected expert on nonprofit finance, suggests that nonprofits examine the issue of financial stability through the lens of sustainability. Can a nonprofit sustain itself if it changes its objectives, such as by creating a for-profit business? Proctor reminds us, "If a nonprofit grows and later cannot sustain its services, it may jeopardize its survival and undermine the constituents who relied upon it to sustain the expansion."[14] Expansion is not to be undertaken lightly.

The Push for Accountability: Watchdog Organizations and Their Standards

Accountability refers to holding people responsible for their actions. Internally, the board and executive director of a nonprofit seek to hold the staff accountable. The literature identifies four core components of accountability:[15]

1. *Transparency,* which involves collecting information and making it available and accessible for public scrutiny;
2. *Answerability* or *justification,* which involves providing clear reasoning for actions and decisions, including those not adopted, so that they may reasonably be questioned;

3. *Compliance,* through the monitoring and evaluation of procedures and outcomes and creation of procedure manuals, combined with transparency in reporting those findings; and

4. *Enforcement* or *sanctions* for shortfalls in compliance, justification, or transparency.

The nonprofit world is a diverse one, with many subsectors and stakeholders, and there is currently no one organization that enforces all four of these components for nonprofits.

Within the nonprofit world, one of the greatest changes in the last 30 years has been the push for accountability by external monitors. Although accountability is now the watchword in the nonprofit world, there is a still a long way to go before real accountability exists. The pressure has come from two groups: (1) government, which has provided contracts and wants to see quantifiable results and (2) the external organizations that evaluate the success of nonprofits. Consequently, nonprofits are under enormous pressure to demonstrate efficiency and effectiveness, and this too costs money.

Federal, state, and local governments fund nonprofits to provide a range of services that government either does not provide at all or does not provide in sufficient quantity to meet the need. As financial resources have become tighter, individual government agencies have demanded more and more accountability from nonprofits. It is not unreasonable for nonprofits to be required to demonstrate that they spend government funds efficiently and effectively. Problems arise, however, when nonprofits are forced to spend countless hours filling out endlessly repetitive or meaningless paperwork to convince governments that they are efficient and effective.

Several organizations exist to evaluate or provide information about nonprofits. Nonprofits that actively seek large donors are well-advised to meet the accountability standards of the following organizations.

1. **GuideStar** (guidestar.org) is the best known, and has recently merged with Foundation Center (candid.org). GuideStar maintains copies of the completed IRS Form 990 for more than 1 million nonprofits so that donors and anyone else interested in learning about the finances of a nonprofit can do so by accessing GuideStar's database.

2. Charity Navigator (charitynavigator.org) and the Better Business Bureau Wise Giving Alliance (give.org) are two "watchdog" organizations that analyze and evaluate nonprofits to provide guidance to donors about which nonprofits are the most efficient. They set accountability standards and measure the service effectiveness of nonprofits, as well as publish information and data that help donors make informed giving decisions.

3. The **Financial Accounting Standards Board (FASB)** is the designated private agency that establishes standards of financial accounting for all nongovernmental entities. It has broadened its accounting measures to include nonprofit accounting (fasb.org/nfp).

With the advent of increased interest by the FASB, the IRS, and other external monitors, nonprofit financial recording has grown and will continue to grow, and nonprofit officers and staff must be alert to new requirements.

One answer to the push for accountability is for nonprofits to provide their staffs with the financial tools they need to document carefully their use of resources and to analyze their financial choices, decisions, and strategies. This book discusses financial management and also presents ways to make it easier for nonprofit executives to document, track, and understand the state of their organizations' financial condition. Careful and close financial data-keeping analysis rewards nonprofits by providing them with the basis for savvy financial strategies. This creates confidence in funders, both public and private.

The Tension between Serving Clients and Protecting the Nonprofit

When a nonprofit faces a fiscal crisis, often the staff must choose between serving the clients and protecting the nonprofit from serious harm. Nonprofits have responded to fiscal crises many times over the years. When the 2008 fiscal crisis hit the United States, nonprofits were faced with large revenue shortfalls in government contracts and a stark decline in contributions. As a result, they had to make choices on how best to fulfill their missions. Perhaps they will use their reserves, and after the reserves are gone, the nonprofit will end a program and lay off staff to preserve the other programs. In 2020, a study of the impact of the Covid-19 pandemic estimated that nonprofit job losses amounted to a 7.3% decline from pre-pandemic levels with a loss of almost 1 million jobs within a year.[16] At some point during a fiscal crisis, a nonprofit has to choose staying afloat and serving some clients over keeping all their staff and running out of money. This is very difficult. Think of a settlement house that had several programs, including day care, breakfast and lunch programs, after-school activities, a cooking workshop, and an employment skills center. During a financial crisis, the settlement house could no longer support all of these programs. But the clients were still in need.

Nonprofits are not trained to lay off staff and end programs. But to fulfill the mission may require a nonprofit to do just that—eliminate a program, which requires laying off staff, so that the nonprofit can continue serving clients in the other programs. It is important that the nonprofit does not lose sight of its mission in order to save one or two programs. In the nonprofit world, in the times of fiscal crises, choices can be very difficult.

Conclusion

Nonprofit organizations have existed in the United States since the nation's founding. The world of nonprofits has grown so large that it is now referred to as the third sector, after government and business sectors. This sector is quite different from business. Unlike businesses, nonprofits are not interested in making profits;

they are interested in fulfilling their missions, and their missions are closely related to their resources.

In the twenty-first century, the third sector has faced tough challenges thus far, first the 2008 Great Recession and then the Covid-19 pandemic of 2020. In order to fulfill their missions in a time of fiscal scarcity, nonprofits must use their resources as effectively and efficiently as possible. They must insist on strict accountability to ensure that they use every dollar wisely. Nonprofits' efficient use of financial accounting, which is complex, has become indispensable. In effect, students who study nonprofits and those who devote their life's work to helping nonprofits fulfill their missions must be knowledgeable and wise concerning financial matters. This book provides such individuals with the financial tools they need to meet the challenges, succeed in the endeavors, and enjoy the adventure of running nonprofit corporations.

KEY TERMS

Financial Accounting Standards Board (FASB)
Form 990
GuideStar
mission
nonprofit corporation
private foundation
prudent investor rule
prudent man rule
public charities
third sector

DISCUSSION QUESTIONS

1. Why does the study of the origins of nonprofits provide useful information?
2. What is the prudent man rule? The prudent investor rule?
3. How is a nonprofit similar to a for-profit business? How do they differ?
4. What is the size of the nonprofit sector in the United States?
5. What is financial management?
6. For a nonprofit, what is the link between mission and money?
7. What organizations are involved in measuring the accountability of nonprofits, and what are the four components of accountability?

SUGGESTED READINGS

Arnsberger, Paul, Melissa Ludlum, Margaret Riley, and Mark Stanton (2008, Winter). "A History of the Tax-Exempt Sector: An SOI Perspective." *Statistics of Income Bulletin*, 105–135 (irs.gov/pub/irs-soi/tehistory.pdf).

Brody, Evelyn (1996). "Agents without Principals: The Economic Convergence of the Nonprofit and For-Profit Organizational Forms." *New York Law School Law Review*, 40: 457–536.

Chisholm, Laura B. (1995). "Accountability of Nonprofit Organizations and Those Who Control Them: The Legal Framework." *Nonprofit Management and Leadership*, 6(2): 141–56.

IRS. *Statistics of Income Bulletin* (irs.gov/statistics/soi-tax-stats-soi-bulletins).
Proctor, Allen J. (2010). *Linking Mission to Money: Finance for Nonprofit Leaders* (2nd ed.). Worthington, OH: LMM Press.

Assignments

Assignment 1.1. Linking Mission to Money

Using the internet, find a mission statement for a nonprofit that interests you. What do you like about the mission statement? Is there a link between the mission and the money in the mission statement? How would you modify that mission statement to provide a link to the money? Discuss what strategies you would propose to finance the nonprofit's mission.

Assignment 1.2. Proposing Improvements to a Nonprofit's Accountability Standards

One of the most famous corruption scandals in nonprofit history is the fall of William Aramony, who served as president of the United Way, one of the largest nonprofits in the United States, from 1970 to 1992. Aramony resigned amid scandal and was convicted and served 6 years in federal prison for conspiracy, fraud, and theft. He spent lavishly, including purchasing a home with United Way funds, and siphoned funds from the nonprofit, directing them to another company for his young mistress. The 33 members of the board of directors, a who's who of America's corporate and labor leaders, were not charged with any crimes, although federal prosecutors said that they were "unduly respectful" of Aramony.

If you were asked by the board of directors of the United Way to help improve the organization's accountability standards, what advice would you give the board? You can assume that the board has several working committees, including a finance committee and an executive committee, as well as an outside auditor who examines the nonprofit's finances and creates audited financial statements.

Assignment 1.3. Researching Two States' Requirements

Choose two of the 50 states and research their legal requirements for nonprofit organizations. What are the legal requirements in each state and how do they differ? Which do you prefer and why?

Assignment 1.4. Response to the Pandemic

When the ABC Settlement House, which was situated in and had a mission of serving a low-income Hispanic community, faced the Covid-19 pandemic in 2020 and closed its doors for six months, the board of directors and CEO applied and received federal funding to continue to pay the staff. The settlement house had several programs including day care, breakfast and lunch programs, after-school activities, a cooking workshop, and an employment skills center. Describe how the settlement house could continue its mission during a time when clients were asked to stay home when possible and when at the facility, to social distance at least six feet apart and wear masks at all times.

Chapter One

NOTES

[1] Proctor, Allen J. (2010). *Linking Mission to Money: Finance for Nonprofit Leaders* (2nd ed., p. 11). Worthington, OH: LMM Press.
[2] Council on Foundations (cof.org).
[3] Friedman, Lawrence J., and Mark D. McGarvie (2002). *Charity, Philanthropy, and Civility in American History* (p. 41). Cambridge: Cambridge University Press.
[4] Quoted in Peter Dobkin Hall (2003). *A History of Nonprofit Boards in the United States* (p. 12). New York: BoardSource (boardsource.org/dl.asp?document_id=11).
[5] Ibid., p. 14.
[6] *Harvard College v. Amory,* 9 Pick. 446, 471, 26 Mass. 446, 471.
[7] Friedman and McGarvie, p. 269.
[8] Salamon, Lester M., and Susan L. Q. Flaherty (1996). Nonprofit Law: Ten Issues in Search of Resolution. In Lester M. Salamon and Helmut K. Anheier (Eds.), *Working Papers of the Johns Hopkins Comparative Nonprofit Sector Project* (no. 20). Baltimore: Johns Hopkins Institute for Policy Studies.
[9] Payton, Robert L. A Defining Moment in American Philanthropy. Payton Papers (paytonpapers.org/output/ESS0044_1.shtm).
[10] National Center for Charitable Statistics (2020, June). *The Nonprofit Sector in Brief 2019* (nccs.urban.org/publication/nonprofit-sector-brief-2019#the-nonprofit-sector-in-brief-2019).
National Council of Nonprofits (2019). *Nonprofit Impact Matters: How America's Charitable Nonprofits Strengthen Communities and Improve Lives* (nonprofitimpactmatters.org/site/assets/files/1/nonprofit-impact-matters-sept-2019-1.pdf).
[11] Ibid.
[12] National Council of Nonprofits (2019).
[13] Perlman, Seth. Advising Nonprofit Organizations 2010. PowerPoint presentation, Practising Law Institute, February 3, 2010 (perlmanandperlman.com/publications/articles.shtml).
[14] Proctor, p. 14.
[15] Ebrahim, Alnoor (2010). *The Many Faces of Nonprofit Accountability* (Working Paper 10-069). Boston: Harvard Business School.
[16] Newhouse, Chelsea (2020, November 16). Nonprofit Jobs Rebound Slightly in October, but Remain Down by Over 900,000 Compared to Pre-Covid Levels. Press Release. Center for Civil Society Studies. Baltimore, MD: Johns Hopkins University.

Part II
Planning and Budgeting

2　Budgeting as Part of the Planning Process

> The essence of budgeting is *choice within constraint*.
> —Dall W. Forsythe[1]

Learning Objectives

The learning objectives for this chapter are as follows:
- Becoming familiar with budgeting vocabulary
- Linking a nonprofit's mission with budgeting
- Understanding the roles of the board and staff
- Recognizing budgeting as a tool for planning, management, and communications
- Identifying different types of budgets: operating and capital
- Formatting budgets: line-item, program, and performance
- Understanding the budget process: preparation, approval, execution, and auditing
- Exploring budget cutbacks

*I*n the nonprofit world, all nonprofit executives and their boards plan how much money their organizations will have and plan how to spend it. Nonprofit executives and board members conduct such budget planning every year and often create multiyear financial plans. These activities represent one of the most rational decision-making processes that nonprofit executives and boards undertake.

Budgeting Vocabulary

When the term *budget* is used, it is often within the context of the budget cycle. When a budget is being prepared, it is referred to as a **proposed budget**. Once it has been approved, it is the **adopted budget**. Throughout the fiscal year, the adopted budget is referred to as the **operating budget** because the adopted budget may be changed (modified) and the nonprofit will thus operate with a budget that is no longer the adopted budget. Other budget terms include *revenue budget* and *expense budget*. A **revenue budget** is simply a plan for all the anticipated revenues in the organization; an **expense budget** is a plan for all the expenses expected.

After the budget is adopted, the finance office of the nonprofit may allocate the resources to different departments. In effect, before funds can be spent, the departments must receive **allocations** from the finance office. Of course, if a nonprofit keeps its budget process centralized, then there may be no allocations to departments; rather, if a staff member wishes to purchase something, permission must be given by the finance office. **Encumbrances** are amounts of money put aside for specific items, such as computers or copying machines. Designating encumbrances is a method used to preserve specific amounts of money for specific items. When preparing the next year's budget, it is common for the executive director to have a **spending baseline**. The spending baseline is how much it will cost to keep the current services going in terms of staff and materials at next year's prices with no additions or subtractions from the current operating budget.

Nonprofits deal principally with two types of budgets: *operating* and *capital*. A nonprofit's operating budget is the day-to-day budget listing revenues and expenses. In addition, often a nonprofit will operate with a **capital budget** that plans the resources for long-term investments, such as land, buildings, and equipment. In this chapter we focus on the operating budget; we discuss capital budgets in more depth in Chapter 11. When a nonprofit board and executive director begin the budgeting process, they should start with their mission.

The Link between Mission and Budgeting

Every nonprofit has a mission. A good example is the American Red Cross's mission statement: "The American Red Cross prevents and alleviates human suffering in the face of emergencies by mobilizing the power of volunteers and the generosity of donors."[2] This mission is wonderful and also enormous. Then the reality sets in. How can the nonprofit afford to fulfill this mission? Clearly, nonprofit executives and staff members cannot fulfill their organizations' missions all at once. Planning becomes very important; the participants must carve out reasonable objectives over a defined period. The American Red Cross has several objectives: first and foremost is domestic disaster relief; other objectives include educational programs that promote health and safety. Nonprofit executives need to be able to show how what they are planning to do relates to their organizations' missions. And their objectives must be closely related to their resources. If the resources are threatened, so are their objectives and also their missions.

Roles of the Board, Executive Director, and Staff

In July 2010 a small, nonprofit liberal arts college, Birmingham–Southern College, announced it had a $10 million deficit. As a consequence, it laid off 51 staff members, froze all hiring, ended contributions to any retirement funds, cancelled all sabbaticals, and required faculty members to take a 10% salary cut.[3] Was this because of the 2008 recession? No. It was the result of human error. For many years, the financial aid office had given away too much financial aid, and the finance office did not know this. In a time of economic growth, the revenue shortfall went unnoticed, but when the recession hit, the finance office detected the shortfall in revenues. An external **audit** was conducted, and the findings were shocking. Obviously both offices, the financial aid office and the finance office, made major mistakes. Other players, however, must consider their roles in this disastrous chain of events.

With the Birmingham–Southern College example, the roles of board members and the executive director come into focus. How can the board of a nonprofit provide proper oversight?

- *Finance committee*: The function of the board's finance committee is to review and monitor the revenues and expenses of the nonprofit carefully, by working closely with the executive director and the finance officer. The board's finance committee must ask the hard questions: How were these revenue projections made? What checks and balances were in place between the financial aid office and the finance office?

- *Audit committee*: The audit committee is charged with overseeing the outside auditor that is hired to review the nonprofit's finances and create the financial statements. In addition, the audit committee is charged with overseeing internal controls—that is, those financial procedures created by an organization to ensure that the assets of the organization are protected. It is during a review of internal controls that the lack of communication between the finance office and the financial aid office would probably have been observed.

- *Outside auditor*: An outside auditor reviews and verifies the finances of a nonprofit. The audit committee, working closely with the executive director, usually chooses the auditor. Although no law requires nonprofits to hire outside auditors, there are external pressures on nonprofits to produce audited financial statements that can be developed only by certified public accountants. The federal and state governments, as well as foundations, often require audited financial statements from nonprofits seeking money from donors or outside sources.

It can be the case that too much oversight on the part of the board also has its problems. One of the most common complaints among executive directors is that the board is too hands-on; that is, the board attempts to manage as well as set policy. Too often, members of the board of directors interfere with the staff. It is always a mistake for a nonprofit to allow board members to become involved in the day-to-day management of the organization. The board should defer such management to the executive director they have hired to run the nonprofit.

The board's work is concerned with policy making, not day-to-day operations. Policy making includes approving the budget, and board members must ensure that they practice due diligence in doing so. Budget implementation is the responsibility of the executive director, but if the Birmingham–Southern College board had paid more attention to the implementation, they might have discovered the financial problems earlier. The relationship between the board and the executive director is a balancing act. There is no easy answer as to where the line should be drawn between board duties and executive director duties when financial matters are involved.

The Tools of Budgeting

Budgeting as a Planning Tool

A variety of actors are involved in creating, approving, and implementing the budget in a nonprofit: the board of directors, the executive director, and the director's key staff. In addition, a variety of external circumstances affect the making of a nonprofit budget—the state of the economy, the growth or contraction of government programs, and the legal environment. Each one of these can have impacts on a nonprofit's budget. With so many internal and external stakeholders, the resources of a nonprofit can change continually.[4] In the case of a national recession, the changes can be abrupt and threatening.

> **Box 2.1**
> **REMEMBER: The Constantly Changing Budget**
> A budget is constantly changing, depending on a variety of external circumstances:
> - The state of the economy
> - The fiscal health of the government sector
> - The legal environment

Budgeting is a process by which nonprofit executives examine external and internal circumstances to determine their resources and how best to use them. It is part of the planning process. If board members and the executive director plan to enlarge the nonprofit's programs by including a new program, they cannot do so without considering whether or not their resources are sufficient, and, if not, where they can get those resources. If the economy is in a downward spiral, that circumstance will affect the decisions made. For example, if the government is cutting its budget that might affect the nonprofit's budget. The severe national recession of 2008 affected U.S. nonprofits in myriad ways. In 2010, the National Council of Nonprofits examined

> the alarming condition of state budget deficits and three resulting threats to nonprofits: (1) governments slashing funds for programs they expect nonprofits to deliver; (2) governments withholding payments from nonprofits for con-

tracted services already delivered; and (3) governments seeking revenue from nonprofits through new fees and taxes.[5]

Part of the planning process is to understand and to operate successfully in the broader environment in which nonprofits live.

If a nonprofit is to succeed, the board and executive director's planning and budgeting must be closely linked. When the board of directors and the executive director are in that annual planning session and board members speak enthusiastically about a new program they are eager to implement, the executive director should ask the realistic question, "Where is the money going to come from to implement this fabulous program?" Often the answer is "We will raise it over a period of time." The planning process for nonprofits must involve a 3–5 year projection and must include specifics about who is going to donate, how much revenue is going to be raised, and how these figures affect the annual giving plans.

Revenues are one side of the coin; the other is expenses. When nonprofit executives think about budgets, they have to think about both sides. Revenues and expenses are equally important, and neither can be neglected. The trick, however, is to find sufficient revenues. When a nonprofit board dreams about a new program, the dream is often without limits—resources are assumed to be plentiful. But making the dream a reality often means shrinking the dream to the resources that the board manages to raise during that year. It is a mistake to limit the thinking about an organization's plans to only a year of revenues and a year of expenses.

Nonprofit executives have to work at thinking beyond a year's time. The immediacy of finances is upon nonprofits, and it is hard to think about 5 years or 10 years in the future, but it is imperative that nonprofit executives think beyond one budget year. They need to think 5, 10, and 20 years ahead, because nonprofits are in business for many years, not just a few years.

Nonprofits can embrace strategic planning and a comprehensive thoughtful approach on a regular basis, year after year. It is not a onetime affair; it must be regular and multiyear. When a nonprofit board and executive staff participate in strategic planning, over a period of time the participants will become quite cognizant of their mission, their goals, and the objectives they embrace to achieve their mission on an annual

> **Box 2.2** **CASE IN POINT: Famous Long-Standing U.S. Nonprofits**
>
> - The National Audubon Society is more than 100 years old. Its mission is to conserve and restore natural ecosystems, focusing on birds and other wildlife and their habitats.
> - Founded in 1909, the NAACP is the nation's oldest and largest civil rights organization. Its members throughout the United States and the world are the premier advocates for civil rights in their communities, conducting voter mobilization and monitoring the public and private sectors to ensure equality of opportunity.
> - Since its founding in 1881 by visionary leader Clara Barton, the American Red Cross has been the nation's premier emergency response organization. As part of a worldwide movement that offers neutral humanitarian care to the victims of war, the American Red Cross distinguishes itself also by aiding victims of devastating natural disasters.

basis. When the participants develop their annual strategic plan, they discuss the resources needed to achieve their objectives. That is budgeting.

Budgeting as a Management Tool

Proper management of a budget leads to control—the control of a nonprofit's internal environment. Proper management of a budget allows the board and executive director to sleep at night. The first rule in managing a budget is to be realistic. This does not mean that the executive director needs to be conservative; rather, it means that he or she must be unbiased and objective. In budgeting, being realistic means the executive director will not count revenues as part of the budget unless those revenues are somewhat secure. For example, the executive director should have a letter or contract from each revenue source pledging the dollar amounts to be given to the nonprofit. If a program is dependent on contributions, then the executive director needs to review the history of fundraising in the organization to understand how realistic the proposed fundraising number is. If a donor's promise to fund the program is only verbal, the executive director should not use that revenue source in the budget.

Table 2.1 displays the hypothetical adopted revenue budget for fiscal year 2020 for Sojourner Truth Settlement House. For each item in the budget, the status of the source of the revenue is noted. The expected revenues must be a realistic expectation and not simply a hope. However, estimated revenues can change. Contracts can be revised; foundations can change their plans. Any changes in estimated revenues must be acknowledged immediately.

The second rule in managing a budget is consistency. There is a routine to managing a budget. The world of budgeting has management reports, which we describe later in this chapter. These reports need to be examined on a regular basis—every month, every quarter—without exception. Just as exercising on a regular basis is a healthy habit, so too is examining management reports. Additionally, the finance director should have a plan to collect the revenue fees in a timely manner. The board's finance committee must ensure that this documentation is in place.

Table 2.1   FY 2020 Adopted Revenue Budget, Sojourner Truth Settlement House

Revenues	Budget FY 2020	
Contributions	$ 1,810,000	estimated
Fees	134,880	estimated
Foundation Grants	1,075,000	confirmed
Government Contracts	2,035,000	confirmed
Investment Income	226,000	estimated
Total Revenues	$ 5,280,880	

The third rule in managing a budget is to tie performance to the budget. This can be very hard to do. The performance of each program must be measured, and then the staff must be held accountable for that performance. Usually, executive directors become friendly with many of their program directors, and it can be very difficult for them to have to sit down with a program director and say that the program is not as good as it should be. In the end, even in budgeting, proper supervision is key.

Effective budgeting as a management tool is a cyclical process. It begins with planning and budgeting; once implemented, an analysis of the results should be reported to key staff and board members. Next comes staff discussions on what they have learned from the reports. Finally, we come full circle—more planning and revised budgeting based on prior results and learned experiences. (See Figure 2.1.)

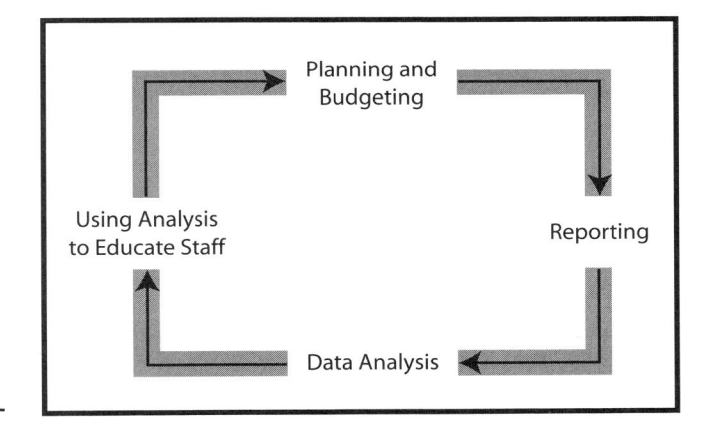

Figure 2.1 The cycle of budgeting as a management tool.

Budgeting as a Communications Tool

For each of these relationships, the nonprofit needs to sell itself. It needs to convince an organization, the sector of people it intends to serve, and individuals that the nonprofit is successful, well run, and focused on its mission. Nonprofits contract with state and federal governments. Monitoring organizations such as the Better Business Bureau, Charity Navigator, and GuideStar[6] evaluate the financial management of nonprofits. Budgeting can be a tool for a nonprofit to sell that message. Contributors, whether from Wall Street or small donors, must be able to read and understand the nonprofit's budgeting information. The way the budget is laid out and explained with understandable charts and graphs makes an indelible impression on the reader, whether that reader is a donor or a client. Imagine the nonprofit at the center of a web of relationships, as illustrated in Figure 2.2.

Figure 2.2 The nonprofit at the center of a web of relationships.

Operating and Capital Budgets

Nonprofits can create operating budgets for the whole organization and usually include a section of the operating budget for each department or program area. In addition, nonprofits may need to create capital budgets if they plan to purchase, lease, or renovate large assets, such as buying or renovating a building. Here we address operating budgets, both for the organization and for individual departments.

Two Sides of a Coin: Revenues and Expenses

All budgets, whether operating or capital, are divided into two parts: revenue and expense. The difference between revenues and expenses is categorized as either a surplus (if there is more than enough revenue to cover the expenses) or a deficit (if there is not enough revenue to cover the expenses). In operating budgets, nonprofits should seek to end the year with a small surplus that they can add to their cushion—their rainy-day fund. Revenues for nonprofits' operating budgets usually come from government contracts or government grants, foundation grants, fees for services, and contributions of all kinds. Revenues for capital budgets usually come from borrowed money or money raised specifically for a capital project. Expenses are divided among personnel services (PS), nonpersonnel services (NPS), and in-kind services.

Personnel Services. PS includes all full- and part-time positions in the program. The salaries and fringe benefits for these positions should be clearly stated. Often you will see fringe benefits listed as a percentage of a salary ranging from 20 to 30%. Fringe benefits are extras attached to a salary, such as retirement benefits, workers' compensation, and health care benefits. More and more nonprofits are providing health care to their employees. The cost of heath care plans differs from employee to employee and is dependent upon the number of people in an employee's family that are covered under the plan.

Another type of benefit is deductions from an employee's salary (in the form of taxes) that contribute to government programs that support individuals. For example, the Federal Insurance Contributions Act (FICA) created a payroll tax mechanism in order to fund social security and Medicare programs. Half of these contributions are paid by the employee and the other half is paid by the employer. Therefore, a nonprofit must budget for both social security and Medicare expenses.

- Social security is a 12.4% dedicated payroll tax in which the employer pays half, or 6.2%.
- Medicare is a 2.9% dedicated payroll tax in which the employer pays half, or 1.45%.

The federal unemployment tax is a 6% tax solely paid by the employer. State unemployment taxes are based on a percentage of the employee's salary. The percentage varies state by state. Often nonprofits do not have to pay unemployment taxes.

Nonpersonnel Services. NPS includes items that are not directly related to an employee position, such as the following:

- Consultants
- Contracts
- Equipment
- Furniture
- Maintenance
- Rent
- Supplies
- Travel
- Utilities

Consultants are contractual workers and thus are part of NPS. By law a consultant cannot receive fringe benefits and is not an employee of the organization.

In-Kind Services. Many nonprofits depend on volunteer workers. Under certain circumstances, volunteer activity needs to be counted as a contribution to the organization. If the services a volunteer provides create or enhance nonfinancial assets, then the volunteer's activities must be counted as a contribution. If the services require specialized skills and are provided by someone with those skills and would have had to be purchased if the volunteer had not come forward, then the volunteer's activities must be counted as a contribution.

In-kind services must be counted on both the revenue and expense sides. If the executive director is preparing a budget for one of the organization's programs, he or she may decide to include in-kind services as revenue. For example, if the program receives space in a building for free and that space is worth $5,000, or the program will use volunteers and the contribution of those hours of labor is worth $5,000. In either of these cases, the in-kind service could be included as revenue because it is a contribution. At the same time, the executive director will include the in-kind service as an expense because the nonprofit will use up this resource.

Link between Operating and Capital Budgets

A capital budget is the long-term budget process used when dealing with fixed assets, such as purchasing very large items, purchasing a building, or renovating a building. The chief characteristics of capital budgets are time duration, costs, and finance method. The time involved for capital budgets is usually more than a year, because long-term projects, such as renovating a building, require more than a year for completion. Capital budgets are usually quite large; the costs involved in buying or renovating a building, for example, can be substantial. Both governments and nonprofits usually finance their capital budgets through borrowing. Sometimes nonprofits run capital campaigns to raise funds to renovate or buy buildings.

We address capital budgets in depth in Chapter 11; for purposes of the discussion in this chapter, it is important to understand that capital budgets are linked to operating budgets. Sometimes the choices made in a capital budget spill over into the operating budget. For example, a nonprofit may renovate a building using a capital budget, but the expenses associated with ongoing costs, such as maintenance, will be in the operating budget. The New York Public Library discovered this linkage when it renovated its beautiful central library and put in very expensive light fixtures. The next year, the budget director witnessed a tenfold increase in the purchase of light bulbs for those very fancy fixtures. These are the kinds of costs that nonprofits need to keep in mind when designing their renovations.

Formatting Budgets: Line-Item Budgets, Program Budgets, and Performance Budgets

Budgets are formatted in different ways. The oldest budget format is the line-item budget created during the Progressive Era of the early 1900s, with its emphasis on government reform. Prior to line-item budgets, most local and state legislatures simply authorized lump sums to administrative offices. Program and performance budgets came later, as government officials sought to understand how funds were being used rather than simply knowing where the money was spent.

Line-Item Budgets

A **line-item budget** is one that has all of the items that are needed for the next year listed in the budget. Each line represents an item, whether that item is a single piece of equipment or several articles that make up an item (e.g., office supplies or travel expenses). Line-item budgets are designed for control; they make it easy for the budget officer to determine whether or not too much has been spent on any one line.

Table 2.2 displays the hypothetical line-item operating budget for the Sojourner Truth Settlement House for fiscal year 2020. The line-item budget lists the staff, but not by program. In the NPS section, all the items are listed, but they are not listed by program. Line-item budgets are very common, and, in large organizations, are usually sorted by department for easier reading. The criticism of line-item budgets for nonprofits is that these types of budgets say little about a nonprofit's programs, although they clearly lay out the major categories of spending. Decision makers need information about their programs in order to make reasonable decisions, and a line-item budget does not provide this type of information. Over time, most nonprofits using line-item budgets have increasingly used supplemental program information along with the line-item budgets.

Program Budgets

A **program budget** divides the projected budget into the various programs offered by the nonprofit. This allows anyone reading the budget to compare easily how much each department or program segment is getting and how much administration is getting. Such program budgets are increasingly popular with nonprofit boards and staff

Table 2.2 FY 2020 Line-Item Operating Budget, Sojourner Truth Settlement House

Revenues	Budget FY 2020
Contributions	$ 1,810,000
Fees	134,880
Foundation Grant	1,075,000
Government Contract	2,035,000
Investment Income	226,000
Total Revenues	$ 5,280,880
Expenses	
PS	
Executive Director	$ 150,000
Facilities Director	100,000
Finance Officer	125,000
Finance Staff	375,000
Administrative Staff	385,000
Development Director	125,000
Development Staff	200,000
Program Director	100,000
Coordinators	240,000
Directors	345,000
Senior Staff	653,000
Staff	957,500
PS	3,755,500
Fringe Benefits (20%)	751,100
Total PS	$ 4,506,600
NPS	
Consultants	232,000
Computer Equipment	40,200
Equipment	83,800
Food	39,000
Maintenance Contract	30,000
Mortgage	60,000
Phones	43,680
Supplies/printing	102,000
Travel	52,900
Utilities	30,000
Total NPS	$ 713,580
Total Expenses	$ 5,220,180
Surplus/Deficit	$ 60,700

Table 2.3 FY 2020 Program Budget, Sojourner Truth Settlement House

Revenues	Budget FY 2020
Contributions	$ 1,810,000
Fees	134,880
Foundation Grant	1,075,000
Government Contract	2,035,000
Investment Income	226,000
Total Revenues	$ 5,280,880
Expenses	
PS	
Administration	$ 1,152,000
Development	439,200
Child Care	819,000
College Prep	258,000
Elementary Volunteer	109,800
Employment and Training	477,000
Foster Care	471,000
Middle and High (After School)	261,000
Middle and High (Summer)	132,600
Parental Education	117,000
Senior Citizen	270,000
Total PS	$ 4,506,600
NPS	
Administration	142,620
Development	47,300
Child Care	15,260
College Prep	88,320
Elementary Volunteer	10,280
Employment and Training	62,700
Foster Care	17,860
Middle and High (After School)	122,200
Middle and High (Summer)	152,060
Parental Education	17,260
Senior Citizen	37,720
Total NPS	$ 713,580
Total Expenses	$ 5,220,180
Surplus/Deficit	$ 60,700

members, because they are so informative. Table 2.3 provides an example of a program budget.

Performance Budgeting or Results-Based Budgeting

Performance-based budgeting links resources (inputs) to measurement of outputs. An **input** is any resource used up during the fiscal year. An **output** is a short-term measure of a result. Performance budgeting links the plan on how resources will be spent to the results of how those resources are spent. Both city and state governments across the United States have moved toward some form of performance-based budgeting. Nonprofits, however, have not widely adopted the linking of performance and budgeting. The city of Concord, California, uses performance measurements as well as efficiency measures (unit costs) for its evaluation process. It characterizes performance-based budgeting as "explicitly focusing on the outcomes, as well as evaluation of programs by measuring the relationship between resources and results. It therefore helps assess performance of a program in terms of its effectiveness and efficiency."[7] Performance-based budgeting allocates resources based on service performance; both planned and actual performances are measured in terms of service effectiveness and efficiency.

The city of Sunnyvale, California, presents program performance statements for each of its program areas.[8] A program's performance is determined according to measures of quality and productivity. (See Table 2.4.) These measures are then compared to the stated goals and objectives of a program area.

Table 2.4 Program Performance Budget, Sunnyvale, California, Program 230—Housing and Human Services

Program Measures	Priority	2006/2007 Actual	2007/2008 Actual	2007/2008 Budget	2008/2009 Current	2009/2010 Adopted
Quality						
Q1 Surveys of the Housing and Human Services Commission rate the overall performance of staff as meeting expectations.	1					
Number of Rating Performance Satisfactory		7	8	4	7	7
Number of Survey Respondents		11	9	4	11	11
Q2 Survey respondents participating in a city-supported housing improvement program rate the program services as satisfactory.	1					
Percent Rating Service Satisfactory		100%	95%	100%	95%	95%
Number of Program Participants		44	65	43	50	50
Number of Survey Respondents		NA	NA	NA	25	25
Productivity						
P1 A share of new housing units will be affordable to very low-, low-, and moderate-income households (3 month moving average).	C					
Percent Affordable		19.6%	13.0%	26.0%	13.0%	13.0%
Number of New Affordable Housing Units		270	91	71	32	32
Total New Housing Units Created		NA	NA	NA	345	345

Cutbacks and Performance-Based Budgeting

Many nonprofits attempt to connect the performance measures of particular programs to their budgets, particularly in times of fiscal stress. If a nonprofit is in financial trouble, what programs should be cut? Often, the answer is those programs that are not performing well—and the nonprofit will know which programs these are if the nonprofit has a performance measurement system. However, cutbacks are not necessarily conducted on unsuccessful programs or on the activities that are the least effective. Often a nonprofit faces the loss of a program because the nonprofit has lost its funding, and the elimination of the program has nothing to do with its effectiveness.

A good example of this is the turmoil that the managers at a major Chicago settlement house went through when the city's child care agency decided to cut its budget. The settlement house operated one of the most effective preschool programs in the city. The state and the city recognized its effectiveness; both had praised the program as one of the most innovative child care programs in the city. The settlement house had not only invested the funds it received from its contract with the city but also sought and received foundation grants and donations to supplement and improve its program. But the city faced budget cuts, and the settlement house's lease for the child care program building had expired. The leadership in the city's child care agency decided that, regardless of how successful the program was, they could save some money by closing the center and, perhaps, moving it to another section of the city.

The settlement house was able to produce numerous performance indicators proving the incredible effectiveness of its program, but that made no difference. The city's child care agency wanted to shut it down. In this case, the executive director and board of the settlement house could either accept the city's decision, or fight it. They chose to fight, using their record of effectiveness as ammunition. After months of endless meetings, parent demonstrations, and countless interviews with journalists, the settlement house leadership won. The executive director said: "This is the mistake that government makes with nonprofits. Too many times government officials only look at the bottom line and do not consider the cost effectiveness of the programs." Such shortsightedness on the part of local government officials is not unusual; many executive directors of nonprofits have witnessed such actions by governmental agencies, particularly during the financial downturn that began in 2008.

The Budget Process as a Cycle

There are four stages to the budget process: preparation, approval, execution, and auditing. Each stage is a vital part of the process. Combined, the four stages take place over a period of 3 years, resulting in a process that always overlaps with that of preceding and succeeding years. (See Figure 2.3.)

Budgeting as Part of the Planning Process   35

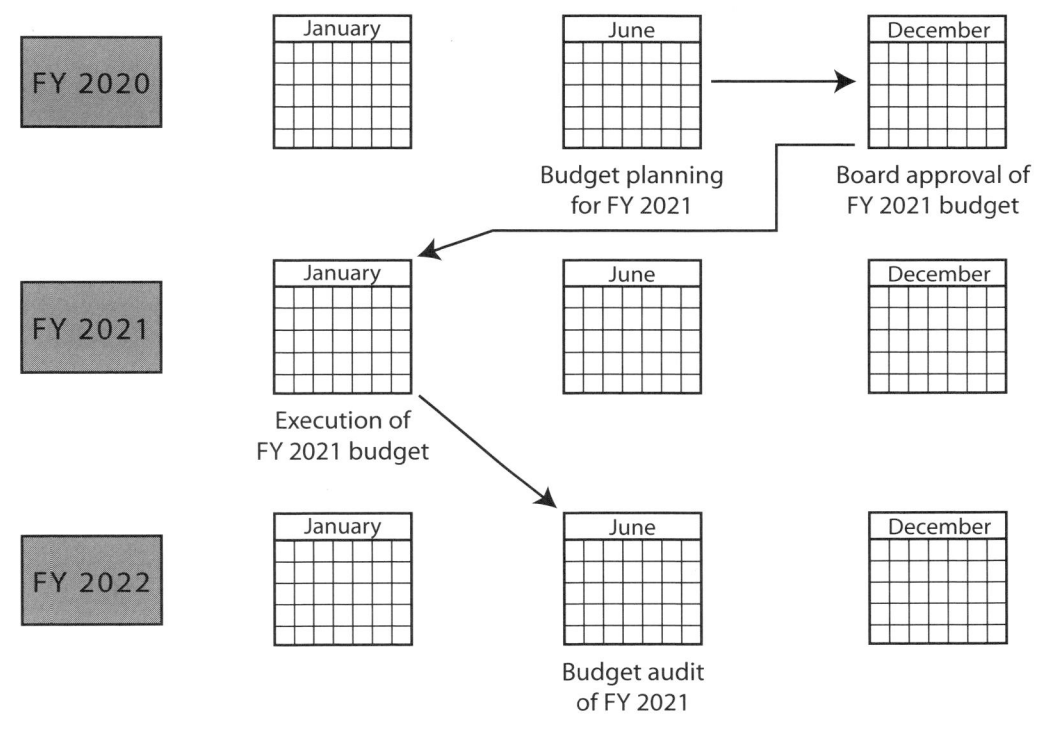

Figure 2.3 The budgeting process.

The Preparation Stage

Once the strategic plan has been developed, that plan must become part of the budget process. When nonprofit executives develop their proposed budgets, they examine both their sources of revenue and their expenses. That preparation stage is the first step in planning next year's budget. The preparation stage begins early. A nonprofit's budget year is called a **fiscal year (FY)**, and it runs for 12 months. Every nonprofit chooses its fiscal year at the time it incorporates. Many choose a calendar year, from January 1 through December 31. Others choose a fiscal year that matches the federal government's fiscal year, October 1 through September 30, or they might choose the fiscal year used by the state in which they are located, which could be any 12-month span, such as July 1 through June 30. Whatever fiscal year is chosen, the preparation process begins several months before the end of the fiscal year because nonprofit executives want to put a new budget in place before the start of the fiscal year.

Let's assume a nonprofit's fiscal year is the calendar year. After the strategic planning weekend, the executive director begins to discuss next year's budget with key staff. This might take place in June, six months before the beginning of the next fiscal year. For the next six months the executive director will work with staff and key board members to create next year's budget.

The preparation stage requires the executive director and staff to review each program's successes and failures as well as consider any new programs that came out of the strategic planning sessions. This review is essential, because it is not enough to say the nonprofit has six programs and these programs cost "X" amount of money; it is important to be able to say these six programs work, they are successful, and these are the positive results. Nonprofits have limited funds, and the last thing they should be doing is operating programs that have lost their effectiveness. Resources are scarce and need to be allocated carefully. Such a review can take up a great deal of the time of every program director and the executive staff.

A useful rule is that programs should drive dollars; dollars should not drive programs. The program needs to make sense before anyone gets too involved in planning a budget for it. Before the items are cost out, these three components should be in place:

- Mission
- Objective
- Program

Another consideration is that often state and federal governments will require certain staffing and other specifics for a program, and the funding source might require a particular set of activities. It is important that these requirements be considered before the budget is created.

Some executive directors keep the budget preparation process closed, including only the finance officer and maybe a staff member. Others talk to their program staff extensively. This is a management choice that an executive director makes. Some manage bottom up and some manage top down. If the executive director operates with a decentralized budget preparation process, then each program will submit its budget. Although our own preference is for a decentralized approach in which many people within the organization are consulted, we recognize that not everyone operates this way. The process can be an open one or a closed one; there is no single right way. What is important in either case is that there is sufficient communication among the staff so that everyone understands what is being planned for the next fiscal year, because the staff will have to prepare for it.

Budget Instructions. Usually in nonprofits, the staff is consulted during budget preparation. The executive director or the finance officer will send out budget instructions asking key program directors to turn in their proposed budgets for next year. Ideally, these budget instructions begin with a delineation of the organization's plans for next year. Then, they ask for the exact amounts of revenue and expenses for each program and what is needed for next year. They ask the program directors to estimate how much they need next year as compared to this year. If, in strategic planning sessions, staff members have proposed expanding a current program, that program director has to cost out the new expansion and pay attention to both the expense side and the revenue earmarked for it. The finance officer will compile the information provided by the program directors and submit a rough draft of a proposed budget to the executive director.

As an example, Sojourner Truth Settlement House has a college preparation program that has as its objective improving academic achievement for students interested in going to college. The program serves 100 students throughout the school year and has space within Sojourner Truth's building. The program has a staff of four and a consultant who is a reading specialist. The staff members spend two hours after school with the students in intensive academic studies and introduce the students to colleges through college trips.

Table 2.5 is the proposed budget for the college preparatory program. It is much more detailed than the Sojourner Truth Settlement House's final operating

Table 2.5 College Preparation Program, FY 2020 Proposed Budget, Sojourner Truth Settlement House

Revenues	Description/# of Positions	Time	Salary	Amount	
Contributions				$ 120,000	to be raised
Fees				2,000	to be raised
Foundation Grants				225,000	confirmed
Government Contracts				—	
Investment Income				—	
Total Revenues				$ 347,000	
Expenses					
PS					
C.P. Coordinator	1	100.00%	65,000	65,000	
C.P. Staff	3	100.00%	50,000	150,000	
Total Salaries				$ 215,000	
Fringe Benefits			20.00%	43,000	
Total PS	4			$ 258,000	

		# of Items/Hr	$ per Item	Amount
NPS				
Computer Equipment	Computers/printers	20	1,800	36,000
Consultants	Reading specialist	40	250	10,000
Equipment	Copier, etc.			7,000
Food		10	500	5,000
Phones	4	12	90	4,320
Supplies	Books, etc.	1,000	10	10,000
Travel	Visit colleges	8	2,000	16,000
Total NPS				$ 88,320
Total Expenses				$ 346,320
Difference				$ 680
Cost per Student	100			$ 3,463

budget. When a budget is in the preparation phase, each program budget needs detail that can be examined by the finance officer and the executive director. These individual program budgets tell the executive director exactly how each dollar figure was calculated. Let's start with the expenses. In the PS side of the budget, there are four full-time positions. Also on the PS side of the budget, fringe benefits are 20% of the PS.

On the NPS side of the budget, there is a clear delineation of how each budget item was calculated. When the PS and NPS are added together, there is a total expense of $346,320. On the revenue side of the budget, some revenues have already been raised, while others have not. There is a built-in surplus of $680, and the cost per student is calculated at $3,463.

Every program within Sojourner Truth Settlement House will have such a proposed budget. These will be examined, altered, and eventually combined into one organizational budget by the finance officer and executive director.

Executive Director's Role. While preparing the budget, the executive director also will meet with the development officer to discuss new revenue streams for the proposed expanded or new programs agreed upon in board planning sessions. A highly competent development director will begin immediately to search out new revenues for these proposed programs even though the board of directors has not yet approved the programs. It takes months to raise new monies, and the development director will start as early as possible.

The executive director and key staff will review the proposed budget, keeping the strategic planning session foremost in their minds. At some point during this 6–9 month preparation stage, the executive director works with key board members, particularly the finance committee. As previously discussed, the board of directors operates with various committees. Certainly the finance committee, led by the board's treasurer, is one of the more important ones.

The Approval Stage

Once the executive director and the finance committee agree on a draft budget, the executive director or the finance committee chair will present the proposed budget to the board. This is the approval stage. This board presentation will usually take place in the last part of the preparation stage; for example, a November board meeting may take place if the fiscal year begins in January. If the board meets only four times a year, then the draft proposed budget would need to be reviewed and approved by the finance committee before the November board meeting. This presentation is important, and usually every attempt is made by the presenter to tie this proposed budget into the strategic planning sessions. Board members may want changes. The executive director will see to it that any needed changes are made and then be sure to get a final proposed budget before the board's December meeting.

The executive director and finance chair must carefully craft the approval stage. Their communication with board members must ensure that there are no surprises in the proposed budget. The most important questions that board members need to ask when presented with the proposed budget for the coming year include the following:

- Does the proposed budget reflect the strategic plan?
- Does the proposed budget reflect all the financial items expected during the next fiscal year?
- What surplus or deficit is projected for the program?
- Is the budget's format one that the board has agreed to and is useful to the board?
- What is the budgeting process? Is it centralized or decentralized?
- Does the budgeting process have a clear calendar?

A common saying in a budget office is "No lies and no surprises." This is a simple way of saying that the executive director ought to communicate early and often with the board, and be accurate.

The Execution Stage

Once the board of directors adopts the proposed budget, the executive director must implement that budget. Usually the executive director will meet with the finance officer and a few key staff members and discuss budget implementation. Some program directors will need to make a few changes in their program budgets that reflect the budget that is being implemented. The executive director will ask the finance officer to send them a memo outlining their budgets for the fiscal year. For program directors who are expanding or implementing new programs, the executive director will have several meetings with them to discuss both the revenue side and the expense side. The budget or finance director is a key player in these meetings, because he or she is the person who must monitor the flow of revenues and expenses.

Unlike government, in which the amount of revenues is often determined by the time the budget is approved, a nonprofit might have new revenues coming in throughout the fiscal year. Expanded programs can be phased in, depending upon the arrival of new revenues. The board of directors and executive director may even adopt an expansion of a new program and spend the next year searching for revenues before implementing the new program. There is no reason why nonprofits have to stick closely to a fiscal year when implementing programs; they can be flexible.

Usually, after the board of directors adopts the budget, the executive director notifies key staff and asks the finance officer to allocate the funds to the program directors. In a decentralized budget process, the program directors will be free to purchase what they need within their budgets, provided that they follow the nonprofit's regulations. Usually program directors may purchase what they need as long as they stay within budget. Large purchases usually require approval from the finance officer or executive director, even when the purchase amount is within the budget.

The executive director must monitor the implementation of the budget. Such monitoring is accomplished through meetings and reports, a system that works quite well if the reports are prepared and reviewed on a regular basis, preferably monthly. The three reports most useful to the executive director are the variance report, the cash-flow management report, and the performance report.

Variance Report. The most common report is the **variance report**. This regular report, monthly or weekly, lists revenue and expense budgets and the actual expenses to date, so that the executive director has an understanding of what revenue has come in and what has been spent. At the end of the first month, no more than one-twelfth, or 8.3%, of the monies should have been expended (unless there were special circumstances that caused an increase or decrease in spending). After two months, no more than 16.7% should have been expended, and so on. Revenues do not come in on a regular basis, so a monthly variance report is more helpful on the expense side than the revenue side.

An example of a typical variance report is provided in Table 2.6. In this example, by the end of February, the Sojourner Truth Settlement House has raised 16.8% of the budgeted revenues. The revenues are almost on track, and the executive director simply has to continue to track when revenues are expended. On the expense side, there are serious issues. If we examine the NPS side carefully, we see that it is clear that this organization overspent. The nonprofit has spent 17.1% of the total expenses, which for the month of February should not exceed 16.7%. Even by the end of January, the executive director could see that this program is spending too much. The PS side of the budget, salaries and fringe benefits, is problematic: the amount of monies budgeted for the staff is insufficient—the nonprofit is spending 8.4% instead of 8.3% in January. It seems that the senior staff and staff positions have been underbudgeted. By the end of the second month, 17% of the monies for the staff positions have been expended instead of 16.7%. The staff positions are underbudgeted by $19,150 and the senior staff positions by $13,060 for the year. Steps must be taken immediately to stop the overspending, either by finding more revenue for these positions or by eliminating one of the positions. The easiest strategy would be to use the surplus to put more money on the staff and senior staff budgeted lines so that the positions are adequately funded. However, if the organization is counting on that surplus for other uses, such as adding to its rainy-day fund in the future, then other strategies must be adopted.

Looking at NPS, the executive director has spent all the computer equipment monies at the beginning of the fiscal year. Supplies have run over budget, as has travel. It may be possible to transfer some of the budgeted amounts from NPS (equipment) to the staff positions on the PS side to help resolve that underfunding and at the same time slow the spending in travel and supplies until they are again in balance. As this example illustrates, the variance report is one of the most vital tools the executive director and finance officer can use to keep control of spending in their organization.

Table 2.6 FY 2020 Variance Report, Sojourner Truth Settlement House (as of end of February 2020)

Revenues	Adopted	January Actuals	% Revenue 8.30%	February Actuals	Cumulative Actuals	% Revenue 16.70%
Contributions	$ 1,810,000	$ 200,000	11.0	$ 125,000	$ 325,000	18.0
Fees	134,880	6,000	4.4	7,000	13,000	9.6
Foundation Grant	1,075,000	100,000	9.3	100,000	200,000	18.6
Government Contract	2,035,000	125,000	6.1	225,000	350,000	17.2
Investment Income	226,000	——	0.0	——	——	0.0
Total Revenues	$ 5,280,880	$ 431,000	8.2	$ 457,000	$ 888,000	16.8
Expenses						
PS						
Executive Director	$ 150,000	$ 12,450	8.3	$ 12,600	$ 25,050	16.7
Facilities Director	100,000	8,300	8.3	8,400	16,700	16.7
Finance Officer	125,000	10,375	8.3	10,500	20,875	16.7
Finance Staff	375,000	31,125	8.3	31,500	62,625	16.7
Administrative Staff	385,000	31,955	8.3	32,340	64,295	16.7
Development Director	125,000	10,375	8.3	10,500	20,875	16.7
Development Staff	200,000	16,600	8.3	16,800	33,400	16.7
Program Director	100,000	8,300	8.3	8,400	16,700	16.7
Coordinators	240,000	19,920	8.3	20,160	40,080	16.7
Directors	345,000	28,635	8.3	28,980	57,615	16.7
Senior Staff	653,000	55,505	8.5	55,505	111,010	17.0
Staff	957,500	81,388	8.5	81,388	162,775	17.0
PS	3,755,500	314,928	8.4	315,462	630,390	16.8
Fringe Benefits (20%)	751,100	62,986	8.4	63,092	126,078	16.8
Total PS	$ 4,506,600	$ 377,913	8.4	$ 378,554	$ 756,467	16.8
NPS						
Consultants	$ 232,000	$ 12,000	5.2	$ 19,256	$ 31,256	13.5
Computer Equipment	40,200	40,200	100.0	——	40,200	100.0
Equipment	83,800	——	0.0	6,955	6,955	8.3
Food	39,000	3,000	7.7	3,237	6,237	16.0
Maintenance Contract	30,000	2,490	8.3	2,490	4,980	16.6
Mortgage	60,000	4,980	8.3	4,980	9,960	16.6
Phones	43,680	3,625	8.3	3,625	7,251	16.6
Supplies/Printing	102,000	10,000	9.8	8,466	18,466	18.1
Travel	52,900	4,500	8.5	4,500	9,000	17.0
Utilities	30,000	2,490	8.3	2,490	4,980	16.6
Total NPS	$ 713,580	$ 83,285	11.7	$ 59,227	$ 142,513	20.0
Total Expenses	$ 5,220,180	$ 461,198	8.8	$ 433,275	$ 894,473	17.1
Surplus/Deficit		$ 60,700				

Cash-Flow Management Reports. It is possible for a nonprofit to have a balanced budget for the year and yet run out of cash. Sometimes revenues do not come in as quickly as staff think they will. That is the most common reason that nonprofits run out of cash even though they have balanced budgets. Another report that is quite useful to the executive director is the **cash-flow management report**, which tells the executive director how liquid the nonprofit is. The degree of a nonprofit's **liquidity**, meaning the extent to which the organization has sufficient cash on hand, is critical. In effect, the executive director creates a cash-flow projection, which is a detailed plan showing revenues expected each month in the fiscal year, planning expenses over the fiscal year, and the difference between the revenues and expenses, which will show either a surplus or a deficit. A cash-flow management report is designed monthly, so that each month the executive director will have some indication when the organization is getting low on cash.

A cash-flow management report is important for several reasons. It is an effective way to track how much cash will be on hand throughout the year. It allows the executive director to make management decisions about when cash needs to be preserved and when sufficient funds are on hand to be spent. Such a report allows the director to determine when the nonprofit might need to borrow money from a lender for a short term because it may run out of cash in a particular month. A cash-flow management report ensures that the executive director and the finance officer know in advance in which months their cash may be low and thus they can make plans to deal with the problem.

Do not confuse the cash-flow management report with the statement of cash flows in a nonprofit's financial statements. Financial statements are formal records of the financial activities of the nonprofit. Usually at the end of the year, a certified public accountant will create four financial statements in a financial report for a nonprofit.

One of these financial statements is the statement of cash flows, which describes the changes in cash from year to year due to operating surpluses or deficits, makes adjustments such as depreciation, and shows increases or decreases in accounts payable and accounts receivable. This is valuable information and is readily available from a nonprofit's accounting system and can be complied every month or every quarter; it provides different information from that provided in a cash-flow management report. We present a more detailed explanation of cash-flow issues in Chapter 3, Liquidity and Managing Cash Flow.

Performance Report. The third report most useful to the executive director is the performance report. It is tied to the performance of each program in a nonprofit. Performance can be determined in terms of the efficiency and effectiveness of a program in relation to a nonprofit's budget. In Chapter 9, we go into detail regarding the measurement of efficiency and effectiveness. In Chapter 10, we discuss other performance indicators in greater depth.

Nonprofits collect a great deal of information about performance, but the crucial aspect for the budget is that the nonprofit is actually serving the number of clients it expects to serve, as these estimations are the numbers upon which the budget is based. It is important to know early in the year whether or not each program has a sufficient number of clients, because the number of clients could have a positive or negative impact on the budget. Revenue can come from fees for each client that participates in a program or if a contract agreement with a state program also relies on client participation. An example of a performance report is provided in Table 2.7. The executive director should receive this report regularly.

Table 2.7 FY 2020 Performance Report, Sojourner Truth Settlement House

Program	Projected Number of Clients	January Actual Number of Clients	February Actual Number of Clients	March Actual Number of Clients
College Prep	100	93		
Day Care Infants	10	8		
Day Care Preschool	65	61		
After School	100	85		
Employment and Training	100	98		
Parent Education	200	155		
Senior Citizens	100	99		
Summer Camp	100	0		
Total	775	599		

Planning for Next Year's Budget. During the execution phase, once decisions are made, the staff must begin the process of looking at next year's budget. This means examining the new programs or the expansion of current programs that came out of the strategic planning sessions. Again, both sides of the coin must be examined: where the revenues are coming from and the costs of the programs being considered. It is common for the executive director to use a spending baseline budget and then expand that baseline budget for new programs. The baseline is how much it will cost to continue the level of services next year with next year's costs of staff and materials. In Chapter 3, we review several factors that affect next year's budget.

Ending the Fiscal Year: The Auditing and Reporting Stage

The end of the fiscal year brings a close to that year's budget, but there is still much work to be done. The executive director and finance officer will prepare a final variance report for the board as well as themselves. It is important for the decision makers to know early into the next year what the problems were with the fiscal year that just closed.

The nonprofit must now create the year's financial statements. The nonprofit usually hires an outside certified public accountant (CPA) who is qualified to issue annual audited financial statements. It is very rare for nonprofits to develop their financial statements themselves instead of using the services of CPAs. It is widely considered best to have an outside expert come in and review the books.

It is the CPA's job to examine the nonprofit's finances and ensure that the organization has faithfully followed **generally accepted accounting principles (GAAP)** in reporting on its financial activities. This is known as a financial audit. Preparing for such an audit requires strong organizational skills on the part of the executive director and the finance officer. On the revenue side, the nonprofit must document every reported revenue source by following a paper trail. On the expense side, every purchase should be linked to a bill or purchase order. The quality of the audit is dependent not just on the auditor's skills but also on the quality of the nonprofit's documentation.

Financial auditors are highly skilled, and undergoing an audit can be very useful to an organization. If asked, an auditor can conduct a management audit—the systematic evaluation of the organization's methods and policies in using all of its resources. In such an audit, the auditor will look at every aspect of the control of the nonprofit's resources. For example, the auditor will examine how petty cash is handled and suggest how the procedures can be improved. It is very common and smart for nonprofits to ask their CPAs to conduct management audits as well as financial audits.

In addition to the CPA, who will issue audited financial statements, the nonprofit may have to deal with federal or state auditors concerning federal or state grants. If a nonprofit receives more than $500,000 from the federal government, the government requires audit information from the nonprofit. This audit includes both a financial audit to ensure that the nonprofit uses GAAP and an internal controls audit to ensure that the nonprofit uses proper procedures and processes for all its assets and transactions. Each state has its own rules about auditing nonprofits that have received state grants, contracts, or loans. We cover internal controls in greater depth in Chapter 13.

Other reports that nonprofits must file include some type of a Form 990, Return of Organization Exempt from Income Tax. Almost always, the CPA who has completed the audited financial statements will complete the Form 990. Many states require nonprofits to file a state form that often requires attaching the Form 990. Rules about filing differ from state to state, and nonprofits must check with their states to ensure that they are in compliance with all the requirements. We discuss reporting requirements in detail in Chapter 5.

Periodic Budget Reviews and Revisions

The executive director and the board of directors must periodically review and, if necessary, revise the budget during the fiscal year. This happens for many reasons. Changing the adopted budget to reflect new revenues or fewer revenues or unexpected expenses is the norm. Revenues can be overstated. An executive director may be optimistic that the nonprofit will get a foundation grant and list that grant as revenue for the fiscal year, but the program officer at the foundation leaves, and the new program officer does not approve the grant. Thus, the nonprofit has a hole in the budget. In this circumstance, the easiest way to revise the revenue side of the budget is to cut the expenses associated with the grant that fell through. If this is not possible, it may be possible to budget other revenues for those expenses if the nonprofit has a stated surplus in its adopted budget.

Sometimes there are errors in calculation. This is common; after all, there are hundreds of calculations in budgets within large organizations. Mistakes are bound to happen. If the fringe benefits rate turns out to be 21% and not 20%, there is a hole in the budget. Nonprofits need to respond quickly to such problems. If there is not enough of a projected surplus in the budget to make up the difference, and if additional revenues are not available, then cuts to the budget must be made. Nonprofits should not use their reserves or rainy-day funds for budget problems unless they see no other alternative. Rainy-day funds should be used for hard times, not to make up for mistakes and miscalculations.

Budget revisions need to be made as soon as possible after problems are recognized. The first monthly variance report is crucial, as are the first cash-flow management report and the monthly performance report. In making all of these adjustments, the executive director's best friend is the finance committee. The finance committee should meet monthly and carefully review these reports with the executive director. The earlier a problem is found, the sooner it can be fixed. Delaying is a mistake because, if a deficit exists, it will build over a period of months.

Applying Indirect Costs for a New Program

Often nonprofits seek funding from foundations and state and federal governments by writing proposals, and with these proposals, the nonprofits must attach proposed budgets. A budget of this type is similar in form to any other operating budget, except it is for a particular program.

A nonprofit can add an **indirect cost** or amount to the total proposed budget to cover expenses that are not in the budget. For example, if a multiservice nonprofit seeks a grant from the federal government to help with its day care center, the nonprofit will write a proposal with a budget and submit it to the appropriate agency. The federal government permits a certain percentage of the expense budget to be indirect, perhaps 4 or 5%. This covers the cost of the central administration of the nonprofit that is not included in the program budget submitted to the federal government. The indirect cost is taken after the PS and NPS is totaled. Then the percentage of that total is calculated, after which the total expenses can be determined. Using indirect cost would look like this:

$$(PS + NPS \text{ expenses}) + \text{indirect costs} = \text{total expenses}$$

Foundations often permit a larger indirect cost when nonprofits seek funding for particular programs. The typical indirect expense for a nonprofit is for central administration, such as the use of the finance and personnel offices, and common nonpersonnel services such as rent and utilities. More information on costs is in Chapter 4.

Cutback Budgeting

Soon after the serious national recession that began in 2008, nonprofits faced a reductionist environment throughout the public and private sector. Recessions are an external factor and must be treated as such. Nonprofits deal with this difficult environment by carefully examining all the factors involved and revisiting their planning strategies. An executive director and staff cannot face a drop in revenues alone; the board of directors must take responsibility and be involved. Board members must educate themselves so that they understand the threats to the budgets. Although it is the role of the executive director to be careful in these times, the board must also be diligent.

The first consideration is the revenue side. During a recession, which revenues will be hit first? Certainly contributions will be affected—contributors will give less because they have less to give. Other reductions in revenue are not far behind. Fees may decrease because clients no longer have that extra $10 to pay for a child's admission to the after-school program. Revenue from foundations may suffer as their endowments shrink. Government contracts also may decrease as state and local governments begin to make cutbacks in their own budgets. Finally, nonprofits' investment income from their endowments may shrink as the stock market falls. Nonprofits are often the hardest hit organizations in a recession because they depend on so many other sectors for funding.

A nonprofit must adopt three strategies that will help it to govern cutbacks. The first strategy is to create savings so that when a recession hits, the nonprofit has a cushion. In a multiyear recession, however, that cushion will not last long. The second strategy is to hire expertise that will help to predict what major funders will do in the future. Planning needs to include donors, whether foundation leaders or government officials. The third strategy is to think through any cutbacks program by program and avoid across-the-board cuts that affect all programs. If a program is bringing in more revenue than it spends, across-the-board cutbacks may damage that program. When a nonprofit operates multiple programs, some may need to be eliminated. Charles H. Levine wrote a series of three essays about retrenchment, emphasizing that choosing cutbacks represents a trade-off between equity and efficiency:

> Equity is meant to mean the distribution of cuts across the organization (across-the-board cuts) with an equal probability of hurting all units and employees irrespective of impacts on the long-term capacity of the organization. Efficiency is meant to mean the sorting, sifting, and assignment of cuts to those people and units in the organization so that for a given budget decrement, cuts are allocated to minimize the long-term loss in total benefits to the organization as a whole, irrespective of their distribution.[9]

Making cuts on the basis of equity is easier because it appears to be fair to all concerned, but efficiency is often the better choice for a nonprofit. When retrenchment occurs, eliminating a program may provide more savings and better results for other programs. It is important to reduce or eliminate programs that do not pay their own way in times of fiscal retrenchment. These are the hard choices that board members and the executive director must make.

It is very difficult to generalize about nonprofit budgeting. The problems and processes depend on what the organization does and the origins and diversification of its revenue streams. For example, budgeting for a college is very different from budgeting for a social service organization. Often colleges have wealthy alumni who help to build the institutions' endowments. Social service organizations rarely have that depth of wealth upon which to draw. Hospitals have financial problems that are very different from those experienced by multiservice agencies. Hospitals must purchase extremely expensive technology; their capital budgets are of major concern. For all types of nonprofits, however, during times of fiscal retrenchment the key is how much unrestricted revenue is available from all sources and how those dollars can be used as efficiently as possible.

Conclusion

Budgeting is not yet a science. The nonprofit environment simply has too many variables—any executive director will find it difficult to plan appropriately in any given year. There are, however, guides to be followed that can make it easier. Budgeting is part of planning, but it must not determine the plan; budgeting must interact with the planning process so that plans have a realistic chance of gathering enough resources to be successful. The board and executive director must work closely together in all phases of the budget process: preparation, approval, execution, and auditing. When nonprofits face a reductionist environment executive directors must carefully track both the revenue and expense sides. Using the various reports discussed in this chapter can help them in that task. When cutbacks are unavoidable, nonprofits should not take the easy way out with across-the-board cuts; rather, they should closely examine each program they are operating and choose wisely as to which one to cut.

KEY TERMS

adopted budget	input
allocation	line-item budget
audit	liquidity
capital budget	operating budget
cash-flow management report	output
encumbrances	program budget
expense budget	proposed budget
fiscal year (FY)	revenue budget
generally accepted accounting principles (GAAP)	spending baseline
indirect cost	variance report

DISCUSSION QUESTIONS

1. How can budgeting be used as a planning tool, a management tool, and a communications tool?
2. Explain each step in the budgeting process.
3. What are the most important reporting tools that an executive director can use during the execution phase?
4. Why is a periodic review of budget data so important?
5. What do we mean when we say that programs should drive dollars and not the other way around?
6. What is the decision-making role of the board of directors as compared to the executive director?
7. Name three budget strategies that an executive director can use during fiscal retrenchment.
8. What is the difference between equity and efficiency in dealing with cutbacks?

SUGGESTED READINGS

Finkler, Steven A., Daniel L. Smith, Thad D. Calabrese, and Robert M. Purtell (2016). *Financial Management for Public, Health, and Not-for-Profit Organizations* (5th ed.). Washington, DC: CQ Press.

Forsythe, Dall W. (2004). *Memos to the Governor: An Introduction to State Budgeting* (2nd ed.). Washington, DC: Georgetown University Press.

Rubin, Irene S. (2019). *The Politics of Public Budgeting: Getting and Spending, Borrowing and Balancing* (9th ed.). Washington, DC: CQ Press.

CASE STUDY

Examining the Hypothetical Budget of the Sojourner Truth Settlement House

Founded by social reformers in 1902, the Sojourner Truth Settlement House (known also simply as the Settlement House) had as its mission to provide a variety of services to the thousands of refugees who were pouring into Chicago from all over Europe. Founded by members of Chicago's upper class who were desperate to provide support for thousands of immigrants, most of whom had never been to school, the Settlement House thrived with multiple services from day care to job training to senior care.

Now more than 100 years later, the Settlement House occupies a large block building on Chicago's South Side. Over the years, the organization has provided education, health care, and job training to thousands. The faces of the poor have changed; clients now come from all ethnicities, including African Americans, Hispanics, Eastern Europeans, and Asians. The Settlement House has grown in stature. Its programs are well regarded in the charity circles of Chicago, and its leaders are respected in the offices of local foundations and city hall.

The board of directors includes many of the oldest and most famous names in Chicago philanthropy. Often board members pass on their membership to their children when they are ready to retire from the world of philanthropy.

In 2020, the executive director retired after 30 years of directing the organization's work. The board hired a dynamic and highly educated Puerto Rican woman, Esther Rosa, seasoned by years of work in the poverty circles of Chicago. Rosa became executive director just as the country was experiencing the biggest recession since the Great Depression, and she had her work cut out for her.

At the time, the fiscal front was not positive. Funding sources and philanthropy by no means kept up with the area's needs for services to children, and the gap was only partially filled by the Settlement House's programs. In FY 2020, the board and the executive director decided to add two new programs, a college prep program and a volunteer program in the elementary schools. Part of the new programs was paid for through cutbacks in other programs. In addition, the Settlement House faced both operating and capital needs as its aging structure required renovation.

Sojourner Truth Settlement House's programs consisted of the following:

1. *Child care programs:* These programs included infant and day care programs as well as a prenatal clinic.
2. *College prep program:* The Settlement House for the first time in FY 2020 implemented a highly enriched after-school component for 100 students.
3. *Elementary school volunteer program:* The Settlement House created a new program in which the Settlement House volunteers tutor needy children in nearby elementary schools.
4. *Employment and job training center:* The Settlement House operated a highly regarded employment and job training center. The center concentrated on training for the skilled trades: electrical, carpentry, and plumbing.
5. *Foster care program:* The Settlement House ran a large foster care program that linked foster parents to the many children in the city who were in need of foster homes.
6. *Middle and high school program:* The after-school and summer programs served the population of middle and high school students in a large gym in the Settlement House facility along with numerous classrooms.
7. *Parental education program:* The Settlement House ran a program that included an adult literacy component to encourage parents in the housing projects near the Settlement House to take an active role in their children's lives.
8. *Senior citizen program:* The Settlement House had an exciting lunch program for seniors that helped to integrate Hispanic, African American, Asian, and Eastern European seniors. The program offered a tai chi session after lunch.

The Settlement House had a large administrative and fundraising (development) team in place—including accounting, personnel, information systems, maintenance, and the executive director's team—to support all of these activities.

The Financial Situation

The Settlement House broke even or generated a small surplus over most of the last 30 years, but in 2020 it ran into trouble because of cutbacks by federal and county governments. In FY 2019 the Settlement House balanced its budget. In FY 2020 the Settlement House began with a balanced budget but was facing difficulties. The pressure on finances caused by slow payments by the federal and county governments added to the problem. Because the board was nervous about collecting revenues, the board changed its rules: it required the executive director to record pledges only when the revenues were received.

The Settlement House owned its large building and recorded this asset at historical value. Space was a problem in some areas but not in others. The employment and job training program was bursting at the seams; it could have easily used twice the amount of space and taken on more clients, and hence produce more revenue. Space was even tighter with the added elementary school volunteer program and the college prep program. The nonprofit was at full capacity. In fact, it had contracted out certain activities, such as payroll, in part to free up space for programs.

The staff and the board differed on how the Settlement House should deal with its financial problems. On one hand, they felt that the mission of the Settlement House included all children's services. The combination of the need for additional space and program financial pressures led the executive director to urge the board to take out a larger mortgage on their building, partly for renovations and partly for operating costs. In 2020, the nonprofit already had a small mortgage at 6% interest for $400,000 taken out more than 15 years ago for renovations. A new renovation program was estimated to cost $3.4 million. A 30-year loan could have been secured at 4.3% if the board acted quickly, but the board members were uncertain about taking this step.

The endowment management had not yet been rethought to accommodate the growing nonprofit. Given the recession, the investment mix was shifted from an equal mixture of common stocks and bonds to 100% bonds as a conservative move to protect the endowment. The finance committee of the board refused to use the endowment principal to alleviate what may be a difficult fiscal year. The board also was content to spend only part of the investment income (interest income and dividends earned) on operating costs (75% spent, 25% saved), and was firmly against any spending of the principal. See Tables 2.8 and 2.9 for the adopted FY 2020 and FY 2019 budgets, respectively.

Case Study Questions

Using the information provided in Tables 2.8 and 2.9, answer the following questions:

1. In FY 2020, which programs bring in the most revenue? Which programs cost the most? Which programs are operating at a deficit? What can you conclude from this limited amount of data?
2. How do these figures compare to FY 2019?

Budgeting as Part of the Planning Process

Table 2.8 FY 2020 Adopted Budget by Program, Sojourner Truth Settlement House

Program	Revenue	Expenses PS	Expenses NPS	Expenses Total	% of Total	Surplus/Deficit
Administration	$ 975,000	$ 1,152,000	$ 142,620	$ 1,294,620	24.8	$ (319,620)
Development	525,000	439,200	47,300	486,500	9.3	38,500
Child Care	905,000	819,000	15,260	834,260	16.0	70,740
College Prep	372,000	279,000	68,840	347,840	6.7	24,160
Elementary Volunteer	100,000	109,800	8,760	118,560	2.3	(18,560)
Employment and Training	585,000	477,000	62,700	539,700	10.3	45,300
Foster Care	535,000	471,000	17,860	488,860	9.4	46,140
Middle and High (After School)	477,880	261,000	122,200	383,200	7.3	94,680
Middle and High (Summer)	315,000	132,600	163,060	295,660	5.7	19,340
Parental Education	161,000	117,000	27,260	144,260	2.8	16,740
Senior Citizen	330,000	249,000	37,720	286,720	5.5	43,280
Total	$ 5,280,880	$ 4,506,600	$ 713,580	$ 5,220,180	100.0	$ 60,700

Table 2.9 FY 2019 Adopted Budget by Program, Sojourner Truth Settlement House

Program	Revenue	Expenses PS	Expenses NPS	Expenses Total	% of Total	Difference
Administration	$ 1,005,000	$ 1,242,000	$ 156,400	$ 1,398,400	28.0	($ 393,400)
Development	600,000	511,200	47,300	558,500	11.2	41,500
Child Care	935,000	855,000	15,260	870,260	17.4	64,740
Employment and Training	615,000	399,000	62,700	461,700	9.2	153,300
Foster Care	540,000	549,000	17,860	566,860	11.4	(26,860)
Middle and High (After School)	482,880	264,000	122,200	386,200	7.7	96,680
Middle and High (Summer)	325,000	132,600	182,760	315,360	6.3	9,640
Parental Education	161,000	118,200	27,260	145,460	2.9	15,540
Senior Citizen	335,000	251,400	37,720	289,120	5.8	45,880
Total	$ 4,998,880	$ 4,322,400	$ 669,460	$ 4,991,860	100.0	$ 7,020

3. Now look at the 2020 and 2019 adopted revenues (see Tables 2.10 and 2.11, respectively). In the Sojourner Truth Settlement House, the nonprofit's leadership decides where contributions should go. Which programs bring in the most revenue from outside the nonprofit—that is, other than contributions? Which revenue uses the nonprofit's internal resources (contributions) more than the others? What can you conclude from this?

ASSIGNMENTS

Assignment 2.1. Creating a Projected Budget for a New Program

Using the following information, create a projected budget for a new program, the After-School Girls Program, for 20 students at the Sojourner Truth Settlement House. Work with others in your class.

Assumptions:

1. *Revenues*: Contributions ($117,000), foundation grant ($150,000), fees of $200 per person for 20 students ($4,000), and in-kind services ($5,000) for rent because the program will use some of the existing space in the after-school program building.
2. *PS expenses*: Executive director @ $150,000 (5% of time), program coordinator @ $100,000 (10% of time), After-School Girls Program coordinator @ $65,000 (100% of time), and one staff person @ $50,000 (100% of time). Fringe benefits for staff are 20% of their salaries.
3. *NPS expenses*: 20 computers @ $2,000 each, 20 printers @ $800 each, equipment (copier and software) for $7,000, two phones @ $950 each, in-kind rent ($5,000), supplies ($10,000), and travel to eight colleges ($12,000).
4. An indirect cost of 10% of all expenses for utilities and administrative support.

Assignment 2.2. Creating a Nonprofit Budget

Create your own small nonprofit with a specific mission, objective, and one program, and then create its revenue and expense budget. Keep it small (below $500,000) so that you do not get lost in the numbers. In effect, you are creating a small business plan. The outline is as follows:

1. Mission
2. Objectives
3. Program to achieve the mission
4. Revenue budget to support the program
5. Expense budget to demonstrate how the funds will be used
6. Variance report, cash-flow management report, and performance report

Assignment 2.3. Serving Seniors

You are the executive director of a social services nonprofit and have just been notified that you are losing your funding from a local foundation for your seniors program. You serve lunch to more than 100 seniors five days a week, in addition to

Table 2.10 FY 2020 Adopted Revenues by Program, Sojourner Truth Settlement House

Revenues	Contributions	Fees	Foundations	Government	Investment Income	Total
Child Care	$ 140,000	$ 50,000	$ 150,000	$ 550,000	$ 15,000	$ 905,000
College Prep	120,000	2,000	250,000	—	—	372,000
Elementary Volunteer	90,000	—	—	—	10,000	100,000
Employment and Training	15,000	20,000	—	550,000	—	585,000
Foster Care	70,000	—	—	460,000	5,000	535,000
Middle and High (After School)	105,000	22,880	125,000	225,000	—	477,880
Middle and High (Summer)	50,000	10,000	250,000	—	5,000	315,000
Parental Education	50,000	10,000	—	100,000	1,000	161,000
Senior Citizen	70,000	10,000	100,000	150,000	—	330,000
Development	300,000	—	125,000	—	100,000	525,000
Administration	800,000	—	75,000	—	100,000	975,000
Total	$ 1,810,000	$ 124,880	$ 1,075,000	$ 2,035,000	$ 236,000	$ 5,280,880
% Total	34.3%	2.4%	20.4%	38.5%	4.5%	100.1%

Table 2.11 FY2019 Adopted Revenues by Program, Sojourner Truth Settlement House

Revenues	Contributions	Fees	Foundations	Government	Investment Income	Total	% of Total
Child Care	$ 170,000	$ 50,000	$ 150,000	$ 550,000	$ 15,000	$ 935,000	18.7
Employment and Training	20,000	20,000	—	575,000	—	615,000	12.3
Foster Care	75,000	—	—	460,000	5,000	540,000	10.8
Middle and High (After School)	110,000	22,880	125,000	225,000	—	482,880	9.7
Middle and High (Summer)	50,000	10,000	250,000	10,000	5,000	325,000	6.5
Parental Education	50,000	10,000	—	100,000	1,000	161,000	3.2
Senior Citizen	75,000	10,000	100,000	150,000	—	335,000	6.7
Development	375,000	—	125,000	—	100,000	600,000	12.0
Administration	830,000	—	75,000	—	100,000	1,005,000	20.1
Total	$ 1,755,000	$ 122,880	$ 825,000	$ 2,070,000	$ 226,000	$ 4,998,880	100.0
% Total	35.1%	2.5%	16.5%	41.4%	4.5%	100.0%	

providing them with a program before the lunch is served. The program is exercise three days a week, and on the other days it is dancing. You decide to approach another foundation to replace the funding you will be losing. Create a proposed budget to attach to your grant proposal (do not write a proposal) to the foundation, using the following information:

1. *Revenue:* Contributions ($122,200), in-kind services ($10,000), foundation grant ($130,000), and senior contributions ($1,250).

2. *Expenses:* Executive director @ $150,000 (3% of time); program coordinator @ $100,000 (5% of time); one senior program director @ $50,000 (100% of time); and one senior program staff member @ $35,000 (100% of time). Fringe benefits for staff are 20% of their salaries. NPS consists of 100 seniors budgeted for 250 days of the year at $5 per meal. The exercise and music staff come in for one hour a day for five days each week for 50 weeks @ $25 each an hour. The in-kind services are for the kitchen @ $10,000. Supplies @ $10,000. The indirect cost is 10% of all expenses.

Assignment 2.4. Calculating Fringe Benefits

You will calculate the fringe benefits for staff at the Senior Day Care Center for FY 2021 based upon the FY 2020 budget. (See Table 2.12.) In 2021, there will be a 5% increase in salary for each staff member, except for the CEO. Fringe benefits are 6.2% for social security, 1.45% for Medicare, and a pension is offered at 20% of salary. Health insurance is $180 a month for all full-time employees; clericals are only part time and *do not* get health benefits. The CEO line has been completed and acts as a guide to complete the rest of the problem.

A specific format is used in Table 2.12. The format is useful information in a budget office in which analysts are often asked how much does it cost to add one more position. If you use this format, the information is readily available.

NOTES

[1] Forsythe, Dall W. (2004). *Memos to the Governor: An Introduction to State Budgeting* (2nd ed., p. 34). Washington, DC: Georgetown University Press.

[2] American Red Cross, Mission Statement (redcross.org).

[3] Epstein, Jennifer (2010, July 16). An Error with Consequences. Inside Higher Ed (insidehighered.com/news/2010/07/16/error-consequences).

[4] See Rubin, Irene S. (1990, March/April). "Budget Theory and Budget Practice: How Good the Fit?" *Public Administration Review*, 50: 179–189. Irene Rubin was the first to divide the budget tools into several categories.

[5] National Council of Nonprofits (2010, March 16). *State Budget Crises: Ripping the Safety Net Held by Nonprofits* (p. 1). Washington, DC: National Council of Nonprofits (councilofnonprofits.org/sites/default/files/documents/Special-Report-State-Budget-Crises-Ripping-the-Safety-Net-Held-by-Nonprofits_0.pdf).

[6] GuideStar merged with the Foundation Center and is now known as Candid.

[7] City of Concord, Performance Based Budgeting (cityofconcord.org/DocumentCenter/View/732/City-Managers-Message-and-Introduction-PDF?bidId=).

[8] City of Sunnyvale, California, Budget Documents (sunnyvale.ca.gov/government/budget.htm).

[9] Levine, Charles H. (1978). "Organizational Decline and Cutback Management." *Public Administration Review*, 38(4): 320.

Table 2.12 Senior Day Care Center Projected 2021 PS Budget

PS	#	Salary 2020	5% increase	Salary 2021	Health	Pension (20%)	SS (6.2%)	Medicare (1.45%)	Total	Individual Salary (w/benefits)	2021 Total Salaries (w/benefits)	Benefits (%)
CEO	1	$ 105,000	$	$ 105,000	$ 2,160	$ 21,000	$ 6,510	$ 1,523	$ 31,193	$ 136,193	$ 136,193	22.9%
Deputy	3	70,000										
Nurses	12	45,000										
Aides	15	35,000										
Clerical	3	25,000										
Total	34		$	$						$	$	

3

Liquidity and Managing Cash Flow

> From a managerial perspective, we believe that liquidity management is one of the most important yet least studied areas in the management of nonprofits.
>
> —John Zietlow, Jo Ann Hankin,
> Alan G. Seidner, and Tim O'Brien[1]

LEARNING OBJECTIVES

The learning objectives for this chapter are as follows:
- Understanding liquidity
- Learning about cash and cash-flow management
- Understanding strategies of cash-flow management
- What do we do when we run out of cash?
- What do we do when we run a cash surplus?
- Managing the level of cash reserves

*T*he operating budget, as discussed in Chapter 2, is arguably the most important financial management tool for all organizations, nonprofits included. A well-developed operating budget, however, does not guarantee that a nonprofit will thrive, or even survive, without good cash-flow management in place. Nonprofits do not fail directly due to and immediately following running a deficit; they fail because they are not able to pay bills and meet payroll. Unlike government, revenues for nonprofits, especially donations and contractual obligations, do not arrive in a predictable fashion. The staff of a nonprofit has to be good enough to know that and to plan for the day when cash does not arrive on time. In other words, we must manage our **cash flow**. Certainly local and state governments can have cash-flow problems, but not to the extent that nonprofits do. Nonprofits face an uncertain future every year—a foundation changes its mind, a large contributor dies, a government contract is cancelled—all of these events can wreak havoc in a nonprofit. This is unlike local and state governments, who can generate revenue by collecting sales and property tax revenue; these revenues may decline in a recession but some of it will still come in.

In this chapter we focus on operational issues in financial management, including liquidity and cash-flow management. We emphasize the development of strategies to forecast cash flow so that management can take preventive or corrective actions if needed. We also discuss investment strategies that nonprofits can implement when short-term surpluses of cash are present. The Financial Accounting Standards Board (FASB) revised accounting rules governing nonprofits in 2016 (Accounting Standards Update 2016-14). One of these revisions concerned liquidity. GuideStar reported that the FASB now requires nonprofits to provide information on how it managed its liquid available resources and liquid risks. "Quantitative information that communicates the availability of a not-for-profit's financial assets at the balance sheet date to meet cash needs for general expenditures within 1 year is required to be presented on the face of the financial statement and/or in the notes."[2] FASB seeks to require nonprofits to be more transparent about their level of liquidity.

Liquidity

Being and remaining liquid are the most important issues for nonprofits. *Liquid*, in the accounting context, means cash or access to cash to meet obligations. When you hear someone say that a "firm is quite liquid," it means that the corporation has a great deal of cash and is not in danger of bankruptcy. **Liquidity** can be calculated as the sum of an organization's cash and cash-equivalent, short-term investments, its unused lines of credit, and committed loans from financing institutions. An organization should establish a target for the level of liquidity in its financial policy and monitor and maintain that target liquidity over time. Achieving and maintaining the target liquidity is a central task of financial managers, especially for nonprofit organizations given the nature of their services (e.g., the separation of clients/customers and payers/supporters and their limited sources of capital as a cushion) relative to for-profit businesses, which can issue stocks and which have better collateral for debt financing.

Timing of Cash Flows and Undercapitalization

Nonprofits often do not have reliable or timely cash inflows because of the separation of service clients and donors. The cash conversion cycle—that is, the time between cash disbursement for program start-up and operation and the receipt of cash from donor support and reimbursement from government contracts—can be long and inconsistent, an issue we discuss further in the section on cash flow. Moreover, nonprofits operate on the edge of solvency; they never have enough funding to do all they want to do. The lack of net assets worsens the liquidity issue, especially when the economy is in recession and government/public support is tightening. Revenues, especially donations, do not arrive in predictable fashion. Yet payroll must be met on a regular basis. Without a reserve/cash balance, a nonprofit has a limited cushion to withstand external shocks, whether these shocks come because of changes in priorities in public support or a lack of synchronization of cash inflows and outflows.

Restricted Monies

Nonprofits often deal with restricted funds, and this limits the choices the nonprofits can make. Financial consultant Allen Proctor has written about the limited liquidity of nonprofits:

> Restricted gifts have limited flexibility or liquidity and, in some circumstances, they can harm existing flexibility and liquidity. For example, a nonprofit manager who receives a $50,000 gift restricted to a new exhibit cannot use this investment to boost attendance, increase working capital, upgrade computer systems, respond to unanticipated events or add fundraising staff. Typically, the expanded program from that exhibit will also increase illiquid receivables, raise payables, probably add more illiquid assets requiring maintenance and expand operating expenses.[3]

Liquidity Targets

To ensure liquidity, nonprofit organizations need to establish liquidity targets in their financial policy statements and plan and manage liquidity consciously and continuously. A rule of thumb is that an organization should set aside six months of operating expenses as a reserve, but most nonprofits do not adhere to this. Different nonprofits, however, have different needs. Hospitals, for example, rarely have large cash reserves, because they operate close to the margin; nevertheless, they have relatively reliable and regular fee revenue and cash flows. Universities may have more cash to put aside as reserves because of alumni and other support, but their revenue and cash inflow can be affected by reductions in government funding. Each organization needs to develop a liquidity target and strategy based on its unique circumstances; although good practices such as cash-flow budgeting and management commonly apply to most nonprofits.

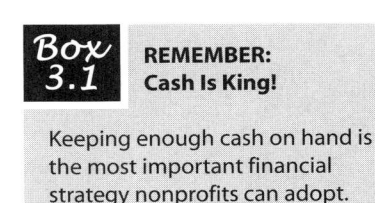

Box 3.1

REMEMBER: Cash Is King!

Keeping enough cash on hand is the most important financial strategy nonprofits can adopt.

Cash and Cash-Flow Management

Cash is king in all organizations, nonprofit and for-profit alike. Strong cash reserves indicate the ability to pay bills, the stability to cope with financial crisis, and the capability to seize opportunities when they emerge. Cash is most liquid assets, and a key component of liquidity. **Cash-flow management** has an impact on the cash balance or cash reserves of a nonprofit, affecting the achievement of established target liquidity.

Cash-flow management is the process of projecting, monitoring, analyzing, and adjusting cash inflows, cash outflows, and cash balances. In most organizations, cash inflows and outflows occur at different times, and cash inflows normally lag behind cash outflows (this is known as the cash conversion cycle in the business world). Many nonprofits do not have large cash reserves, and they "live hand to mouth." A cash shortage can be very disruptive to a nonprofit's ability to carry out its mission. To avoid disruptions of business and to take advantage of temporary cash surpluses, nonprofits should project, monitor, and control cash flows. A nonprofit needs to develop a **cash budget** in addition to, and based upon, its operating and capital budgets for successful cash-flow management.

Cash Budget

A **cash-flow budget**, or *cash-flow forecast*, predicts and estimates cash receipts and disbursements on a quarterly or monthly basis, although weekly and daily budgets can also be used in highly volatile cases. Because of the uncertainty involved in the cash-flow budget, especially in nonprofit organizations, trying to project too far into the future may prove to be futile. At the same time, a cash-flow budget that does not look far enough into the future will not predict events early enough for nonprofits to prepare and take corrective actions.

Strong financial management starts with a well-developed budgeting system, and in recent years many nonprofits have done a good job in developing operating budgets. Meeting operating budget targets, however, does not guarantee the survivability of nonprofit organizations. A nonprofit could appear to be financially healthy based on its balanced budget and financial reports, which conventionally are prepared on an accrual basis, but it could face the challenge of paying its bills—a liquidity and cash-flow problem that, at best, interrupts its operation and, at worst, could force it to go out of business. To illustrate how the issue of cash flow affects nonprofits and the application of cash budgets, we present below an example of a hypothetical case: that of Middle Town Social Services, an otherwise financially healthy nonprofit organization that is facing a cash crisis. You will play the role of financial consultant in this example.

Examples of Cash-Flow Management and Cash-Flow Budget

Middle Town Social Services is a midsize nonprofit that feeds the hungry and shelters the abused. It receives funding from a government contract that covers a major part of the program's costs and conducts fundraising to cover the organization's overhead, including general and management expenses. In recent years, the nonprofit has obtained funding from a national foundation in the amount of $300,000, paid in June, the last month of the fiscal year of the nonprofit. It also receives donations year-round in the amount of $100,000 per month.

The nonprofit spends most of the revenue on its programs. In response to pressure from the general public and from watchdog institutions, it has cut its management spending to the bone, including letting go of a proficient financial manager. The executive director has had to pick up some of the responsibility, focusing and limiting the financial and accounting department function to budgeting (operating budget) and basic accounts management and reporting. The nonprofit has a balanced budget, which is comforting to the executive director and praised and approved by the board. As a matter of fact, the nonprofit is doing well, making a net income of more than $20,000 projected for this fiscal year.

In July, one month into the fiscal year, the executive director found out, to his dismay, that the nonprofit would not be able to pay the salary of its staff the next month. Panic suddenly filled the nonprofit. The executive director immediately contacted you, a financial consultant for nonprofit organization management. Your first step is to recommend that the nonprofit develop a cash-flow budget, based on the pattern of the previous year plus the information that is relevant for the year to come.

After some data crunching and working with the executive director, you produced the cash-flow projection depicted in Table 3.1. The review of the cash-flow forecast provides you with clear information about the reasons for the cash-flow problems. The nonprofit has a strong fluctuation of cash inflows and outflows. For instance, the nonprofit has to pay all personnel expenses and some other expenses in cash prior to receiving its foundation funding at the end of the fiscal year, in addition to the slow, albeit regular, government contract payment. Not paying attention to cash flow has caused problems for Middle Town Social Services even though the budget is balanced for the fiscal year. Cash is king, and without cash, the organization cannot function.

Using the cash-flow forecast, you explain to the executive director and the staff at the nonprofit that they will have a cash shortage in September and October. You suggest that the nonprofit should, with the cash-flow budget in hand, arrange for a bank line of credit to bridge the gap. Failing that, the nonprofit might consider delaying its planned purchase of equipment, speeding up pledge collection, and asking for advances from the foundation and government. You recommend that the nonprofit develop a policy with regard to liquidity management, including a cash reserve fund for a margin of safety. In regard to organizational structure, you suggest that the nonprofit retain a competent financial manager. With the increase in capacity, the nonprofit should create a cash-flow budget, in addition to the traditional annual operating budget and financial statement analysis, which has been conducted commendably in this nonprofit. You emphasize in the consulting report that revenue, expense, cash, and cash-flow tim-

Table 3.1 Cash-Flow Projection for a Nonprofit That Cannot Make Payroll (in thousands)

Cash	Jul	Aug	Sep	Oct	Nov	Dec	Jan	Feb	Mar	Apr	May	Jun
Opening Cash	10	(30)	(70)	(170)	(200)	10	(40)	(90)	(140)	(180)	(210)	(240)
Receipts												
Cash from Service Revenue	200	200	200	200	200	200	200	200	200	200	200	200
Cash from Donations	100	100	100	100	200	100	100	100	100	100	100	100
Cash from Foundation Grants	—	—	—	—	—	—	—	—	—	—	—	300
Cash from Fundraising Events	—	—	—	—	200	—	—	—	—	—	—	—
Total Cash Inflow	310	270	230	130	400	310	260	210	160	120	90	360
Disbursement												
Cash Used for Program	250	250	300	250	250	250	250	250	250	250	250	250
Fundraising Expenses	—	—	—	—	50	—	—	—	—	—	—	—
Administrative and General	40	40	50	30	40	50	50	50	40	30	30	30
Debt Services	50	50	50	50	50	50	50	50	50	50	50	50
Total Cash Outflow	340	340	400	330	390	350	350	350	340	330	330	330
Ending Cash	(30)	(70)	(170)	(200)	10	(40)	(90)	(140)	(180)	(210)	(240)	30

ing have to be considered together. You note that without a financial cushion, the nonprofit may be subject to a constant cash crisis, which is not conducive to mission focus and accomplishment.

Working through a Cash-Flow Analysis

Cash-flow planning and analysis are applicable in the context of program expansion as well as that of daily operation. For example, the (fictitious) nonprofit Hope for All (HFA) is considering whether or not to take on another program. HFA provides services to ex-convicts as they return to the community after their release from prison. Like most small and midsize nonprofits, HFA experienced cash-flow difficulties both during and after the financial crisis of 2008. The disturbance had been mitigated by a small, but adequate, rainy-day fund established in previous years, thanks to the prudent and judicious financial manager who, having been schooled in nonprofit financial management, knows the importance of liquidity and cash management.

HFA has recently been contacted by the state to submit a proposal for a job training program that will prepare convicted drug offenders to be released into the community. The program represents a major policy change in the state, and it fits the mission of HFA very well. The question is, can HFA take on the program financially?

Reviewing the information from the state's request for proposal (RFP) and analyzing the pattern of accounts receivable from the state in the past, HFA estimates that 70% of the accounts receivable of the service to be provided for this program will be collected in the month following the services, 20% of the accounts receivable will be collected in the month after, and 10% of the accounts receivable will be collected in the following month. Using this cash-flow pattern assumption, the chief financial officer of HFA projects the cash inflow from operations for the next six months, as illustrated in Table 3.2.

The program is a match with HFA's mission; however, the financial manager has to look at the cash flow of the project, such as the timing of the inflows and outflows, before determining the feasibility of the project. The financial manager consequently calculates the cash outlays as shown in Table 3.3. Apparently,

Table 3.2 HFA Cash Receipts Projection (in thousands)

	Jan 2009	Feb 2009	Mar 2009	Apr 2009	May 2009	Jun 2009
Revenues	$ 500	$ 600	$ 700	$ 700	$ 700	$ 800
70% First Month		350	420	490	490	490
20% Second Month			100	120	140	140
10% Third Month				50	60	70
Total Receipts	$	$ 350	$ 520	$ 660	$ 690	$ 700

although the government can dictate the terms of payment to HFA, the nonprofit cannot delay the payroll and other payables correspondingly. Combining the two cash-flow projections, the financial manager produces a cash-flow budget for the program that assumes no support from HFA or from other programs; this budget is shown in Table 3.4.

Table 3.3 HFA Program Cash Disbursement (in thousands)

	Jan 2009	Feb 2009	Mar 2009	Apr 2009	May 2009	Jun 2009
Salaries	$ 300	$ 300	$ 300	$ 300	$ 300	$ 300
Fringe Benefits	90	90	90	90	90	90
Supplies	0	60	60	60	60	60
Rent and Insurance	10	10	10	10	10	10
Other	20	40	40	40	40	40
Total	$ 420	$ 500	$ 500	$ 500	$ 500	$ 500

Table 3.4 HFA Program Cash-Flow Budget (in thousands)

	Jan 2009	Feb 2009	Mar 2009	Apr 2009	May 2009	Jun 2009
Cash Receipts	$ —	$ 350	$ 520	$ 660	$ 690	$ 700
Cash Disbursement	(420)	(500)	(500)	(500)	(500)	(500)
Net Cash Flow	(420)	(150)	20	160	190	200
Beginning of the Month	$ 0	$ (420)	$ (570)	$ (550)	$ (390)	$ (200)
End of the Month	$ (420)	$ (570)	$ (550)	$ (390)	$ (200)	$ —

The financial manager concludes that, standing alone, the program has negative net cash flows in the first five months of its start-up. Although the program can sustain itself in the long run, it cannot provide for the cash payments needed to avoid an initial cash crisis because of the different timings of the cash flows. Financial backing from other sources, inside and/or outside the organization, is needed. Given that this is such a high-profile project coming from the state governor, it is a wonderful opportunity for HFA to realize its mission of hope for all. As a result, HFA decides to use its cash reserve to finance the training program in the first two months.

HFA's cash-flow projections and cash-flow management report allow it to discover and then take advantage of an opportunity that fits well with its mission without running into a cash crunch as a consequence. This is an illustration of why maintaining a liquidity target and conducting cash-flow budgeting and analysis are so important for a nonprofit's smooth operation, as well as for allowing it to seize opportunities for mission advancement.

Cash-Flow Budgeting in Practice

Cash-flow budgeting is important; however, less than half of nonprofit organizations prepare and use cash budgets. This is why cash-flow management is the area of financial management that has the most potential to improve the financial health of nonprofits. A well-developed cash-flow budget alerts a nonprofit when cash is excessive and needs to be put into short- or long-term investments. A cash budget can also predict a nonprofit's **cash-flow gaps**, periods when cash outflows exceed cash inflows. When gaps are predicted early, steps can be taken to ensure that they are closed. These steps might include lowering investment in accounts receivable or inventory and looking to outside sources of cash, such as short-term loans.

The preparation of a cash budget includes estimating when collections on year-end receivables will occur, calculating the normal time lag between invoicing/billing for services or pledges and the actual receipt of cash, and predicting the timing of cash payouts when monthly payments are due. A cash budget must also factor in the investment of cash flows in terms of capital spending and financing. A cash-flow budget, moreover, reflects the nonprofit's policies with regard to balancing its service orientation with its desire to survive in the long run. Organizations need to plan from day one to build working capital reserves equivalent to several months' worth of operating expenses. All of these elements are reflected in the cash budget that a nonprofit develops after it prepares the operating and capital budgets, taking into consideration anticipated events and the seasonality of the budget year.

The detailed steps involved in preparing a cash budget vary extensively; however, for many nonprofits cash-flow projections are a natural extension of the budgeting process, meaning they are an extension of the operating budget and the capital budget. The operating budget is broken down from a yearly total into monthly sums, taking into consideration seasonal variations and special events. These monthly revenues and expenditures are then adjusted for timing and non-cash payments, converting the accrual basis of the operating budget into a cash budget, which is then used for planning, control, and evaluation.

Other nonprofits prepare cash budgets by using actual cash-flow figures from previous years. The cash-flow pattern from a previous year is adjusted according to the budgeted program changes and their financial impacts; influences on the pattern caused by special events that occurred in the past and will not occur again are removed. For instance, given the HFA's acceptance of the new program discussed previously, it is anticipating and has budgeted for the government payment delay, recognizing both the payment pattern in the past and the agreement in the contract. New cash inflow is forecast for the second half of the year, recognizing the kickoff of the program in July following the government fiscal year and the conventional 30-day payment schedule from government agencies.

Cash-flow budgets not only help nonprofits to plan short-term credit needs and surpluses; they can also be used to plan capital expenditure and program expansion internally and can serve as tools for external users, such as banks and foundations. The cash budget estimates a nonprofit's future ability to pay debts as well as expenses. For example, preliminary cash budget estimates may reveal that disbursements are lumped together and that, with more careful planning, the nonprofit can spread its payments to creditors more evenly throughout the entire year. As a result, less bank credit will be needed and interest costs will be lower. Banks and other credit-granting institutions are more inclined to grant nonprofits loans under favorable terms if the loan requests are supported by methodical cash plans. Without planning, there is no certainty that a nonprofit will be able to repay its loans on schedule. Also, a monthly cash budget helps pinpoint estimated cash balances at the end of each month, which may aid nonprofits by enabling them to anticipate short-term cash shortfalls and cash surpluses, which should be managed to generate returns.

Updating the Cash Budget with Actuals

Cash-flow forecasts can alert nonprofits to a number of potential issues that need to be addressed. For instance, see the estimated cash flow from the Sojourner Truth Settlement House, which is listed in Table 3.5. The report starts with the actual cash on hand at the beginning of the fiscal year, which is January. All projected revenues and expenses are listed. At the end of January, the estimated amount of cash on hand is listed. That figure becomes the opening cash in February. The entire year is projected by month. The finance staff will track what actually happens each month. What were the actual revenues and expenses in January? How do those figures compare to the estimated cash budget? If the outflow exceeds the inflow, the executive director can take steps to correct the imbalance.

In the projected cash flow for the Settlement House (see Table 3.5), very little ending cash exists at the end of several months. If the revenues do not come in as planned, it will be short of cash even though the budget is balanced for the year. This is why it is so important that the budgeted cash flow be compared to actual cash flow each month. This is also why many nonprofits apply for bank lines of credit to carry them through the tight months.

Cash-Flow Strategies

A number of cash-flow strategies are available to the nonprofit financial manager, such as a line of credit or an operating reserve. In order to meet a projected temporary cash shortage, a nonprofit may want to consider any of the following strategies:

- Arranging for a line of credit or a loan from a bank;
- Speeding up the collection of receivables, to get liquidity from the organization's own working capital;
- Holding a planned fundraising event or campaign earlier than originally scheduled;
- Financing the purchase of equipment by leasing it or paying for it over time;
- Liquidating investments; or
- Delaying payments to vendors.

Table 3.5 Projected FY 2020 Cash-Flow Management Report Sojourner Truth Settlement House

Projected Cash (except for opening cash in January)

	Jan	Feb	Mar	Apr	May	Jun	Jul	Aug	Sep	Oct	Nov	Dec
Opening Cash	$ 50,000	$ 138,305	$ 21,415	$ 33,525	$ 45,635	$ 2,745	$ 84,855	$ 6,965	$ 4,075	$ 4,185	$ 1,895	$ 5,605
Revenues												
Contributions	150,000	175,000	175,000	175,000	150,000	110,000	90,000	80,000	160,000	175,000	150,000	280,000
Fees	11,195	10,000	10,000	10,000	10,000	15,000	15,000	15,000	11,000	8,600	9,600	9,500
Foundation Grant	150,000	75,000	100,000	150,000	45,000	80,000	30,000	50,000	45,000	105,000	135,000	110,000
Government Contract	300,000	100,000	150,000	100,000	175,000	300,000	200,000	275,000	200,000	130,000	70,000	35,000
Investment Income	0	0	0	0	0	0	10,000	0	5,000	0	60,000	151,000
Total Cash Available	$ 661,195	$ 498,305	$ 456,415	$ 468,525	$ 425,635	$ 507,745	$ 429,855	$ 426,965	$ 425,075	$ 422,785	$ 426,495	$ 591,105
Expenses												
Payroll	313,000	313,000	313,000	313,000	313,000	313,000	313,000	313,000	313,000	313,000	313,000	313,000
Fringe Benefits	62,600	62,600	62,600	62,600	62,600	62,600	62,600	62,600	62,600	62,600	62,600	62,600
Consultants	20,000	20,000	20,000	20,000	20,000	20,000	20,000	20,000	18,000	18,000	18,000	18,000
Computer Equipment	50,000	20,200	0	0	0	0	0	0	0	0	0	0
Equipment	50,000	33,800	0	0	0	0	0	0	0	0	0	0
Food	3,250	3,250	3,250	3,250	3,250	$ 3,250	3,250	3,250	3,250	3,250	$ 3,250	$ 3,250
Mortgage	5,000	5,000	5,000	5,000	5,000	5,000	5,000	5,000	5,000	5,000	5,000	5,000
Phones	3,640	3,640	3,640	3,640	3,640	3,640	3,640	3,640	3,640	3,640	3,640	3,640
Supplies/Printing	8,500	8,500	8,500	8,500	8,500	8,500	8,500	8,500	8,500	8,500	8,500	8,500
Travel	4,400	4,400	4,400	4,400	4,400	4,400	4,400	4,400	4,400	4,400	4,400	4,400
Utilities	2,500	2,500	2,500	2,500	2,500	2,500	2,500	2,500	2,500	2,500	2,500	2,500
Total Expenses	$ 522,890	$ 476,890	$ 422,890	$ 422,890	$ 422,890	$ 422,890	$ 422,890	$ 422,890	$ 420,890	$ 420,890	$ 420,890	$ 420,890
Ending Cash	$ 138,305	$ 21,415	$ 33,525	$ 45,635	$ 2,745	$ 84,855	$ 6,965	$ 4,075	$ 4,185	$ 1,895	$ 5,605	$ 170,215

When a nonprofit's cash budget indicates a temporary surplus in its operation, the organization needs to put the money to good use. First and foremost, it should save the cash in a safe and liquid way that also provides returns, such as by making short-term investments in certificates of deposit, money market funds, or U.S. Treasury securities as a liquidity reserve—a good practice in cash management. If several months' worth of cash reserves exists, the nonprofit should think about doing one or more of the following:

- Expanding current programs;
- Developing new programs and taking advantage of opportunities;
- Building up a capital reserve through longer-term investment; or
- Supporting other worthwhile projects in and outside the community.

In the following pages we discuss some of these actions, based on their relevance and importance to nonprofit organizations. We address these topics in more depth in Chapter 11, on capital budgeting, where we discuss long-term financing, and in Chapter 12, on investment strategies, where we discuss long-term investments.

What Do We Do When We Run Out of Cash?

As we have noted above, nonprofits are vulnerable to cash shortfalls. This is not necessarily because of mismanagement; rather, it is often a result of systemic and structural factors that come with being a nonprofit organization. Faced with delayed payments from government contracts and the instability of donations, nonprofits are advised to establish financial cushions by establishing reserves or securing short-term borrowing in advance.

Managing Working Capital. Nonprofits can often get cash from their working capital, e.g., by selling short-term investments and speeding up the collection of receivables. **Working capital** is defined as the difference between current assets and current liabilities. For instance, hospitals have billing and collection systems, or accounts receivable management systems, for timely billing as well as reminding and collecting of unpaid bills from patients, which speeds up the cash conversion cycle and improves the institutions' cash positions.

Other kinds of working capital management techniques are also helpful, although they tend to be less important for nonprofits than for corporations. For instance, inventory control is another way to release cash. However, most nonprofits tend not to carry much inventory, since they are, more often than not, in the service industry. Nonprofits can also withhold money by delaying payment to their vendors, but this practice is not recommended because it can be damaging to the relationship with the vendor and can be contradictory to the public-service orientation of the nonprofit.

Short-Term Borrowing. A potentially quick way in which a nonprofit can meet a financial crunch is by using a line of credit that it has established with a bank. A line of credit is a convenient way to manage risks and reduce the need of keeping a large cash reserve that could subject the nonprofit to public scrutiny. A new or small nonprofit, however, may need to convince the bank as to the nonprofit's creditworthiness, and it may need to obtain collateral or guarantees from credible institutions so that the bank can resort to other sources if the nonprofit fails to repay the loan.

Not all new and small nonprofits have the credibility that banks look for or the types of assets that banks would like to take as collateral. This is one of the difficulties of using borrowing as a cash-flow management tool, apart from the issue of paying interest and the need to pay back the principal at the end of the term of the loan. A unique approach proposed by some consultants is for nonprofits to work with their communities to establish guarantee relationships with organizations and individual philanthropists, and to solicit them to provide backing for any loans the nonprofits intend to seek. Many foundations, for instance, have billions of dollars in assets, and some philanthropists may want to support a nonprofit's cause by providing credit enhancement or by investing in the nonprofit directly. This process can create a win-win-win situation for all the parties involved.

It should be noted that although revenue is not cash, cash flow and revenue are intimately related. In the short run, nonprofits might resort to working capital management techniques, but in the long run, they need to increase revenue and decrease expenses, generating sustainable profits at least to compensate for inflation, so that they can maintain a level of services sufficient to serve their missions and the society at large.

What Do We Do When We Have Too Much Short-Term Cash?

A nonprofit may have short-term surplus cash because of desynchronization of cash inflows and outflows and unexpected windfalls. When this occurs, the nonprofit, as a prudent manager of public funds, should put the cash to good use. The cash could potentially be used in many ways, but here we address only two financial approaches: short-term investments and taking advantage of trade credit terms.

Short-Term Investment. Idle cash can be invested to generate yields that can be used for future nonprofit programs, a common practice of cash management. A nonprofit organization should divert short-term funds from its checking account to its savings account or other short-term investment vehicles as soon as the cash is in hand. Investing is not easy for many busy nonprofit managers, especially for those who are not trained in finance. Some basic knowledge can go a long way toward helping nonprofit managers to manage their cash effectively and efficiently.

In general, a nonprofit should consider three factors in deciding how to invest its cash: safety, liquidity, and returns. Balance has to be achieved through sensible decisions. The board of the nonprofit should develop policies to guide financial decision making and the management of investment practices. A designated financial manager may be required if the amount of the investment is substantial.

Nonprofits by definition have the responsibility to steward public funds in a prudent manner. This entails primarily the protection of the principal of investment. The board consequently needs to be judicious in selecting investment instruments. For instance, for short-term investment, nonprofit organizations should not invest in common stocks or even in long-term treasuries for fear of the risk of interest changes. Many jurisdictions have developed laws that limit the range of investment vehicles in which nonprofits may invest in order to safeguard public resources that are in the hands of nonprofit organizations.

A second major concern of short-term investment is liquidity. Liquidity in the investment context is the ease with which and the length of time in which an asset can be converted into cash without the incurrence of excessive cost. Short-term surplus cash, depending on its planned use, should be invested in an instrument that allows the cash to be available on short notice. Many investment tools meet this requirement neatly. For instance, U.S. Treasury debt has a deep and broad secondary market, so that it can be sold immediately at any time and in any place. However, care should be taken to avoid interest risk (a topic we discuss further in Chapter 12).

Returns are the interest or yield that the investment generates, which is the purpose of investment in the first place. We have put returns last in the hierarchy, however, because returns are the least important of the three criteria for decision making in short-term investing, after safety and liquidity, especially for nonprofits that manage public funds. Some investment instruments, such as stocks, derivatives, and alternative investment vehicles normally managed by hedge funds, are expected to produce high yields, but these instruments are not suitable for short-term investment for nonprofit organizations. They have a higher risk of losing principal, and some of them, such as real estate, are not liquid. Balance among the three criteria—safety, liquidity, and returns—needs to be achieved in short-term investment, although in general, safety and liquidity should take precedence over returns.

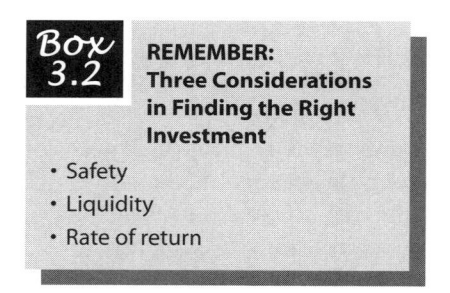

> **Box 3.2**
>
> **REMEMBER: Three Considerations in Finding the Right Investment**
> - Safety
> - Liquidity
> - Rate of return

Taking Trade Discount Incentives. With cash or liquidity enhanced, nonprofits have more flexibility in managing their operations and balance sheets. Cash in hand can not only generate income through short-term investment, but can also make savings by taking advantage of common business payment protocols. Sometimes, paying vendors earlier generates more benefit than investment.

For instance, HFA has just ordered a new set of furniture for its expanded program upon receiving a contract from the state government. The purchasing manager has been offered a credit term of 2/10 net 60, indicating that the store will extend credit to HFA with the incentive of taking 2% off the sales price if HFA pays its bill within 10 days of the invoice date. The furniture is priced at $100,000, so this means a discount of $2,000. If HFA does not pay within 10 days, the bill becomes due within the next 60 days at full price. What should HFA do, assuming it has the cash on hand?

To decide whether to pay the bill in cash now and take the discount, or pay it in 60 days and keep the cash in a bank account that generates 2% annual interest, the financial manager needs to know the implied annual interest rate or, conversely, the savings for this offer to pay the bill within 10 days. The formula to calculate the interest rate is as follows:

$$\text{annual interest rate} = \frac{d}{1-d} \times \frac{365}{t_2 - t_1}$$

where
d = discount (0.02%)
t_2 = credit period (60 days)
t_1 = discount period (10 days)

Inserting the data from above, the financial manager calculated the "would be" annual interest rate for this case as follows:

$$\text{annual interest rate} = \frac{0.02}{1-0.02} \times \frac{365}{60-10}$$
$$= 14.9\%$$

At 14.9%, the opportunity cost of not taking the discount would be very expensive. Given that the alternative use of the cash if saved in the bank is only about 2% annually, HFA would be better off to take advantage of paying the discounted price in 10 days, as opposed to waiting until the 60-day period ends.

More common trade terms include 2/10 net 30 and 2/15 net 40, which offer even more benefits for paying early. The implied annual interest rate is as high as 37.8% for the 2/10 net 30 terms—an advantage that is almost imperative for a nonprofit to take. (Use the formula provided to verify this result and calculate the rate for the 2/15 net 40 terms as well.)

Conclusion

In summary, nonprofits need to manage their cash flow carefully in addition to practicing good financial management through accrual-based budgetary control. Nonprofits should prepare cash budgets at least on a monthly basis, so that shortages and surpluses of cash can be foreseen and management can be ready to take corrective actions if needed.

Nonprofits can deal with short-term cash shortages and surpluses in many different ways, depending on the nonprofit and the situation. Much of this effort should focus on increasing the effectiveness and efficiency of the use of the public funds that have been fiducially granted to the nonprofit to deliver services and to serve the interest of the public at large. Financial managers of nonprofits should establish target liquidity and develop cash budgets to predict future cash shortages or surpluses, so that liquidity can be maintained. Nonprofits can increase liquidity by managing working capital and using short-term borrowing, among other things, when needed. They can also invest surplus cash in safe, liquid, and interest-bearing vehicles following required fiduciary standards and/or take advantage of trade credit, which can often provide great savings, especially when large amounts of money are involved.

KEY TERMS

cash budget	cash-flow gaps	liquidity
cash flow	cash-flow management	working capital
cash-flow budget		

DISCUSSION QUESTIONS

1. Why is "being liquid" so important for a nonprofit?
2. What is a cash-flow budget?
3. Why is a cash-flow budget so important for a nonprofit?
4. Describe several strategies that nonprofits can adopt when dealing with cash-flow issues.
5. Describe how nonprofits can put extra cash to good use.

SUGGESTED READINGS

Blackbaud (2011). *Financial Management of Not-for-Profit Organizations.* Charleston, SC: Blackbaud (blackbaud.com/files/resources/downloads/WhitePaper_FinancialManagementForNPO.pdf).

Dropkin, Murray, and Allyson Hayden (2001). *The Cash Flow Management Book for Nonprofits: A Step-by-Step Guide for Managers, Consultants, and Boards.* San Francisco: Jossey-Bass.

Linzer, Richard, and Anna Linzer (2008). *Cash Flow Strategies: Innovation in Nonprofit Financial Management.* Hoboken, NJ: John Wiley & Sons.

Zietlow, John, Jo Ann Hankin, Alan G. Seidner, and Tim O'Brien (2018). *Financial Management for Nonprofit Organizations: Policies and Practices* (3rd ed.). Hoboken, NJ: Wiley.

CASE STUDY

HOPE FOR ALL (HFA) BORROWS MONEY

This case study is based on the HFA example discussed earlier in this chapter. Upon successfully receiving the contract from the state government, HFA has just ordered a new set of furniture for its expanded job training program. The purchasing manager has been offered a credit term of 2/10 net 60, indicating that the vendor will extend credit to HFA with the incentive of taking 2% off the sales price if HFA pays its bill within 10 days of the invoice date. The difference here is that the nonprofit does not have cash on hand to take advantage of the trade credit, and it does not have other internal financial sources that it can tap into for support. The only option is to borrow from outside the nonprofit; you are HFA's financial manager, and the local bank comes to your mind immediately.

You contact the local bank with an initial inquiry about a line of credit or a short-term loan. The bank is hesitant to lend to nonprofits, but given HFA's good relationship with the bank, the reputation of the management of the nonprofit, and the state contract, the bank is willing to make a short-term loan. The terms of the loan all favor the bank's interests and safety, with a high interest rate of 10% and a covenant that does not allow HFA to sell any assets or to borrow for any purpose from any other institution before the loan is repaid.

Case Study Questions

1. Given these conditions, should you take advantage of the trade credit and go through the trouble of taking out the loan and pay the bill in the credit period, or should you wait and pay after you receive funds from the state within 60 days?
2. Are there any other factors that you should take into consideration before making a decision?

Assignments

Assignment 3.1. Identifying Working Capital and Liquidity

What is working capital? What is included in liquidity?

Assignment 3.2. Developing a Cash Budget

Develop a cash budget based on the following information about a preschool with a fiscal year beginning in January:

- Revenues:
  — Tuition fee: $100,000 paid monthly
  — Event income: $50,000 in November by Thanksgiving
  — Foundation support: $200,000 semiannually (May and November)
- Expenses:
  — Salary and wages: $80,000 monthly
  — Rent and insurance: $100,000 in January
  — Supply and food: $10,000 monthly
  — Administration and fundraising: $10,000 monthly

Assume the board of directors does not allow for short-term borrowing and that the cash safety margin each month is $80,000. How much operating reserve or liquidity should the preschool have? Use the format in Table 3.5 as a guide.

Assignment 3.3. Managing Cash Flow

You are a new purchase manager, and you are offered credit terms of 2/10 net 30 for a piece of medical equipment your nonprofit needs immediately. The nonprofit is short of cash at the moment, but government reimbursement is within 15 days and past history has shown that the federal payment has always been on time. The bank is willing to make a short-term bridge loan for an annual interest rate of 7%. What should you do—take advantage of the trade credit terms and borrow to pay for the equipment and incur interest charges from the bank, or wait for the government payment and pay before the end of the net 30-day term? Make the necessary calculations and report your recommended action.

Notes

[1] Zietlow, John, Jo Ann Hankin, Alan G. Seidner, and Tim O'Brien (2018). *Financial Management for Nonprofit Organizations: Policies and Practices* (3rd ed., p. 30). Hoboken, NJ: Wiley.

[2] *Journal of Accountancy* (2016, August 29). FASB Modifies Not-for-Profit Accounting Rules. GuideStar Blog (trust.guidestar.org/fasb-modifies-not-for-profit-accounting-rules).

[3] Proctor, Allen. Nonprofits Treated Poorly by Restrictions on Funding (linkingmissiontomoney.org/FEB06article.html).

4 Analyzing Costs

> A whole set of techniques revolve around making project or program costs look less expensive by ignoring or underestimating later years' costs, or pushing current costs off into the future.
>
> —Irene S. Rubin[1]

Learning Objectives

The learning objectives for this chapter are as follows:
- Taking an in-depth look at costs
- Direct costs and indirect costs
- Fixed costs and variable costs
- Average costs and marginal costs
- Understanding the relevant costs in financial decision making
- Extension of existing services—marginal analysis
- Potential new services—break-even analysis

*I*n the preceding chapters we have discussed budgeting and cash flow. In order to create next year's budget, a nonprofit needs to be able to determine the costs of the current year's activities and estimate cost changes for the following year. The concept of cost is complex and sometimes confusing for many nonprofit managers.

The term *cost* is used widely in daily lives, in the conducting of business, and in professional discourse, and it can mean different things for different people under different circumstances. In this chapter we focus on cost in the context of economics and financial management in nonprofit organizations. After defining the term in this context, we apply it to cost accounting and financial decision making, which are critical to successful financial management of nonprofit operations.

Direct Costs and Indirect Costs

Costs are often classified into direct costs and indirect costs for costing purposes. **Direct costs** can be easily traced to a cost objective, such as service, project, program, or activity. Typical direct costs include the costs of project staff and project-related supplies, consultants, travel, and training. **Indirect costs** are not readily identifiable with a particular cost objective, but are necessary for the general operation of the organization. Indirect costs benefit more than one project, and the precise benefits to a specific project are often difficult to trace. Typical indirect costs include executive salaries, rent or mortgage payments, utilities, finance, and legal services.

The sum of direct and indirect costs is the total or full cost of a cost objective, a program for instance. Nonprofit organizations need to know the full costs of their services for internal cost control and external reimbursement and reporting purposes. As stipulated in IRS Form 990, nonprofits should prepare financial statements by functional expenses in full costs.

Conceptually, the full costs of a nonprofit's programs and services should be easy to understand and to measure. The accounting system should be set up so that costs can be identified with the programs they benefit. In practice, cost accounting is complex, and many costs are indirect and not easily traced to particular services or programs. For instance, occupancy costs cannot be associated directly with specific services if multiple programs share the same facility. These indirect costs, or overhead, need to be allocated to the service departments, programs, or activities before the full cost of providing a program or a service can be established.

Two concepts, the pool (common) and the base (criterion), are of fundamental importance in allocating indirect costs. The pool or common cost is the accumulation of

> **Box 4.1**
>
> **REMEMBER:**
> **Direct and Indirect Costs**
>
> - *Direct costs* are those that are identified with a cost objective. An example of this would be the salaries of the staff of a senior citizen luncheon program.
> - *Indirect costs* are those that cannot be identified easily with particular cost objectives but are real costs and need to be recognized. For example, the executive director of a nonprofit spends 5% of her time with the senior citizen luncheon program, as does the program director. Hence, 5% of the executive's salary and 5% of the program director's salary would be identified as indirect costs and therefore part of the total or full cost of this program.

indirect costs that are to be allocated, and the base is the criteria upon which the pool is allocated. For example, in the allocation of occupancy costs, the pool could be the total costs of rent, utilities, and maintenance for the nonprofit and the base could be the percentage of square footage that each department occupies. In the allocation of the salary of the executive director, however, the total direct cost for each department may be more reasonably used as the base, since the executive director may spend time proportional to the direct cost of running each department.

Different methods are used in allocating indirect costs. Each nonprofit can choose its own method based on what best supports its operation, although consistent use of the same base over time is highly recommended. Sometimes, funding agencies may require specific methods that nonprofits need to follow. For example, the federal government stipulates a comprehensive methodology to assign indirect costs for those nonprofits that receive federal funding.[2]

Estimating Direct and Indirect Costs

The nonprofit Hope for All (HFA) has four departments: drug treatment, job training, fundraising, and administration. All departments share the same facilities, and the accounting system classifies occupancy-related costs as common indirect costs. You are the financial manager of HFA, and you are asked by the executive director to provide an estimate of the full costs for each department for the next board meeting. The common costs are $200,000 and consist of mortgage interest, utilities, maintenance, depreciation, and phones.

You start the task by discussing the matter with program directors, and collectively you decide to use the square footage of the facility that each department occupies as the base for allocation. You collect the information and calculate the percentage of the space used by each department, as shown in Table 4.1.

Using the available pool of costs and the agreed-upon distribution base of the square footage of the facility, you allocate the common cost ($200,000) and calculate the total cost for each department as shown in Table 4.2. The drug treatment

Table 4.1 Direct Costs and Allocation Base by Department

	Administration	Fundraising	Drug Treatment	Job Training	Total
Direct Costs	$ 50,000	$ 100,000	$ 500,000	$ 300,000	$ 950,000
Allocation Base	10%	15%	50%	25%	100%

Table 4.2 Full Costs by Department

	Administration	Fundraising	Drug Treatment	Job Training	Total
Direct Costs	$ 50,000	$ 100,000	$ 500,000	$ 300,000	$ 950,000
Allocation Base	20,000	30,000	100,000	50,000	200,000
Total Costs	$ 70,000	$ 130,000	$ 600,000	$ 350,000	$ 1,150,000

department is allocated half of the indirect costs, as it accounts for half of the total office spaces.

A single criterion, such as space, may prove to be inadequate for allocating different and diverse indirect costs to each program. Each of the indirect costs may benefit programs differently and/or to varying degrees. This might call for accumulating indirect costs into separate cost pools and then allocating each pool individually to programs using a base that best measures the relative benefits to each program. This method tends to be more accurate; however, increasing the accuracy of the costing scheme has its own cost in terms of system investment, training, and staff time. Financial managers need to balance cost and benefit in designing or extending the cost accounting system between the value of the information it provides and the costs to develop and maintain the system.

Costing Services and Allocating Costs

In costing services, departments are often classified into program (or mission) centers and support (or service) centers. Program centers are those that deliver services directly to clients. Typical program centers in a comprehensive social service nonprofit organization might include soup kitchen, emergency shelter, and job training departments.

Support centers provide services to the program centers. Typical support centers include administration and fundraising. For the full cost of the programs to be measured, the costs in the support centers need to be allocated to program centers. (In this section, we use the terms *department* and *center* interchangeably.)

The process of accounting for the full costs of a program/department is especially important when a nonprofit organization receives government support. In such cases, nonprofits are often required to classify their costs into three basic categories: administration, fundraising, and program. Joint (indirect) costs such as depreciation, rental costs, operation and maintenance of facilities, and telephone expenses are then allocated to each category using a base most appropriate to the particular cost being prorated. The total costs for administration and fundraising are then allocated to program areas to arrive at the full cost of providing various services. Costs are commonly allocated to program centers in one of two ways: through the direct method or through the step-down method.

Direct Method to Allocate Costs

The direct method allocates the costs from support centers to program centers directly. For instance, the Midtown Community Center has two programs, an education outreach program and a day care center. Assume that the day care center occupies 60% of the facility and the education program occupies 20%, with the remaining 20% used by general management. Also assume that the total occupancy cost of the community center, including rental, maintenance, insurance, utilities, and the like, is $100,000 per year and the center has a policy to allocate indirect costs by percentage of occupancy. What would be the amounts to be allocated to education outreach and the day care center for occupancy cost?

To answer this question, we must first divide the square footage of the facility used by each mission center by the total occupancy of the two mission centers combined. Support center occupancy is not included in the calculation, as no common cost is allocated to a support center in the direct method of allocating common indirect costs. In this example, the percentage of day care occupancy in relation to the two mission centers is 75% [60%/(60% + 20%)] and the education occupancy is 25% [20%/(60% + 20%)]. We then factor the proportion of occupancy to the total occupancy cost: the allocated cost to the day care center is calculated to be $75,000 ($100,000 × 75%), and the allocated occupancy cost for the education department is $25,000 ($100,000 × 25%). The full costs of the mission centers would then be the sum of the direct cost of the department plus all the allocated indirect costs, wherein occupancy cost is one of them.

Although relatively simple in conceptualization and application, the accuracy of this allocation method is low. It does not meet the need for more accurate cost measurement that some nonprofits and many supporting foundations and government agencies require.

Step-Down Method to Allocate Costs

The step-down method transfers the cost from service centers to other service centers and then to program centers, following a step-by-step work flow map. It starts from the support center that provides services to the largest number of other centers, both support and mission. The allocated costs are then combined with the direct costs of the service centers of the second tier and allocated to the third tier of service centers (if there is a third tier), and all mission centers. This process continues step-by-step along the descending ladder until costs in all service centers are transferred to mission centers.

This method is more accurate than the direct method of allocating costs, as it reflects the reality of the servicing and benefiting relationships among different centers and programs of a nonprofit. The following case provides an illustration of the step-down method.

Working through the Step-Down Method

Hope for All has two program departments, one for drug treatment and the other for job training. HFA recently received a contract from the state government to provide treatment for former drug offenders. Based on the contract, the Department of Juvenile Justice pays for the full cost of drug treatment but nothing for job training, which is under the jurisdiction of a different department. For budgetary and reimbursement purposes, HFA needs to determine the full cost and unit cost for drug treatment. Given the required accuracy for the purpose of this exercise, you have decided to use the step-down method. You are advised to start with administration, since all other departments require and receive services from administration, but not vice versa. Every department should be assigned a share of the administrative costs in the process of measuring the full cost of delivering the services, since every department benefits from the services of administration.

You select departmental expenses as the basis for allocating costs. Your rationale is that the more expensive a center is, the more help it needs from the central administration department. Even more precise allocation methods can also be applied, such as using full-time equivalent positions as the basis for allocation. For our purposes of illustration, however, we use the simpler expense criteria. This allocation basis and allocation method are acceptable in practice by many nonprofit organizations.

Allocating Administrative and Fundraising Costs. Arguably, the administration department provides services to all departments in HFA and therefore its costs are initially allocated to all other departments in the first step. (See Table 4.3 for the costs for each department.) The cost of administration ($70,000) is allocated to the other three departments based on their expense. The costs of the fundraising department are then adjusted, after the allocated cost of $8,426 from administration is added to the department cost of fundraising of $130,000. The total cost from fundraising of $138,426 is subsequently allocated to the two program centers, drug treatment and job training, based again on relative expenses, as shown in Table 4.4. Adding, across the row, the allocated indirect cost from administration and fundraising to the department cost of the two program centers, we derive the total cost of providing the two services.

Table 4.3   Total Costs by Department

Department	Total Costs
Administration	$ 70,000
Fundraising	130,000
Drug Treatment	600,000
Job Training	350,000
Total Costs	$ 1,150,000

Table 4.4   HFA's Total Costs Using the Step-Down Method of Allocation

Department	Direct Cost	Base	Administration Distribution	Step 1 Total	Base	Fundraising Distribution	Full Cost
Administration	$ 70,000						
Fundraising	130,000	12.04%	$ 8,426	$ 138,426			
Drug Treatment	600,000	55.56%	38,889	638,889	63.16%	$ 87,427	$ 726,316
Job Training	350,000	32.41%	22,685	372,685	36.84%	50,999	423,684
Total Costs	$ 1,150,000	100%	$ 70,000	$ 1,150,000	100%	$ 138,426	$ 1,150,000

Note: To calculate the first base, subtract the administration cost ($70,000) from the total cost ($1,150,000) to get a new total cost ($1,080,000), and then divide the cost of each remaining department by the new total cost to get the base percentage. To calculate the second base, again subtract the fundraising cost ($138,426) from the total cost ($1,150,000) to get a new total cost ($1,011,574), and then divide the cost of each remaining department by the new total cost to get the base percentage.

As shown in Table 4.4, the full costs of the treatment and training programs are $726,316 and $423,684, respectively. The cost measures will be different from and more accurate than the results if the cost measurement is conducted using the direct method. Nonprofit financial managers are advised to weigh their options carefully in conducting cost accounting or cost measurement, including the selection of methods, the pools and the bases, to meet the needs of their nonprofits, and the requirements of external agencies.

Fixed, Variable, and Step Costs

In addition to cost accounting, financial managers are involved in, and often responsible for, cost management. Understanding and being able to predict how costs behave in different contexts is of great importance in financial planning and control. For instance, a soup kitchen needs to know what the costs will be if it extends its services to a new location. In addition to the new location housing costs—rentals, maintenance, insurance, and the like—the managers should know the cost increases in relation to the number of meals the soup kitchen plans to provide. Costs in this context can be classified into fixed, variable, and step costs, depending on their behavior in response to changes in service volume or activities.

Those cost elements that remain constant over a certain volume of activity are **fixed costs**. A typical example of a fixed cost is facility rental, which, within a relevant range of output level and in a certain time period, remains constant.

Variable costs are costs that vary in direct proportion with service volume. For instance, the food cost in a soup kitchen is variable, because total food cost increases with the increase in the number of meals served in a given period of time.

Those cost elements that remain constant but increase to new levels in steps at certain levels of activity or usage within the relevant range are **step costs**. An example is the number of teachers required in a school. When the number of students in a class is lower than the maximum class size—that is, there is unused capacity—the increase of one student will not lead to the hiring of an additional teacher. However, when the school is operating at full capacity, an increase of one student or more will lead to an increase in the number of teachers, a step cost increase at this point of the activity range. Figures 4.1, 4.2, and 4.3 present illustrations of fixed costs, variable costs, and step costs, respectively.

As discussed earlier in this chapter, the cost classification is true only within a relevant volume and time range. As volume increases and time extends, all costs become variable. For instance, if the number of trainees served by a nonprofit job training program exceed the capacity of the facility it currently uses for the training program, new facilities have to be brought online. In response, the fixed facility cost becomes variable due to the overflow of volume beyond the normal, relevant range. The same could be said about time. Although rent is fixed in the short term, it could be, and likely will be, increased over a period of years. Rent, a fixed cost, then becomes a variable cost, as the time frame extends beyond the relevant range.

82 Chapter Four

In sum, the validity of the discussion among fixed, step, and variable cost types holds only when the costs fall within the condition in which the nonprofit managers normally operate—that is, the relevant range.

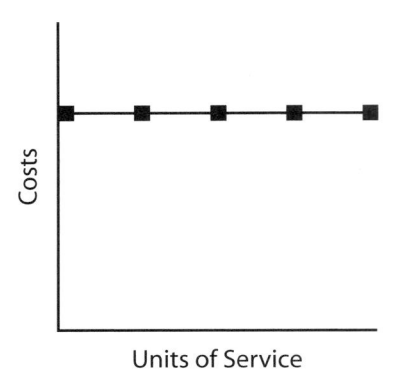

Figure 4.1 Fixed costs.

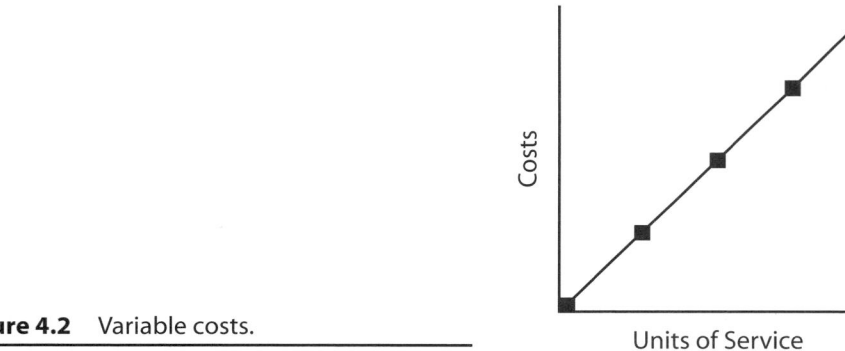

Figure 4.2 Variable costs.

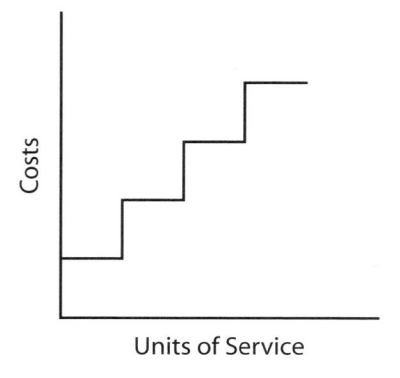

Figure 4.3 Step costs.

Average Costs and Marginal Costs

Average costs are another term that financial managers use regularly. An average cost is the total cost divided by the number of units of goods or service produced. Average cost can be expressed mathematically in the following form:

$$AC = TC/Q$$

where
AC = average costs
TC = total cost
Q = quantity, or the number of units

Average cost is an important measure for operation. Lower average costs reflect higher efficiency in an organization's production of goods or services. Average cost is calculated using historical record. A program will earn a surplus if its average cost is below the reimbursement rate, or the price it can charge. Average cost changes with volume or the level of activities, which is part of the concept of cost behavior, to be discussed further later in this section.

Marginal cost is the cost to produce one more unit of goods or services at a certain level of production. Marginal cost equals the change in total cost that arises when the quantity produced is increased by one more unit. Marginal cost also changes with volume in general, and so at a different level of production, the marginal cost can be different. Within the relevant activity range wherein the fixed and step costs remain constant, however, marginal cost is consistent and equal to variable cost.

For example, adding one more trainee in the HFA program as shown in Assignment 4.1 at the end of this chapter will not require a new classroom or a new teacher, nor will it cause changes in rent or utilities. The additional cost will be just to pay for the textbook and other teaching materials—that is, the variable cost. In this context, the marginal cost would be $1,000, the same as the variable cost.

If the program has exhausted its space and the addition of more students requires the addition of a new classroom, for example, the marginal cost will be the cost of the variable cost plus the additional facilities costs to accommodate the new student or students. In the long run and over a greater volume range, all costs become variable. In daily operation, more often than not, nonprofit managers are concerned about the short run and relevant volume range, wherein marginal costs are equal to variable costs, although verification is always required in cost analysis.

Examples of Average and Marginal Costs

As discussed above, HFA has recently received a contract from the state government to expand its job training program. The expanded program will need an assistant director and a new facility to house the program. As HFA's financial manager, you want to know the behavior of average cost as the number of students increases. Understanding cost behavior is important, as it is the foundation of cost-related analysis and decision making.

You calculate the average costs, as shown in Table 4.5. The average costs are $6,000 when the program serves 40 trainees. That average drops to $4,500 when the number of trainees increases to 100.

Table 4.5 Activity Level as It Relates to Fixed, Variable, Step, and Total Costs

Activity Level (Q)	Fixed Cost (FC)	Unit Variable Cost (UVC)	Variable Cost (VC)	Step Cost (SC)	Total Cost (TC)	Average Cost (AC)
40	$100,000	$1,000	$40,000	$100,000	$240,000	$6,000
60	$100,000	$1,000	$60,000	$150,000	$310,000	$5,167
80	$100,000	$1,000	$80,000	$200,000	$380,000	$4,750
99	$100,000	$1,000	$99,000	$250,000	$449,000	$4,535
100	$100,000	$1,000	$100,000	$250,000	$450,000	$4,500

Notes: Total cost = FC + VC + SC; Average cost = TC/Q

Figure 4.4 graphs the data in Table 4.5. It shows that the average cost of the training program declines as the number of trainees increases. This is because more students are sharing the same facilities, which is a fixed cost. Economists call this economies of scale. This is a major cost behavior that leads to the development of analytical tools, such as marginal analysis and break-even analysis, which we discuss later.

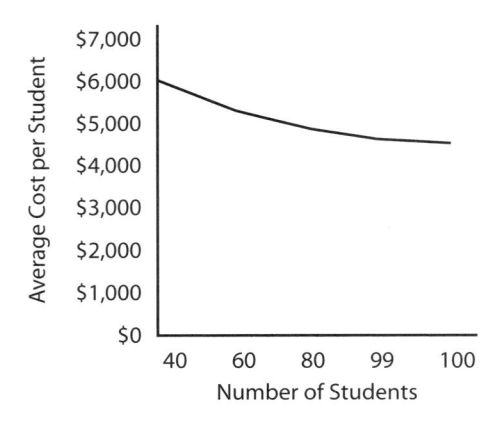

Figure 4.4 Average cost versus activity volume.

An examination of Table 4.5 reveals that when the number of trainees increases from 99 to 100, the total cost increases from $449,000 to $450,000. The difference, or the marginal cost, is therefore $1,000. This is lower than the average cost, which includes a share of the fixed cost. The marginal cost includes only the variable cost of $1,000, as discussed in the preceding section.

Opportunity Costs and Accounting Costs

Arguably, the most confusing part of the concept of **costs** is related to shifts in decision-making contexts between two highly related but different disciplines: economics and accounting. Economic decision making requires the use of opportunity costs, whereas operating financial decision making is often based on information on accounting costs from a given organization's accounting system.

Opportunity Costs

Financial managers participate in decision making in planning, especially in allocating limited resources. In this context, the economic definition of *cost*—that is, the opportunity cost—is most relevant. The term **opportunity cost** refers to the fact that when a decision is made to use a resource for one purpose, the same resource cannot be used for another simultaneously. The value forgone for not using the resource for the second-best alternative is the opportunity cost of the resource concerned in the decision.

For example, a nonprofit manager is considering starting a new program for the community, using an existing building the nonprofit has owned for years. Although the building is currently empty, the organization could rent it out for $2,000 per month. In making the decision from the economic perspective, the nonprofit financial manager should include that $2,000 per month as an opportunity cost. The nonprofit could earn that amount if it were to decide not to use the resource for the new program. Cost is therefore the *monetary value of economic resources used in performing an activity or providing a service,* whether or not money has changed hands. The concept of opportunity has many applications in the nonprofit world. The case study at the end of this chapter presents another example of opportunity cost in a university setting.

Accounting Costs

Another common definition of cost is *the amount of money needed to buy, do, or make something.* Cost is then recorded and recognized in the accounting system when the expenditure is incurred. This is the **accounting cost**, which has applications in the operation of the nonprofit on a daily basis. This cost appears in financial reports and cost accounting systems and is used regularly within and outside the organization for financial decision making.

When the HFA was looking at the possibility of expanding their new job training program, they considered starting the new program in an existing building that it had owned for years. As an example, let's assume that HFA decided to expand their new job training program into their existing empty building. At the end of the fiscal year and after the implementation of the new program, no building cost was included in the calculation of the cost of the new program because there was no transaction recorded in the accounting system. This is different from the concept of opportunity or economic costs. Economic costs are relevant primarily in decision making concerned with allocating limited economic resources, such as in capital budgeting, while accounting costs are used in financial analysis and reporting, which is more related to budgeting and operations. Financial managers need to have the sophistication to discern the difference and use the appropriate concept in different contexts to solve different problems.

In both contexts, a cost is related to a cost objective, or cost object, an organizing concept upon which costs are anchored. Nonprofits consume resources for specific purposes. For instance, to feed the hungry, to improve the environment, and to run the Red Cross are objectives of costs. Cost objectives could be activities, programs, departments, or whole organizations in the study of financial management, especially in cost accounting. Financial managers need to know the various costs of the cost objectives. For example, an accurate full cost accounting of a service is critical for nonprofits that are reimbursed by government programs.

Cost objectives are often presumed or inferred in communications. This can cause misunderstanding and misjudgment between involved parties, as shown in the following example.

A Short Study in Determining Program Costs

The Community Art Group is a performing arts nonprofit that presents programs from street performance to theater events in a midtown metropolitan area. It is facing financial stresses common to many nonprofits during the 2020 Covid-19 pandemic. The box office is not generating the same level of revenues as it had in past years, so the nonprofit needs to explore or enhance other sources of funding. The Community Art Group may have to cut programs if funding is not forthcoming. While going through the list of programs in a planning session, the chief executive officer of the nonprofit asks, "How much does the symphony program cost?" The treasurer produces an estimate that is substantially higher than what the program director has presented. Who is right and who is wrong?

Comparing notes, the treasurer and director realize that they have been estimating costs for different objectives. The program director has considered the costs of the program based primarily on the salaries of the performing artists and supplies for the program only, while the treasurer has considered the costs of the department that houses the program, the only program it runs, including the rental of the theater and the allocated salaries of the executives of the nonprofit. What is the symphony program's cost? It depends. It depends on the cost objective that each party is presuming. Some costs are direct to the production of the program, while others are overhead or indirect and may or may not have to be allocated depending upon the issue and the circumstance. The question is which cost is most relevant.

Relevant Costs in Financial Decision Making

As we have noted, diverse definitions of cost exist. The correct use of the concept in nonprofit financial management depends on the decision context and the knowledge and skills of the nonprofit managers. In this section we survey the most common uses of the cost concept in the nonprofit context. The following are applications of the cost concept used in resolving practical problems.

Extension of Existing Services: Marginal Analysis

Nonprofit organizations are growing in number and in size. In considering expanding existing services, financial managers and executive directors should base their decisions on marginal analysis, in which expected marginal benefits are compared with estimated marginal costs. Those program expansions that produce net surpluses are "stars" or "cash cows" that can advance the missions of nonprofits directly and/or provide financial resources that supplement other programs for mission achievement.

As we explained earlier in this chapter, marginal cost is the additional cost incurred to produce one more unit of goods or services. Marginal benefits are the additional benefits created when one more unit of goods or services is produced. When a nonprofit manager must decide whether to add one more good or service, such as a new client, the relevant decision criterion is net benefit on the margin. It should not be based on a comparison between average costs and average benefits. See Assignment 4.2 at the end of the chapter for an example of the application of marginal analysis in decision support.

Potential New Programs or Services: Break-Even Analysis

Apart from operational decisions, nonprofit managers face planning decisions for programs that are new to their organizations. New opportunities may emerge, and nonprofit managers need the capability to analyze the feasibility and net benefit of new projects for their nonprofits and the constituencies they serve. One of the most common tools used in evaluating the potential financial results of adding a new service or program is the **break-even analysis**.

Break-even analysis is a method of determining the number of units or services that must be sold or in other ways reimbursed at a given price to recover the cost of initiating and operating a new service or program. The break-even point is the service level at which revenue is exactly equal to expenses. The break-even point can be expressed in terms of unit sales or dollar sales. Sales above that number result in net revenue, and sales below that number result in a loss.

The break-even analysis is an excellent tool to help quantify the level of services needed for a new program. To make a sound decision about a proposed new program, a financial manager in a nonprofit organization needs to know if the program can break even, given the projected volume, price, and cost structure. Conversely, the financial manager may be required to answer questions as to what needs to be done if demand for an existing service is declining. The nonprofit may have to change its cost structure to compensate for the reduced volume in order to break even.

Mathematically, the break-even point is the volume or level of activity at which total revenue (TR) equals total costs (TC):

$$TR = TC \tag{4.1}$$

The total revenue can be expressed as follows:

$$TR = P \times Q \tag{4.2}$$

and total cost is determined by

$$TC = FC + Q \times UVC \tag{4.3}$$

where
P = price
Q = volume
FC = fixed cost
UVC = unit variable cost

Inserting Equations 4.2 and 4.3 into Equation 4.1, one gets

$$P \times Q = FC + Q \times UVC \tag{4.4}$$

Solving Equation 4.4, one gets

$$Q = FC/(P - UVC) \tag{4.5}$$

Equation 4.5 indicates that one can calculate the break-even volume by dividing the difference between the price and the unit variable cost, which is also known as the contribution margin, into the fixed cost of a program. See Assignment 4.4 at the end of this chapter for an example of a break-even analysis.

Conclusion

Cost is a complex concept that has different meanings under different circumstances and has broad applications in cost accounting and financial management. Nonprofit financial managers should have a good grasp of the concept. In this chapter we have discussed the cost concept and its application in different contexts, including economic and accounting costs, fixed and variable costs, direct and indirect costs, average and marginal costs, methods of cost accounting to calculate the full cost of a program, marginal analysis in decision making for program expansion, and break-even analysis for new programs. These are all vital elements of an organization's budget and overall financial management; they play a key role in ensuring that a nonprofit has the financial health it needs to carry out its mission.

KEY TERMS

accounting costs	direct costs	opportunity cost
average costs	fixed costs	step costs
break-even analysis	indirect costs	variable costs
costs	marginal costs	

Discussion Questions

1. Why is the concept of opportunity cost important for nonprofits?
2. Explain the difference between direct cost and indirect cost.
3. What is the difference between fixed cost and variable cost?
4. What is break-even analysis? Why is it useful for nonprofits?
5. How is the concept of cost used differently in an accounting context as compared to an economic discussion?
6. Why do most fixed costs in the long run become variable costs?

Suggested Readings

Boardman, Anthony E., David H. Greenberg, Aidan R. Vining, and David L. Weimer (2018). *Cost-Benefit Analysis: Concepts and Practice* (5th ed.). New York: Cambridge.
Chen, Greg C., Lynne A. Weikart, and Daniel W. Williams (2014). *Budget Tools: Financial Methods in the Public Sector* (2nd ed.). New York: Sage.
Mikesell, John L. (2018). *Fiscal Administration: Analysis and Applications for the Public Sector* (10th ed.). Boston: Cengage.
Urban Institute and The Center for What Works (2006). *Candidate Outcome Indicators: Employment Training/Workforce Development Program.* Washington, DC: Urban Institute (urban.org/sites/default/files/2015/04/10/employment_training.pdf).

Case Study

New Program at City University to Help the Unemployed

City University is considering adding a new program to help the unemployed. The program, which is to have a 1-year duration, will provide training in the skills needed for the health care sector in the city and the surrounding area. Initial financial analysis indicates that the fixed cost of the program will be $150,000, which covers the cost of a 1-year rental of the facilities and the utilities, insurance, and administrative cost of the program. The variable cost and step cost is approximately $10,000 per student (to simplify the case), which pays for faculty salary, lunches, teaching materials, and textbooks. The state will kick in $5,000 per student, and the tuition fee, based on the market analysis, is $6,000. The executives of the university are not quite sure how much demand there will be for the program, given that it is new and will be offered in the region for the first time, but they are estimating an enrollment in the range of 100 to 150 students. You are the financial analyst for new programs, and you are asked to do an analysis to generate relevant information that will help executives decide whether or not to add the program.

To address the questions, you plan to use break-even analysis, recognizing that the program is new and the university has major concerns regarding its finances given the current budget constraints in the state and in the university itself. To do a comprehensive analysis, you would also like to provide executives with information on different scenarios so that they are prepared if and when the underlying assumptions do not materialize. In other words, you would like to provide a risk management analysis in addition to a simple break-even analysis to support your decision makers fully.

Assignments

Assignment 4.1. Assessing Fixed, Variable, and Total Costs of a Program

HFA has recently received a contract from the state government to start a job training program. The program will last for 1 year and will likely continue in the future. The program will need a director with a salary of $70,000 per year. The estimated rent for a facility to house the program is approximately $20,000 for the next 12 months. The utilities, insurance, and custodial services are estimated to be $10,000 yearly. The facility can accommodate up to 100 people. The program will also hire teachers/trainers, each of whom can teach up to 20 trainees. The salary for each teacher is $50,000 per year. Each of the program participants will receive a set of textbooks and other teaching materials, estimated at $1,000 per person. For simplicity, other potential costs are not considered for this case.

What are the program's fixed, variable, step, total, and average costs if it enrolls 50 students?

Assignment 4.2. Considering Program Expansion with Marginal Analysis

After a successful start of the job training program, the state government has contacted HFA for an additional 10 new trainee spots, which would expand the current career training program to a total of 60 trainees. The state is willing to pay $3,000 each for the 10 extra spots, which is lower than current average cost, keeping the reimbursement rate for the 50 existing seats unchanged. The facility has the capacity for 100 students and the number of existing teachers can handle an additional 10 students. If only financial viewpoints are considered, should the HFA accept this offer from the state?

Assignment 4.3. Budget a New Program

Given the recent Covid-19 pandemic and the ensuing economic downturn, Midtown Soup Kitchen would like to provide meals in a new location. The initial study shows that the fixed costs, including the rent, equipment, and personnel costs, are $50,000 per month. The facility can serve 1,000 meals per day 30 days a month, and there is more demand than the kitchen can supply. The variable cost is the food cost, which is approximately $2.00 per meal, and the city is willing to support the project. You are preparing a budget application to the city. How much support will you need from the city to make this project break even for your nonprofit financially?

Assignment 4.4. Determining the Break-Even Point for a New Program

The Middle Town Performing Art Theater is planning a new show. The fixed cost is estimated to be $400,000 for the season. The variable cost is $10 per ticket. The box office has set the ticket price at $50. How many tickets does the box office have to sell before the theater can break even?

Assignment 4.5. Considering Opportunity Costs to a Grant Application

HFA is a nonprofit organization established to help ex-convicts during reentry into their communities. HFA is currently preparing a grant application to a foundation to extend its services for former drug offenders by offering a program that will teach them basic skills for employment. The chief financial officer of HFA has collected accounting data and prepared a budget with relative ease, using the organization's well-designed and carefully maintained bookkeeping system. However, when the nonprofit asks for comments on its draft proposal from contacts at City University (with whom HFA has long-standing cooperative relationships), the contacts advise HFA to take into consideration the opportunity costs of the facility that it is going to use to house the new program. The nonprofit has owned the property for years and does not have to pay to use it, but a nearby after-school program has offered $5,000 a month to rent it. In what way can this advice be incorporated into the grant application, given that the nonprofit has revised its financial policy to disallow economically untenable programs with the downdraft of financial resources since the start of the Covid-19 pandemic?

Assignment 4.6. Applying the Direct Allocation Method

HFA has two program departments, one for the treatment of ex-convicts who are drug users and the other for a job training program for ex-convicts. The treatment program hires 40% of the program employees but accounts for approximately 63% of expenses for both programs. HFA also has two support departments, one for general management (administration) and the other for fundraising. These are smaller departments but they provide vital services. Initial allocation of the costs based on square footage notes the direct and indirect costs for each department, as shown in Table 4.6. Using this information, calculate the full cost for the two program departments so that each program can be accurately reimbursed. It is HFA's policy to allocate general management costs by the proportion of employees and to allocate fundraising costs by the proportion of program expenses using the direct distribution method.

Table 4.6 HFA's Direct and Indirect Costs

	Administration	Fundraising	Drug Treatment	Job Training	Total
Direct Costs	$ 50,000	$ 100,000	$ 500,000	$ 300,000	$ 950,000
Indirect Costs	20,000	30,000	100,000	50,000	200,000
Total Costs	$ 70,000	$ 130,000	$ 600,000	$ 350,000	$ 1,150,000

Notes

[1] Rubin, Irene S. (2019). *The Politics of Public Budgeting: Getting and Spending, Borrowing and Balancing* (9th ed.). Washington, DC: CQ Press.

[2] Details are available in CFR Part 200—Uniform Administrative Requirements, Cost Principles, and Audit Requirements for Federal Rewards (ecfr.federalregister.gov/current/title-2/subtitle-A/chapter-II/part-200).

Part III
Financial Analysis in Nonprofit Organizations

5

Basic Principles of Accounting and Reporting Requirements

> At a high level, accounting conventions are artificial constructs designed to ensure some measure of uniformity in financial reporting.
>
> —James Kwak[1]

Learning Objectives

The learning objectives for this chapter are as follows:
- Understanding the basic accounting structure for nonprofits
- Becoming aware of the different users of nonprofit accounting
- Comprehending the basic principles of accounting
- Learning the differences between cash and accrual accounting
- Understanding fund accounting
- Becoming familiar with financial statements
- Understanding reporting requirements
- Learning what constitutes financial responsibility

*A*ccounting is a language that is used to communicate information about financial events that have taken place. Although accounting has its complexities, it is a language that can be learned. With that learning comes an understanding of how financial events affect nonprofit organizations. As we explained in Chapter 2, accounting deals with actual revenues and expenses, whereas budgeting deals with plans and forecasts of revenues and expenses.

Accounting is divided into two parts: financial accounting and management accounting. The first is concerned with financial information, such as debt and past revenues and expenses; the second is concerned with financial information that might be used to improve the effectiveness and efficiency of the organization, such as the costs per client of various programs.

The results of **financial accounting** are often used by those external to the organization. In the case of nonprofits, donors of all kinds—individuals, foundations, and others—examine organizations' **financial statements** to assess their fiscal health. Federal and state governments use nonprofits' audited financial statements in their decisions to make grants. Major contributors to nonprofits closely examine audited financial statements. Certainly, when large nonprofit organizations issue bonds to raise revenue, the bond rating agencies examine the nonprofits' audited financial statements in order to rate the bond issues. Foundations often request nonprofits' audited financial statements before agreeing to any grant proposal.

Management accounting involves using financial data to think through how an organization can be more efficient in its delivery of services or more effective in its accomplishment of program outcomes, and thus is often used by those internal to the organization.

Certain nonprofit stakeholders, such as the board of directors and the executive director, may use both financial and management accounting tools in their role in governance. The board members of a nonprofit have fiduciary responsibility for the organization. They must ensure that the nonprofit remains in good fiscal health, and consequently may focus more on financial reports that report on assets and debt. Certainly executive staff and program directors often focus on managerial reports as they examine the efficiency and effectiveness of their programs.

Accounting Standards Structure

The Securities and Exchange Commission (SEC), under the Securities Exchange Act of 1934, has legal authority to establish financial accounting and reporting standards for nongovernmental entities. The SEC requires that financial statements filed with the SEC be certified by independent public accountants. In 1938 the SEC delegated much of its authority to prescribe accounting practices to the accounting profession. In effect, the SEC relies on the work of the private sector.

As early as 1887, the goal of the American Institute of Certified Public Accountants (AICPA) has been to establish rules and standards for the profession. In 1972, the AICPA set up the Financial Accounting Foundation, an independent nonprofit organization that has responsibility for setting accounting standards for nongovernmental entities, publicly traded companies, and nonprofits. To that end, the foundation established the Financial Accounting Standards Board (FASB) in 1973 to set standards for financial accounting and financial reporting for nongovernmental entities, including publicly held companies and nonprofit organizations. In 1984, the foundation created the Government Accounting Standards Board to establish accounting standards for state and local governmental entities. Given that this book's topic is nonprofits, we focus here on FASB rules and regulations.

The language concerning "private" and "public" companies can be confusing. Privately held companies are those that are owned by only a few shareholders and do not offer stock to the public. One advantage that privately held companies have is that they have no obligation to reveal any financial information to the public. Publicly held companies are those that are owned by many shareholders and trade their stocks publicly. These companies are required to file with the SEC. Of course, an advantage that publicly held companies have is that they can raise a great deal of cash when trading shares.

> **Box 5.1**
> **REMEMBER: Financial Accounting Standards Board**
> Federal law created the SEC in 1934. The SEC relies on the FASB, established in 1973, to set financial accounting and reporting standards for nongovernmental entities, including nonprofits.

Since the nation's financial crisis of 2008, the SEC has come under criticism for not enforcing stricter accounting standards in publicly held companies. Some of that criticism spilled over to nonprofits a decade later. In 2016, FASB tightened accounting rules for nonprofits in several areas, as explained below.

Principles of Accounting

The FASB sets the ground rules for the measurement, reporting, and disclosure of information in financial statements of nongovernmental entities. It has established generally accepted accounting principles (GAAP), the common set of standards and procedures that accountants must use when examining the financial transactions of a publicly held company or a nonprofit. In the United States, whenever financial accounting is involved, it is assumed that these **accounting principles** are followed. GAAP is essential because people who invest in publicly held companies must be assured of a minimum level of consistency in financial recording and reporting from one company to another. The same holds true for nonprofits. When donors, big or small, choose to invest in a nonprofit, they must be assured of the consistency and accuracy of the nonprofit's financial statements. GAAP defines when revenue can be recognized, how assets must be classified on the balance sheet, and other mysteries of financial statements.

While the FASB has established many technical accounting principles, GAAP can be described as being based on four key assumptions, four basic principles, and four basic constraints that must be followed.[2] We discuss these in turn below.

> **Box 5.2**
>
> **REMEMBER: Assumptions, Principles, and Constraints of Accounting**
>
> The four key assumptions:
> - Economic entity
> - Going concern
> - Monetary unit
> - Time period
>
> The four basic principles:
> - Cost
> - Revenue
> - Matching
> - Disclosure
>
> The four basic constraints:
> - Objectivity
> - Materiality
> - Consistency
> - Prudence

The Four Key Assumptions

Economic entity. GAAP requires that each economic entity keep separate financial records. In addition, every transaction, an economic event, must be associated with the specific entity in which that transaction took place.

Going concern. Financial statements are prepared for corporations that are assumed to remain in business indefinitely. Because of the indefinite nature of corporations, corporations divide their assets and liabilities into short-term and long-term periods of time. Since public corporations can assume that they will operate for the foreseeable future, they can calculate the value of their assets using long-term financial tools, such as depreciation and amortization. Nonprofits can carry long-term debt because they are assumed to be in business indefinitely.

Monetary unit. GAAP requires that financial records use one stable currency. If other currencies are used during the fiscal year, those amounts are to be clearly listed. Nonprofit organizations involved in programs overseas must use a single monetary unit in their reporting.

Time period. GAAP requires entities to report any assumptions about the time period that they are using. The assumption is that any and all transactions reported in a specific period occurred in that period. For example, an accountant can report the purchase of equipment over period of years, but he or she must accurately report the transaction in that specific period of time.

The Four Basic Principles

Cost. This principle requires organizations to report their assets at the amount they were originally purchased and not at their current fair market value. Although the value of an asset may not be the same throughout its lifetime, its original value has a simplicity and verifiability that is useful in accounting. GAAP requires that most assets be recorded at the cost at which they were purchased, not their current estimated value. The exception is stocks, which have an actual value at a particular point in time. The FASB, however, now requires nonprofits to report all investments in current fair market value, unlike real estate.

The cost principle is debated regularly among accountants. Reporting some assets at current value makes sense for those assets where it is possible to determine the actual value of the assets at a point in time, such as stocks and bonds. It is more difficult to determine the value of assets like real estate, which in a booming market may be worth a great deal of money but in a down market may be worth very little.

Revenue. This principle requires that all revenue be recognized in the financial statements when earned. That means when a nonprofit receives money from a client to perform a service, that money is not immediately counted as revenue; instead, it can be counted only when the nonprofit earns the money by performing the service. Until that time, that revenue is actually a liability.

Matching. The matching principle is a part of accrual accounting. Revenue and all of its associated costs must be counted in the same accounting period. For example, employees get paid on January 7 for the preceding two weeks, one week of which was December 25 to December 31. The employer should record an expense in December for those wages earned from December 25 through December 31 even though the employees will not be paid until January 7 in the new fiscal year. In effect, accounting pairs revenue with the costs that were incurred to generate that revenue. Depreciation is one example of the matching principle. If an asset, newly purchased, will last a number of years, the cost of that asset is not written off all at once. The value of the asset is depreciated over the asset's estimated useful life. This can be accomplished through the matching of the expense of the asset with the benefits it produces over its lifetime.

Disclosure. This principle requires accountants to disclose all transactions within an accounting period. All expenses must be disclosed—none can be hidden, for example, until the next fiscal year. In addition, significant events, such as a lawsuit that may have financial implications for a corporation, must be mentioned as appropriate notes. Nonprofits cannot hide events that might have a financial impact on them. Auditors and board members often refer to this concept as transparency in financial reporting.

The Four Basic Constraints

Objectivity. The objectivity constraint requires accountants to be objective in their examination of a company's finances. Accountants must include all information that can be supported by independent and provable information.

Materiality. All financial transactions must be recorded, although those transactions that are immaterial need not be counted. The judgment lies in how important the transactions are for the users of the information. For example, if a nonprofit is taking inventory, it need not count individual paper clips, but it must count most supplies.

Consistency. This principle requires accountants to conform to GAAP rules with regard to record keeping—that is, to be uniform from one time period to another. For example, if prepaid expenses run into 2 fiscal years, the prepaid expenses must be recorded as split between the 2 years. Another example is that a nonprofit cannot decide to record its pledge revenues differently from one year to the next. If in one year the nonprofit records pledges as revenue only after the revenue has been received, it cannot decide the next year to record pledges when a written pledge is received but the cash is not yet in hand.

Prudence. The recording of transactions must be done within a prudent framework. This conservatism is important. If accountants must estimate, they must do so conservatively. For example, if revenue for the next fiscal year is received in the present fiscal year, it is essential that the revenue be recorded as restricted and is not available until the new fiscal year. Accountants are required under the principle of prudence to choose an answer that reduces the likelihood that they are overstating the revenue.

Importance of Accounting Principles

All of the above principles of accounting are important. Users depend on financial information to make decisions, and this information needs to be uniform across entities, so that users can compare and contrast the successes and failures of multiple entities. Without uniformity of information, it is impossible to judge the success of any one organization. Remember the Enron Corporation, which lied about its financial worth and fooled the entire investment community for several years. Remember Bernard Madoff, who ran a corporate entity that also falsified its financial records. When such lies are discovered, the result is a crisis of confidence in the entire financial system.

In the nonprofit world, these principles are also very important. With these principles in place, users can compare and contrast one nonprofit with another. Investors can decide where to donate their money. Citizens can decide whether or not to join boards once they understand the financial positions of the nonprofits they are considering. In order to make all of these kinds of decisions, people must have confidence in the financial statements of nonprofits. Financial statements must be uniform for all.

Basis of Accounting

There are three accounting methods: cash, accrual, and modified accrual. The difference between them is when revenues and expenses appear on financial statements. A transaction is a financial event. Whenever a financial transaction occurs, it must be recorded. It is the timing of the record keeping that marks the difference between cash and accrual accounting.

Here is an example: You are the executive director of a new nonprofit providing technical assistance to schools. At the end of the first month, you have paid your first monthly payroll of $15,000. You also have paid your nonpersonnel services (NPS) expense of $1,000 in rent for a total of $16,000 for the first month. You deposit your first client's check of $35,000 and realize that you have a surplus of $19,000. Life is good; you can meet payroll for the first two months. Then you remember that you signed a contract for a copying machine that will be delivered next week and you must pay $5,000. In addition, you ordered supplies from a nearby store for $1,000. This will use up $6,000 of the $19,000 surplus, so that you will only have $13,000 remaining. After taking these two expenditures into consideration, you do not have enough cash on hand to pay the bills that are coming due. In this scenario, the cash accounting method states that you have a surplus, whereas the accrual accounting method states that if you do not have any other financial transactions, at the end of two months, your $13,000 surplus will not cover your payroll.

Cash Accounting

A nonprofit that uses **cash accounting** counts every transaction when cash is received or when cash is spent. If cash is not used, the transaction is not recorded. In cash accounting, revenues are counted in the period (usually monthly) when received, and expenses are counted (usually monthly) when they are paid. Cash accounting is sometimes referred to as "checkbook" accounting. This type of accounting is used rarely in nonprofits. Most nonprofits use accrual accounting, so that the effect of every financial transaction is recorded.

Accrual Accounting

Accrual accounting records the effect of a transaction whenever it occurs, with or without cash changing hands. For example, if a nonprofit agrees to pay for employee vacation time and employees have built up (accrued) vacation days for a period of time, then the nonprofit must record these days as an expense. Even though the nonprofit has not paid for them yet, the nonprofit has incurred an expense. That transaction is counted as an expense even though cash has not yet flowed.

The items are recorded when the nonprofit receives the goods or services. If a nonprofit has performed a service and has sent a bill to the client in order to get paid, that nonprofit has earned revenue even though it has not yet received any money. Revenue is counted when the sale occurs.

Why is accrual accounting so important? It presents an accurate or "true-to-life" picture of a nonprofit's financial state. If accrual accounting is done properly, it creates a record of all of the nonprofit's revenues and expenses. No expenses are hidden. This accurate financial picture allows the decision makers, the board and the executive director, to have a full grasp of the financial condition of the nonprofit, and this knowledge helps them to fulfill the nonprofit's mission. If a nonprofit were using cash accounting, it would count only cash transactions. If it obtained supplies by using a charge account, that charge would not appear in any financial report,

> **Box 5.3**
>
> **REMEMBER:**
> **Accrual Accounting**
>
> A formal definition of accrual accounting is that it that recognizes expenses when incurred and revenue when earned. What does that mean? Accrual accounting records the effect of a transaction whenever it occurs, with or without cash changing hands.
>
> For example, when a nonprofit *orders and receives* supplies from a nearby store and charges the amount to an account, that transaction is recorded as a prepaid expense even though the supplies have not been paid for. This means the transaction is recognized when it is incurred rather than when it is paid.
>
> The same is true for revenues. If a nonprofit organization receives written notification that it will receive a pledge the following fiscal year, accrual accounting recognizes that revenue in an account meant specifically for future revenue.

and the amount of expenses would be underreported. A similar problem would exist on the revenue side. If the nonprofit received a pledge for a donation that would start the next month, then the revenue would be underestimated in any budget. The accrual accounting method demonstrates a nonprofit's long-term profitability.

The principle of matching becomes very important here. Accrual accounting depends on accurate matching of revenues and expenses within the same accounting period, usually the month in which they occur. Consider this problem on the revenue side when dealing with accrual accounting. A nonprofit could overestimate its revenues by claiming revenue it does not have but anticipates getting. This would not happen in cash accounting. The principles of accounting that require matching, however, keep accrual accounting honest. Revenues must be matched with the corresponding expenses in the same accounting period.

Modified Accrual Accounting Method

Government and a few nonprofits use a modified accrual accounting method that involves recognizing revenue when it becomes both available and measurable, rather than when it is earned. This differs from accrual accounting that is required to recognize contributions when made even if donor restrictions make the revenue unavailable. This modified accrual accounting became an important tool for local and state governments when policy makers discovered that local and state officials were declaring revenue that might not materialize.

Differences of Accounting Methods

The basics of all three accounting methods can be summarized as follows:

- *Cash accounting*, used by some small businesses and small nonprofits, recognizes revenue when received and expenses when paid. In fact, the best way to think of this method is as cash receipts (similar to revenues) and cash disbursements (similar to expenses).
- *Accrual accounting*, used by most businesses and nonprofits, requires revenue to be recognized when it is earned and expenses to be recognized when the related benefits are received.
- *Modified accrual accounting* involves recognizing revenue when it becomes both available and measurable, rather than when it is earned. This method is used by many state and local governments.

Fund Accounting

Fund accounting is the heart of nonprofit accounting and is the chief difference between the for-profit sector and the nonprofit sector. A fund allows for a separation of resources. This type of accounting is self-balancing; the intent is to balance dedicated expenses with dedicated revenues. In fund accounting, revenues, expenses, and the difference are tracked for particular purposes in separate accounts. It is largely found in nonprofits and governmental agencies, but it is also sometimes used by for-profit organizations.

Nonprofits often track many separate funds. If a nonprofit receives an education grant that can be spent only for a particular purpose, the finance officer might set up a separate fund to track the revenues and expenses and the difference for this grant. Sometimes nonprofits will bundle a few programs and their funds, such as all their education programs, into one separate fund.

Fund accounting has changed over the years. Since 1973, the FASB has set new accounting standards for nonprofits. These are known as Statements of Financial Accounting Standards (FAS). The standards implemented in 2018 (FASB Update 2016-14 [Topic 958]) divided contributions into unrestricted and restricted funds. This is a major change from previous years when nonprofits used three funds in their financial statements. It is important to note that nonprofits continue to use different funds for different types of programs, but when it comes to financial statements, they must use these two classes of funds.

Unrestricted Net Assets

Nonprofits are required to report their day-to-day operational or general revenues and expenses and the difference in an unrestricted fund. All expenses for the fiscal year must be reported in the unrestricted fund, called **unrestricted net assets**, although revenue can be placed in a restricted fund, called **restricted net assets**. This means when money is to be used from a restricted fund, these monies are moved to the unrestricted fund on the financial statement.

Other than program funds, a subcategory of unrestricted funds is board-designated funds. The board of directors of a nonprofit sometimes decides to segregate a part of the organization's unrestricted funds for a designated purpose of the board's own creation. For example, board members may decide that they want to establish a scholarship fund as a board fund. The IRS does not recognize such a fund as a restricted fund in financial statements because the board cannot create a legal entity; board members can always change their minds, and restricted funds are those funds that are legally restricted to a specific purpose.

Another subcategory of unrestricted funds is fixed asset funds, which many boards create. Again, a fixed asset fund is not a legal entity as much as it is a fund created so that the board is able to separate fixed assets from the unrestricted fund, which then better represents the current program activities of the nonprofit. The creation of a separate fixed asset fund is a board decision. Such a fund can contain land, buildings, and equipment, which are long-term items with a life far beyond yearly financial statements.

Restricted Net Assets

Nonprofits must report all revenues related to restricted funds—that is, funds for which the nonprofits are limited in how the revenue can be used based on the donors' requirements of time and action. These are donor-restricted revenues—they are the ones who determine how the revenue is restricted, not the organization.

There are individual donors and organizations, such as foundations or government entities, that provide funding for a particular purpose and often with a limited period of time. These are restricted funds and when the time arrives to use those funds, the funds are transferred to the unrestricted fund and spent for that purpose.

In addition, there are individual donors who require the nonprofit to keep the principal donation but allow the spending of the investment income (interest and dividends) to support the nonprofit's activities. This is called an endowment where nonprofits will build investments that are permanent. Capital gains or losses on these investments are normally reported in the unrestricted class. Of course, this is not the case if the gains have been explicitly restricted by the donor. Sometimes donors may allow part of the principal to be used. Donors can also restrict the use of investment income to particular activities. When interest income and dividends are ready to be used, these must be transferred to the unrestricted net assets unless restricted by the donor.

Donors sometimes establish term endowments; that is, they require that their original gifts be kept intact for a number of years, after which the monies are unrestricted. Only the donors can formally restrict their monies, and merely expressing a preference is not good enough; for funds to be kept in the restricted category, the amount of the gift must be legally restricted.

Rules Concerning Volunteers

The donated services of volunteers are in-kind services. A volunteer's time is recorded if the time is spent building an asset for the nonprofit or the volunteer donates professional skills, such as those of an attorney or CPA, and, most important, the nonprofit would have paid for the services had the services not been donated. Under these rules, nonprofits that would like to demonstrate a high volunteer component might be restricted in the numbers and kinds of volunteers that they can claim.

As we have noted, nonprofits can use internal accounting for as many funds as they like, but when they report their finances to the outside world in their financial statements, they are required by the FASB to report using the two classes of funds described above and a total of those funds. The discussion of financial statements below will help to clarify the nature of these funds.

Introduction to Financial Statements

Accounting is as old as civilization. Clay tablets recording financial transactions have been found dating to 3500 BCE. Modern accounting's foundations began in Florence in the fifteenth century, when Luca Pacioli, considered the father of modern-day accounting, created double-entry bookkeeping. In 1494 Pacioli, an Italian mathematician and monk, published *Summa*, a book that included several chapters explaining double-entry bookkeeping. In this system every time a financial transaction takes place, the amount of that transaction is recorded twice. For example, if a nonprofit spends $100 on office supplies, the entries include a record of an increase in expense of $100 and a decrease in cash of $100. Double-entry bookkeeping is represented by the **accounting equation** for nonprofits:

Assets = Liabilities + Net Assets (accumulated net revenue)

In effect, the liabilities (debt) and the net of revenues over expenses support the assets of a nonprofit. Assets are created through two inflows: one is debt or the borrowing of money, and the other is net revenue, which is earned in the process of the nonprofit's performance of services. The advantage of recording all transactions twice is that it clarifies for the users of the information both the costs of doing business and the benefits of doing business in a particular corporation. When a financial transaction is recorded in double-entry bookkeeping, it is recorded both as a debit and as a credit. Returning to the example of purchasing office supplies, the transaction is recorded as a debit in expenses on the net asset side and as a credit for cash on the asset side. Both of these transactions are decreases. Before computers, the debits and credits for a given organization were recorded in a book called the general ledger. Although accountants now use computers instead of huge accounting books, accounting systems still use the language of ledgers. Debits and credits are recorded in an electronic general ledger or in one of the subledgers created to track financial transactions. We will discuss the accounting equation in greater depth in Chapter 6.

The best way to understand accounting is to think about your personal finances. Accountants present the worth of a nonprofit organization in four financial statements that are related to one another. Your personal finances include elements that will help you to understand each of these financial statements. In addition to the audited financial statements they must produce yearly, nonprofits usually create monthly trial balances—that is, close examinations of all their accounts to ensure that they balance according to the accounting equation.

Balance Sheet or Statement of Financial Position

The first financial statement is the **balance sheet**, which the nonprofit world calls a *statement of financial position*. We refer to it here as the balance sheet because it is important for those in the nonprofit sector to understand the terminology used in the private, for-profit sector.

Think about all the valuable resources you own—your car, bank account, house, jewelry, clothes, and so on. These are your **assets**. Now list everything you owe—your credit card debt, mortgage, and personal loans. These are your **liabilities**. The difference between your assets and your liabilities is your net worth (often called **net assets**). Usually, younger people have little in terms of assets; college students, in particular, may have accumulated a great deal of debt. After entering the work world full time, people tend to gain more assets.

Let's construct a balance sheet for you. Say that you own a car, jewelry, and stock, and you have some cash. On the other hand, you have a fair amount of debt. You owe money on your car and you have some credit card debt. Table 5.1 pro-

Table 5.1 Example of a Balance Sheet as of December 31, 2019

Balance Sheet
31-Dec-19

Assets		Liabilities	
Cash	$ 1,500	Credit Cards	$ 3,500
Jewelry	800	Car Loan	12,000
Stocks	1,000	Total Liabilities	$ 15,500
Car	15,000	Net Assets	2,800
Total assets	$ 18,300	Total Liabilities + Net Assets	$ 18,300

vides an example of your balance sheet, which describes your financial position at the end of December 2019. The right-hand side lists all the sources of your capital—your debt and net worth (net assets). The left-hand side demonstrates where you invested your capital.

Income Statement or Statement of Activities

Now let's look at your income and expenses. We are going to look at fiscal year 2020, so we can show how the net worth (net assets) changes and how it relates to the balance sheet. Table 5.2 is a version of the financial statement known as the *income statement and changes in net assets*, simplified for illustration purposes. In nonprofit terminology, the income statement is called the *statement of activities and changes in net assets*. The income statement includes all the revenue and expenses for the year being tracked. Let's assume that you received $25,000 from a part-time job and you spent $24,000, leaving you a surplus of $1,000. Table 5.2 shows that you spent $27,000 in expenses because of the depreciation expense of $3,000. (Depreciation is the assessment of property and equipment at the historical cost, with the cost then spread over the life of the asset. We explain depreciation in depth in Chapter 6.)

Table 5.2 Example of an Income Statement and Changes in Net Assets in FY 2020 from January 1 to December 31

Revenues	$ 25,000
Expenses	27,000
Difference	$ (2,000)
Change in Net Assets (net worth)	$ (2,000)
Net Assets at Beginning of the Year	$ 2,800
Net Assets at End of the Year	$ 800

Statement of Cash Flow

The next financial statement is the statement of cash flow. This statement tracks just cash—nothing else. It shows where the nonprofit has received and spent its cash. Cash flow has three categories: operating cash flows, financing cash flows, and investing cash flows. This particular statement, as illustrated in Table 5.3, shows that you used up some of your cash by paying down your car loan. You received cash from selling stock and had more cash coming in during the year. The net decrease in cash at the end of the year was $1,000, shown in parentheses because it is a decrease.

Table 5.3 Example of a Statement of Cash Flow in FY 2020 as of December 31

Cash Flows from Operating Activities	$ 1,000
Cash Flows from Investing Activities	1,000
Cash Flows from Financing Activities	(3,000)
Net Increase or Decrease in Cash	$ (1,000)
Cash at Beginning of the Year	1,500
Cash at End of the Year	$ 500

Connections among Financial Statements

Now let's look again at fiscal year 2020. You managed to pay down your car loan through selling stock ($1,000) and using your cash ($1,500) as well. However, your net worth (net assets) decreased by $2,000 over the 2 years in our scenario, assuming the market value of your car dropped by $3,000. This is reflected in the year-end adjustment of your assets and liabilities that are time-bound. In the nonprofit context, an organization may have to adjust for prepared insurance, accrued salary, and so on. The adjustment for your car is for depreciation, which has the effect of reducing the value of your car on the assets side and reducing the value of your net assets on the liability and net assets side of the balance sheet. The resulting 2020 balance sheet of our simplified case is shown in Table 5.4.

Table 5.4 Example of a Balance Sheet in FY 2020 as of December 31, 2020

Balance Sheet
31-Dec-20

Assets		Liabilities	
Cash	$ 500	Credit Cards	$ 3,500
Jewelry	800	Car Loan	9,000
Stocks	—	Total Liabilities	$ 12,500
Car	12,000	Net Assets	800
Total Assets	$ 13,300	Total Liabilities + Net Assets	$ 13,300

Statement of Functional Expenses

There is one more financial statement required of nonprofits. It is the statement of functional expenses; this type of financial statement is required only of nonprofits that are health or welfare organizations. This statement divides the expenses of the nonprofit during a fiscal year into three categories: program, fundraising, and management/administration. The purpose of this statement is to permit external users to know how much of a nonprofit's efforts are devoted to programs and how much is spent on management and fundraising. Of course, nonprofits have some discretion about whether they categorize particular expenses as program expenses. In any case, the act of categorizing each expense into one of these three categories is a wonderful exercise for nonprofit staff. It forces staff members to examine seriously how they are using their resources.

The Accounting Cycle

As we discussed in Chapter 2, nonprofits organize their financial transactions through time. This begins with the selection of the fiscal year, a choice made by the nonprofit's officials at the time of the nonprofit's creation. The fiscal year often follows the calendar year (January through December), but sometimes nonprofits choose fiscal years that correspond to the fiscal years of the cities or states in which they are located (and from which they expect to get funding). If, for example, a state's fiscal year is defined as July 1 through June 30, a nonprofit in that state might choose that same period.

At the beginning of its fiscal year, the nonprofit starts the recording of all financial transactions for that year, building upon the balance sheet of the year before; that is, the nonprofit's opening balance comes from the previous year's balance sheet. This opening balance is a good example of the going concern principle of accounting. It is assumed that the nonprofit organization will continue to exist, and its history will be taken into account in all transactions.

Usually nonprofit officials choose a monthly cycle for examination of their financial records and creation of a trial balance to ensure that all financial transactions have been recorded correctly. Creating a trial balance involves counting all the financial transactions for a given period of time and checking to see that the debits equal the credits for that period. This is usually done monthly to ensure that the record keeping is as error free as possible. Such a practice does not eliminate all error, but it can catch some kinds of mistakes. For example, if the office supplies transaction referred to previously was recorded by mistake as $10 instead of $100 in both the debit and credit columns, then conducting a trial balance will not find the mistake. Such a mistake would probably be found in the month when an accounting clerk pays the bill for the office supplies. Conducting a trial balance will, however, find any mistakes in which different amounts have been entered in debit and credit columns for a given transaction. As noted in Chapter 2, one key to good financial management is the performance of monthly reviews of the financial state of the organization. Just as the executive director reviews the variance report in budgeting with the finance officer, the executive director reviews the accounting reports with the finance officer.

At the end of the fiscal year, a nonprofit's officials retain an outside certified public accountant (CPA) to review or audit the year's financial activity and create yearly financial statements. The CPA's job is to examine closely the financial transactions of the nonprofit and determine the extent to which the finances fall within generally accepted accounting principles. The CPA produces audited financial statements that the board then reviews. Several entities external to the nonprofit make use of these financial statements in their decision-making processes. For example, if the nonprofit has a line of credit from its bank, the bank will want to review the audited financial statements to verify the organization's financial strength. Donors may want reports to verify that donations are being spent as expected. Potential donors may want to examine financial statements before they commit to making donations.

Reporting Requirements

In the United States, both federal and state governments have passed legislation concerning the reporting requirements of nonprofits, and each state has established its own set of requirements. It is the responsibility of the board of directors of every nonprofit to ensure that their organization is in compliance with federal and state reporting requirements.

National-Level Requirements

Financial Accounting Standards Board. The FASB has moved toward requiring consolidated financial statements; that is, all the funds of a nonprofit must be consolidated into one financial statement. The FASB's concern is that the readers of such financial statements be able to understand the nonprofit as a whole and not simply its parts. Hence, the financial statements of a nonprofit record unrestricted and restricted funds individually, and then consolidate the funds all into one. This gives readers of the statement an understanding of the scope and size of the nonprofit that they may not have if they examined only the statement of the unrestricted fund.

The financial statements of nonprofits today feature columns for the unrestricted and restricted funds and then a total column combining the two funds. The FASB's movement toward consolidated financial statements is based on the accounting principle of full disclosure; that is, readers of financial statements must be assured that all financial transactions that have materiality are in the statements in a way that represents full disclosure of the financial state of the organization.

Sarbanes–Oxley Act. The federal **Sarbanes–Oxley Act of 2002** (Sarbanes–Oxley) was enacted by Congress in response to accounting scandals in the private sector. Since the enactment of Sarbanes–Oxley, the audit committees of corporations' boards of directors have become very important. In addition to audit committees, Sarbanes–Oxley has required greater transparency in financial reporting.

The concerns that gave rise to Sarbanes–Oxley also spilled over into the nonprofit arena, along with a growing demand for transparency in nonprofit accounting. Sarbanes–Oxley includes provisions for audits, disclosure, whistle-blower protection, certified financial statements, and rules on insider transactions; it also proposed a new organization to enforce standards for audits of public companies (but not nonprofits). Sarbanes–Oxley's requirements for nonprofits are only that they have written policies related to employee complaints (whistle-blower policies) and the destruction of documents.

Several states have applied other parts of Sarbanes–Oxley to the nonprofit sector. In California, the Nonprofit Integrity Act of 2004 requires that any charity registered with the attorney general and receiving annual gross revenues of $2 million or more must form an audit committee. Several other states have adopted similar rules, albeit at varying gross revenue thresholds.

The FASB Update No. 2016-14. The new FASB update in 2016 took effect in 2018. Nonprofits were required to change from reporting three funds to two funds on their financial statements: restricted net assets and unrestricted net assets. If donors dictated how monies were to be used, then those monies had to be recognized and moved from restricted to unrestricted in the year of their use. Nonprofits can continue to internally track restricted funds in separate funds such as endowments, foundation grants, etc., but when creating financial statements, all revenues have to be divided between restricted net assets and unrestricted net assets. When monies are moved from restricted to unrestricted in financial statements, then a category, such as "releasing funds from restriction," can be used to designate that move. Even though all the monies with restrictions are placed in the same fund, the nonprofit must disclose a detailed breakout of the different kinds of restrictions in the notes of the financial statement.

FASB No. 2016-14 also made other changes. The tracking and disclosing of liquidity is extremely important. When a grant letter arrives at a nonprofit and states that the nonprofit will receive monies, that grant letter is sufficient to claim a new asset, specifically a pledge receivable, even though monies have yet to be received. The nonprofit has not received the monies and thus cannot use those monies to pay bills. The FASB requires nonprofits to disclose in a notes section what resources it has on hand that can be used to cover expenses in its current fiscal year, and they must point out that such grant monies have not yet been received.

Another major change brought about by FASB No. 2016-14 is the presentation of expenses in the statement of functional expenses. Nonprofits must provide a basis for why each of their expenses was placed into one of three categories: program services, fundraising, and management/administration. For example, nonprofits need to provide more detail about how much of an executive director's time is spent in program services versus fundraising versus management/administration. This can also be done by extensive notes.

Internal Revenue Service. Nonprofits are required by the federal government to file a tax form—IRS Form 990, Return of Organization Exempt From Income Tax (see Appendix A). Nonprofits with less than $50,000 in total receipts must file a Form 990-N; nonprofits with total receipts less than $200,000 and total assets less than $500,000 must file Form 990-EZ; those with gross receipts above $500,000 or total assets more than $500,000 must file Form 990. Although churches are not required to file Form 990, some do. Nonprofits do not pay income taxes except if they are engaged in an unrelated business and subsequently must pay an unrelated business income tax. Form 990 is not an audited financial statement, although it contains the same information. Form 990 gives the nonprofit world the same information in the same way so that one nonprofit can easily be compared to another. Accountants find the Form 990 to be very difficult to prepare but it is required by the IRS.

Form 990 was revised significantly in 2008. A section of the form asks questions about a nonprofit's governance structure, policies, and practices. The revised form also requires disclosure of certain accounting policies, such as policies concerning conflicts of interest, investments, codes of ethics, records retention, gift acceptance, and whistle-blowing. With these changes, the IRS signaled its growing interest in the internal workings of nonprofits.

State-Level Requirements

Individual states have their own reporting requirements for nonprofits. Although these requirements vary from state to state, almost all the states accept a copy of the IRS Form 990. This form satisfies most states' demands for financial reporting by nonprofits, but some states require audited financial statements in addition to Form 990. Some states are quite strict, while others require little from nonprofits. The following are examples from New York, California, and Texas:

- *New York*: Article 7-A of New York State Executive Law requires registration of charitable and other nonprofit organizations with the State Office of the Attorney General's Charities Bureau. Registered charitable and other nonprofit organizations must file with the Charities Bureau every year using form CHAR500, Annual Filing for Charitable Organizations.
- *California*: California requires charities and commercial fundraisers to register with the Office of the Attorney General and to file financial disclosure reports. All charities must file an Annual Registration Renewal Fee Report, and those with gross revenue or assets of $25,000 or more must file annual Form 990 financial reports with the attorney general's Registry of Charitable Trusts. Since 1965, nonprofit schools, hospitals, and churches have been exempted from the law's reporting requirements.
- *Texas*: Under Texas law, most charities or nonprofit organizations are not required to register with the state.

The Task of Financial Responsibility

The IRS determines whether or not a corporation can become a nonprofit and not pay taxes. When the corporation submits its bylaws to the IRS for approval, the corporation must clearly define financial responsibility and the positions of those who oversee the corporation's finances. In a nonprofit, financial responsibility rests with the board, which elects a board member who will serve as treasurer. The treasurer is usually someone who has a budgeting and/or accounting background. Except in the case of very small nonprofits that do not have large enough boards for committee work, the treasurer chairs the finance committee, which comprises of a few members of the board, the executive director, and the finance officer. The treasurer and executive director work closely together to keep and present the financial records that are needed by the board. The board is responsible for retaining an outside CPA to conduct the annual financial audit. Chiefly, the treasurer oversees the work of recording and reporting the finances of the nonprofit in close working relationship with the executive director. This includes complying with federal and state reporting requirements.

Although the board has ultimate fiduciary responsibility, many nonprofits rely heavily on the executive director and his or her staff for the reporting of financial information. That is why the choice of an outside CPA who will create audited financial statements for the nonprofit is so important. The board will benefit annually from an outside view of the nonprofit's finances. The board must exercise its fiduciary responsibility by carefully examining the organization's financial statements.

Conclusion

In this chapter we have introduced concepts, such as accrual accounting and fund accounting, that are important building blocks for a real understanding of financial management. We have also discussed the principles of accounting, an understanding of which is key to learning financial accounting, a system that has been developed over hundreds of years and that, if used consistently, will help nonprofits with their accountability and transparency. The board of directors of a nonprofit retains fiduciary responsibility for the organization. The executive director is, of course, very important in monitoring the nonprofit's finances, but the board must be ever vigilant.

KEY TERMS

accounting equation	cash accounting	management accounting
accounting principles	financial accounting	net assets
accrual accounting	financial statements	restricted net assets
assets	fund accounting	Sarbanes–Oxley Act of 2002
balance sheet	liabilities	unrestricted net assets

DISCUSSION QUESTIONS

1. How does accounting differ from budgeting?
2. Why are principles of accounting so important?

3. Who uses nonprofits' financial information and why?
4. Give an example of cash accounting, accrual accounting, and modified accrual accounting.
5. Why is the principle of matching so important?
6. What is the accounting equation and why is it important?
7. What are the recent trends in government oversight of nonprofits?
8. Describe how the balance sheet and income statement fit together.

Suggested Readings

Gross, Malvern J., Jr., John H. McCarthy, and Nancy E. Shelmon (2005). *Financial and Accounting Guide for Not-for-Profit Organizations* (7th ed.). New York: PricewaterhouseCoopers.

Miranti, Paul J., Jr. (1990). *Accountancy Comes of Age: The Development of an American Profession*. Chapel Hill: University of North Carolina Press.

Reid, Glenda E., Brenda T. Acken, and Elise G. Jancura (1987, May). "An Historical Perspective on Women in Accounting." *Journal of Accountancy*, 163(5): 338–355.

Case Study

Fraud and the Importance of Accounting Principles

In 2008, a bookkeeper working for the Heart of Texas Council on Alcoholism and Drug Abuse was fired for stealing money from the nonprofit. The employee, who had been with the nonprofit for 12 years, had check-writing authority. In 2010, he was found guilty of felony theft; he was sentenced to 10 years of probation and was required to pay back $41,394 to the council.[3] The nonprofit's executive director, who had served the nonprofit for 21 years, was fired.

When the fraud was uncovered, the state conducted an audit of the agency's finances. As a result, the state demanded that the nonprofit pay back about $100,000 to the Texas Department of State Health Services. The state review found that the agency had billed two staff members' time simultaneously to multiple contracts in 2008 and had billed for bonuses and other outlays that were not chargeable.[4] Officials of the nonprofit shut down the agency in 2010 because they could not repay the money, and they were fearful of more state audits uncovering additional problems. The nonprofit's budget was $650,000, mainly coming from the state. The current officials of the nonprofit sued both the past executive director and the employee convicted of fraud to pay the state's demands.

Such a case is a nightmare for nonprofit executives. Imagine having labored as an executive director for 21 years while a longtime employee steals money, resulting in multiple state audits and ending in the agency owing the state money it cannot possibly repay. If the employee had not committed fraud, it is probable that the state would have never audited the agency in such detail, and other discrepancies would not have been uncovered. As it was, the career of the executive director was wrecked and the nonprofit closed its doors. Audits are serious business; nonprofits must track and record transactions carefully and review their records frequently to be sure that the record keeping is as accurate as possible.

Such a case is also a nightmare for board members. Imagine being on the board and being told that the state wants the nonprofit for which you hold fiduciary responsibility to pay back more than $100,000. It is no wonder that this small nonprofit closed its doors. The board of directors and the executive director may have been covered by liability insurance, but great harm was still done. The tragedy of this situation is that the community lost the program services of the nonprofit, and its mission would no longer be fulfilled. Thinking about the events that took place in the case of this nonprofit, discuss the accounting principles that are useful for executive directors.

Assignments

Assignment 5.1. Identifying Financial Terms

Identify each of the following as an asset, a liability, a revenue, an expense, or a net asset (unrestricted or restricted):

1. The land on which the nonprofit is located and which it owns.
2. Salaries owed to employees.
3. A $100,000 grant to be paid next year for a specific purpose by a foundation.
4. Government bonds owned by the nonprofit.
5. Prepaid insurance expenses.
6. A 15-year mortgage on the organization's building.
7. Salaries paid to employees.
8. Supplies in the closet.
9. A bill from a utility company.
10. Money owed to the nonprofit but not yet paid.

Assignment 5.2. The Assumptions, Principles, and Constraints of Accounting

List the four assumptions, four principles, and four constraints of accounting. Give examples.

Assignment 5.3. Identifying Cash and Accrual Accounting

Define and give examples of cash and accrual accounting.

Assignment 5.4. Creating Balance Sheets

Create a balance sheet of your own financial situation. List your assets and all your liabilities, and then find the difference: your net worth or net assets.

If you create all four of your own financial statements this semester and turn them in at the end of the semester, you will earn five points toward your grade. To complete this project, you will need to track all your revenues and expenses for the semester and then project out those revenues and expenses for the fiscal year.

Assignment 5.5. Reconciling Surplus and Deficit in Wisconsin's Budget

On February 1, 2009, the *Washington State Journal* reported that the governor of Wisconsin claimed that he had a surplus for the year ending in June 2008 of $130.7 million. However, according to Wisconsin Taxpayers Alliance, Wisconsin had a deficit of $2.5 billion. Since the state constitution requires Wisconsin to have a balanced budget, the governor needed to be able to make the announcement he did. How, then, could the state run a deficit?

NOTES

[1] Kwak, James (2009, January 3). The Importance of Accounting. The Baseline Scenario (baselinescenario.com/2009/01/03/sec-report-mark-to-market-accounting).

[2] See Wagner, David A. (2007, August 20). Accounting Assumptions, Principles, and Constraints: A Short Review. MBAFAQ (mbafaq.blogspot.com/2007/08/accounting-assumptions-principles-and.html).

[3] Witherspoon, Tammy (2010, August 3). "Waco Nonprofit Suing Two Former Employees to Help Repay Money State May Seek." *Waco Tribune* (wacotrib.com/news/99817444.html).

[4] State of Texas, Auditor's Office (2011, May). *An Audit Report on Substance Abuse Program Contract Monitoring at the Department of State Health Services* (Report 11-030, p. 41). Austin: State Auditor's Office.

6

Understanding Financial Statements

> Fund accounting is widely used by not-for-profit organizations because it provides the ability to ensure compliance with legal restrictions, to report on the organization's stewardship of amounts entrusted to it by donors, and to manage operations in accordance with the expressed wishes of the governing board.
>
> —Malvern J. Gross, Jr., John H. McCarthy, and Nancy E. Shelmon[1]

LEARNING OBJECTIVES

The learning objectives for this chapter are as follows:
- Understanding the statement of financial position (balance sheet)
- Understanding the statement of activities (income statement)
- Understanding the relationship between the statement of financial position and the statement of activities
- Learning about the cash-flow statement and the statement of functional expenses

*T*his chapter explains the content of financial statements as well as how these statements relate to each other. It is important for nonprofit executives to understand the basics of each financial statement and its relationship to the others.

Financial statements are one of the key ingredients in a nonprofit's ability to determine how successful it has been in fulfilling its mission. A solid performance in the financial statements can go a long way toward demonstrating that a nonprofit is using its resources carefully and effectively. The four financial statements are the statement of financial position (the balance sheet), the statement of activities (the income statement), the statement of cash flow, and the statement of functional expenses. The last of these is required only for health and welfare organizations. Readers who wish to learn about financial statements in more detail are referred to Appendix B, Debits and Credits. However, it is not necessary to learn how to apply debits and credits in order to have a basic understanding of financial statements.

Knowledge of some accounting terms is helpful for understanding financial statements, but a deep background in accounting is not necessary. One such term frequently used in accounting is *fund*. In accounting, a fund is any part of an organization that keeps separate accounting records. Often people unfamiliar with accounting will confuse assets and funds. Assets are those resources owned or controlled by the organization. Another basic term is *net assets*, also referred to as *fund balance*. This is "the mathematical amount obtained by subtracting total liabilities from total assets of a particular fund."[2] We will discuss this concept in more depth later in this chapter.

The Statement of Financial Position (Balance Sheet)

A nonprofit's balance sheet (or statement of financial position) displays assets on one side and liabilities and net assets on the other. This can be expressed mathematically as follows:

$$Assets = Liabilities + Net\ Assets$$

This equation is the heart of financial accounting. It allows accountants to track, categorize, and present the finances of organizations in accurate and useful ways.

Assets are those resources that the organization owns or controls. **Liabilities** are the debt incurred in pursuit of assets. Net assets are the difference between the assets and the liabilities and represent the cumulative net revenue of the nonprofit. Consider the nonprofit Access to Learning, which provides after-school tutoring for elementary school students. It has a budget of more than $500,000, which pays for a director and her assistant as well as two full-time teachers, a part-time bookkeeper, and several part-time teachers. The nonprofit owns a small building close to two elementary schools. In addition to the teachers on staff, the nonprofit hires teachers at an hourly rate to provide tutoring after school. Its statement of financial position (balance sheet) over a 2-year period, shown in Table 6.1, indicates that the organization is financially healthy. It has cash on hand and little debt.

Understanding Financial Statements

Table 6.1 Access to Learning, Statements of Financial Position (Balance Sheets) as of December 31, 2019 and 2020

Assets	2020	2019	Liabilities	2020	2019
Current Assets			**Current Liabilities**		
Cash	$ 20,000	$ 5,000	Accounts Payable	$ 7,950	$ 17,000
Marketable Securities	18,000	3,000	Salaries Payable	5,000	3,000
Accounts Receivable	12,000	2,000	Mortgage Payable	5,000	5,000
Pledges Receivable	1,150	12,000	Total Current Liabilities	$ 17,950	$ 25,000
Supplies Inventory	2,000	2,000			
Prepaid Expenses	1,000	—	**Long-Term Liabilities**		
Total Current Assets	$ 54,150	$ 24,000	Mortgage Loan	$ 20,000	$ 25,000
			Total Liabilities	$ 37,950	$ 50,000
Long-Term Assets			**Net Assets**		
Equipment (net)	$ 8,800	$ 6,800	Unrestricted	$ 69,800	$ 60,800
Building (net)	98,000	100,000	Temporarily Restricted	—	—
Investments	130,000	121,000	Permanently Restricted	183,200	141,000
Total Long-Term Assets	$ 236,800	$ 227,800	Total Net Assets	$ 253,000	$ 201,800
Total Assets	$ 290,950	$ 251,800	Total Liabilities and N.A.	$ 290,950	$ 251,800

Assets

Assets are those things that have value, can be measured, and are owned or controlled by the nonprofit. Assets can be divided between current, or short-term, assets and fixed, or long-term, assets. Assets are always listed in order of liquidity, with those most liquid coming first (*liquid* refers to the ease with which assets can be turned into cash).

Current Assets

In the example of a balance sheet shown in Table 6.1, the short-term or **current assets** are cash, marketable securities, and accounts receivable. Other categories of current assets are pledges receivable, supplies inventory, and prepaid expenses. Current assets are those assets that are cash or can be turned into cash within a fiscal year. Current assets must be easily available to pay off existing obligations.

Cash. Cash is the most liquid asset; it can easily be used to pay off obligations. Cash can be kept in a checking, savings, or money market account. Cash equivalents such as U.S. Treasury bills can also be counted as cash.

Marketable Securities. Monies invested on a short-term basis (less than 1 year) are called **marketable securities**. In this example, marketable securities of $18,000 are those monies invested in short-term securities, such as stocks and bonds, which can be bought and sold quickly in the market. Stocks are shares of a corporation, and their value can grow or decline. Bonds, notes, and U.S. Treasury bills are debt instruments issued by corporations or government (the issuers). These issuers pledge to repay those who buy their bonds plus interest over a period of time. This interest is called investment income. Marketable securities must always be recorded at their market value and not their historical cost.

Accounts Receivable. Money that other organizations or individuals owe the nonprofit is called **accounts receivable**. The $12,000 in accounts receivable in Table 6.1 could refer to contributions that have been promised but not yet delivered. Other types of receivables are monies due because of contracts, membership dues, grants, and pledges. Accounts receivable often reflects monies owed to the nonprofit by government agencies, since many nonprofits contract with federal or state governments for money that is provided at specific times.

Often the nonprofit must wait months for payment; meanwhile, that nonprofit records the contract money as an asset in accounts receivable. In a 2013 survey of nonprofits that contract with government, the Urban Institute found that 45% of the nonprofits surveyed said late payments were a problem.[3] Nonprofits with government contracts can thus have very large accounts receivables.

Box 6.1

REMEMBER: Characteristics of Assets

Assets must
- have value,
- be measured, and
- be controlled by the nonprofit.

Pledges Receivable. Pledges receivable is money that has been promised to the nonprofit unconditionally. Pledges receivable must be recorded for the amount that the nonprofit thinks it is going to collect. For example, the nonprofit may collect 95% of its pledges, so 95% is the net amount of pledge receivables the nonprofit can record. The remainder of the pledges (5%) is placed in an account called "allowance for bad debts," and this amount is deducted from the total pledges receivable. It would look like this on a balance sheet:

Pledges Receivable	$ 100,000
5% Allowance for Bad Debt	(5,000)
Pledges Receivable (net)	$ 95,000

Inventories. The costs of materials and supplies owned by the nonprofit that the nonprofit wishes to sell to the public are called inventories. Examples of inventories would be the materials sold in the gift shops of museums, books in college bookstores, food in snack bars and refreshment stands, and T-shirts and other promotional items for sale. If supplies and materials are used in the course of business, these are not recorded as inventory; rather, they are counted as expenses as soon as they are purchased.

The accounting for inventories can be fairly complicated and is beyond the scope of this introduction to accounting. For purposes of this discussion, it should be noted that there are different methods of accounting for inventories. These methods differ in the flow of inventories; that is, which inventories are sold first. The first-in, first-out (FIFO) flow assumption simply means that the oldest items in the inventory will be the first items sold. This is the most common method used by nonprofits. The alternative flow assumption is last-in, first-out (LIFO). LIFO assumes that the last items brought in will be the first ones sold. These flow assumptions are related to inflation. For example, net income, the difference between revenue and expenses, is lower under LIFO than under FIFO because expenses are matched against revenue. The ending inventory figure in the balance sheet will be lower under LIFO than FIFO because inventory is being stated in older dollars. A company can increase or decrease its earnings through the timing of inventory acquisitions. Older inventory items will have a lower cost assigned to them because of inflation, so there could be a larger profit realized when last items are sold first.

Prepaid Expenses. Another short-term asset is **prepaid expenses** (expenses that are paid before they are incurred). This is an asset that can be reimbursed. Insurance policies often are prepaid expenses, as are internet and telephone services.

Long-Term Assets

A nonprofit's **long-term assets** are property and equipment, as well as long-term investments; often, property and equipment are called fixed assets. Fixed assets are those that cannot be easily turned into cash.

Property and Equipment. A common long-term asset is property (vehicles, land, and buildings) and another is equipment, including computers. Any tangible item that has an operational life of more than a year should be listed as a fixed asset. In practice, small items such as staplers and tape dispensers are not listed as fixed assets but are accounted for as supplies and expenses when purchased. Usually a nonprofit sets a price threshold over which an item is named as a fixed asset. For example, a nonprofit may decide to call a fixed asset any item that costs more than $5,000 and has an operational life of more than a year.

Whenever fixed assets are recorded, it is possible to use depreciation expense for the use of fixed assets over time. **Depreciation** involves assigning a value to the useful life of a capitalized fixed asset and expending those assets over its economic life. Land is valued at historical cost, its cost at purchase. Equipment and buildings are assets recorded at their historical cost minus the accumulated depreciation. As Gross et al. note, although

> it seems absurd for an organization to present the cost of an old building on land that has in fact appreciated to many times its value over the course of time, . . . the intended purpose of this same building and its use and enjoyment by the organization are independent from the market value until the time comes when the organization changes its purpose and places the asset for sale.[4]

The balance sheet reflects the asset's value at a particular point in time.

The capitalization of this fixed asset begins with the determination of a depreciation method. Nonprofits usually use straight-line depreciation, which is depreciation for a limited number of years. For example, if a nonprofit buys a truck for $30,000 and chooses to depreciate the truck over 6 years, the nonprofit will have a depreciation expense of $5,000 ($30,000/6) a year for those 6 years. Each year, the nonprofit will reduce the cost of the asset on the balance sheet by the accumulated depreciation over the 6 years. This is straight-line depreciation. The balance sheet would look like this:

Equipment	$ 30,000
Less Accumulated Depreciation	($5,000)
Total Equipment (net)	$ 25,000

At the same time, the income statement would look like this:

Depreciation Expense	($5,000)

The drawback to calculating depreciation is that it is a method for allocating the original cost of a fixed asset over time and not a method for determining the current cost of replacing that item. A new truck 6 years from now might cost $35,000, but depreciation is calculated on the historical cost. Often nonprofits will consider a salvage value for their equipment; that is, before determining the yearly depreciation, the accountant subtracts an amount from the purchase price that will be the approximate value of the equipment once it is fully depreciated. For example, the truck costs $30,000 and the salvage value is determined to be $2,500, which leaves $27,500 to be depreciated over 6 years. This would be a depreciation expense of $4,583 per year over 6 years.

Why bother to depreciate at all? Over time, fixed assets deteriorate. If we depreciate the fixed assets, we include depreciation expense, which is the cost that properly reflects the cost of that particular asset. In addition, for-profit corporations can use depreciation to show "paper" expenses. This costs a corporation nothing, yet it gets to add in more expenses, which means that, on paper, its profits are lower and hence its taxes are lower. So there is great incentive for for-profit corporations to calculate depreciation expense, and a great deal of time and effort is spent in determining the highest depreciation expense a corporation can take for a given piece of equipment or building. Nonprofits, in contrast, need to depreciate fixed assets because this means that the costs of the fixed assets are properly reflected in the financial statements.

Investments. Long-term investments are usually related to a nonprofit's restricted endowment—a fund to which donations have been made and from which only the interest and dividends (investment income) on those donations can be spent. If the endowment is limited in time, then those monies still belong in the restricted fund. Gains on the investments will be treated as unrestricted income unless the donor requires any gains to be kept with the original donation as part of the restricted fund.

Liabilities

Liabilities are sources of capital used to finance the assets, and they are debts the organization owes to third parties and must be paid. For a debt to be counted as a liability, it must be measurable.

Current Liabilities

Short-term or **current liabilities** are usually called payables. These are debts that are to be paid off within a year.

Accounts Payable. The unpaid bills of a nonprofit fall under the category of accounts payable. The accounts payable could be bills from other businesses, such as an office supply store or computer store. Usually these bills are paid within 30 days (if not, the supplier will charge interest).

Accrued Salary Expenses. Remember from Chapter 5 that accrual simply means transactions have occurred but cash has not been used—these transactions represent money the nonprofit owes. Salaries payable are salaries owed to staff at the end of an accounting period, also called **accrued salary expenses**. This often happens in a nonprofit when the pay period does not coincide with the end of the accounting period. Accrued liabilities such as accrued salaries are incurred at the end of the reporting period but not yet paid. The accrued liability is shown under current liabilities in the balance sheet. For example, assume that the last payroll date was January 28 and the next payroll date is February 11. For the last few days of the month (January 29–January 31), the company owes its employees $500 in salaries. The appropriate journal entry on January 31 is to debit salaries expense and credit salaries payable for $500. Other accrued expenses such as vacation accruals and payroll taxes accruals are treated similarly to salaries accrued.

Mortgage Payable. The portion of the mortgage principal that is to be paid in the current year is termed mortgage payable. The remainder of the mortgage debt is recorded in long-term liabilities.

Deferred Revenue. Unearned revenue is called deferred revenue. Sometimes, a nonprofit receives revenue in advance of a service the nonprofit is to provide. For example, a nonprofit provides training workshops on mediation and receives the revenue before providing the service. This is the converse of prepaid expenses as an asset. The nonprofit records the cash and also records a liability—deferred revenue. When the nonprofit provides the service, the deferred revenue listed in liabilities is eliminated. The money then becomes revenue.

Long-Term Liabilities

A nonprofit's **long-term liabilities** usually consist of a mortgage, a lease, or some other form of long-term debt. Long-term liabilities are those unlikely to be paid off in a year.

Mortgage Loans. Mortgages on buildings are among the most common long-term liabilities. The portion of the principal to be paid during the fiscal year is recognized as a current liability. The remainder is recognized as a long-term liability.

Bonds and Notes Payable. Nonprofits sometimes take out loans that are not related to buildings. The most common notes payable is a nonprofit equity line that the nonprofit uses when its cash flow is low. Many larger nonprofits apply for bank equity lines in anticipation that one day they will have cash-flow problems.

Net Assets (Fund Balance)

Net assets are the difference between an organization's assets and its liabilities; they are the accumulation of the difference between the cumulative revenues and cumulative expenses over the life of an organization. In any one year, the change in net assets is all the revenue minus all the expenses, which the nonprofit hopes will result in a surplus. That surplus is added to all the surpluses and deficits accumulated over the life of the nonprofit. This is the cumulative balance.

As we explained in Chapter 5, the FASB issues guidelines to nonprofits. In 2018, FASB changed some definitions and issued guidelines requiring nonprofits to divide their net assets into the categories of unrestricted and restricted. Each of these categories has a specific purpose.

Unrestricted Net Assets

Unrestricted net assets are the running totals for the nonprofit, representing money that was donated without any restrictions for spending it, including timing.

Restricted Net Assets

Restricted net assets are all those revenues given by donors year after year that are not to be spent but are to be invested in long-term stocks, bonds, and other instruments that will produce interest and dividends. The endowment is a permanent fund provided by donors; usually the principal cannot be touched, but the interest income, dividends, and gains (investment income) can be used by the nonprofit in accordance with the wishes of the donor. The rule is that the donor decides how and when the principal and the investment income can be spent. Nonprofits must measure their investments at market value and not at historical cost (price of purchase).

Revenues being held temporarily until they can be spent are also restricted net assets. When the nonprofit is ready to spend those funds, the funds are transferred to the unrestricted net assets fund. For example, a nonprofit's girls' program is planned for the next fiscal year, but the monies for it are being raised in the current fiscal year. These monies are in the restricted fund until they can be spent. Another example is when a nonprofit receives money from a foundation for a program that is not due to start until the next fiscal year. Such revenue would be placed in restricted funds and transferred to the unrestricted fund in the year it can be spent.

> **Box 6.2**
> **CASE IN POINT:**
> **Unrestricted or Restricted Revenue?**
>
> If a nonprofit receives a foundation grant in December and its fiscal year runs from January to December, the nonprofit cannot count that grant in its unrestricted fund.
> Since the unrestricted fund is the day-to-day operating fund, the unrestricted fund must have its revenues matched to its expenses, and it cannot count revenue intended for the next fiscal year. Remembering that the unrestricted fund is the day-to-day operating fund makes it easy to understand the distinctions among the funds.

Nonprofit Financial Statements: The Statement of Activities (Income Statement)

The statement of activities records the revenues, expenses, and the difference in a given period, usually a fiscal year. All expenses are recorded in the unrestricted net assets.

The difference between revenues and expenses is the change in net assets in unrestricted net assets. Table 6.2 displays a statement of financial activity from the Access to Learning nonprofit corporation for fiscal years 2019 and 2020. The nonprofit has a healthy surplus (more revenues than expenses) for both years ($9,000); that surplus is called the change in net assets.

Table 6.2 Access to Learning, Statements of Activity (Income Statement) for FY 2020 and FY 2019

Revenues	2020	2019
Foundation Grant	$ 150,000	$ 125,000
State Education Contract	250,000	250,000
Contributions	90,000	80,000
Investment Income	25,000	23,000
Special Events	50,000	55,000
Total Revenues	$ 565,000	$ 533,000
Expenses		
Salaries	$ 377,000	$ 350,000
Fringe Benefits	24,000	21,800
Computer Equipment	5,000	2,000
Copier Contract	300	300
Depreciation Expense	3,000	3,000
Equipment	800	800
Mortgage Expense	500	500
Phones	400	400
Supplies	10,000	10,600
Travel	4,800	4,800
Teachers (5 part time)	96,000	96,000
Utilities	10,200	9,800
Reading Consultant	24,000	24,000
Total Expenses	$ 556,000	$ 524,000
Change in Net Assets	$ 9,000	$ 9,000

Revenues

Revenues come in many different forms: contributions (gifts), pledges, grants and contracts, fees, interest income and dividends, investment gains, donated services, and donated materials and securities. These revenues may be categorized as either unrestricted or restricted, unlike expenses, which can appear only in the unrestricted net assets fund. Most revenues are also in the unrestricted funds. Donors may restrict the use of the money, in which case, the funds are placed in the restricted fund.

Contributions (Gifts). Contributions are counted as revenue when received. They are considered unrestricted unless the gift is not to be spent and is part of a permanent endowment, or if the gift is to be spent later. Gifts for a specific purpose to be spent during the current accounting period are part of the unrestricted category. Of course, gifts can be restricted for specific purposes, but in the accounting world, purpose-restricted gifts are classified unrestricted if they are being spent currently.

Donated Services. In special circumstances, volunteer time must be counted as a contribution. FASB requires that if the volunteer services enhance nonfinancial assets, such as construction, or if the task requires special skills (such as attorney services) and the nonprofit would have to purchase those skills if they had not been volunteered, then the volunteer time is a contribution.

Pledges. A **pledge** is a promise to give something (cash, property, or the like) to an organization in the future. In order for a pledge to be counted as revenue at the time the pledge is given, the pledge must be collectable and material in its amount during the accounting period. Accounting rules require that an allowance for bad debt be established for the portion of pledges that the nonprofit believes is uncollectible. Over time, nonprofits become adept at calculating how much of their pledges will be uncollectible. If pledges are given over several years in advance, accounting rules require that pledges payable beyond the current accounting period be discounted to their present value (see Chapter 11 for a discussion of present value).

Grants and Contracts. If revenue is received as part of a contract, it is recorded as such. Contracts are for the purchase of goods or services, with a specific time and place for the delivery of those goods or services. Grant revenue is recorded in the unrestricted fund unless it is for a future time, in which case it belongs in the restricted fund.

Fees and Business Income. Nonprofits are allowed to collect fees from their services, and they do not need to pay taxes on that revenue. The services for which a nonprofit collects fees, however, must be related to the organization's mission. For example, if a nonprofit opens a bakery and nonprofit clients who are part of an employment and training program staff the bakery, then the revenue earned from the bakery is not taxable because the bakery is intimately connected to the organization's mission. However, all nonprofits are subject to normal corporate taxes when earning unrelated business income. The key is the word *unrelated*. If the activity is not related to the nonprofit, the burden of proof to exclude tax is on the nonprofit.

Expenses. Expenses occur when an asset is used up or a liability is incurred. Expenses are only shown as unrestricted. Each expense is categorized. The list of accounts that an organization uses to classify and record transactions is called the chart of accounts. For example, when employees earn salaries, their pay is recorded as salaries expenses. When a supply bill is paid, it is recorded as a supply expense. A chart of accounts explains how all of these expenses and revenues are categorized. In the chart of accounts each category has its own object number so that the categories can be easily tracked. Table 6.3 presents a typical chart of accounts for a small nonprofit.

Table 6.3 Typical Chart of Accounts

1	**Assets**	4	**Revenues**
10	Cash	40	Contributions
11	Temporary Investments	41	Fees
12	Receivables	42	Grants
13	Prepaid Expenses	43	Contracts
14	Buildings	44	Other Revenues
15	Equipment		
16	Other Assets	5	**Expenses**
		50	Salaries
2	**Liabilities**	51	Fringe Benefits
20	Accounts Payable	52	Computers
21	Taxes Payable	53	Equipment
22	Salaries Payable	54	Copier Contract
23	Mortgage Payable	55	Phones
24	Notes Payable	56	Office Rental
25	Other Liabilities	57	Supplies
		58	Travel
3	**Net Assets**	59	Consultants
30	Unrestricted	60	Per Diem
31	Restricted	61	Depreciation
		62	Other Expenses

Relationship between the Statement of Financial Position and the Statement of Activities

The statement of activities records every transaction that has taken place over the entire fiscal year. At the end of the fiscal year, the profit or loss from all that revenue and expense becomes the change in net assets in the unrestricted fund for that year. The change in net assets is then added to the unrestricted net assets on the statement of financial position for the start of the next fiscal year. The easiest way to understand this is to look at transactions. Remember that the equation Assets = Liabilities + Net Assets must always balance. Let's consider how to record transactions using the data listed below.

The Access to Learning nonprofit has begun its 2020 fiscal year. At the end of January, the financial officer created a trial balance sheet (see Table 6.4). The first line is the ending balance from FY 2019. Net assets have been divided among unrestricted and restricted. The total assets and the total liabilities plus the net assets are listed so that we can see that the equation is balanced. The following transactions occurred in the month of January:

1. On January 2, the nonprofit uses $1,000 in cash to pay down accounts payable. The transaction is listed as a decrease in cash and a decrease in accounts payable. Because this transaction is recorded on both sides of the equation, the balance sheet remains balanced.
2. On January 5, the nonprofit receives $50,000 in revenue from a foundation. The transaction is recorded as an increase in cash and an increase in revenue (listed unrestricted net assets). (You will see as we go through these transactions that revenues and expenses are listed under unrestricted net assets. Revenues are recorded as increases, and expenses are recorded as decreases.) Because this transaction is recorded on both sides of the equation, the balance sheet remains balanced.
3. On January 6, the nonprofit pays $1,000 for an insurance policy for the year. This transaction is recorded as a decrease in cash and an increase in prepaid expenses. Note that the accounting equation remains balanced.
4. On January 8, the nonprofit receives $20,000 in a grant not to be spent until the next fiscal year. The transaction is recorded as an increase in cash and an increase in the restricted fund.
5. On January 10, the nonprofit charges $1,000 in supplies. This transaction is recorded as an increase in accounts payable and an increase in inventory of $1,000. No cash changes hands. Again the equation remains balanced.
6. On January 15, the nonprofit pays its teachers $20,000, which reduces its cash by $20,000 and also is an expense of $19,000; in addition, the nonprofit pays down salaries payable by $1,000. Again the equation remains balanced.
7. On January 20, the nonprofit sells $2,000 of its marketable securities, which increases cash by $2,000 and decreases marketable securities by $2,000.
8. On January 25, the nonprofit is awarded a $50,000 foundation grant, and the check will come within the fiscal year. The nonprofit increases accounts receivable by $50,000 and also increases unrestricted net assets as revenue by $50,000.
9. On January 26, the nonprofit is awarded a $25,000 foundation grant, and the check will not come until next year. The nonprofit increases restricted net assets by $25,000 and increases accounts receivable by $25,000. The revenue will not be recognized as part of the currently unrestricted fund until the next fiscal year.
10. On January 28, the nonprofit receives $2,000 in cash from money owed in accounts receivable. This transaction increases cash by $2,000 and decreases accounts receivable by $2,000.
11. On January 28, the nonprofit spends $500 worth of supplies. This transaction decreases inventory by $500 and increases expenses by $500, which is a negative. Therefore, both sides balance.

Table 6.4 Access to Learning January 2020 Transactions

Beginning Balance 2020	Cash	Market Securities	Accounts Receivable	Pledges Receivable	Prepaid Expenses	Equipment	Inventory	Investments	Building	=
Last Year's Balance	$ 5,000	$ 3,000	$ 2,000	$ 12,000	$—	$ 6,800	$ 2,000	$ 121,000	$ 100,000	=
2-Jan	(1,000)									
	Paid $1,000 in cash to pay down accounts payable.									
5-Jan	50,000									
	Received $50,000 in revenue from a foundation.									
6-Jan	(1,000)				1,000					
	Prepaid insurance policy for the year.									
8-Jan	20,000									
	Received $20,000 grant not to be spent until the next fiscal year.									
10-Jan							1,000			
	Charged $1,000 in supplies.									
15-Jan	(20,000)									
	Paid teachers $20,000 and included $1,000 in salaries payable.									
20-Jan	2,000	(2,000)								
	Sold $2,000 in market securities for cash.									
25-Jan			50,000							
	Awarded a $50,000 foundation grant, no check yet, but will come within the fiscal year.									
26-Jan			25,000							
	Awarded a $25,000 foundation grant, but payment will not occur until next fiscal year.									
28-Jan	2,000	(2,000)								
	Received $2,000 in cash from money owed in accounts receivable.									
28-Jan							(500)			
	Spent $500 worth of supplies.									
29-Jan	10,000									
	Received $10,000 for services to be rendered in the future.									
30-Jan	10,000		(10,000)							
	Received first payment of $10,000 from $50,000 foundation grant.									
Jan. Ending Balance	$ 77,000	$ 1,000	$ 65,000	$ 12,000	$ 1,000	$ 6,800	$ 2,500	$ 121,000	$ 100,000	=

Table 6.4 (continued)

Accounts Payable	Salaries Payable	Mortgage Payable	Deferred Revenue	Mortgage Loan		Unrestricted	Restricted	Total Assets		Total Liabilities + Net Assets
$ 17,000	$ 3,000	$ 5,000		$ 25,000	+	$ 60,800	$ 141,000	$ 251,800	=	$ 251,800
(1,000)										
						50,000 R				
							20,000			
1,000										
	(1,000)					(19,000) E				
						50,000 R				
							25,000			
						(500) E				
			10,000							
$ 17,000	$ 2,000	$ 5,000	$ 10,000	$ 25,000	+	$ 141,300	$ 186,000	$ 386,300	=	$ 386,300

R = Revenue
E = Expense

12. On January 29, the nonprofit receives $10,000 for services to be rendered in the future. This transaction increases cash by $10,000 and increases deferred revenue by $10,000.

13. On January 30, the nonprofit receives $10,000 in its first payment from the foundation grant of $50,000. This transaction increases cash by $10,000 and decreases accounts receivable by $10,000.

This is double-entry bookkeeping. Every transaction is recorded twice. No transaction is neglected; every transaction that takes place during FY 2020 is recorded. At the end of each month, the nonprofit's financial officer creates a trial balance, which is a method of ensuring that the equation is balanced. (For more about the trial balance, see Appendix B.)

The statement of financial position and the statement of activities are connected through net assets. If you examine the unrestricted net assets on the balance sheets used here as examples for both FY 2019 and FY 2020, you will see that the increase between the two years was $9,000—the change in net assets or profit on the statement of activities for FY 2020.

Remember that the unrestricted net assets fund is the fund in which expenses are listed. The restricted fund never lists expenses, although it can reflect revenue. Expenses take place during the current fiscal year and thus are recorded only in the unrestricted net assets.

Assignments 6.1 and 6.2 at the end of this chapter allow you to record and categorize transactions for the Access to Learning nonprofit. This is a good time to try these assignments, which is best conducted as a group activity.

Cash-Flow Statement

The cash-flow statement is a summary of all cash available to the nonprofit during the year and how the cash was received and used. The cash-flow statement is divided into three categories: operating cash flows, investing cash flows, and financing cash flows.

1. *Operating activities*: The cash flow from operating activities consists of cash received from revenue sources such as contributions, grants, investment income, contracts, and special events. In addition, cash flow is related to expense sources—the largest of which is employee salaries and other operating expenses such as utilities and phone service.

2. *Investing activities*: The cash flow from investing activities consists of cash for the purchase or sale of equipment or the purchase or sale of investments.

3. *Financing activities*: The cash flow from financing activities consists of those transactions concerning the repayment of debt, such as borrowing from a bank.

Cash in a cash-flow statement includes cash and cash equivalents. Cash equivalents are short-term investments that can be readily converted into cash, such as marketable securities, short-term certificates of deposit, and U.S. Treasury bills. Table 6.5 presents the cash-flow statement for the Access to Learning nonprofit in FY 2020.

Table 6.5 Access to Learning FY 2020 Statement of Cash Flow

Operating Activities	FY 2020
Cash received from grants	$ 150,000
Cash received from contracts	275,000
Cash received from contributions	90,000
Cash received from special events	50,000
Cash received from investment income	25,000
Cash paid to employees	(497,000)
Cash paid to suppliers	(34,000)
Cash paid to utilities, travel, phone	(15,400)
Subtotal Operating Activities	43,600
Investing Activities	
Purchase of equipment	(800)
Purchase of investments	(15,000)
Proceeds from sale of investments	700
Subtotal Investing Activities	(15,100)
Financing Activities	
Investment in endowment	(9,000)
Payment on mortgage	(4,500)
Subtotal Financing Activities	(13,500)
Net increase or decrease in cash	$ 15,000
Cash at beginning of the year	$ 5,000
Cash at end of the year	$ 20,000

Statement of Functional Expenses

The statement of functional expenses categorizes expenses into categories, either programmatic services or support services. Support services are further divided into management and fundraising. This division of expenses gives the reader of the statement an understanding as to where the nonprofit is spending its money. This kind of categorization raises a host of helpful questions: How much goes to mailings? How much to travel? How big is the payroll? How much is spent on fundraising as compared to programs? The statement of functional expenses can be very helpful to the board and executive director of a nonprofit, enabling them to make conscious decisions that align with the goals of the nonprofit; for example, only 20% of the organization's funds should go to management, or only 15% of funds should go to fundraising, and so forth. Such a statement allows those who lead the nonprofit to think seriously about where the organization's money goes. It also allows the executive director to think about how his or her time is spent. Should the director spend 30% of his or her time in program activities? 50%? How much time does the director spend on fundraising? Every staff member's salary is divided among these three categories. If the statement of functional expenses is realistic and honest, the executive director and the board can learn a great deal from it about where the nonprofit's resources are going.

Conclusion

An understanding of the basic language of accounting is an important part of managing a nonprofit's finances. Nonprofit executives do not need to be accountants, but they do need to be well versed in the terminology of receivables and payables and must understand the difference between a statement of financial position and a statement of activities. They must also make sure that all financial data are timely and accurate, because timeliness and accuracy in such data are keys to the well-being of any nonprofit. Without accurate financial data, the leadership of a nonprofit is seriously handicapped, and the nonprofit's mission may suffer. When solid financial data are available, the responsibility of the nonprofit's leaders is to take time to understand what the data are telling them. In Chapter 8, we discuss the financial tools that nonprofit leaders need to interpret the data.

KEY TERMS

accounts receivable	depreciation	net assets
accrued salary expenses	liabilities	pledges
assets	long-term assets	prepaid expenses
current assets	long-term liabilities	revenues
current liabilities	marketable securities	unrestricted net assets

DISCUSSION QUESTIONS

1. What is the difference between current and long-term assets? Why is this important?
2. What is the difference between marketable securities and long-term investments?
3. Why is it necessary to distinguish between current liabilities and long-term liabilities?
4. Why does the mortgage appear as part of a current liability and a long-term liability?
5. What are the two categories of net asset funds? Which one is used as the operating fund?
6. What is depreciation and why is it important?
7. Why does a nonprofit need a chart of accounts?
8. When does a nonprofit pay federal taxes?

9. If only asset accounts are affected by a transaction, why is the accounting equation still balanced?
10. Why is deferred revenue a liability?

SUGGESTED READINGS

Gross, Malvern J., Jr., John H. McCarthy, and Nancy E. Shelmon (2005). *Financial and Accounting Guide for Not-for-Profit Organizations* (7th ed.). New York: PricewaterhouseCoopers.

Keating, Elizabeth K., and Peter Frumkin (2001, October). How to Assess Nonprofit Financial Performance (webs.wofford.edu/gonzalezle/Acct411/Chapter%2018%20Communication%20Case.pdf).

McNamara, Carter (n.d.). All about Financial Management in Nonprofits. Free Management Library (managementhelp.org/nonprofitfinances/index.htm).

Sangster, A., G. Stoner, and P. McCarthy (2007). "Lessons for the Classroom from Luca Pacioli." *Issues in Accounting Education*, 22(3): 447–457.

ASSIGNMENTS

Assignment 6.1. Recording and Categorizing Transactions in February

Using Table 6.4 as a guide, create a transaction report for the following February transactions for the Access to Learning nonprofit organization:

- On February 1, the nonprofit paid $20,000 in salaries.
- On February 2, the nonprofit used $5,000 in cash to pay down its accounts payable by that amount.
- On February 5, the nonprofit received $5,000 in cash from a foundation, and that donation had previously been recorded in accounts receivable.
- On February 10, the executive director talked to a foundation program officer who said that the foundation would be giving a $25,000 grant to the nonprofit within the next 2 months.
- On February 15, the nonprofit incurred another $1,000 in salaries payable.
- On February 20, the nonprofit received $5,000 in cash from pledges.
- On February 22, the nonprofit received a second payment of $10,000 from the $50,000 foundation grant.
- On February 23, the nonprofit conducted the workshops that were paid for in January ($10,000), and the payment had been recorded as deferred revenue.
- On February 24, the nonprofit made a mortgage payment of $5,000 plus $500 in mortgage interest.
- On February 25, the nonprofit bought $500 worth of books with cash.

Assignment 6.2. Recording and Categorizing Transactions in March

Complete the March transactions report for the Access to Learning nonprofit organization:

- On March 1, the nonprofit paid $20,000 in salaries.
- On March 5, the nonprofit charged $10,000 worth of supplies.
- On March 7, a foundation program officer told the executive director that the nonprofit would receive a $25,000 grant from a foundation.
- On March 10, the nonprofit received the third payment of $10,000 from the $50,000 foundation grant.
- On March 15, the nonprofit received $8,000 in cash from pledges receivable.
- On March 20, the nonprofit paid $5,000 in cash to reduce accounts payable.
- On March 25, the nonprofit sold $1,000 in marketable securities.
- On March 30, the nonprofit incurred $2,000 in salaries payable.
- On March 31, the nonprofit consumed $1,000 worth of supplies.

Assignment 6.3. Determining Marketable Securities

A nonprofit has a balance sheet of cash $10,000, accounts receivable $2,000, prepaid expenses $1,000, marketable securities of an unknown amount, accounts payable of $2,000, salaries payable of $1,000, and current unrestricted net assets of $12,000. Set up the balance sheet and determine how much is marketable securities.

Notes

[1] Gross, Malvern J., Jr., John H. McCarthy, and Nancy E. Shelmon (2005). *Financial and Accounting Guide for Not-for-Profit Organizations* (7th ed., p. 19). New York: PricewaterhouseCoopers.

[2] Ibid., p. 34.

[3] Pettijohn, Sarah L., Elizabeth T. Boris, Carol J. De Vita, and Saunji D. Fyffe (2013). *Nonprofit-Government Contract and Grants: Findings from the 2013 National Survey*. Washington, DC: Urban Institute (urban.org/research/publication/nonprofit-government-contracts-and-grants-findings-2013-national-survey/view/full_report).

[4] Gross et al., p. 50.

7 Financial Analysis

> Financial statements should enable readers to evaluate the organization's financial performance. Financial analysis is the process of using the information provided by the financial statements to calculate the financial ratios and other measures that enable such judgment.
> —Regina E. Herzlinger and Denise Nitterhouse[1]

LEARNING OBJECTIVES

The learning objectives for this chapter are as follows:
- Understanding financial analysis
- Learning how to conduct ratio analysis
- Gaining an understanding of red flags
- Learning about rating agencies

*E*xecutive directors and board members who wish to understand a nonprofit's finances usually start by conducting a financial analysis. Such an analysis will contribute to the understanding of the extent to which the nonprofit is using its resources wisely to achieve its mission. Financial analysis is the study of the information in an organization's financial statements to determine that organization's fiscal health. Financial analysis uses ratios to clarify the financial condition of a nonprofit by asking questions about liquidity, solvency, efficiency, profitability, matching of revenues and expenses, and diversification of revenues. Financial analysis also uncovers other information, such as the existence of red flags. Financial ratios have been used for many years in both the public and private sectors. Over time, numerous financial ratios have been created. The ones discussed here represent only a small part of the rich and varied history of financial analysis. Readers are encouraged to examine other textbooks and to cruise the internet to find other financial ratios that might help them to understand their nonprofits' finances.

Financial Resources

Nonprofits need to use their resources in ways that are efficient and effective so that the resources can be used to fulfill their missions. Nonprofits can understand how efficient and effective they are in their use of resources by measuring their use as carefully as possible. This is where financial analysis comes in. Nonprofits use ratio analysis to examine several key elements.

Liquidity

In the last decade of the twentieth century, nonprofits became used to an ever-increasing stream of revenue pouring into their coffers. Then, with the 2008 recession, nonprofits had to drastically revise their revenue estimates downward. Because of the recession, many nonprofits found themselves in the unenviable position of having overcommitted their resources, and they had to cut back their programs. In effect, they were undercapitalized and did not have enough cash (liquidity).

Of course, the opposite can also be true. A few nonprofits are extremely fiscally conservative and tend to save their monies and not spend them on programs. Such a nonprofit may be overcapitalized, which can be a mistake—after all, the mission of nonprofits is to provide services, not save money. The answer is to find the correct balance. Few nonprofits are overcapitalized; usually nonprofits have to deal with being undercapitalized because they try to do so much with so little.

Long-Term Solvency

Solvency differs from liquidity in that solvency is not about how much cash is on hand but about the ability of the nonprofit to meet its long-term obligations. The long-term solvency of a nonprofit is crucial for its long-term development. If a nonprofit has sufficient long-term solvency, it can think about long-term expansion and growth.

Long-term solvency is closely related to liquidity. Certainly the amount of debt a nonprofit is carrying will affect the ability of the nonprofit to keep sufficient cash on hand to meet its financial obligations. **Leverage** is the amount of debt used to finance a nonprofit's assets. If a nonprofit has a great deal of debt as compared to its assets, it is considered highly leveraged.

Efficiency

Efficiency compares what is actually produced against the resources used to produce it. In effect, efficiency is how much output can be produced given all the resources used to produce the output. For nonprofits, efficiency has become increasingly important, because governments are requiring nonprofits to produce estimated efficiency ratios when submitting grant proposals and because as resources become tighter, nonprofits must use their resources carefully.

Efficiency ratios are used to determine the extent of an organization's efficiency, such as measuring how long it takes for a nonprofit to pay its bills or to collect its receivables, or the cost of an after-school program per student enrolled. These types of ratios are useful in determining the extent to which the nonprofit is efficient in its use of resources.

Profitability

For many years, nonprofits have thought that most of their resources should be spent, not saved. It was believed that at the end of the year, a nonprofit should have no surplus, because this would be an indication that the nonprofit is devoting all the revenue the donors have given to the nonprofit's mission. Now, however, a more sophisticated understanding of nonprofits has led to a change in this thinking.

Executive directors want to end with a surplus for the year. The question becomes how much of a nonprofit's resources should be spent in the current year. Remember: If a nonprofit spends its resources now, it will not have the resources in the future; that is the "going concern" accounting principle. Nonprofits assume they will be in business indefinitely. It is essential that they plan for the future. If the board and the executive director of a nonprofit do not husband their resources carefully, they will not have sufficient resources in the future to provide the same level and quality of service they are providing now.

Nonprofits should be ending each year with a surplus that can be saved for future programming. This is referred to as **intergenerational equity**; in effect, a nonprofit will save some of its current revenues for future generations who will benefit from the nonprofit. In the end, spending every dollar of a nonprofit's resources in a given year for vital programming is the wrong strategy. Remember the conservative principle in accounting. Again, the key is balance. Board members and executive directors must come to agreement about the balance between resources spent and resources preserved for the next generation.

Matching

The conservative principle applies as well to matching as it does to profitability. As part of the matching principle, matching revenues with expenses goes one step further. Revenues and expenses must match within the same accounting period. For example, salaries are an expense when the nonprofit's staff members work, not when they are paid. The revenue is linked to the expense when the expense occurs.

Planning for the matching of funding for programs and services helps a nonprofit better manage its financial resources. The nonprofit world is very diverse—hospitals, colleges, and both huge and small multiservice organizations. It is difficult to generalize across all of these different types of nonprofits. Most nonprofits, regardless of size or complexity, have both long-term and short-term goals, and with those goals the nonprofits have long-term and short-term resources. A multiservice nonprofit may operate a day care center that is funded by a city or state contract. The revenue from the government should cover the costs of the day care center, and those monies should not be used for other programs. The nonprofit matches the source of the resources to the use of the resources during the same time period. Of course, the board and executive director may have made a decision to deepen the programmatic experience for those children in the day care center by raising extra monies, and those monies are dedicated to that day care center. A college may be building its endowment so that it may endow a chair in the history department. Those funds are set aside for that purpose.

Revenue Diversification

The concept of revenue diversification is not as widely understood as other concepts discussed here because some nonprofits have no need of it. If a nonprofit is largely dependent on one source of revenue, such as a government contract, that nonprofit could be vulnerable when changes occur in government fiscal policy. Thus, for many nonprofits, it is reasonable to pursue several sources of revenue so that if one source shrinks, the nonprofit has only a moderate funding problem rather than a massive one.

Diversification of financial resources, however, can have its own set of problems. Sometimes a nonprofit will pursue a revenue source that is well outside its mission simply because that revenue source is available. A nonprofit might be tempted to do this because it is not liquid enough, and it is looking for revenues wherever it can get them. Of course, in the long term it is folly for a nonprofit to accept revenue from a source outside the nonprofit's mission. If a nonprofit loses sight of its mission, it will find that it is much more difficult to deliver a coherent message to donors about the nonprofit. The situation becomes confusing for all who identified with that mission.

Conducting Ratio Analysis

Financial analysts developed ratio analysis for the private sector for the purpose of determining the financial condition of a corporation—information needed by those considering whether to buy corporate stocks. Ratio analysis has also come to be useful in determining the financial condition of nonprofits. The many available books on ratio analysis provide endless examples of ratios. The ratios we discuss here are those that we consider the most useful for nonprofits. In using these ratios, we will examine a small nonprofit that we will call the ABC Nonprofit Corporation. This organization provides educational training services to elementary and secondary schools in Ohio.

Ratios and Liquidity

We will address here three ways to measure liquidity: current ratio, working capital, and quick ratio. Liquidity is king; without it, nonprofits will fold. You actually only need to use one of these measures to determine the liquidity of a nonprofit. Each one can be used to determine the extent to which a nonprofit need not worry about its cash flow. In order to calculate these measures, a nonprofit's statements of financial position are needed; these statements for FY 2020 and FY 2019 for the ABC Nonprofit Corporation are reproduced in Table 7.1.

Current Ratio. The current ratio determines whether or not a nonprofit has sufficient cash for the fiscal year. It is calculated by dividing current assets by current liabilities (i.e., bills that must be paid in the coming months, not years). Using

Table 7.1   Statements of Financial Position, ABC Nonprofit Corporation as of December 31, 2020 and 2019

	2020	2019
Assets		
Current Assets		
Cash and Cash Equivalents	$ 66,799	$ 26,402
Short-Term Marketable Securities	125,000	75,000
Accounts Receivable	47,907	15,130
Grant Receivable	15,000	—
Other	317	317
Total Current Assets	$ 255,023	$ 116,849
Long-Term Assets		
Equipment at Cost	55,790	55,790
Less Accumulated Depreciation	(50,156)	(49,191)
Total Long-Term Assets	$ 5,634	$ 6,599
Total Assets	$ 260,657	$ 123,448
Liabilities and Net Assets		
Current Liabilities		
Bank Line of Credit	$ 11,641	$ —
Accounts Payable	9,492	33,608
Accrued Expenses	3,000	2,000
Other	6,250	18,250
Total Current Liabilities	$ 30,383	$ 53,858
Net Assets		
Unrestricted	$ 108,639	$ 34,847
Restricted	121,635	34,743
Total Net Assets	$ 230,274	$ 69,590
Total Liabilities and Net Assets	$ 260,657	$ 123,448

the statements of financial position from the ABC Nonprofit in Table 7.1, the current ratio for FY 2020 and FY 2019 for the ABC Nonprofit Corporation are:

$$\text{Current Ratio} = \frac{\text{Current Assets}}{\text{Current Liabilities}}$$

$$\text{Current Ratio FY 2020} = \frac{\$255,023}{\$30,383} = 8.4$$

$$\text{Current Ratio FY 2019} = \frac{\$116,849}{\$53,858} = 2.2$$

It is important to have a ratio of at least 1 so that the resources cover the liabilities; however, 2 is more comfortable in terms of having resources that can quickly be turned into cash to cover outstanding current liabilities. In both years, the ABC Nonprofit has sufficient liquidity to cover its current liabilities, although in FY 2020, a current ratio of 8.4 is extremely high and needs to be explained.

Working Capital. Like the current ratio, working capital is a method of determining how liquid an organization is. Again, the rule of thumb is to have more current assets than current liabilities. Working capital is the difference between current assets and current liabilities:

$$\text{Working Capital} = \text{Current Assets} - \text{Current Liabilities}$$

$$\text{Working Capital FY 2020} = \$255,023 - \$30,383 = \$224,640$$

$$\text{Working Capital FY 2019} = \$116,849 - \$53,858 = \$62,991$$

Quick Ratio. A more conservative ratio, the quick ratio, measures fewer assets, only using those assets that can be quickly changed into cash.

$$\text{Quick Ratio} = \frac{\text{Cash} + \text{Marketable Securities} + \text{Accounts Receivable}}{\text{Current Liabilities}}$$

$$\text{FY 2020 Quick Ratio} = \frac{\$66,799 + \$125,000 + \$47,907}{\$30,383} = 7.9$$

$$\text{FY 2019 Quick Ratio} = \frac{\$26,402 + \$75,000 + \$15,130}{\$53,858} = 2.2$$

The quick ratio demonstrates a similar result to the current ratio. This nonprofit has a ratio of over 1, and over 2 is best. The nonprofit has sufficient liquidity.

Ratios and Long-Term Solvency

The concept of long-term solvency involves leverage; that is, if all of a nonprofit's assets and debt were included in calculating a financial ratio, what would be the measure of fiscal health in the nonprofit? Could the nonprofit afford the amount of debt it is carrying? Such a ratio helps to determine long-term fiscal health. In effect, long-term solvency is about the amount of leverage, which is the amount of debt used to finance activities. If you are highly leveraged, it means you have a great deal of debt as compared to your resources. Banks use leverage ratios to help determine whether an individual or corporation is solvent enough to be given a loan. The bank wishes to be repaid. The major ratios that are useful in the consideration of solvency are the debt-to-asset ratio and the debt-to-equity ratio.

Debt-to-Asset Ratio. The debt-to-asset ratio measures the nonprofit's total assets financed by all borrowing.

$$\text{Debt-to-Asset Ratio} = \frac{\text{Total Liabilities}}{\text{Total Assets}}$$

$$\text{FY 2020 Debt-to-Asset Ratio} = \frac{\$30,383}{\$260,657} = 0.12$$

$$\text{FY 2019 Debt-to-Asset Ratio} = \frac{\$53,858}{\$123,448} = 0.44$$

In FY 2019, the ABC Nonprofit had a fair amount of debt for its assets. By the next year, FY 2020, the debt had been reduced and the assets increased. A rule of thumb is that the debt-to-asset ratio should be below 0.4. This example illustrates why it is important to have at least two years of financial data. Measuring 2019 alone would provide a less than favorable picture of ABC Nonprofit's debt-to-asset ratio. Five years of data is preferable; data gathered over a greater amount of time allow the analyst to understand the financial trends in the nonprofit. One year of data is insufficient.

Debt-to-Equity Ratio. Similar to the debt-to-asset ratio is the debt-to-equity ratio (also called the debt-to-net-assets ratio). This ratio considers the long-term resources provided by debt in relationship to those provided internally by the net assets.

$$\text{Debt-to-Equity Ratio} = \frac{\text{Total Liabilities}}{\text{Net Assets}}$$

$$\text{FY 2020 Debt-to-Equity Ratio} = \frac{\$30,383}{\$230,274} = 0.13$$

$$\text{FY 2019 Debt-to-Equity Ratio} = \frac{\$53,858}{\$69,590} = 0.77$$

The assessment of the debt-to-equity ratio is similar to the assessment of the debt-to-asset ratio. This ratio demonstrates even more clearly the difficult financial position the ABC Nonprofit was in during FY 2019. These long-term solvency ratios help nonprofits determine whether they are able to meet their long-term commitments. Again, the rule of thumb is that the ratio should be below 0.4. In this case, FY 2020 demonstrates that the nonprofit is secure.

Ratios and Efficiency

The main ratios that are useful for considering a nonprofit's efficiency are known as asset management ratios (AMRs). These ratios provide a picture of how

Chapter Seven

soon bills are being paid and how quickly revenues are being received. AMRs were first used to pick stocks, but these ratios are also useful to nonprofits because they are indicators of efficiency within an industry. Some industries require a great many assets to conduct their activities; therefore, it is best not to compare nonprofits from different industries. For example, a hospital's asset management ratio should not be compared to that of a social service agency. It is useful, however, to compare the AMRs among hospitals. We examine below two asset management ratios: the asset turnover ratio and the days receivable ratio.

Asset Turnover Ratio. A high asset turnover ratio is desirable because it indicates that the organization provides many services for every dollar invested in its assets. In order to measure the asset turnover ratio, we need to use both the statements of financial position over two years and the statement of activities for the newest year. The statement of activities for the ABC Nonprofit in FY 2020 and FY 2019 is presented in Table 7.2.

The asset turnover ratio is calculated by dividing the total unrestricted revenues by the average total assets. Using the total unrestricted revenues instead of the total revenues allows the ratio to represent what occurs during the day-to-day operations of the nonprofit. The average total assets is determined by combining the total liabilities and net assets for a fiscal year (see Table 7.1).

$$\text{Asset Turnover Ratio} = \frac{\text{Total Unrestricted Revenues}}{\text{Average Total Assets}}$$

$$\text{FY 2020 Asset Turnover Ratio} = \frac{\$637{,}852}{\$260{,}657} = \$2.48$$

$$\text{FY 2019 Asset Turnover Ratio} = \frac{\$503{,}169}{\$123{,}448} = \$4.08$$

The ABC Nonprofit generates $2.48 in revenue for every dollar of investment in assets, which is a strong ratio. This result is quite healthy. The nonprofit is providing many services for every dollar invested. Any asset turnover ratio over $1.00 indicates revenue generated for every dollar invested.

Days Receivable Ratio. The days receivable ratio measures the average number of days between the beginning of an accounts receivable and when it is collected. This is useful in social service agencies that deal with a great many receivables because of pledges or government contracts.

$$\text{Days Receivable Ratio} = \frac{\text{Accounts Receivable} \times 365 \text{ Days}}{\text{Unrestricted Revenue}}$$

$$\text{FY 2020 Days Receivable Ratio} = \frac{\$47{,}907 \times 365}{\$637{,}852} = 27.4 \text{ days}$$

$$\text{FY 2019 Days Receivable Ratio} = \frac{\$15{,}130 \times 365}{\$503{,}169} = 10.9 \text{ days}$$

Table 7.2 Statements of Activities, ABC Nonprofit Corporation, during FY 2020 and FY 2019

	FY 2020			FY 2019		
	Unrestricted	Restricted	Total	Unrestricted	Restricted	Total
Revenues						
Contributions	$ 172,100	$ —	$ 172,100	$ 158,705	$ —	$ 158,705
Corporate Contributions	191,395	310,550	501,945	161,190	—	161,190
Special Projects	1,160	—	1,160	29,285	119,500	148,785
Seminars, Workshops	10,940	—	10,940	18,558	—	18,558
Subscriptions, Publications	4,645	—	4,645	5,398	—	5,398
Grants Released from Restrictions	223,658	(223,658)	—	119,257	(119,257)	—
Investment Income	15,698	—	15,698	10,776	—	10,776
Other	18,256	—	18,256	—	—	—
Total Revenues	$ 637,852	$ 86,892	$ 724,744	$ 503,169	$ 243	$ 503,412
Expenses						
Program Services	$ 483,409	—	$ 483,409	$ 424,115	—	$ 424,115
Support Services						
Management	41,491	—	41,491	26,473	—	26,473
Fundraising	39,160	—	39,160	28,819	—	28,819
Total Expenses	$ 564,060	$ —	$ 564,060	$ 479,407	$ —	$ 479,407
Change in Net Assets	$ 73,792	$ 86,892	$ 160,684	$ 23,762	$ 243	$ 24,005
Net Assets						
Beginning of Year				$ 23,191	$ 231,368	$ 254,559
Adjustment to Return Restricted Funds				$ (12,106)	$ (196,868)	$ (208,974)
Beginning of Year Restated	$ 34,847	$ 34,743	$ 69,590	$ 11,085	$ 34,500	$ 45,585
End of Year	$ 108,639	$ 121,635	$ 230,274	$ 34,847	$ 34,743	$ 69,590

In this particular case, the nonprofit has an excellent days receivable ratio. Any ratio under 30 days is sensible because it is an indication that the nonprofit has sufficient liquidity to pay its bills on time.

The ratios above indicate that the ABC Nonprofit Corporation is efficient enough to collect its revenues in a timely manner. One caveat: These ratios may be almost too good. Nonprofits need to spend their resources in achieving their missions. Stockpiling resources rather than using them can be too conservative. It could also be a reaction to the previous year's problems with returning restricted funds.

Ratios and Profitability

Remember the "going concern" principle of accounting. A nonprofit, if its board and executive director are careful, can exist for a hundred years. It is important in the life of the nonprofit that budgets are balanced, expected revenues are collected, and expenses are monitored so that the nonprofit ends each year in a surplus. There is nothing wrong with a nonprofit earning a profit for the year, for several reasons:

- A nonprofit may seek to expand, and it is not necessarily wise to finance expansion totally by debt.
- A nonprofit must have a cushion because of the uncertainness of the economy.
- A nonprofit must replace equipment that has worn out, and it can do that only if it has a surplus to direct to that end.

All of these reasons are part of the larger picture of preparing the way for the next generation to take over a thriving nonprofit. Ratios that provide a picture of a nonprofit's profitability include the profit margin ratio and the return on assets.

Profit Margin Ratio. The profit margin ratio is calculated by dividing the unrestricted surplus by the unrestricted revenues. The surplus can be determined by subtracting the total expenses from the total revenues for the fiscal year. This calculation requires the use of the statement of activities (see Table 7.2).

$$\text{Profit Margin Ratio} = \frac{\text{Unrestricted Surplus}}{\text{Unrestricted Revenue}}$$

$$\text{FY 2020 Profit Margin Ratio} = \frac{\$73,792}{\$637,852} = 11.6\%$$

$$\text{FY 2019 Profit Margin Ratio} = \frac{\$23,762}{\$503,169} = 4.7\%$$

In both years, the ABC Nonprofit Corporation had a surplus that it could add to its net assets as a cushion in the future. Think of it this way: If revenues are $100 and profits are $3, then the nonprofit has earned three cents of operating profit for every dollar of revenue generated.

The rule of thumb is not to run deficits, in which case the nonprofit would be unable to support the next generation, and also to retain a large enough surplus that inflation does not interfere. If inflation was 5% in 2019, then even though the ABC Nonprofit had a surplus, it did not have a large enough surplus to cover inflation. There is no guideline regarding how big the surplus should be, although it is certainly possible that contributors may question a surplus of 20% or more, since nonprofits exist to provide services, not to protect large surpluses.

Return on Assets. Another similar ratio that evaluates a nonprofit's return is the return on assets, which measures the operating surplus over assets that are used to generate the revenue. In this case, both the financial position statement and financial activities statement are needed (see Tables 7.1 and 7.2).

$$\text{Return on Assets} = \frac{\text{Operating Surplus}}{\text{Total Assets}}$$

$$\text{FY 2020 Return on Assets} = \frac{\$73,792}{\$260,657} = 28.3\%$$

$$\text{FY 2019 Return on Assets} = \frac{\$23,762}{\$123,448} = 19.2\%$$

In effect, the return on assets evaluates the nonprofit's return relative to the assets used to generate that income. Although these returns on assets are high, it is not unusual for a nonprofit to show such high returns when it is being conservative about its savings in the midst of a recession.

Matching

Nonprofits receive revenue from many sources, and most of these revenues are dedicated to particular activities. If a nonprofit receives a grant for a girls' after-school program, those revenues cannot be used for the day care center. If the nonprofit receives a government contract to operate an employment and training program, then the nonprofit cannot use those funds to finance a computer center. The purposes for the resources must match the uses. That is why executive directors are always seeking revenues that are completely unrestricted, that can be used for anything—because regulations, laws, and contracts bind so many of nonprofits' revenues to specific purposes.

Questions about appropriate matching are difficult to answer using financial statements. Such questions are best answered through discussion with a nonprofit's executive director and finance officer. Financial ratios are useless for tracking this type of matching; however, such analysis must be done. Executive

> **Box 7.1**
> **CASE IN POINT: Matching Revenues with Expenses**
> Nonprofit executives who treat all revenues alike can find themselves in a great deal of trouble. Revenues must be spent according to the agreements originally made about those revenues.

directors who do not carefully match the dedicated purpose of resources to their uses can find themselves in a great deal of financial trouble when outside auditors examine their finances.

Another kind of matching involves looking at total assets versus long-term assets. The ABC Nonprofit's total assets for FY 2020 are $260,657, and its long-term assets are $5,634, which means that 2.2% of its capital was invested in long-term assets (see Table 7.1). The ABC Nonprofit has most of its assets in cash or receivables, which is unusual. Most nonprofits would not carry this much cash; they would spend the cash to provide more services or put it in long-term investments. The ABC Nonprofit's capital investment practice is questionable and needs to be brought to the attention of the board members.

Diversification

When a board of directors and executive director measure the fiscal health of their nonprofit, they must consider whether their current resources are sustainable. The way to measure sustainability is to measure **diversification** of the nonprofit's resources. It is assumed that, in most cases, the more dispersed the resources, the more sustainable the resources. Research has found that "a diversified portfolio encourages more stable revenues and consequently could promote greater organizational longevity."[2] What this means is that if a revenue stream is reduced—for instance, the state government cuts back its funding of employment and training programs—then the nonprofit will have its resources reduced. The extent to which the loss of a revenue stream affects a nonprofit is partly dependent on the proportion of resources dedicated to the program for which funding was cut. If the program was only 10% of the nonprofit's revenues, then the cutbacks are sustainable. If the program was half of the nonprofit's revenue stream, the nonprofit is in a great deal of trouble. The best way to measure diversification is to determine the percentages of a nonprofit's revenue sources. The more diverse the revenue, the more protected the nonprofit's resources.

Common Size Ratio

The common size ratio is the proportion of an expense or revenue item to the total expenses or revenues. It can be important, particularly on the revenue side, because it is an indication of what proportion each revenue stream is to the total revenue.

$$\text{Common Size Ratio (Proportional \%)} = \frac{\text{Line Item}}{\text{Total Category}}$$

For ABC Nonprofit, the data show that individual and corporate contributions make up about 60% of its revenue, while grant money is a third in FY 2020 and less than a quarter in FY 2019 (see Table 7.3). The diversification seems ample.

Diversification varies across the nonprofit sector. Advocacy groups may have significantly more revenue from private sources than from public sources, while

Table 7.3 Examining Revenues, ABC Nonprofit Corporation, during FY 2020 and FY 2019

	FY 2020	% of Total	FY 2019	% of Total
Contributions	$ 172,100	27.0	$ 158,705	31.5
Corporate Contributions	191,395	30.0	161,190	32.0
Special Projects	1,160	0.2	29,285	5.8
Seminars, Workshops	10,940	1.7	18,558	3.7
Subscriptions, Publications	4,645	0.7	5,398	1.1
Grants Released from Restrictions	223,658	35.1	119,257	23.7
Investment Income	15,698	2.5	10,776	2.1
Other	18,256	2.9	—	0.0
Total Revenue	$ 637,852	100.0%	$ 503,169	100.0%

certain social service nonprofits may receive more public funding. The importance of diversification thus varies according to nonprofit type.

Contributions Ratio

Another part of a nonprofit's financial analysis is the measurement of the effectiveness of the fundraising office, which has the responsibility of raising funds from contributors. This measurement involves the use of the contributions ratio and revenue data (see Table 7.3).

$$\text{Contributions Ratio} = \frac{\text{Revenue from Individual and Corporate Contributions}}{\text{Total Revenue}}$$

$$\text{FY 2020 Contributions Ratio} = \frac{\$172,100 + \$191,395}{\$637,852} = .57$$

$$\text{FY 2019 Contributions Ratio} = \frac{\$158,705 + \$161,190}{\$503,169} = .64$$

This gives the analyst some understanding of how successful the nonprofit's fundraisers are. Yet, it is difficult to judge the results. If a nonprofit has a fundraising ratio of 0.52, what does that mean? It depends on the industry. Churches will have very high donor ratios, sometimes 0.90. Social service agencies will have ratios that hover in the 0.30 to 0.50 range. Hospitals will have very small contribution ratios, often below 0.10, since they receive most of their revenue from fees and government sources. For social service agencies, a large contribution ratio of 0.50 to 0.60 can be quite helpful because donors become a buffer against cutbacks that might come from government contracts and grants. Particularly during a recession, nonprofits with an excessive dependence on government contracts and grants may get into trouble. Donations are not recession proof either, but a strong fundraising office can pursue high-end donors during any type of economy.[3]

Program Services Expense Ratio

The program services expense ratio measures the amount of money spent on programs as compared to total expenses, which include administrative and fundraising expenses. The Wise Giving Alliance of the Better Business Bureau (BBB) has set a standard of at least 65% for this ratio. Such a standard is arbitrary, however, and does not take into consideration the nonprofit sector in which a given organization must operate. Most social service agencies have no problem reaching at least 65%; they keep administrative and fundraising expenses low. Advocacy nonprofits, in contrast, must put a great deal of money into fundraising because far fewer people and foundations are interested in funding advocacy. Such nonprofits may have program services expense ratios of 60%.

Red Flags

In financial analysis, red flags are indications of trouble, and all red flags should be explored. These include large changes in administrative expenses, increases in short-term liabilities, losses in fixed assets, large gifts, and losses in the annual surplus. Each of these kinds of red flags needs to be examined to determine why it is occurring.[4]

- Large reductions in administrative expenses could be an indication that the nonprofit is in financial trouble and is attempting to solve its problems by cutting back its administration. This can be problematic because the administrative side of an agency is key to the agency's success.

- Increases in accounts payable could be an indication that the nonprofit does not have sufficient cash flow to handle its payables. Conversely, an increase in accounts receivables collection time may indicate problems in collecting and have an adverse effect on cash flow (especially if cash on hand is low).

- Losses in fixed assets could be an indication the nonprofit is selling its assets, which could be the result of a financial crisis.

- If the nonprofit has received a large contribution, this can become a problem if the nonprofit expands services without long-term guarantees of additional revenue.

- Losses in the annual surplus are of serious concern. Nonprofits must add to their intergenerational equity every year and can do this only if the surplus is above the level of inflation. If the surpluses are very small, then the nonprofit is endangering future generations.

Box 7.2

REMEMBER: Red Flags

- Large changes in administrative expenses
- Increases in short-term liabilities
- Losses in fixed assets
- Large gifts
- Losses in the annual surplus

Financial Health of the ABC Nonprofit Corporation

The ABC Nonprofit Corporation's current and long-term assets ratios indicate that although FY 2019 was financially difficult, the nonprofit has recovered. It is profitable. Its matching between sources and uses of resources is difficult to determine. Diversification of revenue is not a problem. What must be addressed is the large amount of assets in cash or in short-term securities. Is the nonprofit preparing for an endowment campaign or for the purchase of a building? It is unusual for a nonprofit to retain so much cash and cash equivalents, so this aspect of the organization's financial status should be investigated.

Ratios and Rating Agencies

Rating agencies closely examine the financial condition of nonprofits. The two most widely known among such agencies are Charity Navigator and the BBB. High-end donors use the information provided by these agencies to help decide to which nonprofits they should donate. Hence, it is best for nonprofit executives to know what these monitors are saying about their nonprofits.

Charity Navigator uses information such as the average annual growth of program expenses, average annual growth of primary revenue, and working capital. Unfortunately, Charity Navigator uses only 1 year of data—a practice that we believe is a mistake. No single year provides an accurate description of a nonprofit's financial condition. It is best when conducting a financial analysis of a nonprofit to use at least 2 years of data, and 3–5 years is much better. Any nonprofit can have a multitude of reasons that 1 year of financial data is not representative of its financial condition. Events such as a change in executive director, the purchase of real estate, or the loss of a major donor can be reasons why 1 year of data is skewed. Information obtained over a period of multiple years provides a far more accurate representation of a nonprofit's financial condition.

The Wise Giving Alliance has established standards for nonprofit accountability that it uses to determine how specific nonprofits are doing in terms of their governance and oversight, effectiveness, finances, fundraising, and informational materials. Donors can easily access the BBB's website to see what rating a particular nonprofit has received. Such ratings are helpful to those wishing to make donations, but potential donors should understand the standards used and not take any single standard out of context. For example, it certainly sounds reasonable that the BBB has set as a standard that a nonprofit must spend at least 65% of its total expenses on program expenses. However, this standard is actually meaningless, as it is easy for nonprofits to manipulate what they call program expenses as compared to administrative or fundraising expenses. In addition, the BBB, like Charity Navigator, uses only one fiscal year to calculate its ratios. However, despite the shortcomings we have noted regarding their methodology, both of these rating agencies provide a valuable service to donors and others interested in nonprofits.

Conclusion

Financial analysis is an important management tool for determining the financial health of a nonprofit. Such analysis is conducted chiefly through the use of financial ratios, which can inform the executive director and board of directors about just how good the financial management is in their nonprofit. The better the financial management, the more success the nonprofit will have in fulfilling its mission. Recognizing red flags is also an essential part of financial analysis.

Financial ratios are guides, and often a single year's worth of ratios may be misleading. A nonprofit may be saving its cash for a particular project starting the next year, so that it ends the year with a current ratio of 10, which is far too large. A nonprofit could end a year in a deficit because it decided to amply fund its retirement account, and every other year has been and will continue to be fine. It is important to examine ratios over a period of 5 years, 10 years, or even more, and not make snap judgments about a nonprofit based on one year's ratios.

The financial analysis is about balance. How much of a nonprofit's resources should be spent and how much should be saved? This is not an exact science, and nonprofit executives need to conduct this kind of financial analysis to improve their own understanding of their organizations' finances. National monitoring agencies use ratio analysis to judge the financial condition of nonprofits, so this kind of analysis is key to a nonprofit's future.

KEY TERMS

diversification	intergenerational equity	solvency
efficiency	leverage	

DISCUSSION QUESTIONS

1. Why are financial ratios useful in financial analysis?
2. Explain the difference between a current ratio and working capital in relation to examining liquidity.
3. What is the difference between the liquidity ratio and the long-term solvency ratio?
4. Why does profitability matter to nonprofits?
5. Why do nonprofits need to bother with matching revenues to expenses?
6. Why is revenue diversification important for nonprofits?
7. What are the limits to revenue diversification?
8. Explain why one should be cautious when using a contributions ratio to measure the success of a fundraising office.
9. Why is financial analysis of a nonprofit more accurate if several years of data are available rather than only data from a single year?
10. What ratios are the most useful for clarifying the financial condition of a nonprofit?

Suggested Readings

Carroll, Deborah A., and Keely Jones Stater (2008). "Revenue Diversification in Nonprofit Organizations: Does It Lead to Financial Stability?" *Journal of Public Administration Research and Theory*, 19: 947–966.

Herzlinger, Regina E., and Denise Nitterhouse (1994). *Financial Accounting and Managerial Control for Nonprofit Organizations.* Cincinnati: South-Western.

Zietlow, John, Jo Ann Hankin, Alan G. Seidner, and Tim O'Brien (2018). *Financial Management for Nonprofit Organizations: Policies and Practices* (3rd ed.). Hoboken, NJ: Wiley.

Case Study

Financial Analysis of the Montana Mentoring Nonprofit

Montana Mentoring is a small nonprofit with no permanent endowment and no long-term debt. You know little about the nonprofit but you do have its financial statements. Conduct a financial analysis of this nonprofit using the financial statements provided in Tables 7.4 and 7.5.

Table 7.4 Statements of Financial Position, Montana Mentoring Nonprofit, December 31, 2020 and 2019

	2020	2019
Assets		
Cash and Cash Equivalents	$ 154,000	$ 100,000
Marketable Securities	500,000	400,000
Accounts Receivable	44,000	13,000
Prepaid Expenses	1,000	500
Total Current Assets	$ 699,000	$ 513,500
Long-Term Assets		
Property and Equipment, at Cost	$ 50,000	$ 44,000
Less Accumulated Depreciation	(36,000)	(27,000)
Net Total Long-Term Assets	$ 14,000	$ 17,000
Total Assets	$ 713,000	$ 530,500
Liabilities		
Accounts Payable	$ 91,000	$ 51,000
Unearned Income	6,000	12,500
Total Current Liabilities	$ 97,000	$ 63,500
No Long-Term Liabilities		
Net Assets		
Unrestricted	$ 476,000	$ 392,000
Restricted	140,000	75,000
Total Net Assets	$ 616,000	$ 467,000
Total Liabilities and Net Assets	$ 713,000	$ 530,500

Chapter Seven

Specifically, in paragraph form, explain the financial condition of this nonprofit using the data you have analyzed and review the red flags. Create a spreadsheet that demonstrates that you calculated the ratios necessary for your answers.

Table 7.5 Statements of Activities, Montana Mentoring Nonprofit, FY 2020

	Unrestricted	Restricted	Total
Revenues			
Grants	$ 58,300	$ 478,000	$ 536,300
Contributions	44,700	—	44,700
Fees	19,600	—	19,600
In-Kind Donations	68,300	—	68,300
Special Events	26,800	—	26,800
Interest	24,700	—	24,700
Net Assets Transferred	413,000	(413,000)	—
Total Revenues	$ 655,400	$ 65,000	$ 720,400
Expenses			
Salaries	$ 185,200	$ —	$ 185,200
Fringe Benefits	61,400	—	61,400
Fund Development	4,300	—	4,300
Public Relations	6,500	—	6,500
Conferences	1,300	—	1,300
Meetings	800	—	800
Office Rent	26,800	—	26,800
Program Training	127,500	—	127,500
Telecommunications	8,500	—	8,500
Postage	2,900	—	2,900
Travel	3,300	—	3,300
Supplies	6,300	—	6,300
Staff Training	2,600	—	2,600
Audit	8,500	—	8,500
Support Services	11,600	—	11,600
Miscellaneous	600	—	600
Depreciation	8,700	—	8,700
Facilities Charges	89,600	—	89,600
Special Events	15,000	—	15,000
Total Expenses	$ 571,400	$ —	$ 571,400
Increase in Net Assets	$ 84,000	$ 65,000	$ 149,000
Net Assets at Beginning of the Year	$ 392,000	$ 75,000	$ 467,000
Net Assets at End of the Year	$ 476,000	$ 140,000	$ 616,000

Assignments

Assignment 7.1. Using Ratios to Assess Current and Long-Term Liabilities

In FY 2020, the ABC Settlement House had total assets of $1.2 million and current assets of $300,000. Its current liabilities were $200,000 and its long-term liabilities were $800,000. What ratios can be used to conduct a financial analysis of this nonprofit? What would the answers be? Given the fact that there is only one year's worth of data, what conclusions can you draw?

Assignment 7.2. A Second Year's Worth of Data

In FY 2019, the ABC Settlement House had total assets of $900,000 and current assets of $350,000. Its current liabilities were $240,000 and its long-term liabilities were $1,000,000. Conduct a financial analysis and compare it to the analysis done in Assignment 7.1. What conclusions can you draw now that you have 2 years' worth of data?

Assignment 7.3. The ABC Settlement House and Its Profits

In FY 2020, the ABC Settlement House had $800,000 in unrestricted revenues and $780,000 in unrestricted expenses. In the previous year, FY 2019, the ABC Settlement House had $700,000 in unrestricted revenues and $685,000 in unrestricted expenses. What ratios would you use to conduct a financial analysis of this nonprofit? What are the answers and what conclusions would you draw?

Notes

[1] Herzlinger, Regina E., and Denise Nitterhouse (1994). *Financial Accounting and Managerial Control for Nonprofit Organizations* (p. 133). Cincinnati: South-Western.

[2] Carroll, Deborah A., and Keely Jones Stater (2008). "Revenue Diversification in Nonprofit Organizations: Does It Lead to Financial Stability?" *Journal of Public Administration Research and Theory*, 19: 947.

[3] Zietlow, John, Jo Ann Hankin, Alan G. Seidner, and Tim O'Brien (2018). *Financial Management for Nonprofit Organizations: Policies and Practices* (3rd ed.). Hoboken, NJ: Wiley. Zietlow et al. discuss Chris Robinson's master's thesis, which examines contribution ratios from 479 audited financial statements from nonprofit organizations in San Jose, California.

[4] Information in this section comes from Herzlinger and Nitterhouse, p. 165.

PART IV

Financial Management

8 Understanding Revenues

> Remember that a revenue forecast is based on a prediction that a certain sequence of events or a specific scenario will occur.
>
> —Allen J. Proctor[1]

LEARNING OBJECTIVES

The learning objectives for this chapter are as follows:
- Understanding the theoretical development of nonprofit finance
- Learning about all the sources of revenues
- Understanding the distribution of revenues
- Understanding revenue strategies

*N*onprofit organizations play a key role in solving social problems in places where markets and governments fail. In this chapter we discuss nonprofit revenues, including a theoretical foundation for understanding how the benefits provided by nonprofits affect their revenues, main revenue sources, and revenue strategies. Nonprofit managers use these strategies to develop, expand, and diversify financial resources in the context of mission achievement.

Theoretical Development of Finance for Nonprofits: The Benefits Theory

Although nonprofits have developed and received revenues from diverse sources for centuries, attempts to establish a theoretical foundation to explain this phenomenon is relatively new. The economic base for nonprofit organizations is founded on the concepts of market failure and government failure. Macroeconomics tells us that resources are not efficiently allocated to produce all the goods and services that society values in a free market economy. **Public goods** and services, such as clean water and air, are fundamental to the survival and development of a society. The poor and the unfortunate need basic services that a rich society, such as that of the United States, should provide. Market failure means a capitalistic society is unable to provide services that citizens want and need. The question of when to intervene in the markets occurs frequently in political debate as some citizens define market failure narrowly and others quite broadly.

One way to address these consequences of market failure is through government intervention. Government can levy taxes and use them to finance or to directly produce public goods and services. However, there must be an interest by government to participate in the financing and/or production of public goods and services. A political reality in many countries arguably precludes governments from setting levels of taxation high enough to produce an adequate supply of public goods and services by government alone. This is called government failure.

Another form of intervention is when governments engage and support the private sector, especially the nonprofit sector, in financing and delivering public goods and services. The nonprofit sector, when providing public goods and services, develops financial resources from diverse sources, including contributions from individuals, corporations, foundations, and governments, as well as earned revenue from private sources. Each nonprofit organization, new or mature, has its own mix of revenue sources and strategies to acquire resources over time. These strategies are of great theoretical and practical interest in the fast-growing and increasingly competitive nonprofit environment.

Theories in other disciplines—for example, finance, accounting, organization analysis, and political science—provide insight into nonprofit revenue conceptualizations, and scholars have attempted to adapt these theories to the nonprofit world.[2] Although we cannot address all of these constructions here, the benefits theory developed by Dennis Young (professor emeritus at Georgia State University) and his colleagues is useful to nonprofits because it integrates interdisciplinary thinking into a broad, albeit rudimentary, framework to understand revenue and the formation of revenue strategies for nonprofits.

Based on the foundational concepts of public goods and exchanges, the **benefits theory** focuses on the connections among a nonprofit's mission, its services, the beneficiaries, and the sources of financial support. It classifies nonprofits based on the benefits they generate, and it directs nonprofits to seek financial support from those sources that demand their services. We explore the benefits theory throughout this chapter.

Types of Benefits

The benefits theory postulates that nonprofits provide four basic types of benefits: private, group, public, and trade. *Private benefits* are those that accrue to clients and consumers of the nonprofits' services. These goods and services are of a private nature, meaning they are rival (or competing) and excludable (nonpayers can be easily excluded from the services). For instance, nursing home services are primarily private services, benefiting elderly persons and their families. While a nursing home caretaker serves one client, he or she often cannot take care of another client at the same time. Those who do not pay for these services can be refused for the services.

Group benefits accrue to specific constituencies associated with causes that potential donors may value and are willing to support. These goods and services tend to be private but include significant positive externalities. Externalities can be defined as involuntary third-party impacts, or spillover effects, arising from the production and/or consumption of goods and services wherein no appropriate compensation is paid. A positive externality benefits a party that was not a part of the original transaction, and a negative externality does just the opposite. For instance, access to live classical music can benefit not only the audience but also civil society at large. Some interest groups would like to see young people have greater exposure to classical music as an extension of cultural heritage, and they are willing to donate resources so that young people can enjoy orchestral performances at reduced fees or at no cost at all.

Public benefits accrue to the general public. These goods are public in nature. They are nonrival and nonexcludable; that is, the consumption of such benefits by one person does not diminish their consumption by another person, and no one can be excluded from consumption practically, once the benefits are produced. Examples include clean air and public radio.

Trade benefits accrue to organizational partners in a quid pro quo relationship. Nonprofits may enter mutually beneficial relationships with corporations and governments. For instance, in exchange for a grant from a financial company a major city symphony orchestra includes the name of the financial company on all its advertisements for the upcoming season, so that the supporting financial company gains recognition for good corporate citizenship and potentially acquires more clients from the public and corporate sectors.

Box 8.1

REMEMBER: What Is a Public Good?

Public goods are benefits that are public in nature; they are open to the public. They are nonrival and nonexcludable; that is, one person's consumption of the benefit does not exclude or prevent others from utilizing the same benefit. A good example of a public good is clean air.

Matching Benefits and Revenues

The concept of exchange is a building block of the benefits theory, which directs nonprofits to seek revenues from those who demand/benefit from their goods and/or services. Specifically, it suggests that a nonprofit's beneficiaries should pay for private benefits through user fees, to the extent that collection is congruent to the nonprofit's mission and the collection is feasible. Nonprofits should seek donations from interest groups and concerned citizens who benefit from and/or value the services the nonprofits provide, such as specific causes or specific social groups. Governments should finance public benefits, as these benefits accrue to society at large. Benefiting parties should pay reciprocally for trade benefits, although the forms of payment tend to vary in terms of services, equipment, know-how, and grants that come from corporations and foundations.

The benefits theory also contends that nonprofits should seek funding from diverse sources. Many nonprofits provide multiple services, and each service benefits multiple groups/clients. Consequently, nonprofits should seek a mix of revenue sources corresponding to the degree or percentage of benefit the beneficiaries receive. The theory recognizes that there are many practical factors, internal and external to nonprofits, that affect the feasibility and desirability of selecting and diversifying revenue sources. Each nonprofit should make its own decisions regarding revenue strategy given its mission, size, maturity, capacity, and environment. In the following sections, we discuss the existing sources of nonprofit revenues and the revenue strategies used by different types of successful nonprofit organizations, in reference to the benefits theory outlined above.

Existing Sources of Revenue

Public charities receive funding from diverse sources, including private donations, public support, and earned revenues. Approximately 35% of nonprofits registered with the IRS in 2016 were required to file a Form 990, Form 990-EZ, or Form 990-PF. These reporting nonprofits received $2.62 trillion in revenues in total.[3] Figure 8.1 presents a breakdown of these revenues by sources. Among the total revenue, 8.7% was donated from individuals; 3.8% was donated from foundations and corporations; 31.8% came from government sources, including grants and fees for services; and 49% was earned from private fees for services. Investment returns constitute a special type of earned revenue for a relatively small number of nonprofits; such revenue normally accounts for less than 5.2% of their total revenue.[4] Given the unique nature of investment revenue for nonprofits and the special financial management techniques it requires, we discuss this topic in more depth in Chapter 12. The following discussion focuses on the key revenue sources from an operating standpoint—the donations, government support, and earned revenues that are common to most nonprofits.

Understanding Revenues 163

| 49% EARNED Private Fees for Services | 31.8% EARNED Government Grants/Contracts | 8.7% DONATED Individuals | 2.9% DONATED Foundations | 1.5% DONATED Bequests | .9% DONATED Corporations | 5.2% Other |

Figure 8.1 Revenue sources for charitable nonprofits in 2016.

Source: Reprinted with permission from the National Council of Nonprofits.

Donations

A key revenue category for nonprofits is charitable donations. In 2019, Americans gave $449.64 billion to charities and religious organizations.[5] Although donations provide a smaller portion of total nonprofit revenue when compared with funding from government sources and from nonprofit earned revenues (see Figure 8.1), donations are vitally important to the fiscal health of certain nonprofits, and provide symbolic significance for all public charities. Donations come from many sources, including individuals, foundations, and corporations (see Figure 8.2).

Individuals. Individuals play the most significant role in charitable donations. Giving from individuals was estimated to be $309.66 billion in 2019, accounting for 69% of all donated revenues. In addition, individual charitable bequests were estimated to be $43.21 billion, accounting for another 10% of total giving from individual sources. The total donations from individual sources, combining both, makes up 79% of total giving in 2019.[6]

Individual giving was in recovery after the devastating 2008 financial crisis. It dropped between 2007 and 2008 by 5.8% in real terms and declined further in 2009 by 3.3% during the recession.[7] When compared to 2018, in 2019 individual giving rose 4.7% for a total of $309.66 billion.[8] However, in 2020, 83% of mid-size nonprofit organizations (500–5,000 employees) reported a decline in individual giving due to the impact of the Covid-19 pandemic and the resulting economic shutdown.[9]

Foundations. Relative to individual giving, foundations play a smaller role in supporting nonprofit organizations. In 2019, foundations distributed $75.69 billion, representing 17% of total donations.[10]

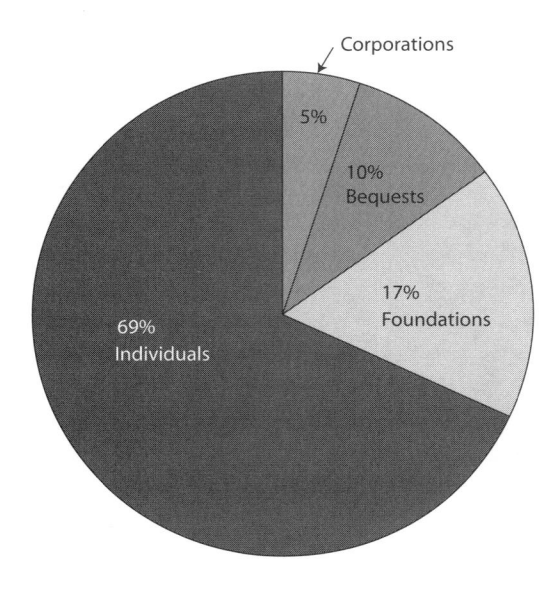

Figure 8.2 Giving contributions by source in 2019.

Source: Giving USA (2020, June). *Giving USA 2020: The Annual Report on Philanthropy for the Year 2019*. Chicago, IL: Giving USA Foundation.

The revenue from foundation sources increased early in the twenty-first century. Grant dollars from foundation sources doubled in the 10-year period between 1997 and 2007. Foundation assets decreased during the 2008 financial crisis nevertheless. Foundation funding resumed its upward trend with the recovery of the economy and asset price after the Great Recession.

Within foundation giving, the vast majority comes from independent foundations. According to the Foundation Center, in 2015 70% of the total foundation giving in the United States came from independent foundations. The three other types of foundations—community foundations, corporate foundations, and operating foundations—contributed 11%, 9%, and 10%, respectively.[11]

Corporate Giving and Strategic Alliances. After a 5.8% decline in 2008 from the previous year, corporate giving increased by 11.8% in 2009 and further rose by 8.8% in 2010 in real terms.[12] In 2019, corporate giving was up 13.4% from 2018. Corporations gave $21.09 billion to public charities, making up 5% of the total giving.[13] The strength or weakness of the U.S. economy seems to play a role in corporate giving, however, corporations can uniquely benefit from working with nonprofits.

Corporate grants can be classified into one of two categories based on motivation: charitable giving or strategic alliances. In recent years, charitable giving has been dwindling while strategic alliances between corporations and nonprofits are on the rise. Corporations sponsor events for strategic commercial purposes, funded by their marketing budgets. When strategic alliances are done properly, both parties benefit: the corporations gain name recognition, and the nonprofits get the funds.

Not all nonprofits can tap into corporate financing, however. New and small nonprofits are unlikely to be sought after for partnerships, and even large nonprofits may not have access if they are not nationally recognized. Established nonprofits that are considering partnering with corporations have to evaluate the pros and cons of lending support to companies that may not be mission compatible. An alliance with a company that is a poor fit can damage the name of the nonprofit and the financial support it receives from other sources, including from the community it serves. However, successful cooperation can enhance the mission achievement of a nonprofit in addition to securing financial support.

Distribution of Donations among Types of Nonprofits. The funds that are donated support diverse nonprofit organizations. The distribution, however, is skewed, as Figure 8.3 shows. Religious organizations received the largest share of donated money in 2019, accounting for 29% of the total amount. A distant second was education, which received 14% of the total giving. Gifts to foundations and human services were the third highest-ranking recipient category, receiving 12% each of all charitable giving. Other subsectors of nonprofits each received 9% or less of the total contributions.[14]

Although relatively small in amount, charitable giving is an important source of funds for many nonprofits. By providing more reliable and often unrestricted revenue that can support administration and fundraising, donations, especially donations in small amounts and stable-flow donations, allow nonprofits to sustain themselves and possibly accumulate capital for expansion. For religious groups, individual donations are a lifeline. Foundations and the corporate sector represent new and increasing sources of giving, sometimes with strings attached. The nonprofit world is experiencing a changing institutional philanthropy that seeks mutual benefits and sometimes active involvement in policy setting and program deliveries. Nonprofit managers need to take this into consideration in revenue development.

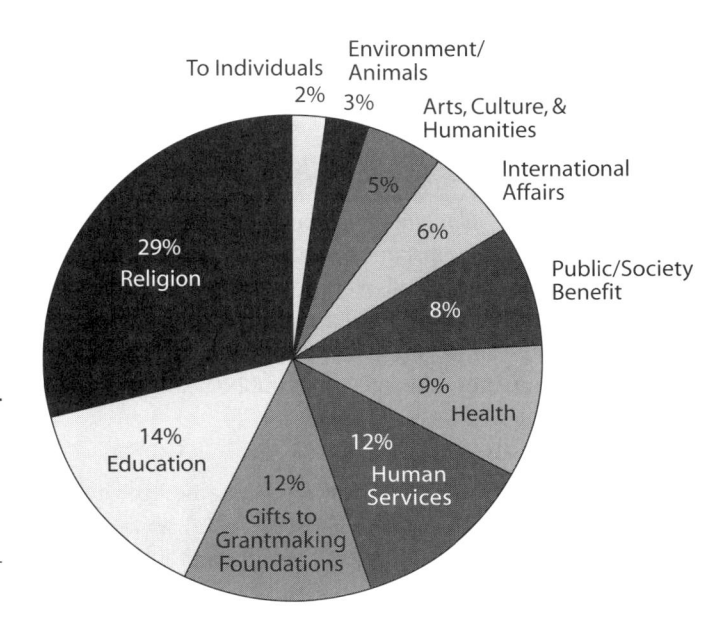

Figure 8.3
Distribution of contributions by type of nonprofit, 2019.

Source: Giving USA Foundation (2020, June). *Giving USA 2020: The Annual Report on Philanthropy for the Year 2019*. Chicago: Giving USA Foundation.

Government Grants and Payment of Fees for Services and Goods

Various levels of government fund nonprofit organizations to provide public goods and goods with substantial positive externalities.[15] As discussed in the benefits theory, public goods and services would not be supplied efficiently in an unbridled free market economy. During the Industrial Revolution, new types of government-funded programs and services were developed and the level of government funding increased. These policies and programs shifted the concentration of the population from rural areas to major urban areas, resulting in a number of social and environmental issues. Between the 1960s and the 1990s, once again government funding for nonprofits grew, corresponding to the Great Society period of new public programs and the contracting out of government services under the name of new public management.

Amount of Government Support. The amount of government support for charities in the United States is difficult to measure because such support comes in different forms and is reported on the IRS Form 990 in different locations. Most government funding support for nonprofits takes two main direct forms: contracts and grants. In addition, governments provide indirect support through nonprofit tax exemptions and tax deductions for donations to public charities. In total, in 2016 revenues from government sources accounted for 31.8% of total public charity revenue, second only to services revenue (see Figure 8.1).[16]

After the start of the financial crisis in 2008, the federal government, facing trillions of dollars in national debt, did not approve any increases in nonprofit support, except for short-term stimulus plans. State governments struggling to balance their budgets also reduced funding for nonprofits. Given the economic impacts of the Covid-19 pandemic, nonprofits believe "additional assistance is needed to help sector organizations continue to provide essential services to our communities and restore their operations and employment levels, through additional grant, loan, or payroll tax relief programs."[17] The CARES Act (passed in March 2020) and the RELIEF Act (passed in December 2020) provide some assistance, but more legislation would be required to avoid major financial shortfalls.

Distribution of Government Funding among Nonprofit Subsectors. Government funding is not equally dispersed throughout the nonprofit sector. Health and human services charities are favored over those that work in the humanities, the environment, and education. State and local funding for health and human services nonprofits remain relatively stable due partly at least to the emphasis and mandate of different levels of government in the interest in public health and the common good.

Earned Revenues

Earned revenues are any revenues obtained through the sale of goods and services—a business transaction. The goods and services tend to be private in nature, benefiting individual consumers and clients. They are rival and excludable; for example, many preschools charge fees to attend. The revenue is earned because it is acquired through an exchange in the marketplace as opposed to coming from a third-party donation or a grant.

Amount of Program Revenues. Earned income has played a large role in nonprofit revenue in recent years. In 2018, 49% of nonprofit revenue came from earned revenue from private sources.[18] Today, many nonprofits are considering social ventures as potential revenue sources to supplement their mission-related endeavors and revenues, in addition to charging fees for mission services.

Distribution of Earned Income among Nonprofit Subsectors. The importance of earned revenue varies among nonprofit subsectors. One study shows that fees account for 27% of revenue for civic organizations and for more than 65% of revenue for educational institutions.[19] This could be explained by the benefits theory outlined earlier. Civic organizations promote the interests of the general public, whereas education arguably benefits primarily individuals, so fees should account for a smaller share of revenue for civic services and a larger share of revenue for educational institutions.

Nonprofit Revenue Strategies

Nonprofit organizations need to develop revenue strategies that allow them to sustain and expand resources for mission activities and achievement. The benefits theory provides a starting point for this planning and decision-making process. The rationale is that nonprofits that provide public goods, such as environmental protection, public safety, and social services, should consider seeking revenue from public sources through different levels of government. Nonprofits that provide group or collective goods and services, such as churches and breast cancer research, should focus on donations, individual and institutional, as sources of funding. Nonprofits that provide **private goods**, such as higher education, health care, and arts and culture, should first develop revenues from fees and other commercial revenues. Well-known nonprofits might consider generating revenue through trade relationships with businesses and/or other nonprofits. Moreover, the benefits theory suggests that most nonprofits provide multiple services, each with diverse benefits. The theory thus supports a portfolio approach to strategizing nonprofit financing approaches. Each nonprofit should develop revenue strategies based on its own specific circumstances.

Funding Models of Large Nonprofits: The Benefits Theory in Practice

The benefits theory seems to have found empirical support from nonprofit financing practices in the real world. Examining the funding models of large nonprofits, William Landes Foster, Peter Kim, and Barbara Christiansen identified 10 prototypes, or benchmarks, of successful nonprofits that generated $50 million in annual revenue. Foster and his colleagues named the 10 models as follows: heartfelt connectors, beneficiary builders, member motivators, big bettors, public providers, policy innovators, beneficiary brokers, resource recyclers, market makers, and local nationalizers.[20] The 10 funding models illustrate how successful large nonprofits finance and grow their operations. They demonstrate the correspondence and congruence between the benefits theory and the practical strategies used by these benchmark nonprofit organizations (see Table 8.1). Nonprofit managers are therefore advised to consider this theory in selecting and structuring their revenue strategies. We briefly discuss each model below and cross-reference them with the benefits theory.

Table 8.1 Correspondence between Benefits Theory and Funding Models

Funding Models	Fees	Donations	Governments	Partners
Heartfelt Connectors		X		
Beneficiary Builders	X	X		
Member Motivators	X	X		
Big Bettors		X		X
Public Providers			X	
Policy Innovators		X	X	
Beneficiary Brokers			X	
Resource Recyclers		X		
Market Makers	X	X		
Local Nationalizers	X	X	X	

Sources of Revenue

Heartfelt Connectors. Nonprofits that acquire finances and grow large by focusing on causes that resonate with large numbers of people and by creating structured ways for these people to connect and donate are the heartfelt connectors. The causes on which they focus include environmental issues, international issues, and medical research. Foster et al. use the Susan G. Komen organization to fight breast cancer to illustrate the model.[21] Consistent with the benefits theory, the foundation has successfully funded and expanded its programs primarily by seeking and acquiring contributions and has provided group, and to some extent public, benefits.

Beneficiary Builders. Nonprofits that are identified as beneficiary builders are financed by reimbursements for services they provide to specific individuals, but at the same time they rely on people who have benefited from their services in the past for contributions. Examples of nonprofits in this category include universities that solicit contributions from alumni and hospitals that contact previous patients for contributions. These nonprofits not only serve their current clients, but their success also benefits their previous customers. For instance, a university's good reputation will likely enhance the career advancement of its graduates. From the point of view of the benefits theory, these nonprofits provide private benefits and group benefits and so they should, and they do, develop and receive funding from both fees and donations.

Member Motivators. Member motivators rely on individuals who donate money because the issues addressed by these nonprofits are important to the donors in terms of value or in terms of private and group benefits. These organizations are often involved in religion, the environment, arts and culture, and humanities. Examples of this funding model include the National Wild Turkey Federation, which protects and expands the habitats of wild turkey populations and promotes the hunting of wild turkeys. Members of the organization hold thousands of banquets that generate more than 80% of its revenue through membership dues and merchandise sales. This model corresponds well to the group benefit and private benefit categories of the benefits model. Interest groups that value and benefit from an issue create the demand.

Big Bettors. Nonprofits that are big bettors rely on major grants from a few individuals or foundations to address major issues with promising solutions. An example is the Stanley Medical Research Institute, which aligns its mission (research into schizophrenia and bipolar disorder) with the missions of foundations that want to tackle an issue that is deeply personal for their founders. This model demonstrates a combination of group benefit and trade benefit, where the nonprofit provides services that benefit a defined group of people with an identifiable condition, which may or may not include the founders or their family members but is nevertheless of importance to the founders. Financial managers may consider this approach when the missions of their nonprofits are matched with the missions of major funding foundations, or the nonprofits' missions can be adjusted within reason so that they can establish partnerships for mutual benefit.

Public Providers. Nonprofits that provide essential social services that are traditionally supported by governments are identified as public providers. These nonprofits benefit the general public as well as specific clients. Their services often are valued by groups of people who benefit directly or indirectly from positive externalities of the services. The Success for All Foundation, which provides services in housing, human services, and education, is an example of this funding model.

In the late twentieth century, all levels of governments in the United States outsourced service delivery functions to the private sector, leading to the expansion of this subsector of nonprofits. Early in the twenty-first century, however, government funding has tapered off, causing the need for diversification of finances among this group. Given the collective nature of the benefits rendered, these nonprofits could build into their future revenue strategies donations from various sources that value the group benefits of the services that are provided. In addition, they might charge fees for services if feasible, based on the prescription of the benefits theory.

Policy Innovators. Policy innovators develop novel methods to address social issues. These nonprofits finance their operations primarily through government support. Examples include HELP USA, which provides transitional housing for the homeless and develops affordable permanent housing for low-income families in New York City as an alternative to paying hotels to house the homeless. This is a very interesting niche of services that benefit the government and the society at large through the development and implementation of effective and efficient policies, and may also benefit the general public in terms of improving society and lowering taxes. Such nonprofits' seeking of public support through government sources is therefore justified based on the benefits theory.

Beneficiary Brokers. Those nonprofits that compete to match up government services with intended beneficiaries are identified as beneficiary brokers. They often manage voucher programs, primarily in the areas of housing, employment services, health care, and student loans. The beneficiaries are free to choose the nonprofits through which they get the services. The Iowa Student Loan Liquidity Corporation is an example. This nonprofit provides services for students who apply for student loans, offering free help to high school students, their parents, and high school counselors. Nonprofits of this type receive broker fees from the government agencies with which they work, supplemented by contributions. These nonprofits provide services that benefit the government and the public in general and, not incidentally, they are supported financially by government.

Resource Recyclers. Resource recyclers are those nonprofits that collect donations from corporations and individuals and distribute these donated goods to other nonprofits that provide direct services to needy recipients. The Greater Boston Food Bank, which distributes 98 million pounds of food annually to more than 600 local organizations, including food pantries, soup kitchens, day care centers, senior centers, and homeless shelters, is an example. In-kind donations typically account for the majority of revenues for resource recyclers, but these nonprofits also need to raise additional funds to support their operations. Their services benefit groups of needy persons; thus, they seek and receive support in the form of donations from individuals and corporations. However, given the social service orientation of these nonprofits, government also provides funding, which is consistent with the prediction and recommendation of the benefits theory.

Market Makers. Nonprofits that provide services where there is a need but no market to fill the need are identified as market makers. The services they provide are mostly in the area of health care, where laws and regulation are restrictive and complex. For example, the mission of the American Kidney Fund is to fight kidney disease through direct financial support to patients in need, health education, and prevention efforts. The organization generates the vast majority of its revenues through donations from such corporations as Amgen and American Kidney Services. This funding model again corresponds to the benefits theory, wherein group benefits are funded by contributed support, although trade benefits are likely present to a varying degree for different donors.

Local Nationalizers. Nonprofits that are local nationalizers focus on local issues that are also common and important across the nation. An example is Big Brothers Big Sisters of America, which has grown large by creating a national network of locally based operations to help poor children, a group that has national significance. Given that the beneficiary is an identified group, the service provides a group benefit as defined by the benefits theory. The funding is indeed raised locally, often from individual and corporate donations and special events. This funding model corresponds to the combination of group benefits with some public and private benefits. It demonstrates the blurred demarcation between group and public benefit in the benefit model, wherein revenue could come from either or both sources. Based on the benefits theory, local nationalizers could direct their revenue development efforts at government and private sources as a strategy to improve funding.

Diversification: Revenue Strategies and Risk Management

The benefits theory also lays a foundation for revenue diversification. Diversification is one of the key tools that nonprofit managers use to manage financial risks. The future of a nonprofit that relies on a single source of revenue is risky and subject to economic fluctuations and changes in societal demands and values. Countless nonprofit failures have demonstrated the danger of relying on a sole source of revenue; when the single source of support is terminated, the nonprofit is devastated, regardless of its quality and the effectiveness of its services. Moreover, nonprofits tend to provide multiple services, and each service benefits multiple constituencies. Consequently, they should pursue revenue strategies that tap into multiple sources and potentially in multiple forms.

The opposite argument, however, has also found support in nonprofit finance. Rather than diversifying, some nonprofits have chosen to focus their development efforts on a few funding sources, establishing deep and lasting relationships and cultivating mutual dependence and trust. This argument is empirical, not only theoretical, and nonprofits should decide on revenue strategies based at least partly on their experience, given the nature and capacity of the organization and the environment they are working in place and in time.

Nonprofits do not solely base their revenue strategies on the analysis of beneficiaries. Other factors are also at work. For example, the maturity of a nonprofit organization often affects its diversification decisions. The lack of experience in managing and reporting financial results often found in new nonprofits limits their success in securing government funding. Lack of experience, funding, and name recognition may prevent nonprofits from entering into a commercial venture coalition. The size of a nonprofit organization also correlates with its decisions on revenue source selection and diversification. The larger the nonprofit, the more likely it is to have reserves and investments as additional income and a cushion in bad times. Consequently, large nonprofits may limit their diversification efforts, focusing instead on their key mission programs and stable constituencies.

Advantages and Disadvantages of Different Funding Sources

As discussed earlier, different financing sources are available to nonprofit organizations. Each of the sources has its unique features and is suitable to certain types of nonprofit organizations based on the services they provide and the benefits they generate. Practical concerns require nonprofit financial managers to consider their capabilities and the feasibility of successfully implementing the strategies derived from the benefits theory. When making decisions on revenue strategies, nonprofit managers are advised to assess their organizations and environment in addition to other financial factors.

Numerous studies have investigated the benefits and difficulties of nonprofits' pursuance of different funding sources. Table 8.2 presents a brief summary of the findings regarding small nonprofits. Financial managers need to take these practical matters into consideration in developing their revenue strategies.

Table 8.2   Advantages and Disadvantages of Different Funding Sources

Source	Potential Value	Difficulties and Risks
Clients/Beneficiary	• Largest source of revenue • Unrestricted	• Crowding out donations • Dilution of missions
Unrelated	• Potential revenue with flexibility • Unrestricted	• Complexity of tax and related issues • Requires business skills in the selected field
Individuals	• Potential for large and continuing revenue source • Build support from grassroots/community	• Expensive and time-consuming to develop a broad base • Difficult and risky as issue, appeals, and task change
Foundations	• Potentially large sums of money from one source • Clear guidelines and professional staff	• Often support start-up or with restricted purposes • Lengthy process and need professional capacity
Corporate Charitable Giving	• Potentially large sums of money from one source • Stable, smaller amounts of money for operation	• Must be within their guidelines • Often limited to headquartered locations
Federal	• Stable source of relatively large sums of money • Professional staff and clear process	• Not for start-up organizations • Limited to social services and crowding out donations
Local	• Stable source of relatively large sums of money • Professional staff and clear process	• Lengthy entry process/complex reporting requirements • Slow reimbursement
Corporate Strategic Alliance	• Clear business objectives • Source of cause-related marketing • Partners trade expertise with mutual benefits	• May need adjustment of mission • May damage image if partner is not well selected • Finding partner(s) with complementary skills set

In sum, nonprofits should include multiple considerations when making revenue strategy decisions. First, they should review their missions, services, and beneficiaries based on the benefits theory. Second, they should decide on the degree of diversification they intend to seek. Many factors should enter the decision-making process, and nonprofits that conduct thorough and systematic analyses and deliberations will have a better chance of planning and implementing successful revenue strategies. Finally, nonprofits should consider the practicalities of pursuing certain funding sources, taking into consideration their own internal capacities and the overall external operating and economic environment.

Conclusion

Nonprofit organizations at aggregate receive revenues from diverse sources, including donations, government support, program fee revenues, and investment income. These revenues are distributed among a wide variety of nonprofits, such as social services, health care, education, arts and culture, etc. The distribution of revenues is not even among revenue sources and nonprofit types. For example, commercial nonprofits, represented by hospitals and universities, receive revenue primarily from fees, whereas social service nonprofits are funded primarily by government support and donations.

Nonprofit managers need to study this skewed funding pattern in order to understand the underlying reasons for it and to develop revenue strategies in response for their organizations. The benefits theory lays out a comprehensive, though rudimentary, framework that describes and explains the phenomenon. The theory identifies four types of benefits—private, group, public, and trade benefits—and suggests that nonprofits should consider the beneficiaries of their programs in designing and implementing their revenue strategies. The existing successful funding models and practices seem to support the benefits theory, nonetheless financial managers need to consider their mission, internal capacity, and the larger social economic environment in making finance decisions.

There is an added urgency to explore diverse finances at the present time due to the ongoing Covid-19 pandemic. Nonprofits not only need to develop effective revenue strategies and explore potential revenue sources as discussed in this text, but also mobilize to contact government and public offices, to the extent legal and appropriate, to solicit legislative support. The world is changing. Nonprofits need to adjust to continue and better serve their missions, especially for underserved populations in time of extreme difficulties and when the markets and government fail.

KEY TERMS

benefits theory   private goods   public goods

Discussion Questions

1. What is the benefits theory and how is it organized?
2. What are the major sources of revenue for nonprofits?
3. What are heartfelt connectors as compared to beneficiary builders?
4. Explain what member motivators are and give an example of what they do.
5. Which nonprofits can be considered big bettors?
6. Compare public providers with policy innovators. Give an example of each.
7. What are beneficiary brokers, resource recyclers, market makers, and local nationalizers?
8. Why is diversification so important for some nonprofits?

Suggested Readings

Fischer, Robert L., Amanda L. Wilsker, and Dennis R. Young (2007). *Exploring the Revenue Mix of Nonprofit Organizations: Does It Relate to Publicness?* (Working Paper 07-32). Andrew Young School of Policy Studies, Georgia State University.
Foster, William Landes, Peter Kim, and Barbara Christiansen (2009, Spring). "Ten Nonprofit Funding Models." *Stanford Social Innovation Review*, 23 (ssireview.org/articles/entry/ten_nonprofit_funding_models).
Proctor, Allen J. (2010). *Linking Mission to Money: Finance for Nonprofit Leaders* (2nd ed.). Worthington, OH: LMM Press.
Salamon, Lester M. (2012). *America's Nonprofit Sector: A Primer* (3rd ed.). New York: Foundation Center.
Salamon, Lester M., ed. (2012). *The State of Nonprofit America* (2nd ed.). Washington, DC: Brookings Institution Press.
Sherlock, Molly F., and Jane G. Gravelle (2009). *An Overview of the Nonprofit and Charitable Sector.* Washington, DC: Congressional Research Service.
Young, Dennis R., ed. (2007). *Financing Nonprofits: Putting Theory into Practice.* Lanham, MD: AltaMira Press.

Case Study

An Environmental Nonprofit Considering Extending Its Cleanup Program

You are the chief financial officer of an environmental nonprofit located in a rust belt community. Your organization is considering extending its services toward the cleanup of local land polluted by industries over the past century. The nonprofit is an established public charity with a good reputation, and your board is influential in the local community. Local citizens, federated fundraisers, and foundations have expressed support for the intended program. The CEO of the nonprofit has called you to his office and raised a couple of questions with regard to seeking extra funding from sources including federal, state, and local governments. He has also proposed that the nonprofit should open a restaurant in the downtown area, which needs rehabilitation and economic development. He has convinced you that he knows how to run a restaurant.

You know that currently government funding is in decline. Economic development in terms of opening a restaurant in the downtown area is good, but it is not directly related to the mission of your organization, which is to raise the quality of life for members of the local community by protecting and improving the environment. The proposed restaurant could be run as a nonrelated business, but that has tax complications. How are you, as chief financial officer, going to respond to the CEO's ideas? Would the internal capacity of your nonprofit facilitate or hinder the chance of success, given the external competition of established businesses already there? What are the pros and cons of soliciting government support and/or starting a new venture? What are the major points you need to cover if you decide to pitch your cleanup project in order to secure government funding? Thinking outside the box, what are other and potentially larger factors, such as a possible economic recession, that you can explore to help you form your opinion and answer questions?

Assignments

Assignment 8.1. Identifying Main Revenue Sources and Trends

What are the main sources of revenue for nonprofit organizations? Analyze the effectiveness of each resource within the context of before, during, and after the Covid-19 pandemic.

Assignment 8.2. Using the Benefits Theory in Revenue Strategy

You are starting a nonprofit that will provide public safety benefits to society at large. Utilizing the benefits theory, which revenue sources would you consider as primary and/or secondary opportunities to obtain financial support? What other considerations might you have?

Assignment 8.3. Considering a Deal for Corporate Support

You are the financial manager of a nonprofit and a corporation in your community has approached you for a potential joint marketing project, wherein the corporation will use your nonprofit's name as a means to promote its product. In return, your organization will receive a substantial grant. What steps would you take in order to determine whether or not to join the marketing project?

Assignment 8.4. Decision on a Newly Contemplated Nonrelated Business

The City Museum, for which you work as financial manager, is considering enhancing its business revenue by opening a restaurant in the facility. The restaurant, however, could be considered a nonrelated business for the museum. What factors should you take into consideration in deciding whether to go forward with the restaurant?

Chapter Eight

NOTES

[1] Proctor, Allen J. (2010). *Linking Mission to Money: Finance for Nonprofit Leaders* (2nd ed., p. 49). Worthington, OH: LMM Press.

[2] See, for example, Chang, C. F., and H. P. Tuckman (1994). "Revenue Diversification among Nonprofits." *Voluntas*, 5: 273–90. Grønbjerg, Kirsten A. (1993). *Understanding Nonprofit Funding: Managing Revenues in Social Services and Community Development Organizations*. San Francisco: Jossey-Bass. Weisbrod, Burton A. (1998). *The Nonprofit Economy.* Cambridge, MA: Harvard University Press.

[3] Urban Institute, National Center for Charitable Statistics (2020, June). *The Nonprofit Sector in Brief 2019.* Washington, DC: Urban Institute (nccs.urban.org/publication/nonprofit-sector-brief-2019#the-nonprofit-sector-in-brief-2019).

[4] National Council of Nonprofits (2019). *Nonprofit Impact Matters: How America's Charitable Nonprofits Strengthen Communities and Improve Lives.* Washington, DC: National Council of Nonprofits.

[5] Giving USA Foundation (2020, June). *Giving USA 2020: The Annual Report on Philanthropy for the Year 2019.* Chicago: Giving USA Foundation (givingusa.org/giving-usa-2020-charitable-giving-showed-solid-growth-climbing-to-449-64-billion-in-2019-one-of-the-highest-years-for-giving-on-record).

[6] Ibid.

[7] Giving USA Foundation (2011). *Giving USA 2011: The Annual Report on Philanthropy for the Year 2010.* Chicago: Giving USA Foundation (givingusareports.org/products/GivingUSA_2011_ExecSummary_Print.pdf).

[8] Giving USA Foundation (2020, June).

[9] Independent Sector (2020, June 15). Impact of COVID-19 on Mid-Size Nonprofits.

[10] Giving USA Foundation (2020, June).

[11] Foundation Center (2015). Foundation Stats. Aggregate Fiscal Data of Foundations in the U.S., 2015 (data.foundationcenter.org/?_ga=2.125303882.1758314186.1594671137-513109550.1594671137).

[12] Giving USA Foundation (2011).

[13] Giving USA Foundation (2020, June).

[14] Ibid.

[15] As noted previously, a positive externality occurs when someone does something that unintentionally results in benefit to others.

[16] National Council of Nonprofits (2019).

[17] Independent Sector (2020, June 15).

[18] National Council of Nonprofits (2019).

[19] Salamon, Lester M. (1999). *America's Nonprofit Sector: A Primer* (2nd ed.). New York: Foundation Center.

[20] Landes Foster, William, Peter Kim, and Barbara Christiansen (2009, Spring). "Ten Nonprofit Funding Models." *Stanford Social Innovation Review* 23 (ssireview.org/articles/entry/ten_nonprofit_funding_models).

[21] Ibid.

9

Performance Measurement in Financial Management

> The law simply requires that we chart a course for every endeavor that we take the people's money for, see how well we are progressing, tell the public how well we are doing, stop the things that don't work, and never stop improving the things that we think are worth investing in.
>
> —President Bill Clinton[1]

Learning Objectives

The learning objectives for this chapter are as follows:
- Defining performance measurement
- Purpose of performance measurement
- Relating performance measurement and program evaluation
- Explaining ingredients used to measure program performance
- Developing performance measurement systems
- Comparison between performance measurement and program evaluation

*T*here are different ways to define performance measurement. The Urban Institute, a nonpartisan economic and social policy research center, defines performance measurement as "measurement on a regular basis of the results (outcomes) and efficiency of services or programs."[2] The definition by the Urban Institute is brief, however, it touches upon the core intension and extension of performance measurement. The following sections in this chapter discuss the role performance measurement plays in mission achievement and the financial management of nonprofits, survey elements in performance measurement systems, outline the process of developing performance measures in the context of key stakeholders, and compare performance measurement with program evaluation. An abbreviated case study summarizes these discussions.

Purpose of Performance Measurement

As discussed in earlier chapters, mission drives money. Mission also drives performance measurements. Performance measurement is integral to a nonprofit's decision-making process during strategic planning, implementation, and monitoring of a program. Throughout these stages performance measurement should occur within the context of mission achievement. A nonprofit often uses performance measurement for different purposes: for example, to solicit funding by convincing potential donors that the nonprofit is achieving its mission goals and to help in budgeting and financial management in a technically complex, multiperspective context.

Planning Programs and Securing Funding

In the context of mission pursuance and strategic planning, the development and revision of a performance measurement system are embedded in the planning process with the participation of key stakeholders. Thinking about how to measure performance must take place early in the process of strategic planning and program development. Performance measures must be valid and reliable, addressing the goals of the programs within the context of the organization's mission. Linking performance measures to program goals and to the nonprofit's mission with fidelity will help demonstrate program effectiveness and efficiency, and will also help secure funding from diverse sources now and into the future.

External stakeholders are invested and interested in nonprofit performance measurement development not only because it is a determining factor for their continued support, but also because they need some valid way to evaluate the extent to which the nonprofit has achieved its stated goals within the established parameters. Policy makers and founding agencies can be quite unreasonable about measuring performance nonetheless. Countless nonprofits complain that government officials are unrealistic about what can be measured and how it can be measured. Since nonprofits have limited budgets, they often find it difficult to measure performance in ways that policy makers would consider meaningful. Therefore, nonprofits must carefully educate their external stakeholders so they understand why particular performance measures have been chosen.

Linking Performance to Budgets

Performance measurement is about the past and budgeting is for the future. Performance information and its related costs therefore inform budgeting and financial management decisions. When considering budgeting resources for a program for the next year, it is helpful to measure its performance, the extent of its activities, the number of people served, the quality of the program, and the costs incurred. Performance measurement allows the executive director and the board to consider changing a program in order to improve its performance, adjust the quantity and quality of its services, or even cancel the program in response to changes in circumstances.

If the budget process is to use performance data, however, two conditions must be met. One is that accurate performance data are available, and the second is that the data must be timely. Beginning in 1970, New York City has produced a yearly Mayor's Management Report that has supported the formation of a city budget ever since.[3]

Key Elements in Performance Measurement Systems

To attract resources and to facilitate budgeting effectively in a competitive environment, nonprofit managers need to have a functioning performance measurement system. Performance measures/indicators should be organized in a systematic manner in terms of inputs, process, outputs, outcome/effectiveness, and efficiency An example of a performance measurement system is provided in Figure 9.1.

Inputs are those resources used to implement and operate a program. For example, the number of positions that have been budgeted for a specific program is an input. The number of computers and their cost is also an input. Another important input that is somewhat unique and important to nonprofit organizations is volunteer time, which is often measured in terms of money. Time and other forms of existing resources, including technology, are also used by different scholars and organizations.

A **process** is the programs and the activities within those programs that the nonprofit operates. It is possible to create process indicators to determine how well a particular program has been implemented, operated, and its activities delivered. Some indicators are more qualitative than quantitative, descriptive than prescriptive. For example, a process/activity variable could include a teacher raising a question after reading a chapter of a textbook, or a student group discussion and report to class of their conclusions in a high school literature program. Process variables, which use resources as inputs, differ from result variables, which are outputs and outcomes.

An **output** is the specific service or product produced by the process/activity/program. It is the quantification of the activities of a program, it is what has been directly produced by the program in natural/physical terms. For a soup kitchen, an output could be the number of meals served on a weekly basis.

Outcome/effectiveness refers most often to the impact of the program upon its clients/recipients within the framework of the program's intended or stated goals. Unintended consequences also should be measured when possible and appropriate. As a performance measure, effectiveness can be determined in the short or long term. For example, in a summer tutoring program for high school students, a shorter term outcome indicator might be an increase in reading comprehension of program participants, and the long-term outcomes could be graduation rates from high schools.

Efficiency is often defined as inputs/resources/costs per unit of output/outcome produced, or the relationship/ratio between the amount of input and the amount of output/outcome. Efficiency measures can also be concerned with the cost of the activities per unit of output.

It should be mentioned that within the academic and professional worlds there are different definitions, terminology, and methods used in the structuring of per-

INPUTS
Resources are money and what it can buy, as well as time

- Money
- Staff
- Volunteers
- Facilities
- Equipment

PROCESS

- Activities
- Programs

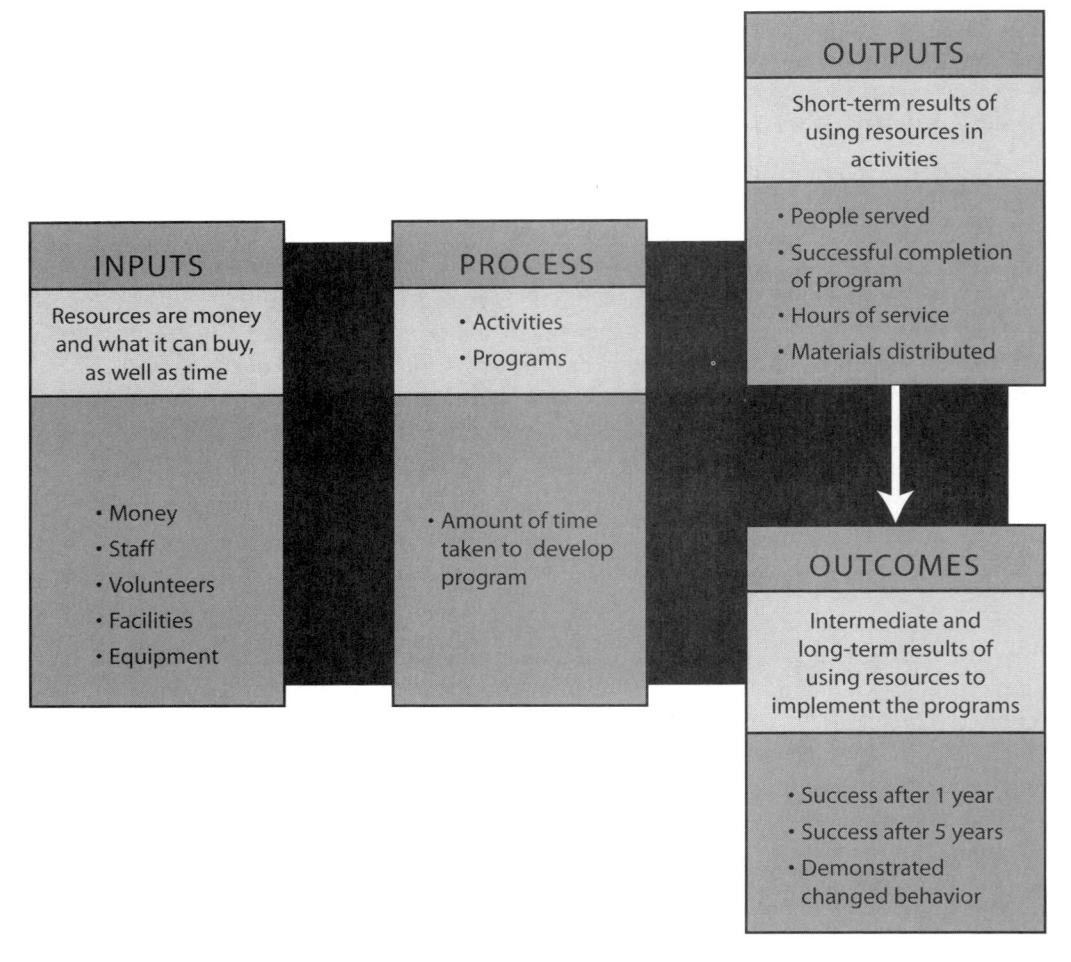

- Amount of time taken to develop program

OUTPUTS
Short-term results of using resources in activities

- People served
- Successful completion of program
- Hours of service
- Materials distributed

OUTCOMES
Intermediate and long-term results of using resources to implement the programs

- Success after 1 year
- Success after 5 years
- Demonstrated changed behavior

Figure 9.1 Understanding performance measurement.

formance measurement systems and to classify performance measures. There is no hard rule in defining and/or organizing performance measures. It is acceptable, even preferable, if the terms selected by a nonprofit serve the purposes of its mission statement and support strategic planning within the context of the general construction of a performance measurement system. We would like you to be alerted to and knowledgeable of these ongoing academic and professional discussions, but we will not get bogged down in these nomenclatures in this textbook.

Outcomes as Compared to Outputs

There are different definitions and distinctions made among scholars with regard to output and outcome measures; some distinguish them by a program's product versus its impact on intended recipients, and others define them along a timeline. For example, in the early 1960s, Dr. David Weikart and his colleagues developed the HighScope Perry Preschool Project, which was Michigan's first publicly funded preschool program. The project went on for 5 years, and evaluation of the results continues today. The participants were surveyed annually from ages 3 to 11, and again at ages 14, 15, 19, 27, and 40. The program identified and used long-term effects (termed as outcomes) of early educational programs as a key measure in assessing the program. Over this extended time period, children who were in the program had better school attendance than a comparison group, had fewer behavioral problems in school, and had lower dropout rates. Following the children into adulthood, the program found that they had greater economic success than a comparison group over an even longer term.[4]

Efficiency as Compared to Effectiveness

Efficiency measures are concerned with the costs of the activities per unit of output. For example, let's measure the cost per unit for a child who successfully completes a year of Head Start. If the Head Start program costs $300,000 to operate for 30 children who successfully complete the year, then the cost per unit is $10,000. This efficiency measure can be used to compare one Head Start program to another in terms of cost effectiveness, albeit the quality of the program is not necessarily reflected in efficiency measures.

A Head Start program may have a lower cost per unit than another, but that may say nothing about its effectiveness. Too often, state and federal governments look at the cost per unit of nonprofit programs without giving enough consideration to the effectiveness of the programs. Effectiveness is measured by successful output and outcome indicators. Effectiveness is about the quality of outputs and impacts of the program with regard to the stated objectives more often than not. If a nonprofit decides to invest more resources into a program than other nonprofits do, that nonprofit will have a greater cost per unit than other nonprofits, which may suggest to the unsophisticated mind that this program is lower in efficiency measures. But if the nonprofit has been careful in the program design, it may have a more effective program, and this effectiveness can be demonstrated through the careful measuring of outputs and outcomes.

Application of Performance Measurement

To illustrate performance measurement in a real life application, let's continue to look at Head Start as an example. Head Start is a program that seeks to improve the educational performance of preschool children from low-income families. The inputs in this context are all those resources that Head Start uses to educate the children, such as the teachers' salaries, the physical plant, supplies, materials, and equipment. Their resources are used to conduct processes/activities that will improve the children's educational performance, such as singing songs, learning the alphabet, and playing games. The outputs are the specific services or products that are produced by the process. These outputs can be measured, for example, by the number of hours spent in teaching songs, or the number of meetings/time between the instructors and the students in teaching/learning the alphabet. The short-term outcome can include the percentage of children able to recite all of the alphabet, to do complicated puzzles, to recognize numbers, and to use improved vocabulary. These are all indicators that when the Head Start children begin elementary school, they will be more likely to be successful in learning to read, write, and calculate. An intermediate outcome may be research showing that the children do better in school than similar children who do not attend Head Start. A long-term or end outcome could be that, compared with children who did not attend Head Start, more of the Head Start children graduate from high school and more attend college.

> **Box 9.1**
> **CASE IN POINT:**
> **The HighScope Perry Preschool Project**
>
> Although the Perry Preschool Project enriched the education of 3- and 4-year-olds for 2 years, the early results were disappointing. The children did not retain their gains as compared to a similar group in elementary school.
>
> "However," researchers later noted, "the Perry Preschool children had substantial improvements over their lifetimes in many critical outcomes, including graduating from high school, earning more income, and committing fewer crimes as compared to those who were not chosen to participate in the Perry Preschool program."[5]
>
> Preschool education has a profound effect on children's life success, but measuring this kind of effectiveness is costly. Most nonprofits cannot sustain post-program evaluation of their clients for many years, as was done in the case of the HighScope Perry Preschool Project, which studied the program participants for 40 years.

Development of Performance Measurement Systems

The development of a performance measurement system includes the identification of objectives and key performance measures, the institutionalization of a system, the way the data are collected and processed to produce the performance measures, the protocol for interpretation of the performance measures, and the computer system that will store, manage, and process the data over time for comparison. External stakeholders (funders, policy makers, foundations, and the like) and internal stakeholders (board members, staff, and clients) shape this process and the product.

The major institutions involved in researching, developing, and promoting performance measurement systems (or its extension into performance management) in the nonprofit sector are the Robert Wood Johnson Foundation, the Urban Institute, the Lilly Endowment, the W. K. Kellogg Foundation, and the United Way of America. The United Way has more than 1,200 community partners, and as such is insistent upon setting accountability standards. Every 3 years all local United Way partners are required to conduct a self-assessment of its financial management. Contact these institutions if you have questions or concerns in developing a performance measurement system as needed for your own organization.

The Urban Institute's Steps to Develop a Performance Measurement System

The Urban Institute, a recognized leader in performance measurement, describes it as "a process in which governmental or nongovernmental public service organizations undertake regular collection of *outcome* and/or *output* data (preferably both) throughout the year (not only at the end of the year) for at least many of its programs and services." In addition, performance management refers to "the practice of public service managers using performance data to help them make decisions so as to continually improve services to their customers."[6] These concepts conclude that data should be used to support or revise a program as needed in order to improve the efficiency or the results of that program.

According to the Urban Institute, performance measurement should be based on a nonprofit program's approach, or mission. The mission can be a road map that outlines how the nonprofit's actions can bring about the desired outcomes. Also, the mission can be visualized in the form of a logic model and depict a path toward the goals of the mission. A logic model is a chart outlining all inputs, processes, outputs, and outcomes for a particular program. It will make clear what resources are needed, what activities are required, and what short- and long-term changes will be needed to fulfill the mission of a program.[7]

Performance measurement/management systems should be maintained and reassessed on a periodic basis, so that new information and changes in circumstances are reflected in the system, although every effort should also be made, to the extent reasonable, to keep the definition of the performance measures consistent over time for comparison and interpretation.

Recognizing the difficulties in measuring outcomes and current disparities in nonprofit capacity, the Urban Institute and the Center for What Works have jointly developed a series of common outcome measures in 14 program areas. An example from one of these areas is presented in Table 9.1 and provides a glimpse of the performance outcome indicators for this area—employment and training programs.

A great deal of thought and effort goes into the creation of performance measures/indicators. Nonprofits often struggle to create performance indicators that they can afford to measure and continue to follow up on. There is still debate on

Table 9.1 Performance Outcome Indicators for Employment and Training Programs

Common Outcome	Program-Specific Outcome	Indicator	Data Collection Strategy	Outcome Stage
1. Increase access to services	Clients enroll in the program	Number and percentage of clients enrolling in the program	Internal program records	Intermediate
2. Increase participation and attendance	Clients enroll in the program	Number and percentage enrolled after the first week	Internal program records	Intermediate
3. Build skills knowledge	Increased skills	Percentage of clients passing job skills competency exams	Internal program records	Intermediate
4. Increase employment	Increased sustainable employment/retention	Number and percentage of clients in same job after X months	Surveys of clients after program completion	Intermediate/end
5. Economically empower individuals	Increased earnings	Average hourly wage of clients who become employed after training	Surveys of clients after program completion	End

Source: The Urban Institute and the Center for What Works. Outcome Indicators Project (urban.org/policy-centers/cross-center-initiatives/performance-management-measurement/projects/nonprofit-organizations/projects-focused-nonprofit-organizations/outcome-indicators-project).

the value of spending limited resources to measure and demonstrate success, although a shift to performance measurement can be observed due partly to government/funder requests and partly to the drive within nonprofits toward improvement over the long run.

The Balanced Scorecard System

Several popular performance management systems are widely used in the nonprivate and public sectors. One of the best known is the balanced scorecard system, which monitors the performance of an organization using both financial and nonfinancial information. First developed in 1992 by Robert Kaplan and David Norton, the balanced scorecard is a strategic planning and management system that uses strategic measures in addition to financial data to produce a more balanced view of performance.[8] The balanced scorecard examines an organization from four perspectives: financial (or stewardship), customer and stakeholder, internal process, and organizational capacity (or learning and growth). Designing a balanced scorecard requires selecting 3–6 good measures for each perspective. For example, the organizational capacity perspective views human capital, infrastructure, technology, and culture as key capacities for successful performance.

An example of this system is presented in Table 9.2, which illustrates an application for the United Way of Southeastern New England. As the table shows, the nonprofit developed three areas in which they wished to focus and to collect data about: financial, customer, and internal. Within each area, they created several outcomes and strategic objectives. The balanced scorecard system is comprehensive because it includes both financial and nonfinancial areas of concern for an organization, linking to strategic plan and objectives. Once the objectives are identified, the nonprofit can decide which particular performance indicators are useful for each strategic objective.

Table 9.2   Example of a Balanced Scorecard, United Way of Southeastern New England

Areas	Outcomes	Strategic Objectives
Financial	External growth	Increase net amount of funds raised
	Internal stability	Balance internal income and expenses to maintain our 100 percent guarantee to others
	Community building	Increase amount of funds that go to services Increase amount of funds that go to proprietary products
Customer	Customer satisfaction	Recognition Ease of giving
	Market growth	Products that customers care about and that will improve the community
	Customer retention	Information on results Quality, timely service
Internal	Key internal business processes based on quality	Improve processes in these areas: fundraising, fund distribution, community building, information processing, pledge processing, product development, volunteer/staff development, customer service, interdepartmental communications
	Innovative products	Develop a research and development process to come up with new, innovative products
	Viable product line	Develop a consistent process for evaluating existing products and services

The Challenges of Selecting Performance Measures/Indicators

To illustrate the development of a performance measurement/management system, let's look at a hypothetical preschool program. Many key stakeholders should be involved in the process, including potentially a steering committee, a working group, and internal and external experts in measurement and research/evaluation. The executive director may initiate the process and be on board in some fashion to establish and empower a structure and the process. The mission of the program is to prepare 3- and 4-year-old children (customers) for a successful school experience. The strategic objective is to improve the children's educational achievement; therefore, the working group needs to identify the inputs, processes, outputs, and outcomes that they wish to measure. For example, the input measures may include resources of human, financial, and technical indicators. The process measures may cover the activities the program creates in applying the resources to address and to achieve the intended objectives of the program. The output and outcome measures may include the curriculum for the children, the number of teacher-student meetings, improved attendance and behavior, and comprehension of learning material. The working group needs to specifically create pre- and posttests to measure the children's educational progress. It potentially needs to find and verify reliable tests by consulting early childhood experts. The internal and external experts, and other stakeholders involved, may need to find other programs in the area with which they can compare their children with. Only after all the performance measures and measurement techniques are considered, tested, and key stakeholders satisfied, can they start implementing the performance measurement program.

Data Collection

It is essential that nonprofit managers develop and/or select performance measures and collect valid and reliable data carefully. For example, a nonprofit wishes to start an after-school recreational program. Two of the nonprofit's performance measures include attendance rate and improved behavior. This sounds reasonable until we consider how these two indicators are to be measured. Attendance is easy—the staff can take and log attendance every day. Getting a handle on improved behavior proves to be more difficult. In addition to selecting proven and established valid and reliable measures, the staff would need to be trained on these measures in order to identify and keep track of changes in the behavior of children who are participating in the nonprofit's program. Performance indicators are important, but how to measure these indicators should also be taken into consideration when developing performance measures in advance.

Relationship between Performance Measurement and Program Evaluation

Managers and donors want to know if their programs are successful: Are the programs implemented as planned? Do the programs accomplish what they intend to do? Program evaluation is a highly related approach to, or an extension of, performance measurement, with a focus on accurately establishing attribution of the observed changes on outcome measures of the program. A good program evaluation answers the following questions:

- What are the program's cost and efficiency?
- What are the program's outcomes?

- Has the program been implemented as planned?
- What is the program design and logic model associated with this program?
- To what extent is there a need for the program?[9]

Performance measurement is often considered an important part of program evaluation (and vise versa) by performance management and evaluation scholars. Performance measurement and program evaluation have become more and more significant for nonprofit managers from the perspectives of both program improvement and accountability. In addition to ongoing performance measurements, many foundations, institutions, and government agencies require nonprofits to perform periodic program evaluations. As measuring performance has become more sophisticated, so too has program evaluation.

Program evaluation not only measures performance but also analyzes and quantifies the extent to which the results, if there are any, can be attributed to the program, and not to other factors that may confound the results. A well-designed program evaluation can provide a clear picture of a program's performance in the context of a confluence of many changes/covaries that directly and indirectly affect the issues that the program intends to address.

Economic evaluation, including cost-benefit analysis (to be discussed in more detail in Chapter 10), calculates the net value that programs create and justifies the programs in terms of resource generation and allocation. Cost-benefit analysis requires the quantification of social benefits and societal costs in common monetary terms so that comparisons can be made economically and consistently across programs. The results of the cost-benefit comparison can be used to judge the economic value of a program, which supports program decision making.

Social and environmental benefits are often difficult to measure and even more difficult to quantify in monetary terms. Small nonprofits can call upon institutions and consultants for help in these areas; for nonprofits that can afford it, in-house expertise in program evaluation is handy. An excellent example of providing a performance measurement system and evaluation of a program's effectiveness is the work of Metis Associates in Georgia. In 2006, the Foster Family Foundation worked with Georgia's Department of Family and Children Services to create EMBRACE, an initiative that worked to recruit and support foster families. Metis conducted an implementation and impact evaluation of the program and found that the retention of foster care families had increased significantly. Not surprisingly, the Georgia legislature wanted to know how cost-effective this highly successful program was. How much more did these enhancements benefit the state and were they worth the cost? In response, Metis Associates implemented a return on investment (ROI) model, a simple method in quantifying cost-effectiveness. In calculating ROI, the return produced by an investment is divided by the cost of the investment. The exact formula is as follows:

$$\text{ROI} = \frac{\text{Gain of Investment} - \text{Cost of Investment}}{\text{Cost of Investment}}$$

Using data from their performance measurement system, Metis determined that the EMBRACE program produced a 22% ROI in the first year of statewide implementation. The Georgia legislature continued to fund EMBRACE across the state in part because of the work of Metis Associates, which linked the dollars spent to performance, an economic program evaluation.[10]

This brief discussion on program evaluation does not do justice to such an important and complex subject and its practices. For continued studies, interested readers should seek out the many textbooks available on performance measurement and program evaluation.

Conclusion

Performance measurement for nonprofits can be commonly defined as the process of collecting, analyzing, and/or reporting information regarding the performance of a nonprofit on a regular basis. Designing a performance measurement system of performance measures/indicators, defining the frequency, sources, and method for data collection, securing the system/software to manage, analyze, and report the resulting information properly requires leadership and technical support from within the organization and potentially from external sources. There is no right or wrong performance measurement system that all nonprofits should adhere to. There is no system that is cast in stone in its conceptualization, the definition of terms, the process of its development, or its application, although general ideals to advance the mission of the nonprofit in terms of program improvement and stakeholder accountability in the context of strategic planning and budgeting is often involved. Each nonprofit develops and uses a performance measurement system differently, as long as it serves its purposes well in the particular context it operates.

Over time, nonprofits have learned a great deal about how to develop and apply performance measurement systems, but many nonprofits still face challenges, including serious cost issues when implementing performance measures. Too often, data are collected but never analyzed, so making sense and good use of the data is difficult. Nonprofits generally find it hard to raise funding to specifically put a performance measurement system in place, which is often deemed as channeling resources away from actual program delivery, but performance measurement systems must be in place before nonprofits can fully measure and demonstrate program accountability and effectiveness, and improve the program as needed.

KEY TERMS

effectiveness   efficiency   inputs   outcomes   outputs   process

DISCUSSION QUESTIONS

1. What is performance management?
2. What are inputs? Give an example of one.

3. What are outputs? Give an example of one.
4. What are outcomes? Give an example of one.
5. What is efficiency?
6. What is effectiveness?
7. What is performance-based budgeting?
8. What role has the U.S. government played in promoting performance measurement?
9. Describe the balanced scorecard system and explain its value.
10. What is the difference between program evaluation and performance measurement?

SUGGESTED READINGS

Brown, Madeline, Matt Eldridge, and Brian Bieretz (2019, July). *Performance-Based Strategies: Defining Terms and Comparing Common Strategies*. Washington, DC: Urban Institute (urban.org/sites/default/files/publication/100452/performance-based_strategies_defining_terms_and_comparing_common_strategies_2.pdf).

Hatry, Harry P. (1999). *Performance Measurement: Getting Results*. Washington, DC: Urban Institute Press.

Hatry, Harry P. (2014, July). *Transforming Performance Measurement for the 21st Century*. Washington, DC: Urban Institute (files.eric.ed.gov/fulltext/ED559312.pdf).

Kaplan, Robert S. (2001). "Strategic Performance Measurement and Management in Nonprofit Organizations." *Nonprofit Management & Leadership*, 11(3).

National Council of Nonprofits (2020). Evaluation and Measurement of Outcomes (councilofnonprofits.org/tools-resources/evaluation-and-measurement-of-outcomes).

Zietlow, John, Jo Ann Hankin, Alan G. Seidner, and Tim O'Brien (2018). *Financial Management for Nonprofit Organizations: Policies and Practices* (3rd ed.). Hoboken, NJ: Wiley.

CASE STUDY

MENTORING PROGRAM TO REINTEGRATE EX-PRISONERS INTO THE COMMUNITY

The U.S. Department of Justice has announced that it is seeking applications/request for proposals for funding for nonprofits to start a mentoring program. The grants are based upon Public Law 110-199, the Second Chance Act of 2007, which authorizes grants to nonprofits that create mentoring programs to promote the reintegration of people released from prison into the community. *Mentoring* is defined loosely; it can be a one-on-one or a small group relationship, but it must take place in both prerelease and post release environments. Nonprofits can provide transitional services, which can include, but are not limited to, prerelease mentoring relationships, housing, education, substance abuse treatment, mental health treatment, family reunification, job training, and case management. If you are responding to this request for proposals, what kinds of performance measures would you propose to be included in the submission?

Assignments

Assignment 9.1. Measures/Indicators of Program Performance

Identify each of the following as an input, process indicator, output, intermediate outcome, or long-term outcome.

1. The number of students completing an employment and training program
2. The number of staff hired for the nonprofit's computer lab
3. The number of students who were placed in a job after graduating from an employment and training program
4. The number of students who stayed on a job for 6 months after graduating from an employment and training program
5. The supplies used in the employment and training program
6. The attendance rate of the students in the employment and training program
7. The process used to screen unwanted applicants from the program
8. The copier used in the employment and training program
9. Number of children attending an after-school program
10. Number of staff needed for an after-school program
11. Amount of materials used in an after-school program
12. Graduation rate of students who attended a preschool program as compared to a control group
13. Improvement in behavior at a high school
14. Graduation rate from a high school

Assignment 9.2. Working within the Balanced Scorecard Framework

Within the balanced scorecard framework, what could be the outcome, the strategic objective, and performance indicators for the problem of overspending in a nonprofit?

Assignment 9.3. Developing a Performance Management System

You are the chief financial officer (CFO) of a nonprofit that has just received a conditional grant to expand its probation program for newly released prisoners in a major urban center of Virginia. Each probation officer carries a caseload of 10 prisoners on probation. In addition, the nonprofit operates 5 days of meetings each week for an Alcoholics Anonymous program as well as for a Narcotics Anonymous program for any prisoners on probation.

The foundation that supports your nonprofit has requested that your organization develop a performance measurement system. The foundation is particularly interested in doing what it can to improve the morale of probation officers, who are struggling with high caseloads. The nonprofit must create input, output, and outcome measures. As CFO, you are asked to work with program staff to develop a set of performance measures that will be included in the foundation's performance measurement system.

1. What steps should you take to develop the performance measurement system?
2. What types of performance measures/indicators should you use for inputs, outputs, and outcomes?
3. Are there any process performance indicators you can develop?
4. What about efficiency measures?
5. What about effectiveness measures?

Assignment 9.4. Identifying Similarities and Differences

Discuss briefly the key similarities and differences between performance measurement and program evaluation.

Notes

[1] President Bill Clinton, statement at the signing of the Government Performance and Results Act, August 3, 1993.
[2] Hatry, Harry P. (1999). *Performance Measurement: Getting Results.* Washington, DC: Urban Institute.
[3] Mayor's Office of Operations, New York City (2020). Mayor's Management Report (nyc.gov/site/operations/performance/mmr.page).
[4] For more information about the HighScope Perry Preschool Study, see highscope.org/?s=highscope+perry+preschool+study.
[5] Schweinhart, Lawrence J., Jeanne Montie, Zongping Xiang, W. Steven Barnett, Clive R. Belfield, and Milagros Nores (2005). *Lifetime Effects: The High/Scope Perry Preschool Study through Age 40.* Ypsilanti, MI: High/Scope Press.
[6] Hatry, Harry P. (2014, July). *Transforming Performance Measurement for the 21st Century.* Washington, DC: Urban Institute (files.eric.ed.gov/fulltext/ED559312.pdf).
[7] Tatian, Peter A. (2016). *Performance Measurement to Evaluation.* Washington, DC: Urban Institute (urban.org/research/publication/performance-measurement-evaluation-0).
[8] Balanced Scorecard Institute. Balanced Scorecard Basics (balancedscorecard.org/bsc-basics-overview).
[9] Rossi, Peter H., Mark W. Lipsey, and Gary T. Henry (2018). *Evaluation: A Systematic Approach* (8th ed.). Thousand Oaks, CA: Sage.
[10] Metis Associates (2009). *Georgia's Foster Family Initiative: EMBRACE.* New York: Metis Associates.

10
Time Value of Money and Cost-Benefit Analysis

> A nickel ain't worth a dime anymore.
>
> —Yogi Berra

Learning Objectives

The learning objectives for this chapter are as follows:
- Understanding the concepts and formulas of the time value of money
- Applying the time value of money in financial analysis
- Learning about cost-benefit analysis in the nonprofit sector
- Applying cost-benefit analysis in investment decision making in nonprofit organizations

*T*ime value of money is an important concept in financial analysis and management. It applies to almost every aspect of long-term financial planning, from household mortgage applications, to government decisions to build transportation facilities, to business investment in new production lines. In this chapter we introduce the concept of the time value of money and provide examples of typical applications of it in nonprofit organizations. We then use time value of money as a building block to introduce cost-benefit analysis, an economic evaluation method for project and investment decision making.

The Time Value of Money

The concept of the **time value of money** reflects the fact that money available at the present time is worth more than money of the same amount to be available in a distant future. Financial managers in nonprofit organizations can benefit from understanding and using this concept in long-term financial planning and investment decision making. For instance, a new program often makes cash outflows for start-up costs in anticipation of future operational net cash inflows as a result of the investment. Given that money differs in value at different points in time, however, future cash flows must be adjusted, i.e., discounted, before the net gain or loss of an investment can be determined.

> **Box 10.1**
>
> **REMEMBER: The Time Value of Money**
>
> A core principle of finance is that, since money can earn interest under normal economic and financial circumstances, it is worth more to have a dollar in hand than a dollar to be received in the future.

The concept of the time value of money is rooted in not only financial applications, but also personal beliefs. It can be demonstrated from several different perspectives. First, people are concerned about inflation. The purchasing power of money decreases as the general price level of goods and services rises over time. Second, people are concerned about opportunity cost. Money can be invested for future gains if not used for current consumption. For example, when money is put into interest-bearing vehicles, such as a savings account in a bank, it earns interest; over time, the balance will grow, and a dollar today will become more than a dollar in the future. Third, people in general prefer to receive benefits sooner rather than later—this gives rise to higher valuations of money at present than of money to be received in the future. The degree of preference varies between cultures and among demographic and social groups. Finally, all future monies are promises that bear a degree of uncertainty. We do not know for sure what economic conditions lay ahead, nor do we know what our own life events will entail. This is especially true as people age.

Time value of money is an important concept in financial decision making. Most nonprofits have had the experience of borrowing money from banks to cover short-term cash fluctuations; the lenders are paid back the principal with interest. In addition, a central consideration of time value of money is long-term financial planning, such as capital budgeting. A set of terms has been developed around this concept, including *present value, future value, annuity,* and *net present value*. A series of computational methods and computer applications have also been developed to facilitate the conversion of future value and present value, among other related calculations used in financial analysis and management.

A key concept in the time value of money calculation is interest. Interest is paid to compensate lenders, as well as savers, for the use of their money over a specified duration. The **interest rate** is the percentage rate at which interest is calculated. It reflects the societal valuation of the time value of money and often is determined in the marketplace, such as bank lending rates for different risks and different maturities. Interest rate is a fundamental parameter in investment decision making and capital budgeting.

A related concept is the number of periods when the interest is calculated. Periods are evenly spaced intervals of time, not necessarily in years, although that is often the case. The length and number of periods relate to the frequency of compounding, which we will discuss further in the next section.

An **annuity** is a series of equally spaced payments made in equal amounts. Payments may be positive (i.e., receipts) or negative (i.e., outlays). Again, an annuity does not necessarily imply annual. The time period for payment can, for example, be quarterly, monthly, or daily. For instance, you probably pay your office or home rent in equal monthly payments.

Using this framework, analysts and decision makers can calculate the future value, present value, and net present value of cash inflows and cash outflows. In the following sections we introduce the formulas for these values, followed by examples of applications in the nonprofit world.

Calculating Future Value

Future value refers to the amount of money at a specified date in the future that is equivalent in value to a specified amount today. Future value can be calculated from the current amount, the interest rate, and the number of periods into the future. There are two ways to calculate the future value of a present amount: the simple interest rate method and the compound interest rate method, depending on the circumstance.

Simple Interest Rate Method. The simple interest rate method adds the interest to the principal at the end of the period. The interest is calculated based on the principal only, without taking into consideration any interest that has been earned over the prior periods. The simple rate method is not commonly used in financial decision making in real applications.

Compound Interest Rate Method. In the compound interest rate method, interest is earned not only on the principal but also on any interest accumulated in previous investment periods. Suppose that you put $100 in a bank account at a yearly 10% interest rate. At the end of 1 year, you will earn $10 interest. With the interest added to the $100 original principal, you will have $110 in your account. This is expressed mathematically as follows:

$$FV = \$100 \times (1 + .10) = \$110$$

If you invest the $110 (i.e., the initial principal plus the interest) next year at the same 10% interest rate, you will get $11 interest. Adding it to the $110 principal, the account will grow to a total of $121.

$$FV = \$100 \times (1 + .10) \times (1 + .10) = \$100 \times (1 + .10)^2 = \$121$$

If you continue to invest the principal plus interest in the third year, the account will be $133.10 at the end of the year:

$$FV = \$100 \times (1 + .10) \times (1 + .10) \times (1 + .10) = \$100 \times (1 + .10)^3 = \$133.10$$

If you simplify the method shown above, the following formula (Equation 10.1) can be used to calculate the total future value of your bank account at the end of year n:

$$FV = PV \times (1 + i)^n \qquad (10.1)$$

where

FV = future value of your investment
PV = present value of your investment (the principal)
i = the interest rate
n = the number of compounding time periods

The future value calculation has plenty of applications in financial decision making in nonprofit organizations. For example, suppose you are the CFO of the ABC Nonprofit Organization and you establish a reserve fund for future equipment replacements. You can invest in a fund that pays a 5% interest rate on an annual basis. You would like to know what the amount will be in 5 years if you invest $5,000 today. This question can be solved easily if you apply Equation 10.1.

$$FV = \$5,000 \times (1 + .05)^5 = \$6,381.41$$

A more involved future value calculation involves a series of cash flows in future time periods. Suppose that your nonprofit organization does not have a lump sum to invest now for the reserve fund but can regularly put a small amount of money into it for future equipment replacements. For example, how much would the nonprofit have if it puts $2,000 in a bank account at the end of each year for 5 years if the bank interest rate remains the same (5%)?

This type of problem involves periodic equal investment/payments at evenly spaced intervals into an interest-bearing account that permits interest to be reinvested at the same rate for compounding. This is an annuity, as defined earlier, and its calculation for future value is expressed in Equation 10.2:

$$FV = PMT \left[\frac{(1+i)^n - 1}{i} \right] \qquad (10.2)$$

where

PMT = amount of payment or receipt
i = interest rate
n = number of compounding time periods

Using Equation 10.2, the future value of the $2,000 annual investment at end of each year for 5 years will be:

$$FV = \$2{,}000 \left[\frac{(1+0.05)^5 - 1}{0.05} \right]$$
$$= \$11{,}051.26$$

The future value of annuities formula can be rearranged to solve for regular payments, given the amount that will be required or expected at a specified future time. Suppose that you need to replace a delivery truck for meals for homebound persons in 5 years, and the cost of the truck is $100,000. Assume also that the nonprofit could put money at the end of each year into its bank account at a 5% interest rate. How much money does the nonprofit need to put into the bank account yearly so that it will have enough funds to purchase the truck at the end of the fifth year?

You can answer this question by making a minor modification to Equation 10.2. You can solve for the amount of the yearly payment by dividing the future value by the compounding interest calculation.

$$PMT = \frac{FV}{\left[\frac{(1+i)^n - 1}{i} \right]} \quad (10.3)$$

Returning to our example, plug in the interest rate, the future value, and the number of years into Equation 10.3 and you get

$$PMT = \frac{\$100{,}000}{\left[\frac{(1+0.05)^5 - 1}{0.05} \right]}$$
$$= \$18{,}097.48$$

This is a bit more involved mathematically. Fortunately, most spreadsheet software programs, such as Excel, have ready-made functions for time value of money calculations. What you need to do is to select any cell in an Excel spreadsheet, click on the Formulas tab found near the top of the screen, click on the Financial dropdown menu and select PMT, and input the required parameters: i, n, and FV in this case. (See Figure 10.1. The negative sign in the results indicates a cash outflow.) In the Excel formula bar, you should see the following entry: "=PMT(0.05,5,,100000)". This will produce the same results as Equation 10.3. (See Figure 10.2.)

Calculating Present Value

We have discussed the concepts and developed formulas to calculate the future value of a single present amount and an annuity, and applied them in financial analysis cases in nonprofit organizations. Conversely, we can calculate the **present value** of a future amount and an annuity. The derivation of the present value formula

198 Chapter Ten

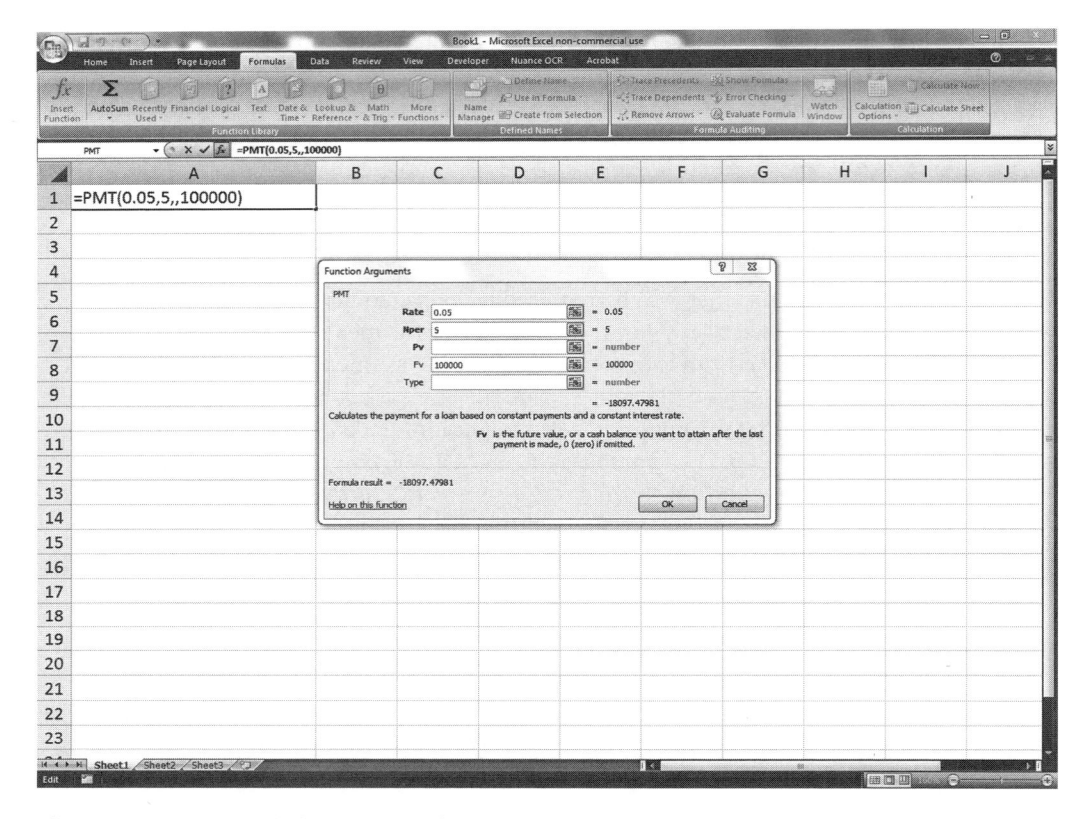

Figure 10.1 In Excel, the Payment function calculates the payment for a loan based on constant payments and a constant interest rate.

(Equation 10.4) is simple, it is accomplished just by dividing the factor, $(1 + i)^n$, from both sides of Equation 10.1.

$$PV = \frac{FV}{(1+i)^n} \qquad (10.4)$$

This formula, among many other applications, can be used to calculate the present value of future cash flow(s), so that different cash flows at different times can be compared using the same metrics of the present time.

For example, a donor promises a $1 million contribution in 10 years. The nonprofit, however, has been offered the alternative option of receiving $800,000 if it would like to have the contribution now. Knowing that you can invest the money in an interest-bearing account that earns 5% interest per year, is it a good idea to ask for the cash now ($800,000) and invest it, or wait to receive the full amount ($1,000,000) in 10 years?

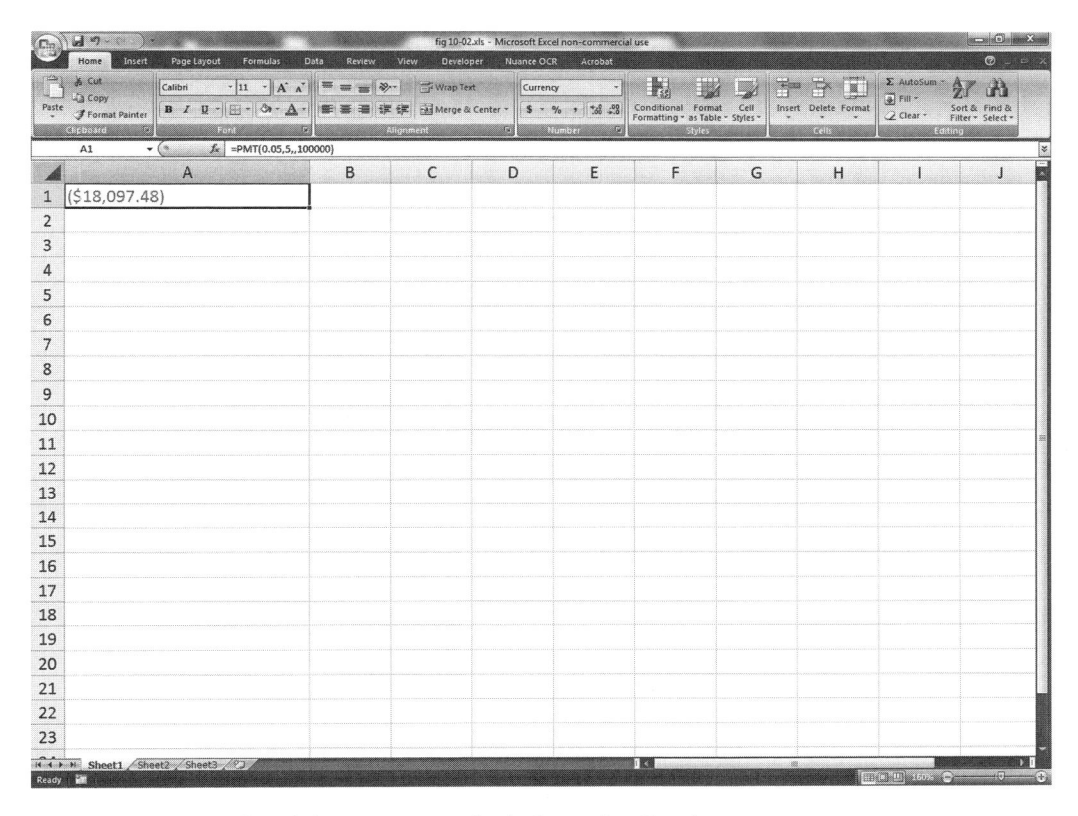

Time Value of Money and Cost-Benefit Analysis   199

Figure 10.2   Results of the payment calculation using Excel.

You can answer this question by calculating the present value of the future amount and then compare it with the amount offered at present. Using Equation 10.4 you get the present value of this future amount:

$$PV = \frac{\$1,000,000}{(1+0.05)^{10}}$$
$$= \$613,913.25$$

The present value of $1,000,000 that could be received 10 years from now is $613,913.25. Given that the present value is lower than what has been offered to you as the alternative option, it is wise for you to accept the $800,000 now. This formula can also be found in Excel. As discussed earlier, you can click on the Formulas tab found near the top of the screen, click on the Financial drop-down menu and select PV, and input the required parameters—that is, i, n, and FV in this case. See Figures 10.3 and 10.4.

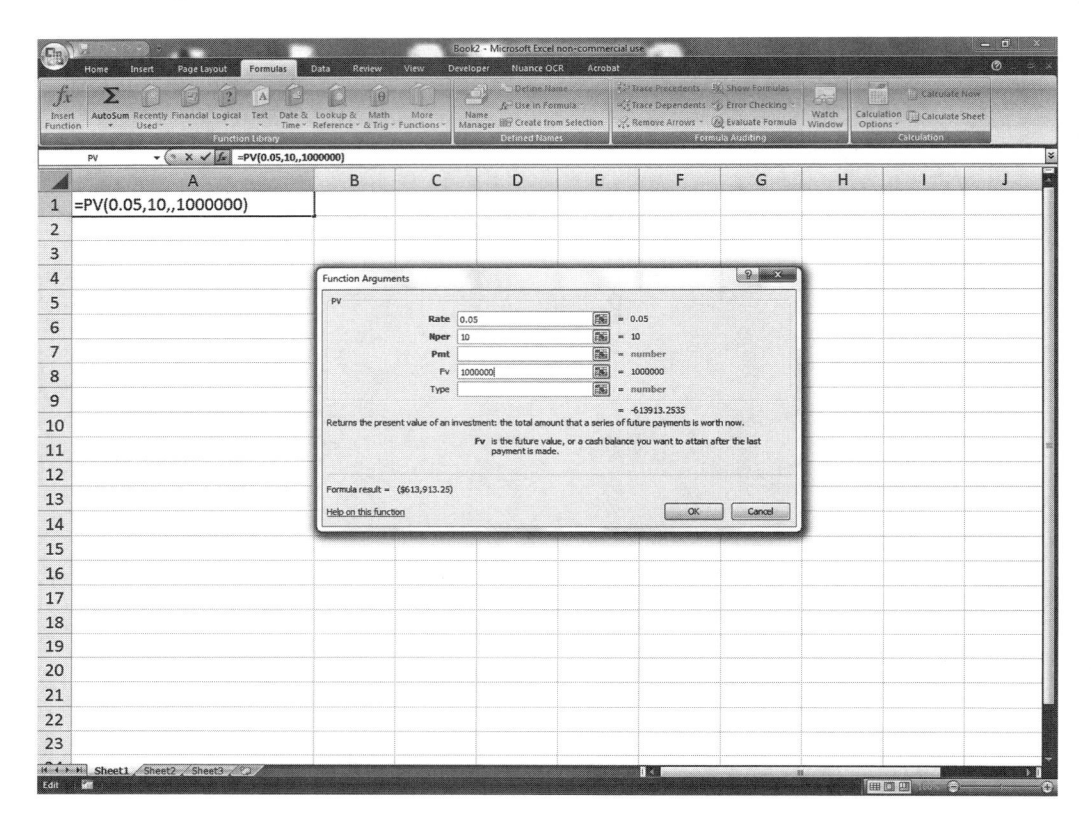

Figure 10.3 In Excel, the Present Value function calculates the total amount that a series of future payments is worth now.

The present value of an annuity, similar to the future value of an annuity, can be expressed in the following formula:

$$PV = PMT \times \left[\frac{1 - \frac{1}{(1+i)^n}}{i} \right] \tag{10.5}$$

Nonprofits need to calculate the present value of annuities under many different circumstances, such as making purchase decisions when the main concern is determining the most economical choice. This is often called discounted future cash-flow investment analysis. For instance, the executive director of a nonprofit is considering the purchase of a refrigerator for the nonprofit's soup kitchen. The choices have been narrowed down to two brand names, both of which could serve the nonprofit equally well. The main consideration, therefore, is costs, both the initial purchasing price and operating costs. Given that the equipment will last for 5 years, the timing of the cash flows should be taken into consideration.

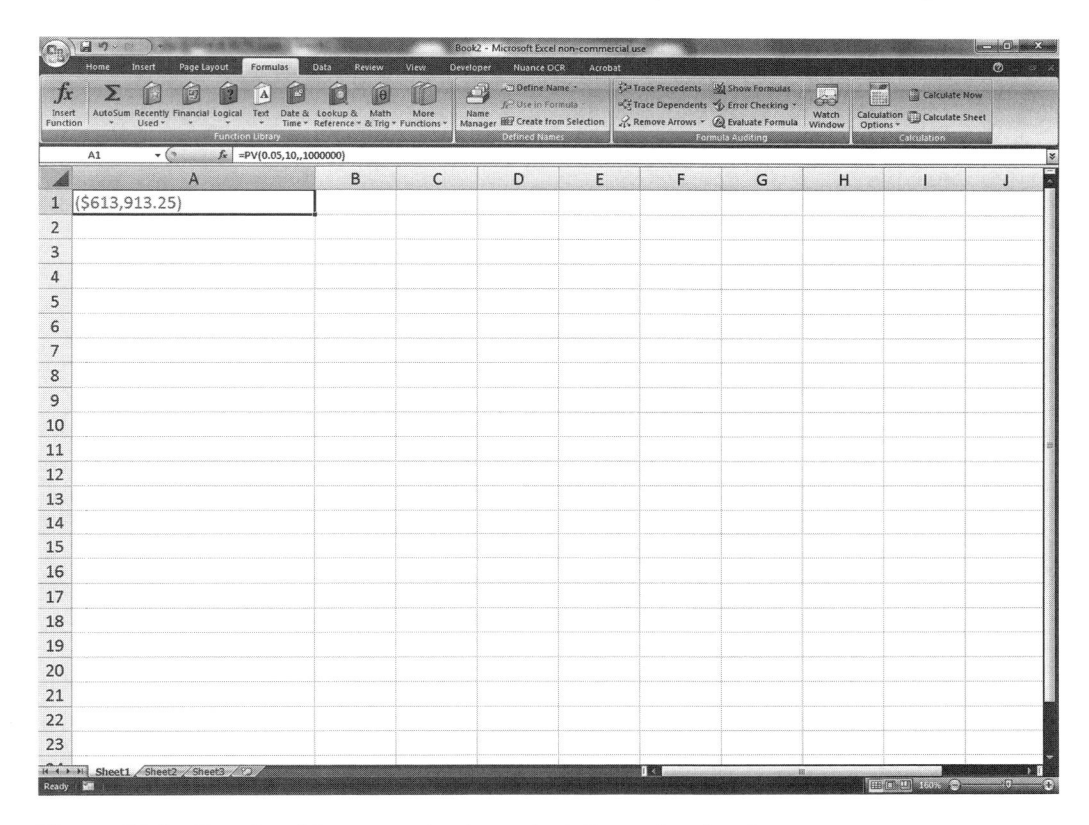

Figure 10.4 Results of the present value calculation using Excel.

Based on information collected, the two refrigerators would incur cash outflows as shown in Table 10.1. Apparently, model A is more expensive to buy but less costly to operate and maintain. Model B is just the opposite, less pricey but more expensive to run. Which one will be more economical to own and operate by the nonprofit organization? Or which one should the organization buy, taking into consideration the initial costs and operating expenses?

Table 10.1 Purchasing and Operating Costs of Alternative Refrigerators

Year	Cost	Model A	Model B
0	Purchasing	$5,000	$4,000
1	Operating and Maintenance	$1,000	$1,200
2	Operating and Maintenance	$1,000	$1,200
3	Operating and Maintenance	$1,000	$1,200
4	Operating and Maintenance	$1,000	$1,200
5	Operating and Maintenance	$1,000	$1,200

The solution to this problem requires the calculation and summation of two present values of costs, the purchasing price and the operating costs. At year 0, the present value of the purchasing price is the same as the list price. The present value of the operating costs for subsequent years requires the calculation of the present value of annuities, with the known yearly interest rate of 5% over a period of 5 years. If we plug these parameters into Equation 10.5 and add to that the initial purchasing price, we get the following results:

For refrigerator A:

Present value of costs = $5,000 + $1,000 × {1 − [1/(1 + 0.05)^5]/0.05} = $9,329

For refrigerator B:

Present value of costs = $4,000 + $1,200 × {1 − [1/(1 + 0.05)^5]/0.05} = $9,195

Given that the two refrigerators function equally well and refrigerator B costs less, the executive director decides to purchase model B, based purely on economic considerations. This is a simplified, even trivial case for illustration of the concept and procedure of the present value of annuities. Much more complex and substantive cases, including the construction or purchase of large facilities, are resolved regularly using the principle and method of the time value of money.

Net Present Value: A Decision Criterion

The above examples illustrate financial decision making when taking into consideration the time value of money in the nonprofit organization context. Not all cases, however, are as simple as these. Often both cash inflows and cash outflows occur at different points in time in long-term financial planning and analysis. The cash flows are not necessarily evenly spaced and in equal amounts. Moreover, decision makers are most concerned about net gains or losses of an investment, relative to the net gains or losses of other alternatives, within the constraints of their budgets and the condition of the larger economy. These questions require the calculation of the net present value of a project or investment, taking into account the time value of money.

Net present value is defined as the difference between cash inflows and cash outflows, both of which are discounted to their present values. It measures the net gain or loss of an investment, project, or program. The general formula to calculate net present value is presented in Equation 10.6.

$$NPV = \sum_{t=0}^{n} \frac{(b_t - c_t)}{(1+i)^t} \qquad (10.6)$$

where
NPV = net present value
b = cash inflows
c = cash outflows
i = discount rate
t = time period
n = number of time periods

It also is used as a criterion in decision making based on common sense, although economists may call it efficiency. Depending on the results of a NPV calculation, it can tell us how to view an investment:

- If NPV is greater than 0, then the project/investment creates value, and consequently we accept the project.
- If NPV is less than 0, then the project/investment destroys value, and we therefore reject the project.
- If NPV is equal to 0, then the project/investment neither creates nor destroys value, and consequently we are indifferent to the project.

For example, let's assume you are the chief financial officer of a university. The university is considering establishing a new research center for green energy corresponding to a new federally sponsored initiative. Your initial analysis indicates that this new research center will bring $3 million per year in operating revenue to the university. It will cost the university approximately $1 million to run the center each year. The start-up cost of the center is estimated to be $10 million, primarily for equipment acquisition, and the center will end its operation in about 5 years, with no residual value for the equipment purchased. From an initial investigation of financing, you are aware that the best loan you can get from banks will have an interest rate of 5%. (See Table 10.2 for the relevant data.) Would establishing the center be a good investment from the university's financial viewpoint?

You can answer this question by using Equation 10.6 (see the last column of Table 10.3). Adding the present value over time (netting the present value of the cash inflows of the cash outflow, the initial investment), you can find the net present value of the potential investment (see the bottom row of Table 10.3). Given that the net present value is negative, which indicates there is a net loss if the new research center project is undertaken, you recommend that the university not accept the project in its present form. Negotiations of better terms to increase revenues or possible ways to decrease costs should be investigated and pursued if appropriate.

It should be noted that the above analysis is based purely on financial considerations. The green energy project may potentially have substantial impacts on the economy and the environment in addition to its effects on the university, and so it should also be evaluated from a societal benefit perspective. If such an evaluation

Table 10.2 Future Cash Flows for Research Center Project (in thousands of dollars)

Year	Cash Out	Cash In	Net Cash Flow
0	($10,000)	$0	($10,000)
1	($1,000)	$3,000	$2,000
2	($1,000)	$3,000	$2,000
3	($1,000)	$3,000	$2,000
4	($1,000)	$3,000	$2,000
5	($1,000)	$3,000	$2,000

Table 10.3 Discounted Cash Flows and NPV for Research Center Project (in thousands of dollars)

Year	Cash Out	Cash In	Net Cash Flow	Present Value
0	($10,000)	$0	($10,000)	($10,000)
1	($1,000)	$3,000	$2,000	$1,905
2	($1,000)	$3,000	$2,000	$1,814
3	($1,000)	$3,000	$2,000	$1,728
4	($1,000)	$3,000	$2,000	$1,645
5	($1,000)	$3,000	$2,000	$1,567
Net Present Value				($1,341)

determines that the project is likely to have sizable positive impacts on the society at large, the university could use this information in negotiating with local and/or federal governments for improved funding. Moreover, nonprofit financial managers should keep in mind that financial resources are always a means to achieve the mission of the nonprofit, and therefore rules that determine financial decisions can and sometimes should be overridden internally when conflict with the mission arises.

Introduction to Cost-Benefit Analysis

The preceding sections have discussed time value of money, a technique and a foundation in financial management with applications in discounted future cash-flow investment analysis. In this section we utilize the time value of money technique in the development of an analytical framework: cost-benefit analysis. The exposition of cost-benefit analysis is necessarily brief given the breadth of this textbook. However, this section will introduce you to the basic concepts and demonstrate step-by-step applications so that you can perform the basic analysis by yourself or be able to select the right internal or external evaluator with an appreciation of his or her quality of work.

Conceptual Framework of Cost-Benefit Analysis

Cost-benefit analysis (CBA), or social cost-benefit analysis, as it applies to public and nonprofit organizations, constitutes a more comprehensive form of economic evaluation than the discounted future cash-flow investment analysis discussed above. While some forms of analysis focus on the financial impacts of a program or investment on the nonprofit organization, a CBA seeks to quantify both the costs and benefits from a broader perspective, including the benefits and costs to society at large. Moreover, CBA by definition quantifies impacts into a common monetary denominator, allowing policy makers to compare projects, programs, or investments in diverse policy and program domains. For example, CBA enables government decision makers and foundation grant reviewers to compare programs from different service areas, such as health care, education, arts, and social and human services.

CBA is often the tool decision makers use when choosing which programs to support on an allocative efficiency basis. Programs are chosen based on the value they create, as measured by net present value. Although governments and foundations have many other criteria in making project decisions, such as cost-effectiveness analysis (where the cost is monetized while the effect remains in substantive units), CBA provides the consistent conceptual framework and the economic rationale. Nonprofit organizations, especially larger ones, also use this framework in their investment decisions internally, for example, in facility investment and equipment purchasing.

Two main categories of CBA are ex ante analysis and ex post analysis. They are easily distinguishable, and they serve different purposes. *Ex ante CBA* allows the analyst to investigate and compare potential programs or program components to inform decision makers as to which program to choose, or none at all. *Ex post CBA* is performed after the fact, and its main purpose is to assess the efficiency of an implemented program, usually as part of an overall program evaluation. It is used primarily for accountability auditing, deciding on the net worth of the program concerned. The information generated can be used for decisions regarding expansion, improvement, or termination of an existing project, program, or investment.

Steps in Conducting Cost-Benefit Analysis

CBA is a complex and iterative process, but given that this textbook is designed for nonprofit managers, we will introduce the methods in a linear, step-by-step fashion. Taking the risk of oversimplification, we believe this approach will give you hands-on knowledge and skills that you can practice immediately at work. "Practice makes perfect" makes great sense in nonprofit financial management.

As Boardman et al. explain, a cost-benefit analysis can be broken down into the following key steps:[1]

- Determining standing and perspectives
- Determining alternatives or basis for comparison
- Listing impacts
- Monetizing impacts, including both costs and benefits
- Discounting future impacts
- Calculating and using net present value as decision rule
- Performing sensitivity analysis
- Selecting the alternative with the largest net social benefits

Determining Standing, Perspectives, and Alternatives or Basis for Comparison. CBA starts with deciding standing, that is, whose interests count. In economic evaluation of nonprofit projects, the concept of social cost-benefit analysis is often invoked, wherein the interests of all the people in the jurisdiction are taken into consideration. In reality, the decision about who has standing is often determined by the project sponsor and the nonprofit organization that provides the services. Clients of the program should have standing, although in plenty of cases their interests are not given adequate attention. Multiple perspectives—from the sponsoring agency, the nonprofit organization, the clients, and the society at large—are encouraged in comprehensive CBA, if deemed useful and feasible.

A basis for comparison must also be selected. In order to generate meaningful information, a proposed capital investment or new program should be evaluated in comparison with existing investments or programs. At least two explicitly expressed and commonly used bases for comparison are the status quo and an alternative. Status quo refers to the continued allocation of resources to an existing program—a theater needs maintenance, an old refrigerator costs electricity to run. An alternative refers to a new recipient of those resources; instead of maintaining a piece of worn-out equipment an evaluation is done based on the potential replacement cost and the potential savings the new equipment may bring. All the costs and the benefits of how resources are spent should be estimated or calculated incrementally for the organization as a whole, with and without the proposed change.

Listing, Monetizing, and Discounting Impacts. An appropriately designed CBA strives to identify and assess all material program impacts. It is relatively easy to identify financial impacts; however, nonfinancial or societal costs and benefits (for example, impacts on the environment) may not be identified as easily. Other challenges in identifying impacts include establishing cause-effect relationships and determining what might happen if the program is not implemented. In some cases, neither the nature of the relationship nor the type of impact is readily known. This is especially true when the investment or program addresses complex social issues. For example, determining whether a given program reduces crime is difficult to quantify in some instances because the causal factors underpinning crime are plentiful, and the interactions among them to determine crime rates are not well understood. Given these factors, many nonprofits focus on financial impacts in their limited uses of cost-benefit analysis. Nonprofit financial managers should strive to include all impacts in the future when resources and knowledge render it feasible.

All identified impacts should be monetized for CBA into cash flows. Appropriate economic valuation methods—that is, opportunity cost and willingness to pay—should be used to assign monetary values to inputs and impacts. For example, the implementation of public policies or the decision to invest in capital assets requires the use of resources, often referred to as start-up costs. These inputs, if not used for the particular program under consideration, could be used for other productive ends. Consequently, the resources used as inputs for investments or interventions should be valued at their opportunity cost. The opportunity cost of a resource represents the value that society must forgo, which could be measured theoretically by the second-best use. For example, the limited funds used for a drug treatment program cannot simultaneously be used for housing the homeless drug users. The valuation of the resources used for drug treatment should be assessed in the context of values forgone for not providing housing (assuming that housing is another mission of the nonprofit and assuming that housing is the second-best use of the organization's resources). Opportunity cost is the appropriate way to value inputs in CBA and should always be considered the first choice in cost estimation.

When a nonprofit develops a public project or capital investment it intends to generate positive impacts for the clients, the nonprofit organization, and society at large. Theoretically, willingness to pay is the appropriate method by which to value the impacts of policies. For goods and services that are traded in a well-functioning market, the demand curve estimated from market studies can be used to assess the willingness to pay value for market goods. For goods and services not traded in the market, other inferential methods are needed. Two main approaches are used in current practice: inferring value from observed behavior (the revealed preference approach) and inferring value from public surveys (the contingent valuation approach). (For greater detail on these approaches, see the specialized texts listed in the Suggested Readings section at the end of this chapter.)

Nonprofits' programs and capital investments often span long periods, and the monetized impacts need to be converted into a common metric using the concept of the time value of money, as discussed earlier in the chapter. Future costs and benefits need to be discounted so that their present value can be determined before their summation and comparison. Although discounting future benefits and costs to derive their present values for policy valuation is a relatively straightforward mechanical process, the selection of an appropriate social discount rate is much more involved theoretically.

We do not intend to debate the correct approach to selecting discount rates; instead, we focus on the application of CBA, using widely accepted and sometimes mandated methodologies. In practice, CBA uses a number of **discount rates**. For example, different offices in the U.S. government set discount rates for government projects. The Office of Management and Budget (OMB) updates annually the discount rate for federal government agencies in conducting CBA.[2] The Government Accountability Office (GAO) uses a more flexible approach;[3] it bases its discount rate on the real rate of interest on federal borrowing. Theoretically debatable, this approach uses the cost of the source of funds as opposed to the use of the funds. Local governments often use this method in determining discount rates, in part because their borrowing cost is relatively easy to determine and in part because it provides a link to interest costs in financial statements and other reports.

Calculating and Using Net Present Value as Decision Rule. In CBA, net present value is the preferred decision criterion in accepting or rejecting a project. Net present value, as discussed earlier, is the difference between the present value of the benefits (the cash inflows) and the present value of the costs (the cash outflows). It is the most theoretically sound and practically consistent criterion in evaluating public programs. If the net present value of a project is positive, the program generates more benefits than the resources it uses and therefore is economically efficient relative to the alternative, which is the basis for comparison. It generates a net benefit and therefore the program should be recommended for acceptance.

Other rules or criteria used in making investment decisions include **benefit-cost ratio (BCR)** and **internal rate of return (IRR)**. The BCR expresses the total benefit and the total cost of a program in a ratio form. When multiple programs are evaluated, they can be ranked by the BCR. The program with the highest BCR should be considered for adoption first, before programs of lower ranks. The information from the BCR criterion, however, can be insufficient under certain circumstances. It may require the supplement of net present value to inform decision making.

The IRR is another approach, and it is used more by corporations. It is intuitive and can be used easily in comparing different potential investment options as it measures a program's return on investment. To calculate a project's IRR, one solves for the discount rate in the net present value equation (see Equation 10.6) so that the net present value equals zero. The use of IRR as an evaluation criterion can run into conceptual and practical difficulties. The IRR implicitly presumes that the monetary returns of a project can be reinvested at a rate that is equal to the IRR, which is untenable theoretically and practically. The IRR method can also run into difficulties because multiple discount rates can sometimes be found as the solution to zero net present value for Equation 10.6. Choosing among multiple IRRs for a project becomes a subjective endeavor. Nonprofit managers are therefore advised to use net present value as a determining criterion in making investment decisions. Other easy-to-calculate but theoretically unsound metrics, such as payback period (not discussed in this chapter), can be used to supplement decision making, but their usefulness is contingent on budgetary issues and other specific contexts.

Performing Sensitivity Analysis. The recommendations and/or decisions suggested by a positive net present value need to be checked for robustness, with recognition of the potential imprecision and uncertainty in estimations and assumptions. Often the net present value of a project is influenced by the estimates of impacts, as shown in projected future cash flows and the selection of parameters, such as discount rate. When assessing the impacts of the important parameters under different assumptions, or while evaluating estimate errors, partial sensitivity analysis is most applicable and convenient.

Partial sensitivity analysis varies one factor at a time, holding all other factors constant. It is easy for an analyst to do and easy for decision makers to comprehend. It is the most frequently used method for sensitivity analysis in current practice, especially in nonprofit organizations. The drawback of partial sensitivity analysis is its inability to investigate the joint effects of changes in several key parameters concurrently. In reality, parameters often change simultaneously, and the interactions of those effects may render the analysis results untenable.

Best-case (most likely) and worst-case scenarios can be created to test the robustness of a CBA conclusion. More advanced sensitivity analyses, such as simulation, are available for use if the distribution of relevant input parameters is known. (Interested readers are referred to specialized textbooks listed in the Suggested Readings section at the end of this chapter for more detailed discussion of such analyses.)

Selecting the Alternative with the Largest Net Social Benefits. Based on the base case CBA and the sensitivity analysis, the financial manager makes a recommendation to decision makers as to the most economically efficient and robust actions to undertake. Theoretically, all independent projects with a positive net present value should be selected for recommendation. Practically, budget constraints often limit the number of projects. When more than one project has a positive net present value, the combination of projects with the highest net present value should be considered, subject to budget limitations and other practical considerations. When projects are related, especially when they are mutually exclusive, the project with the largest net present value should be selected, followed by the second largest, within the constraints of budget and other potential considerations.

We should note, before we end this discussion of CBA, that although a nonprofit's financial manager often performs the CBA, he or she is not in the position of making the decision. The financial manager makes a recommendation to the executive director and the board, who make decisions as the fiduciary of the organization. Nonprofits sometimes decide to take on programs with negative net present values based on the programs' projected significant impacts. This is justifiable, given the limitations of CBA, where some social benefits are not easily and accurately estimated or quantified. Some decisions not consistent with CBA criteria may be rooted in political considerations, organizational interests, or the self-interests of the persons involved. Economic efficiency, while important, is just one consideration among several others in nonprofit and public sector decision making. The case study for this chapter, which addresses whether a nonprofit hospital should adopt new health information technology, illustrates that large net social benefits may outweigh a negative net present value from a narrow financial perspective and prompt a nonprofit to explore more funding options in pursuit of fulfilling the organization's mission.

Conclusion

This chapter has introduced fundamental concepts and technical skills useful in financial analysis for nonprofit organizations: the time value of money and CBA. Time value of money is a fundamental concept and method in financial analysis when the decision has long-term impacts. The basic steps of CBA—determining standing, perspectives, and alternatives or basis for comparison; listing, monetizing, and discounting impacts; calculating net present value; performing sensitivity analysis; and selecting the alternative with the largest net social benefits—provide a systematic tool for decision making, including capital budgeting.

KEY TERMS

annuity	interest rate
benefit-cost ratio (BCR)	internal rate of return (IRR)
cost-benefit analysis (CBA)	net present value
discount rate	present value
future value	time value of money

Discussion Questions

1. Why is the concept of the time value of money important to a nonprofit?
2. If you were an executive director of a social service agency offering several different programs to many disadvantaged groups, when would you use the concept of the time value of money?
3. Give examples of an annuity from your own experience.
4. If you were an executive director of a small nonprofit offering programmatic technical assistance to other nonprofits, when would you use cost-benefit analysis?

Suggested Readings

Boardman, Anthony E., David H. Greenberg, Aidan R. Vining, and David L. Weimer (2018). *Cost-Benefit Analysis: Concepts and Practice* (5th ed.). New York: Cambridge University Press.
Chen, Greg G., Lynne A. Weikart, and Daniel W. Williams (2014). *Budget Tools: Financial Methods in the Public Sector* (2nd ed.). Washington, DC: CQ Press.
Frankel, Todd C. (2020, May 23). "The Government Has Spent Decades Studying What a Life Is Worth. It Hasn't Made a Difference in the Covid-19 Crisis." *The Washington Post* (washingtonpost.com/business/2020/05/23/government-has-spent-decades-studying-what-life-is-worth-it-hasnt-made-difference-covid-19-crisis).
Van Horne, J., and John M. Wachowicz (2008). *Fundamentals of Financial Management* (13th ed.). Essex, England: Pearson Education.

Case Study

Cost-Benefit Analysis for a Nonprofit Hospital Considering Adopting New Technology

As a part of proposed health care reform, the federal government is encouraging hospitals to use new health information technology as a means to reduce health care costs and increase quality of services. You are the treasurer of a nonprofit hospital and need to conduct a CBA of the idea to present to the board. Being well trained in economic evaluation, especially CBA, you have happily accepted the challenge of this task.

You have collected some relevant information. You know that the new system will enable the hospital staff to make more timely diagnoses and interventions, will reduce medical errors, and will improve communication within the care team. The initial start-up cost for your hospital is estimated to be $10 million, which includes planning, purchasing of information systems (hardware and software), and staff training, among other things. You also estimate that the operating and maintenance cost of the new system will be about $1 million per year After the system is implemented, the hospital is expected to benefit financially from cost savings and revenue enhancement. It is estimated that cash inflow will increase by $2.4 million. The information system will be obsolete in about 10 years, and no residual value is expected.

The improved quality of diagnosis and appropriate treatment will also have broader social and human consequences. Studies show that for hospitals similar in size to yours, the system has saved an average of two lives per year because of reduction of errors, plus a likely decrease in injuries and long-term disabilities to patients.

Based on the information collected, you decide to study the matter from the perspectives of both the hospital financials and the larger social impact. In consultation with the CEO and other key personnel, you specify the current hospital status quo as the basis for comparison, which dictates that all costs and benefits are incremental from that of current practices of the organization. Working with your evaluation team, you identify key impacts, such as cost savings and increased revenue, that are to be included in the benefit accounting when studied from the hospital perspective. From the societal perspective, one of the benefits includes the lives saved. You search the literature and decide to use $7 million as the statistical value for a human life.

You could borrow money, with the help of the local government, by issuing municipal bonds at a 4% real interest rate. You decide to use this as the discount rate in the analysis. You also decide to conduct a sensitivity analysis, in which you change the discount rate to 8%, in case you need to borrow from the financial markets directly. If the net present value of the analysis is positive at either discount rate, you will have more confidence of the robustness of the results.

Case Study Questions

1. Describe the results of your base case CBA from the hospital perspective using a 4% discount rate.
2. Describe the results of your sensitivity analysis from the hospital perspective using an 8% discount rate.
3. Conduct a CBA from the societal perspective using 4% and 8% discount rates. What are your results?
4. What is your recommendation to the CEO with regard to the adoption of the new system?

It should be noted that this case is a simplified analysis of the very complex issue of hospital investment in adopting advanced health care information technology. For instance, there are many other costs and benefits that are not included in this study. We present this case here to give you practice in the step-by-step application of CBA in nonprofit organizations. The case is educational and illustrative in nature, and you are advised to delve deeper into other impacts of such a project on the hospital, the locality, and the society at large in the real application of this economic evaluation technique.

Assignments

Assignment 10.1. Calculating Future Value with Yearly Compounding

Your nonprofit organization has received a restricted fund of $100,000 to be used in 5 years. You can deposit it in a bank to earn 6% interest compounding yearly. How much will you have in 5 years?

Assignment 10.2. Calculating Future Value with a Faster Compounding Scheme

Your nonprofit organization has received a restricted fund of $100,000 to be used in 5 years. You negotiated with the bank for a 6% yearly interest rate, but it is compounded on a monthly basis. How much will you have in 5 years? How does this compounding scheme compare to the future value calculated in Assignment 10.1? What are your conclusions regarding the benefits and drawbacks of the future value of large investments, more frequent compounding periods, and longer investment horizons?

Assignment 10.3. Budgeting for Debt Service Payment

You are the financial manager for the nonprofit Mobile Health, which needs to replace its mobile medical unit to continue providing diagnostic services and preventive medicine to city residents. The van costs $120,000 and a city bank is willing to lend the nonprofit the money at an interest rate of 6% amortized over 5 years in an equal debt payment schedule. Payments are due at the end of each month, and interest is compounded monthly. How much should you budget for the monthly payment?

Assignment 10.4. Evaluating Property Purchase

The nonprofit Classic Performer, for which you serve as financial director, is considering purchasing a space for year-round performances. An old theater in the city center is for sale for $80 million, and an initial costs analysis has revealed that to get the theater up and working would require another $20 million. The average operating costs for the planned activities is estimated to be $5 million per year. The ticket sales are estimated to be $10 million per year for the next 10 years. The theater will need major renovation after 10 years, and the residual value at that time will be $90 million, considering the increase in real value of city property over the past several years. Do you recommend that Classic Performer purchase this property? Why?

NOTES

[1] Boardman, Anthony E., David H. Greenberg, Aidan R. Vining, and David L. Weimer (2018). *Cost-Benefit Analysis: Concepts and Practice* (5th ed.). New York: Cambridge University Press.

[2] Federal Register. Discount Rates for Cost-Effectiveness Analysis of Federal Programs. Revisions to Appendix C of OMB Circular A-94 (federalregister.gov/documents/2019/12/23/2019-27575/discount-rates-for-cost-effectiveness-analysis-of-federal-programs).

[3] U.S. Senators Kamala D. Harris (D-CA) and Dianne Feinstein (D-CA) (2020). Harris, Feinstein, Whitehouse, Senators Release GAO Report: By Misrepresenting Cost of Carbon, Administration Underestimates Cost of Climate Change to Economy. Press Release (harris.senate.gov/news/press-releases/harris-feinstein-whitehouse-senators-release-gao-report-by-misrepresenting-cost-of-carbon-administration-underestimates-cost-of-climate-change-to-economy).

11

Capital Budgeting and Financing

> Programs spawn projects, and these projects often involve large capital allocations with multiyear cash-flow effects. These will affect your organization's target liquidity level for years to come.
> —John Zietlow, Jo Ann Hankin, Alan G. Seidner, and Tim O'Brien[1]

LEARNING OBJECTIVES

The learning objectives for this chapter are:
- Understanding capital projects and capital assets
- Comparing the capital budget and its impact on the operating budget
- Applying the concept of capital budgeting, using an example of life-cycle costing
- Understanding capital financing: pay-as-you-go and debt financing
- Understanding the types and steps in borrowing
- Understanding the importance of payment schedules
- Understanding capital budgeting policy and debt policy

A comprehensive master budget for a nonprofit organization includes an operating budget, a cash budget, and a capital budget. We have discussed operating budgets and cash budgets in previous chapters. In this chapter we focus on the capital budget, its relationships with other budgets, as well as on the financing method to pay for capital assets that can be used by nonprofit financial managers.

Capital Budgeting and Capital Assets

Capital budgeting is the process of making long-term capital asset investment and financing decisions. At a minimum, capital budgeting includes the identification and justification of the capital needs of a nonprofit based on its mission and strategic plan, the selection among alternative projects or asset purchasing to meet capital needs, and the decision on the financing of the capital project and/or asset acquisition. Capital assets are long-lasting and big-ticket assets, including typically land, facilities, and equipment. Consequently, capital budgeting is an important management planning activity. A mistake made in capital decisions will have enduring and potentially devastating financial impacts on a nonprofit, big or small.

Capital budgeting involves making decisions regarding capital projects, that is, the construction or acquisition of capital assets. To qualify as a **capital asset**, the asset should last more than a certain length in time and cost more than a threshold dollar amount. Different nonprofits have different criteria in defining capital assets. For some small nonprofits, computers may be classified as capital assets, while for some large nonprofits, only assets that cost more than $5,000 and last more than 5 years qualify. This could be justified on materiality grounds. For example, whether to expense a new computer out in 1 year or capitalize it and amortize it over a 3-year period may not make a difference for a hospital in terms of the effects on its financial position or activities. The choice, however, may affect the financials of a small, new nonprofit that is struggling to make ends meet.

The Relationship between Capital Budgets and Operating Budgets

Although both capital and operating budgeting support the organization's mission by planning and managing financial resources, methodological and procedural differences do exist between the two. For example, while the operating budget allocates funds to departments/responsibility centers or projects by categories or as line items, the quantifiable unit of the capital budget is the capital asset.

The capital budget and operating budget, however, have a close relationship. Investing in a fixed asset often results in extra expenses in operation and maintenance. For instance, a new swimming pool will require extra personnel to operate and clean and maintain the facility. Borrowing money to finance the asset will incur interest costs, which have to be accounted for in the operating budget as a debt service item. These items commit future revenues of the organization for extended periods, and therefore reduce its flexibility to seize other opportunities or to cope with future unpredicted events. Nonprofits need to understand and be prepared for the impacts of capital acquisitions on their operating budgets, even if the assets are donated. Failure to consider the impact of a capital acquisition on the operating budget could put a nonprofit into a financial tailspin. The operating budget may have impacts on the capital budget as well; a surplus in the operating budget can provide the pay-as-you-go financing for capital projects, which we discuss later in this chapter.

Accepting or Not Accepting a Donated Capital Asset: An Example

Mr. Goodwill is a regular donor to Hope for All (HFA), a hypothetical nonprofit organization that provides services to ex-convicts for their return to the community. Mr. Goodwill is concerned for the safety of the community and for the future of convicted juvenile delinquents. He has approached HFA's chief financial officer and proposed a planned gift of his mansion, a large heritage house with plenty of rooms, after he moves to a nursing home in the coming year. He insists that the house be used for the HFA drug treatment program he cherishes so much, and he stipulates that the house not be sold or used for other programs. The house, however, would need substantial updating and maintenance. What should the CFO consider in advising HFA's leadership about responding to this offer?

Before going to the CEO and the board, the CFO needs to do some preliminary but serious investigation, taking the restricted nature of the contribution into consideration. The CFO determines that the capital expenditures for remodeling the mansion into a facility for the treatment program will be approximately $100,000, and the operating and maintenance costs of the remodeled facility will be about $10,000 per month. The CFO compares these findings to the current facility rental arrangement cost of $5,000 per month, which is paid to another nonprofit organization. The CFO is also cognizant of the potentially substantial contribution that most nonprofits pay to the city in lieu of property taxes.

From a financial standpoint, the CFO finds that accepting this property would reduce HFA's capacity to deliver its mission program in a balanced fashion, since more funding would need to go to maintaining the property than is currently being spent on the rental facility. This would divert funds, which are already limited because the government contract reimburses program expenses only, from the clients' treatment. On the other hand, the property would provide the nonprofit with the stability and the feeling of having a home to run the program, where it would not be subject to rental decisions made by outside organizations and would avoid the disruption of moving around.

Balancing the pros and cons, the CFO recommends to the CEO and the board that they contact and enlighten the appropriate government agencies about how helping a nonprofit to build sustainability is in the best interests of both the government and the nonprofit in the long run. Building up a nonprofit instead of just purchasing services from it can not only improve service delivery, but also reduce the government's contracting transaction costs. The HFA could apply to foundations that provide continued support for unrestricted general operating expenses and capacity-building grants. Some foundations have realized the importance of the capital needs of nonprofits and are willing to provide longer-term unrestricted funding for capacity building.

Other steps that HFA might take include conducting an internal and external assessment for the potential of a capital campaign for the capital improvement and permanently ratcheting up fundraising activities in some other ways to cover the already tight operating budget. Failing that, the nonprofit may have to forgo the contributed property, explaining the reason to Mr. Goodwill and thanking him for his generosity. A nonprofit, by definition, is in the business of serving its clients and the public interest, not of accumulating assets, unless the assets provide benefits for its mission programs.

Capital Budgeting Process

A nonprofit's decisions about whether to fund capital projects should be made in the context of mission achievement. Capital budgeting should be derived from the organization's long-term capital improvement plan (CIP), which is developed through the nonprofit's strategic planning process (although most small nonprofits do not adopt this formal process for human resource or financial reasons). After decisions are made concerning which programs are mission critical and what assets are needed to support the programs, alternative capital assets should be cost out using a standard format. Consideration should then be given to the selection of vendors and/or contractors. An example of procurement decision making follows.

Life-Cycle Costing

Life-cycle costing (LCC) is one example of a technique used in capital budgeting when making fixed asset purchasing decisions. It is a special cost-benefit analysis case, in which the benefit is known and fixed while the costs are variable among alternative options. For instance, you may find that a number of industrial kitchen ranges can serve your soup kitchen's operation requirements equally well in terms of functionality, appearance, and longevity. The ranges, however, vary in terms of price, energy efficiency, and required maintenance. Which one do you choose based on economic considerations? In this context, the purchasing decision should be based on total costs, assuming all the alternatives are within your financial range.

The core idea of LCC is that purchasing decisions should be based on the total costs of ownership, including purchasing, operating, maintenance, and disposal throughout the economic life of the asset, and not on the purchasing price alone. Using the lowest price as the only criterion can be faulty, costing the organization more resources than optimal over the asset's lifetime. The concept and process of LCC should be applied in making procurement decisions.

In a thorough LCC analysis, each cost must be estimated in terms of both amount and time of incurrence, unless the life cycle of the asset is short, and the effect of timing is negligible from the time value of money consideration. Costs that will be incurred in the future need to be discounted to their present value before summarization and comparison among alternatives, following the time value of money techniques discussed in Chapter 10. Mathematically, LCC can be represented by the following equation:

$$LCC = A + O + M + D \qquad (11.1)$$

where
- A = acquisition cost, which includes the initial capital expenditure for the capital asset, the system design, engineering, and installation. These costs typically incur at the beginning of the project; therefore, discounting is not normally required.
- O = operating costs, including personnel cost, energy cost, material cost, overhead cost, and the like. Given the nature and timing of the incurrence, operating costs need to be discounted to their present value.
- M = maintenance costs, which are the total maintenance and repair costs discounted over the life of the project.
- D = disposal costs, which happen at the termination of the project and when the project involves toxic materials that may have negative impacts on the environment. Disposal can also be a benefit when the project has a terminal value. Disposal costs or benefits need to be discounted to the present value from the termination time.

The criterion used in the LCC method is the present value of costs. When faced with a number of alternatives, the project with the lowest life-cycle costs in present value is most cost-effective and should be recommended for acquisition.

The method of LCC can be illustrated by the following example. A midtown soup kitchen is considering an update to its kitchen facilities. After an initial search, the administrators have identified two sets of equipment, both of which meet the needs of the kitchen equally well and both of which will last for 10 years. The first set costs $100,000 to purchase and install, $5,000 to operate, and $2,000 to maintain annually; the second set costs $90,000 to buy and install, $7,000 to operate, and $3,000 to maintain annually. Assuming both sets of kitchen equipment will have no economic value or disposal cost at the end of their life cycle, which set of equipment should the soup kitchen buy?

The financial manager, knowing the method of LCC and how to do time value of money analysis, calculates the present value of the operation and maintenance costs for each of the equipment sets using the present value formula in Excel. The financial manager selects any cell in an Excel spreadsheet, clicks on the Formulas tab found near the top of the screen, clicks on the Financial drop-down menu and selects PV, then enters in the parameters for the asset (see Figures 11.1 and 11.2).

> **Box 11.1 REMEMBER: Life-Cycle Costing**
>
> Purchasing decisions must be made based on costs over the entire life of an asset, not just the initial cost. Nonprofits need to consider all the costs, including maintenance and disposal costs for example, not just the purchasing price in making purchasing decisions.

Chapter Eleven

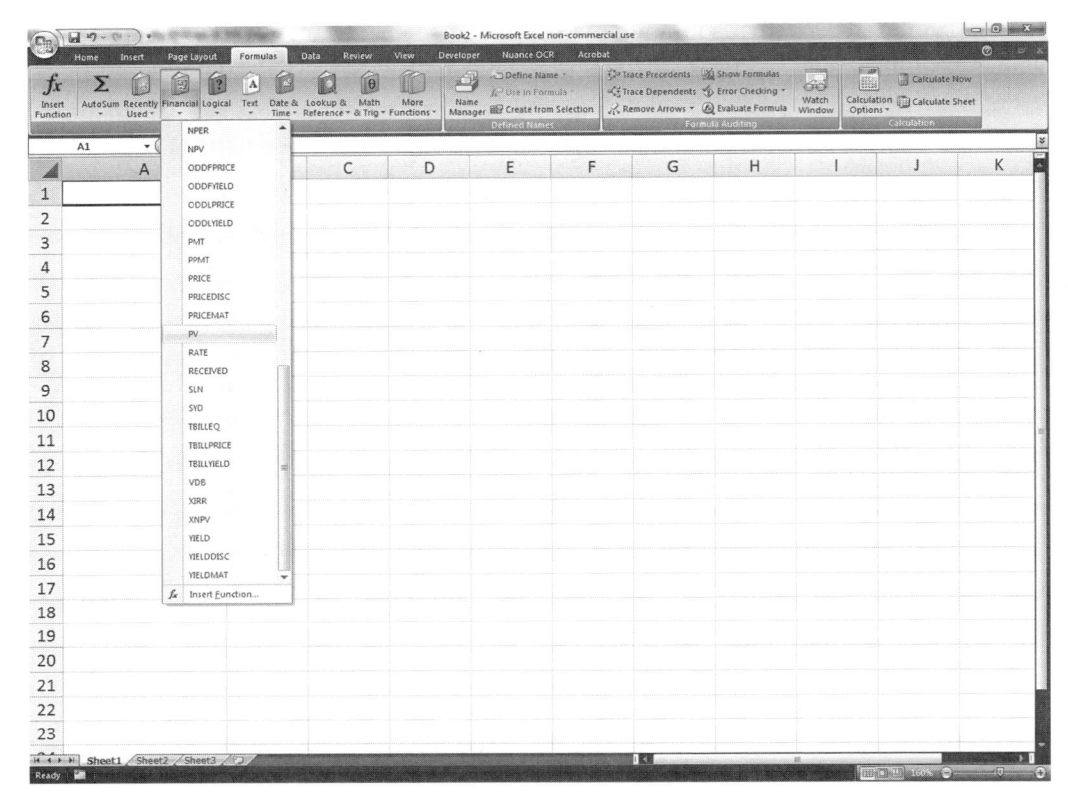

Figure 11.1 The criterion used in the LCC method is the present value of costs.

The Excel program calculates the present value of operating and maintenance costs for the two sets of kitchen equipment as follows:

- Operating cost (set 1) = PV(0.04, 10, –5,000) = $40,554.48
- Maintenance cost (set 1) = PV(0.04, 10, –2,000) = $16,221.79
- Operating cost (set 2) = PV(0.04, 10, –7,000) = $56,776.27
- Maintenance cost (set 2) = PV(0.04, 10, –3,000) = $24,332.69

Now that the present values are known, the financial manager calculates the LCC for each set using Equation 11.1:

LCC (set 1) = $100,000 + $40,554.58 + $16,221.79 + 0 = $156,776.37

LCC (set 2) = $90,000 + $56,776.27 + $24,332.69 + 0 = $171,108.96

Given that the LCC of kitchen set 1 is lower than that of kitchen set 2, the financial manager recommends that the CEO of the soup kitchen purchase set 1. It should be noted that set 2 is cheaper to buy. Had the financial manager limited his comparison to purchase prices, he might have recommended the less costly alternative. The use

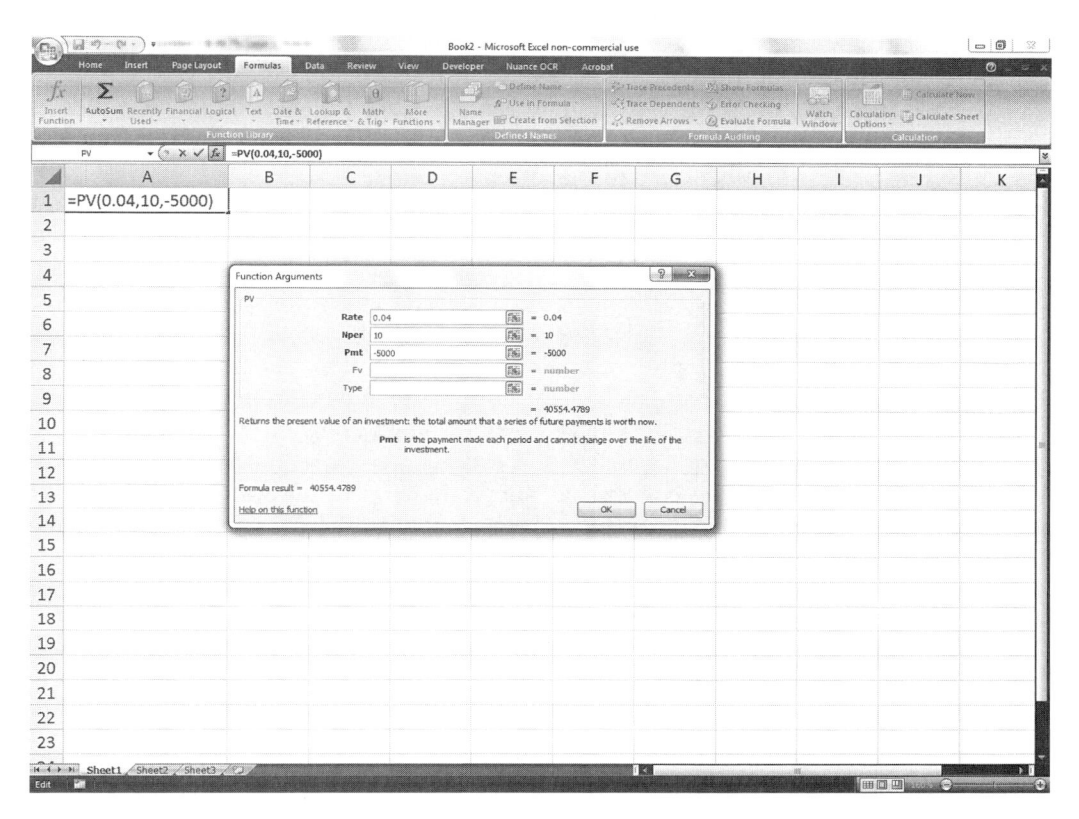

Figure 11.2 The present value of the operating costs for set 1.

of the time value of money technique, however, makes the calculation and conclusion more accurate than simply adding the operation and maintenance costs over the next 10 years, although the conclusion would be the same in this particular case.

Capital Financing: Pay-as-You-Go and Debt Financing

After decisions are made on capital projects, the next issue is to decide on their financing. Capital finance can be obtained from two primary sources: equity financing and debt financing. Equity financing, often called pay-as-you-go in the government and nonprofit context, refers to funding through internal sources: current revenues, fund balance, reserve funds, designated endowment, or capital campaigns/donations. Debt financing is borrowing from external sources. Funding can come from conventional taxable borrowing through a bank or from the capital markets, or it can be obtained from tax-exempt debt instruments, by issuing municipal bonds sponsored by state or local governments. **Pay-as-you-go financing** is cash financing. It does not add debt to the nonprofit, and this is important if the policy of the nonprofit disallows debt incurrence or if the debt load of the nonprofit is already of concern. For instance, a local Meals on Wheels may decide to raise cash through fundraising for the purchase of a delivery van, although a loan is readily available from a local bank because of the relationship the nonprofit has established with the bank over the years.

Using equity/pay-as-you-go to finance capital projects has some advantages. It encourages nonprofits to live within their means, and it preserves debt capacity and supports a stronger credit rating, assuming that credit history has already been established. Pay-as-you-go financing also avoids the added cost of interest payments, giving the nonprofit a healthier financial condition and better flexibility to take on new programs and take advantage of other opportunities when they emerge.

For large-ticket items, such as facilities and equipment, nonprofits may need large amounts of capital that can be obtained only through debt financing. Pay-as-you-go capital can take a long time to establish, as far as fundraising and designated endowments are concerned. Nonprofits tend to have limited net revenue each year, and retained income is hard to accumulate. This is partly because of the philosophy of many nonprofits that the objective of their financial management is to break even, and partly because of the reality that donors and their watchdogs discourage capital accumulation. Financial managers therefore should be aware of debt financing, especially when they are considering significant capital spending for facilities and major equipment.

Debt Financing: Bank Loans and Bond Issuance

Bank loans and bond issuance are two key sources of debt financing.[2] The decision between bank loans and bond issuance depends on feasibility and cost comparison. Many commercial banks hesitate to lend to nonprofits, especially when suitable collateral is unavailable and when cash flows are dependent on unpredictable donations. Bank loans can also be more expensive, relative to bond issuance, for large nonprofits that need significant amounts of capital.

Securing a Bank Loan

For many small and midsize nonprofits, the most familiar source from which to borrow money is a bank. For nonprofits, banks tend to finance small amounts of money and for relatively short terms. To borrow from a bank, the nonprofit financial manager needs to be familiar with the process and must have the required documents to increase the chances of securing a loan. A consistent and predictable cash flow and a strong balance sheet are always helpful, although not all nonprofits have these. Some nonprofits also find it difficult to provide the collateral for security for a loan, which is a less attractive alternative. A good reputation—of the nonprofit, its board, and its executive director—is also important. Many nonprofits do have good relationships with local banks, especially small ones. In any case, the financial manager needs to know the criteria and the thinking of the bank loan officers in making loan decisions. Putting in the effort to establish a good relationship with the bank and preparing evidentiary documents constitute an excellent investment of the financial manager's time. In doing so, the financial manager demonstrates for loan officers not only the financial strength of the nonprofit, but also its professionalism, which to some extent reassures loan officers that the nonprofit will repay its loan on time.

For large amounts of money and long-term capital financing, bank loans, even if they are available, are often not the first choice nonprofits should consider. Bank loans can be expensive. Banks are intermediaries, and they profit from the spread of borrowing and lending interest. As a general principle, borrowers should seek direct financing sources, reducing the cost associated with going through intermediaries.

Issuing Bonds

For a large amount of long-term financing, issuing bonds is likely to be more cost-effective than taking out a loan. This is especially true for those nonprofits that have good credit or credit support from other trusted institutions. A **bond** is a debt security, a long-term contract between the issuer (the borrower) and the investors (the lender) wherein the borrower promises to repay the principal, plus interest (called *coupon*), at specified times. The interest rate of the bond, i.e., the cost of borrowing, depends on the economy at large and the demand and supply of the bond security, as well as the credit quality of the borrower and its potential insurer/guarantor. The effective interest rate can be different from the **coupon rate**, which is derived by dividing the coupon amount by the par value (or face value) of the bond, as bonds could be sold at a premium or discount.

Nonprofits can take advantage of a bond's tax-exempt status, which attracts investors and reduces the interest rate and therefore the cost of borrowing for the nonprofit. The initial fixed cost of bond issuance, however, is high and can easily reach tens of thousands of dollars. This can be viewed as the downside of disintermediation (e.g., removing the intermediary, such as banks, from the financial process). Bonds are sold directly to the public, both individuals and institutions, through primarily public offerings, which require strict regulation and standardization to protect the interests of the investors (private placement is also possible, but this makes up less than 10% of total bond issuance). Financial managers should note that the cost of bond issuance is sometimes relatively fixed no matter how much capital is raised. Consequently, nonprofits should not issue bonds unless the total amount to be financed is in the multiples of millions of dollars. Pooling bond issuance with other nonprofits sponsored by governments may be a possibility in some jurisdictions. In addition, the many budget shortfalls and market changes created due to the Covid-19 pandemic in 2020 encouraged the federal government to make accommodations in policy for bond issuance.[3]

Issuing bonds is a complex process, involving legal counseling and financial advisement, the service of investment bankers/dealers as the underwriters, and many administrative supports, such as bond registration and printers. If a nonprofit is considering bond financing, the financial manager needs to consider many issues and conduct many initial investigations. The financial manager should understand bond types and bond structure, along with their cost implications in general. The financial manager should have a general understanding of the process of issuing municipal bonds, although much of the detailed work needs to be done by a sponsoring government agency and professionals in the municipal bond market.

Bond Types: Corporate/Conventional and Municipal Bonds. Two major types of bonds in bond financing are corporate bonds and municipal bonds. A corporate bond is an obligation issued by a corporation. It is a financial instrument that a corporation issues to raise money in order to expand business operations. **Municipal bonds** are debt obligations issued by states, cities, counties, and other public entities. The bond proceeds are used to fund public projects, by government and by nonprofits. Nonprofits cannot issue municipal bonds by themselves; based on Internal Revenue Service code, they must have the help of state, city, or county governments. Municipal bonds are attractive for investors because they are exempted from paying tax on interest income from these bonds. Consequently, municipal bonds pay lower interest rates than corporate bonds for the same credit quality, saving the nonprofits in capital financing. Cost consideration is one of the key reasons that nonprofit organizations finance capital projects through issuing municipal bonds. Moreover, in comparison to corporate bonds, fewer regulations and registrations are involved in the issuance of municipal bonds, which potentially reduces issuance cost.

Two major types of municipal bonds are **general obligation (GO) bonds** and **revenue bonds**, although other special obligation bonds are available in some jurisdictions. Both usually have tax exemption from the federal government and from the state in which the bonds are issued. GO bonds are issued to finance projects for the general public's benefit, such as libraries and schools. Revenue bonds are issued for public enterprises that generate revenue by charging fees for services, such as airports and toll roads. GO bonds are secured by the "full faith and credit" of the issuing government. GO bonds thus have lower risk and therefore lower interest costs from the borrower's viewpoint. Revenue bonds have higher risk in general in that the bonds are secured with and repaid from limited revenue sources of the public enterprise. Revenue bonds tend to have a higher borrowing cost relative to GO bonds.

Municipal bonds, however, have restrictions and limitations in regard to who can issue them and what projects can be funded by their proceeds. The tax exemption is intended to support programs for public interests, not private gains, and the projects have to be safe in terms of repayment to protect the interest of the investors and the public in general. For instance, nonprofits should use the proceeds of municipal bonds for mission purposes only. Municipal bond financing cannot be used to finance risky projects. Arbitrage or nonrelated businesses are not qualified for municipal bond financing. Change of use of a facility financed through municipal bonds may result in disqualification of the tax benefits. The average maturity of a nonprofit bond issue is limited to 120% of the expected economic life of the project. Again, nonprofits that intend to issue municipal bonds should consult bond counsel and responsible government authorities first to determine the qualifications and restrictions of issuing tax-exempt municipal bonds.

Bond Structure: Term and Serial Bonds. Bonds differ in terms of their structure of maturity. **Term bonds** are a class of bond that matures on the same date as the end of the bond term. Corporations often issue term bonds. **Serial bonds** are a class of bond that matures at different points in time, meaning a serial bond periodically pays on the principal owed to investors, usually at the end of each year of the bond term. This can smooth out the debt service payments over the term of issue, which is helpful for state and local governments to avoid tax or fee fluctuations, and is also helpful for some nonprofits to manage their cash flows. Municipalities and nonprofits often issue combinations of serial and term bonds with periodic retirements of the serial bonds. The rest of the bonds are paid out at the end of the term as term bonds. The structure of bonds can be flexible, especially for large and multiple offerings, which is another feature that nonprofits should consider when issuing bonds. With the combination of term and serial bonds, the repayment of principal and interest can be structured to accommodate potential financial prospects and future financing needs.

Payment Schedules

Debt, whether bank loans or municipal bonds, needs to be repaid with interest. Different schedules of debt repayment can have significant impacts on the financing cost, cash flow, and financial health of a nonprofit. Two basic types of payment schedules are common for bond repayment: the level debt service payment schedule and the level principal payment schedule.

Level Debt Service Payments

Many nonprofits issue bonds with a level debt service payment plan. A level debt service plan repays a debt through a fixed number of installments of a fixed amount. This payment arrangement is easy to understand because it is similar to a fixed-rate home mortgage. It also makes budgeting easy by leveling the debt service amount over the term of the bond. Spreadsheet programs make it simple to calculate annual debt service for a level debt service schedule. For example, Excel's PMT function gives a quick and accurate estimate of the total principal and interest payment required to retire debt on a given schedule.

Let's look at an example of level debt service payment to demonstrate the process. In response to the heightened demand for outpatient services, City General Hospital is planning to issue bonds to finance a new wing in its medical building. The addition will cost $10 million for construction and $1 million for design and other preliminary preparations. The cost for the bond issuance is estimated to be 2% of the total costs, and the interest rate is 6%, based on similar projects. A simplified capital budget is presented in Table 11.1.

As with a typical tax-exempt bond, the nonprofit pays interest twice a year and pays the principal once a year. Methods of calculating the amount of payments and the debt remaining at the end of each period vary slightly. The CFO chooses the

Table 11.1 Simplified Capital Budget Form with Consideration of Bond Financing

Project Name: City General Hospital Construction

Project Cost Components and Other Key Assumptions

Acquisition or Construction Cost	$ 10,000,000
Design Cost	1,000,000
Subtotal	11,000,000
Costs of Issuance at 2%	220,000
Total Capital Cost	$ 11,220,000

following steps for the level debt service repayment plan. First, she calculates the annual payment using the PMT function in Excel and the required parameters. (Please refer to Chapter 10 if you need to refresh your memory of PMT in Excel.) Then she computes the interest by multiplying the principal outstanding at the beginning of the period by the annual interest rate. Subsequently, she subtracts the interest payments from the debt service calculated by PMT to arrive at the principal payment. The yearly interests are divided by two (since in this case, the bond was issued with the twice a year interest payment schedule). A more detailed illustration of the level debt payment schedule for the City General Hospital is illustrated in Table 11.2.

As Table 11.2 shows, the total payment is composed of both principal and interest, and like mortgage or car payments, the interest portion is always higher in the earlier years. With the amortization of the principal over time, the interest portion in the debt services declines. Conversely, the principal portion of the payment starts low early in the bond term and increases as the interest portion decreases to keep the level debt services constant. The principal portion of the payment gradually increases and makes up most of the payment as the maturity date of the debt approaches. At the end of the repayment period, the organization will pay $8,344,215 in interest using the level debt service payment option.

Level Principal Payments

A level principal payment schedule, as the name suggests, repays the debt principal consistently in equal installments over the debt maturity period. Compared to the level debt payment schedule, the level principal method loads the payment more at the front end. Statutes in some jurisdictions require this kind of debt repayment by mandating equal principal repayments. Investors often like this structure, as they have less risk in getting their investment back.

The level principal payment method divides the principal amount (borrowed by the issuer) by the maturity of the debt issuance to come up with the required principal payment in each year. Interest amounts are calculated by multiplying the principal outstanding at the beginning of the period by the interest rate. These interest outlays are added to the level principal payments to arrive at the semiannual and annual debt service in each period. As the principal is paid off, the calculated interest outlays decline, and so do the total debt service payments. Compared with level debt payment structure, a level principal payment schedule requires high annual debt service initially with descending amounts as the term matures. The

Table 11.2 Level Debt Payment Schedule

Project Cost Components and Other Key Assumptions
Principal Amount   11,220,000
Interest Rate   6.000%
Term in Years   20

Year	Principal Outstanding	Interest	Principal Repaid	Total Semiannual Service	Total Annual Debt Service
0.5	11,220,000	336,600		336,600	
1		336,600	305,011	641,611	978,211
1.5	10,914,989	327,450		327,450	
2		327,450	323,311	650,761	978,211
2.5	10,591,678	317,750		317,750	
3		317,750	342,710	660,460	978,211
3.5	10,248,968	307,469		307,469	
4		307,469	363,273	670,742	978,211
4.5	9,885,695	296,571		296,571	
5		296,571	385,069	681,640	978,211
5.5	9,500,626	285,019		285,019	
6		285,019	408,173	693,192	978,211
6.5	9,092,453	272,774		272,774	
7		272,774	432,664	705,437	978,211
7.5	8,659,789	259,794		259,794	
8		259,794	458,623	718,417	978,211
8.5	8,201,166	246,035		246,035	
9		246,035	486,141	732,176	978,211
9.5	7,715,025	231,451		231,451	
10		231,451	515,309	746,760	978,211
10.5	7,199,716	215,991		215,991	
11		215,991	546,228	762,219	978,211
11.5	6,653,488	199,605		199,605	
12		199,605	579,001	778,606	978,211
12.5	6,074,487	182,235		182,235	
13		182,235	613,742	795,976	978,211
13.5	5,460,745	163,822		163,822	
14		163,822	650,566	814,388	978,211
14.5	4,810,179	144,305		144,305	
15		144,305	689,600	833,905	978,211
15.5	4,120,579	123,617		123,617	
16		123,617	730,976	854,593	978,211
16.5	3,389,603	101,688		101,688	
17		101,688	774,835	876,523	978,211
17.5	2,614,769	78,443		78,443	
18		78,443	821,325	899,768	978,211
18.5	1,793,444	53,803		53,803	
19		53,803	870,604	924,407	978,211
19.5	922,840	27,685		27,685	
20		27,685	922,840	950,526	978,211
Total		8,344,215	11,220,000	19,564,215	19,564,215

level principal structure also produces lower total debt service payments, reflecting the lower financial interest costs resulting from faster principal amortization.

Table 11.3 shows the level principal payment schedule for the City General Hospital's proposed bond issuance. The total repayment is indeed higher in the earlier years of the bond term, compared with the level debt service payment schedule. The debt service payment declines as it moves to the later years of the bond term. The total interest is lower in the level principal payment schedule, totaling $7,068,600. The CFO, after reviewing the pattern of the cash flow of the hospital, decides to go with the level principal financing payment structure, which saves the hospital more than $1.2 million nominally over the financing period and extends the debt capacity of the hospital for potential future financing needs.

This is a simplified case for discussion purposes; in the real world, CFOs potentially have many other issues to consider in making repayment decisions, including other uses of funds, and the financial market usually demands higher interest rates for longer-term principal repayment, as in the case of the level debt service schedule relative to the level principal schedule.

Capital Budget Policy and Debt Policy

A nonprofit organization needs to develop capital budget policy and debt policy as part of the overall policies that guide its financial decision making and debt management. This is a challenging task that requires considerable time and competence, including proficiency in deciding on and managing capital structure, operating reserve, and cash flow so that the nonprofit can build up debt capacity and a good credit rating for lower costs and higher financing flexibility.

Capital budgeting policy and debt policy should address the capital budgeting process. The processes of capital budgeting and financing differ among nonprofit organizations, depending on their sizes and how long they have been established, among other things. Large and well-established nonprofits may have a structured process in which the capital projects are identified regularly through the long-term strategic planning process and formalized in the capital improvement plan. Departmental requests to draw on capital assets are justified on a mission, urgency, and efficiency basis and approved by management and/or the board, depending on the size of the investment as stipulated in the policy statement. Small and new nonprofit organizations may not have formal structures in place for capital budgeting and financing. Their processes can be more fluid and work in combination with the annual operating budgeting process. Given the long-lasting and high-cost nature of capital projects, and to the extent feasible, nonprofits are well served by developing 5–6-year capital improvement plans as part of their routine strategic planning processes and prioritizing the projects to fund based on mission impact and urgency each year in their capital budgets.

Nonprofits need to compare and/or balance between equity/pay-as-you-go and debt financing in developing and implementing their capital budgeting and debt management policies. A debt policy should stipulate the instrument and the amount of debt that is allowed and how risk is managed. Maturity is another issue

Table 11.3 Level Principal Payment Schedule

Project Cost Components and Other Key Assumptions
Principal Amount   11,220,000
Interest Rate   6.000%
Term in Years   20

Year	Principal Outstanding	Interest	Principal Repaid	Total Semiannual Service	Total Annual Debt Service
0.5	11,220,000	336,600		336,600	
1		336,600	561,000	897,600	1,234,200
1.5	10,659,000	319,770		319,770	
2		319,770	561,000	880,770	1,200,540
2.5	10,098,000	302,940		302,940	
3		302,940	561,000	863,940	1,166,880
3.5	9,537,000	286,110		286,110	
4		286,110	561,000	847,110	1,133,220
4.5	8,976,000	269,280		269,280	
5		269,280	561,000	830,280	1,099,560
5.5	8,415,000	252,450		252,450	
6		252,450	561,000	813,450	1,065,900
6.5	7,854,000	235,620		235,620	
7		235,620	561,000	796,620	1,032,240
7.5	7,293,000	218,790		218,790	
8		218,790	561,000	779,790	998,580
8.5	6,732,000	201,960		201,960	
9		201,960	561,000	762,960	964,920
9.5	6,171,000	185,130		185,130	
10		185,130	561,000	746,130	931,260
10.5	5,610,000	168,300		168,300	
11		168,300	561,000	729,300	897,600
11.5	5,049,000	151,470		151,470	
12		151,470	561,000	712,470	863,940
12.5	4,488,000	134,640		134,640	
13		134,640	561,000	695,640	830,280
13.5	3,927,000	117,810		117,810	
14		117,810	561,000	678,810	796,620
14.5	3,366,000	100,980		100,980	
15		100,980	561,000	661,980	762,960
15.5	2,805,000	84,150		84,150	
16		84,150	561,000	645,150	729,300
16.5	2,244,000	67,320		67,320	
17		67,320	561,000	628,320	695,640
17.5	1,683,000	50,490		50,490	
18		50,490	561,000	611,490	661,980
18.5	1,122,000	33,660		33,660	
19		33,660	561,000	594,660	628,320
19.5	561,000	16,830		16,830	
20		16,830	561,000	577,830	594,660
Total		7,068,600	11,220,000	18,288,600	18,288,600

that should be addressed. A mix of longer and shorter term debt in relation to the yield curve and in consideration of the match between the economic life of the assets and the maturity of the debt should be addressed in capital budgeting and debt policy for cost and safety. Large and long-term debt can be financed through municipal bonds, which are often less expensive to have. However, federal and state regulations provide restrictions, including a limit of the amount per year that a nonprofit can borrow and eligibility requirements for the purpose/use/applications of the financing (e.g., unrelated business is not allowed to be financed by municipal bonds). Nonprofits are well advised to check with experts and authorities before delving into this potential option to finance projects.

Conclusion

Capital budgeting and financing are key financial management functions that support nonprofits' mission critical programs; they also need special attention during each stage of their development. Mistakes in capital budgeting and financing can have significant impacts on the survival and growth of nonprofits, large or small. Nonprofits should consider developing their capital budgets in the context of capital improvement plans established through the strategic planning process and should consider financing capital projects through a combination of internal and external sources as deemed appropriate, taking into account cost, future financing, and potential impacts on long-term organizational sustainability and growth. Given their lower costs, municipal bonds could be considered if the asset is extensive and meets the requirements of federal and state governments. Specific capital budget policies in the context of federal and state laws should be developed to consistently guide the process of capital budgeting and financing.

KEY TERMS

bond	general obligation (GO) bonds	revenue bonds
capital asset	life-cycle costing (LCC)	serial bonds
capital budgeting	municipal bonds	term bonds
coupon rate	pay-as-you-go financing	

DISCUSSION QUESTIONS

1. Why and when is it necessary for a nonprofit to create a capital budget?
2. What impacts can a capital budget have on an operating budget?
3. For what purpose might you use life-cycle costing techniques?
4. What is the difference between a corporate bond and a municipal bond?
5. What are the similarities and differences between a revenue bond and a general obligation bond?
6. What is the difference between a term bond and a serial bond?

Suggested Readings

Blackbaud (2011). *Financial Management of Not-for-Profit Organizations.* Charleston, SC: Blackbaud (blackbaud.com/files/resources/downloads/WhitePaper_FinancialManagementForNPO.pdf).

Dropkin, Murray, Jim Halpin, and Bill La Touche (2007). *The Budget-Building Book for Nonprofits: A Step-by-Step Guide for Managers and Boards* (2nd ed.). San Francisco: Jossey-Bass.

Hamilton Foley, Elizabeth (2009). Budgeting for Capital. Nonprofit Accounting Basics, GWSCPA Nonprofit Financial Accountability Task Force (nonprofitaccountingbasics.org/reporting-operations/budgeting-capital).

Internal Revenue Service (2019). Tax-Exempt Bonds for 501(c)(3) Charitable Organizations. Publication 4077 (Rev. 9-2019). Washington, DC: Department of the Treasury (irs.gov/pub/irs-pdf/p4077.pdf).

Marlowe, Justin, William C. Rivenbark, and A. John Vogt (2009). *Capital Budgeting and Finance: A Guide for Local Governments* (2nd ed.). Washington, DC: ICMA Press.

Zietlow, John, Jo Ann Hankin, Alan G. Seidner, and Tim O'Brien (2018). *Financial Management for Nonprofit Organizations: Policies and Practices* (3rd ed.). Hoboken, NJ: Wiley.

Case Study

The Drug-Free Center Municipal Bond Repayment Schedule

The Drug-Free Center, a growing nonprofit, is currently considering the construction of a new treatment building. After consulting with a law firm that specializes in municipal bonds, the nonprofit has decided to issue a tax-exempt municipal bond, taking advantage of the potentially lower financing costs. The initial consideration of the bond issue is $50 million, and the bond issuance cost is estimated to be $1 million, which includes all professional services of the bond counsel and financial adviser and the underwriting firm. The full term of the bond issue is 20 years in consideration of the economic life of the facility before major renovation is needed. The interest rate is 6% based on the market rate for tax-exempt municipal bonds for similar projects at the time. Local authorities have agreed to issue the bond based on a signed inducement.

You are the nonprofit's financial manager, and you are asked to prepare a bond structure and payment schedule that is efficient and feasible. You decide to consider a serial bond with either a level debt service payment schedule or a level principal payment schedule, and you will base your decision on which one is more financially favorable, knowing that your cash flow can cover either of the schedules. Moreover, you are aware that the organization is growing, and based on the Drug-Free Center's capital improvement plan, you expect to need to finance new projects over the next 10 years. How do you proceed with your evaluation of each payment schedule? What is your final recommendation?

Assignments

Assignment 11.1. Conducting Life-Cycle Costing

A Catholic school is considering refurbishing the lighting system in its administration building. After an initial investigation, the school procurement office has narrowed down the options to two: option 1 is an Ergolight system that costs $500,000 to purchase and install; option 2 is a conventional system that costs $100,000 to purchase and install. Both systems are expected to last for 20 years. The energy and maintenance costs for option 1 are $20,000 and $2,000, respectively. The energy and maintenance costs for option 2 are $50,000 and $10,000.

Assume that all costs are to be paid at the end of the year and the real discount rate is 4%. Which lighting system should the school select based on financial considerations? Use the LCC method to address this question.

Assignment 11.2. Preparing a Level Debt Service Bond Payment Schedule

The City General Hospital has to issue a bond to finance the upgrade of its emergency department. The bond issuance is $100 million for 20 years bearing an interest rate of 8%, paid semiannually. Prepare the payment schedule based on a level debt service bond.

Assignment 11.3. Understanding Capital Budgeting

Explain what capital budgeting is and how it relates to the mission and strategic planning of a nonprofit. What are the major sources of financing for capital projects?

Assignment 11.4. Understanding Capital Financing

You are the financial manager for a midsize museum that is considering opening a restaurant to subsidize revenues, which have been unstable (to say the least) in recent years. The restaurant will need a separate structure with appropriate equipment. The capital expenditure will be high—in the millions of dollars. The executive director would like to join with the municipality to issue bonds for financing the restaurant, considering its lower costs. What would be your response when asked about the issuance?

Notes

[1] Zietlow, John, Jo Ann Hankin, Alan G. Seidner, and Tim O'Brien (2018). *Financial Management for Nonprofit Organizations: Policies and Practices* (3rd ed., p. 418). Hoboken, NJ: Wiley.

[2] Author's note: Some of the examples in the next section are adapted from the original work of Dr. Dall Forsythe. I have benefited greatly from knowing and working with him [Greg Chen].

[3] Federal Reserve Bank of New York (2020). Municipal Liquidity Facility (newyorkfed.org/markets/municipal-liquidity-facility).

Mercado, Darla (2020, April 28). Here's How the Coronavirus Is Threatening This Source of Tax-Free Income. Smart Tax Planning. CNBC.com (cnbc.com/2020/04/28/how-the-coronavirus-is-threatening-this-source-of-tax-free-income.html).

Abello, Oscar Perry (2020, July 7). The Fed Makes Groundbreaking Purchase of Municipal Bonds, But Is it Enough? The Bottom Line. Next City (nextcity.org/daily/entry/the-fed-makes-groundbreaking-purchase-of-municipal-bonds-but-is-it-enough).

12 Investment Strategies

> Even a modest increase in return on investment can, over many years, make an enormous difference in the financial health of an organization. To obtain such benefits an organization must integrate investment policies into all aspects of organizational and financial life.
>
> —Robert P. Fry, Jr.[1]

Learning Objectives

The learning objectives for this chapter are as follows:
- Understanding investment policies and guidelines
- Understanding short-term investment strategy and investment vehicles
- Understanding long-term investment strategy and investment vehicles

*O*perating nonprofits and charitable foundations have both working capital and longer term funds. For instance, short-term surplus cash from unsynchronized cash inflows and outflows may swell the cash position on a nonprofit's balance sheet. Long-term endowments and pension funds that accumulate over the years can be substantial financial resources for established organizations. These funds can generate income for nonprofits through well-developed financial investment strategies. The success or failure of investment strategies can have significant consequences for some nonprofits, such as colleges and universities, in carrying out their mission programs.

In this chapter we discuss investment principles and guidelines, emphasizing the key role of the board as the fiduciary in developing a policy statement and overseeing its implementation. We then address short-term and long-term investment separately, recognizing the different priorities in investment objectives and the different strategies needed to achieve these objectives.

Investment Policies and Guidelines

A well-developed investment policy and guidelines are the prerequisites of a successful investment program. The key elements for investment policy and guidelines include management structure; investment objectives; asset allocation and rebalancing guidelines; permissible instruments; consultancy, custodian, and manager selection and evaluation; reporting requirements; and policy review. Given the limitation of space for this discussion, we will address the most essential elements only. For nonprofit investment programs, the roles and responsibilities of the nonprofit board are of special significance. We therefore start this section by discussing the fiduciary responsibility of the nonprofit board.

Role and Responsibilities of the Board

The board of directors of a nonprofit organization has the fiduciary responsibility to steward the organization's financial resources and to ensure that funds are used to further the organization's mission and goals. In addition, the board must ensure that donors' intentions and designations are honored. Federal and state laws institutionalize the board as the fiduciary for tax-exempt organizations. A **fiduciary**, by definition, is an individual or organization holding assets for another party. The board of directors has the fiduciary duty for all the assets of a nonprofit; including investing funds in trust for the benefit of the nonprofit's constituencies, so that the organization can deliver its mission on a sound financial basis.

A board, in discharging its fiduciary responsibilities, establishes policies and guidelines, selects key officers and managers, oversees policy implementation, evaluates results against benchmarks, and initiates changes as needed. It is common for a board to set up an investment committee to assist in policy development while delegating the operation of the investment program to the management of the nonprofit internal staff or external investment advisers/managers. Large organizations often hire external consultants and fund managers to operate their programs under the supervision of their investment committees or designated internal financial managers. Selecting appropriate and proficient external professionals is critically important for the success of investment programs, and time and resources are needed for a carefully run recruiting process. As demonstrated by exposed investment fraud schemes, such as the notorious Ponzi scheme by Bernie Madoff that came to light in

2008, nonprofits need to be very careful in selecting individual advisers and investment funds, especially when these are not associated with reputable firms.

Investment Policy Statement

The **investment policy statement** is a major tool for regulating the investment behavior of the parties involved. It is the key document that the board creates to discharge its fiduciary responsibility in nonprofit investment. An investment policy statement outlines the objectives and strategies of a nonprofit's investments; provides an organizational structure, including delineation of responsibilities and discretions; establishes accepted risk level and the subsequent strategic asset allocation guidelines regarding allowed and prohibited investment vehicles; specifies the criteria and process for selecting investment consultants, managers, and custodians, if needed; outlines methods and benchmarks to be used in monitoring and evaluating investment performance; and stipulates procedures for corrective actions. The policy statement also includes a schedule for policy review, which is often conducted annually.

The specific content and format of investment policy statements vary among nonprofit organizations, but the statements are commonly composed of general policies and specific guidelines. More often than not, an investment policy statement begins with information on the nonprofit and the environment in which it operates. The statement then stipulates a spending policy and an investment policy (objectives and strategies) based on the mission of the nonprofit and applicable laws of the federal and state governments. The statement then specifies asset allocation guidelines (to be discussed in detail later in this chapter) and establishes parameters within which investments are allowed and/or prohibited. These specifications are often followed by guidelines for management selection if external fund managers are involved. Reporting and evaluation procedures are specified, with selected benchmarks, depending on the specific portfolio. The typical statement often closes by outlining the policy review process, which keeps the investment program up to date.

An example of an investment policy for short-term investments for nonprofits is presented in Appendix C. More complete and complex examples are available from investment firms and from textbooks that focus specifically on the investments of nonprofits.

Short-Term Investment Strategy

Nonprofits have liquidity and operating reserves. Liquidity reserves are financial resources set aside to smooth out operations and to provide a cushion against cash-flow fluctuations. An **operating reserve** is a rainy-day fund—that is, a fund for unexpected events. These funds need to be invested in safe and liquid investment vehicles to generate market returns. The proficient management of liquid and operating reserves can make a significant contribution to a nonprofit's finances, especially when excess cash is substantial.

Issues in Short-Term Investment

To manage liquidity and operating reserves, the financial manager needs to know the amount and the duration of available cash that the nonprofit has at present and/or is expected to have in the future. Thus, a prerequisite of effective short-term investment management is a cash-flow forecasting system. As part of the annual budgeting process (discussed in Chapters 2 and 3), a financial manager should develop a cash-flow forecasting system, estimating as accurately as possible and feasible the amount of cash inflows, cash outflows, and the resulting cash balances over an extended time period. With regard to the investment program, the most relevant information consists of the amounts and the durations of surpluses. The cash-flow budget should give the financial manager a good idea of when the nonprofit will have cash to invest and when it will need to liquidate (sell) investments to fund operations and other cash needs. The manager should also be aware that an unexpected cash shortfall can occur and should make sure that operating reserves or rainy-day funds are available upon relatively short notice.

Investment Objectives: Safety, Liquidity, and Yield

Financial managers in general consider three objectives in managing investment programs: safety, liquidity, and yield (return). *Safety* refers to the probability that the investors will get the principal back at the end of the investment period, *liquidity* represents the extent to which the investment can be converted back into cash in a timely manner and without incurring undue losses to the principal, and *yield* refers to the returns from the investment, net of expenses. Ideally, a nonprofit organization should seek to invest in a safe (as opposed to a risky) place, to have access to the cash on short notice, and to earn high returns—all at the same time. Investment theory and experience, however, have shown that risk, liquidity, and yield are not independent. Higher return is associated with higher risk and often with lower liquidity. The three objectives of short-term investment need to be prioritized in the investment policy statement to provide clear guidance for investment decisions.

As fiduciaries of public assets, the nonprofits' first and overriding objective for short-term investment is safety, meaning the protection of principal to deliver mission programs. This is followed closely by liquidity, given the potential unpredictability of unexpected events of various types of nonprofits and the short-term nature in investing operating reserves. Return, in relative terms, is not as important an objective as the other two and should be given lower weight in investment decision making. Major losses can result if this rule is not followed closely. There is no free lunch, as economists often proclaim. Nonprofit financial managers need to understand the concept of risk and the methods for managing risk if they are to manage investment programs successfully.

Default and Market Risks

Risks can come from different sources. The two key risk sources are default risk and market risk. **Default risk** relates to the safety of an individual security or to the company that issues the security. Investors may lose part or their entire invested principal if the financial soundness of the investment vehicle or the issuing company deteriorates materially or, in the worst scenario, declares bankruptcy. Financial managers should thoroughly research the expected future performance of the securities and the issuing company's financial soundness carefully before investing.

A number of security rating agencies provide information on credit quality, and traditionally nonprofit organizations rely on the judgments of such agencies in making investment decisions. Standard & Poor's, Moody's, and Fitch are the three major companies that provide this type of service. The quality of credit is represented by a scheme of letters and numbers, depending on the rating agency issuing them. For instance, the investment grades used by Standard & Poor's are, in descending order of credit quality, AAA, AA, A, and BBB. C-grade securities are speculative, and D-grade securities are in default. Financial managers of nonprofits are advised to make short-term investments in investment-grade instruments only. The questionable performance of the rating agencies prior to the Great Recession of 2008 has shaken trust in the system. The misgivings are epitomized by the indiscriminate high ratings given to securitized financial assets, including collateralized debt obligations, which are composed often of risky mortgages of varying qualities. It is generally recommended now that nonprofits do their own credit investigations, if resources allow, or stay with conventional investments that are within the knowledge range of their financial managers.

Market risk, or interest risk, relates to interest rate changes in the marketplace that go beyond an individual instrument or the organization that issues the security. Future investors will request higher yields when market interest is rising or is expected to rise, pushing down the value of existing securities with fixed coupon payments or interest and causing the loss of principal if the existing securities have to be sold before they mature to meet operating or emergency needs.

In this sense, high-quality securities with little default risk are not necessarily risk free, especially with securities of longer maturities. Even the safest investment instruments possible, that is, U.S. Treasury securities, are not exempt from market risk because of interest rate changes. The best way to increase safety is to match the maturity of the security to the forecast time for the use/needs of the funds, whenever possible, to avoid the liquidation of the investment prematurely. Other strategies, such as laddering or interest hedging, can be used to reduce market risk to a lesser degree and/or with a cost. **Laddering** is the structuring of security terms so that a certain proportion of the investment matures every year over a few years. The mature investment is then reinvested, laddering behind the last one to mature. For instance, an investment could be arranged in a 5-year ladder, where the matured investment is reinvested for another 5-year term, if not needed for current use. In this way the impact of interest change on security value can be mitigated.

Hedging is another method of reducing market risk. Hedging often assumes the form of taking an offsetting position in a related security. For instance, the financial manager can purchase an interest swap or credit default swap to protect against potential loss caused by an interest rate change. An in-depth discussion of the complex hedging approach is beyond the scope of this introductory text. We recommend that interested readers seek out specialized texts to learn more about this topic.

Shortening investment terms can reduce market risk, as it is easier for nonprofits to wait for maturity when interest rates rise. Consequently, the investment policies of nonprofit organizations often stipulate a maximum length of investment for their short-term investment securities.

Given the safety and liquidity for short-term investments, high quality, short maturity, fixed-income instruments seem to fit the bill well. Fixed-income investment vehicles are those that obligate the borrower or the issuer to make payments on a fixed schedule of a fixed amount. Contrasted with equities (which we will discuss in more detail later), fixed-income securities are less affected by the performance of the issuers, as the income is guaranteed by the issuers as long as it is an ongoing concern. The debt holders take precedence in asset claims even if the issues are under restructuring or liquidation. Fixed-income securities of high quality, such as U.S. Treasury bills, also have a deep and broad secondary market and thus meet the needs of liquidity for short-term investment.

Key Short-Term Investment Vehicles

A variety of short-term investment securities are available and suitable for nonprofit organizations in the financial market. The following is a brief introduction to selected key investment vehicles sorted by safety, banks, government and government agencies, and other corporations/investment vehicles.

Bank Offerings. Banks offer a variety of checking accounts, savings accounts, and money market accounts wherein nonprofits traditionally park their working capital. The Federal Deposit Insurance Corporation (FDIC) insures these investments up to a certain amount, and the money is available on demand. For those nonprofits that have limited cash and time to invest, these are safe vehicles to manage cash and cash flows. Little or no return can be expected from checking, savings, or money market accounts, especially during times of economic recession, although banks can make some adjustments when large volumes of short-term cash are involved. Some banks give higher interest rates with limited services, such as internet-based banks. Nonprofits may take advantage of the somewhat higher returns if the limited services meet their banking needs.

Certificates of deposit (CDs) can be short-term investment vehicles that are safe (FDIC insured); however, they are less liquid than some other options. When compared with checking and savings accounts, CDs offer marginally higher fixed rates on funds deposited for specified periods of time. If such an instrument is considered, the financial manager should review the organization's cash-flow needs before deciding on the appropriate maturity term, because withdrawing funds from a CD before the maturity date can incur substantial penalties, offsetting the potential gain in return. Many banks now offer negotiable CDs, which can be traded in a secondary market and therefore have increased liquidity. One downside of a negotiable CD is the required size of investment to take advantage of the secondary market. CDs are often traded in millions of dollars. Small nonprofits often do not have this amount in their cash account in order to take advantage of this instrument.

U.S. Treasury Securities. U.S. Treasury securities are obligations of the U.S. government. These investment vehicles are backed by the full faith and credit of the U.S. government for timely repayment of principal and interests. Treasury securities are issued in three maturity ranges: Treasury bills, Treasury notes, and Treasury bonds. Treasury bills (T-bills) are offered in 4-week, 3-month, and 6-month terms; Treasury notes have maturities between 1 year and 10 years; and Treasury bonds mature up to 30 years. As a short-term investment, Treasury bills can be obtained directly from the Federal Reserve Bank or from security dealers.

As far as default risk is concerned, treasuries are the safest securities, given the size of the U.S. economy and the financial strength of the U.S. government (an exception is a bank account with an FDIC insured amount). Treasuries also have a deep and broad secondary market for liquidity, and thousands of dealers across the world are ready to trade U.S. Treasury securities. Consequently, treasuries have very low returns, especially at the short end of the maturity spectrum. In January 2020 the U.S. Department of the Treasury announced it would resume the issuance of the 20-year maturity bond, which was last issued in 1986.[2] The issuance was in response to the Covid-19 pandemic and the ensuing economic downturn and federal deficit, which could amount to $4–$5 trillion for the 2020 fiscal year. Although it has a historically low interest rate, priced to yield 1.22% at auction, it still has a higher margin than the yield of the 10-year Treasury note, which in much of 2020 was lower than 1%.

> **Box 12.1**
> **REMEMBER: Treasuries**
>
> Treasuries are considered risk-free investments with regard to default risk, but they are not beyond market risk. Investments in treasuries could lose principal, especially in difficult economic and financial environments wherein the 10-year interest rate falls below its normal range. As the interest rate climbs back to its normal range, the value of these securities will drop. If a nonprofit that has invested in treasuries has to redeem securities before they mature, it could lose a substantial part of its investment. Thus, U.S. Treasury securities are not completely risk free. Nonprofit financial managers must be careful in interpreting financial terms and make decisions that follow the board's investment policies and are suitable to their financial context.

Treasuries are not exempt from market risk, and longer term treasuries therefore tend to have higher interest rates to compensate for the risks. Nonprofit financial managers should be cognizant of this market risk in investing in longer term treasuries. Interest rates will eventually go up and the price of U.S. Treasury securities will go down, causing the potential loss of principal for security holders who have to liquidate their securities before maturity. This is especially significant for those who have invested in the longer term.

Other Government Agency Securities and Municipal Bonds. Certain government agencies, such as Fannie Mae and Freddie Mac, issue agency securities. Some of them are second only to treasuries in terms of safety and liquidity, with a somewhat higher yield. Financial managers should research government agency securities, as not all of them are guaranteed by the U.S. government. Municipal and state governments also issue bonds to finance government and nonprofit expenditures. As discussed in Chapter 11, many such bonds are tax-exempt. A tax-exempt bond has a lower interest rate because the investors do not have to pay federal taxes—or, under some circumstances, state taxes—on the earned interest. Tax-exempt securities may not be the first option for nonprofit investment programs because these securities offer low interest rates for already tax-exempt organizations.

Commercial Paper. High-quality industrial companies and financial institutions issue commercial paper. Large nonprofits that have sizable cash for short-term investment may invest in such instruments. Maturities on commercial paper range normally from a few days to 270 days. For longer maturities, costly Securities and Exchange Commission (SEC) registration is required. Commercial paper is a relatively safe, liquid, and efficient investment vehicle in terms of yield, but the minimum denomination requirement, $1 million or more, is out of the reach of many small and medium nonprofits.

Repurchase Agreements. Repurchase agreements, or repos, are contractual agreements between investors and security dealers, commercial banks, or the Federal Reserve System. The issuers in a repurchase agreement enter into a contract to sell the investors securities while simultaneously agreeing to purchase the securities back at predetermined dates and prices. Repos can constitute a very efficient investment tool for nonprofits that have cash for overnight investment. They are relatively safe and liquid, although not totally without risk. Recent amendments of laws and regulations require adequate collateral from the borrowers, which increases the safety of the instrument. Repos share the same downside with commercial paper in that a large denomination is required, which can be a hurdle for nonprofits of limited size and money for short-term investment.

Money Market Mutual Funds. Money market mutual funds, or money market funds, are a relatively newer investment vehicle in the short-term financial management marketplace and are becoming more and more attractive to investment managers working for small nonprofit organizations. Money market funds are different from money market accounts offered by banks, which are a type of bank deposit, similar to checking and savings accounts. Money market funds are mutual funds that invest in short-term, relatively safe investment vehicles, such as investment-quality bonds and short-term commercial paper, known as "the money market." Money market funds are often denominated in amounts of $1,000 or less and often can be redeemed on short notice. Money market mutual funds also offer convenience—they often allow the investors to write checks. Small nonprofits can consider these vehicles for liquidity and returns, although it should be mentioned that they are not insured against loss by the FDIC.

Many other investment vehicles are available in the money markets for short-term investment. Unless these investment vehicles are deliberately decided upon and specifically listed in their investment policy statements, however, nonprofit organizations should in general avoid them. This is especially true for small nonprofits that have limited resources to enable them to understand the nuances of the instruments and to follow the ups and downs of the prices of these investment vehicles in the financial markets.

Long-Term Investment Strategy

Long-term investment is suitable for funds that are not to be used for at least one year's time. These include endowment funds, pension funds, self-insurance funds, etc. Among them, an endowment is arguably the most significant one, with regard to designated programs and in terms of pure size. In this section we focus on endowment investment management, although we also touch on other long-term investments in passing.

Endowment funds are often restricted funds in which the principal is invested for perpetuity and income from the investment, and sometimes a specified proportion of the fund, is used to support the operation of the nonprofit. Endowments may be categorized into a number of types: true endowments, term endowments, and quasi-endowments, for example. True endowments, also known as permanent endowment funds, are restricted by the donors in perpetuity. Term endowments differ from true endowments in that they are limited by terms. In a term endowment fund, the gift as well as the investment returns can be spent after a stipulated passage of time or upon the occurrence of some specified event. There is also a classification of a quasi-endowment, where the principal as well as the income of the fund can be used at the discretion of the nonprofit. The board of the nonprofit rather than a donor often designates a quasi-endowment. Legally, a quasi-endowment is not an endowment fund. Most endowment funds are true endowments, and we focus here on such funds.

An **endowment fund** is created when a donor or donors give private resources to a nonprofit as a permanent investment fund, often with specifications and/or restrictions. Endowment funds play a significant role in financing some nonprofit organizations, including education and health care institutions, for which endowments provide a substantial proportion of financial resources for operation and capital investment. Having an endowment gives a nonprofit a cushion that protects the organization from unexpected events, such as in the time of economic recession or a global pandemic. The value of the endowment investment fund itself, however, may undergo substantial swings up and down due to financial market fluctuation and economic cycles.

Key Issues in Endowment Investment: Spending Policy

The management of endowment funds differs from the management of liquidity and operating reserves. The key concerns in endowment management are spending policy and investment policy. Combined with the acquisition of new donations, these policy decisions determine the processes and outcomes of the endowment program. In this section, we explore spending and investment policies, their specific investment vehicles, fund manager selection, and risk management. Developing new donations falls more in the domain of fundraising, which is not addressed in this chapter.

Spending policies affect the results of endowment programs and are affected by the legal framework of federal and state governments. They reflect the mission of the nonprofit and the decisions of the nonprofit that allocate resources between current and future programming in the context of a donor's intentions. The financial implications of these decisions can be significant; overly conservative spending policy may deprive current clients of urgently needed services and potentially slow the advancement of education, health care, and scientific development for future generations. The large size of some universities' endowment funds are one example; in fiscal year 2019, Harvard's endowment fund was valued at $40 billion and ended that year with an operating surplus of $298 million.[3] This is in contrast with the exploded high level of student loans in recent years. Many nonprofit professionals and client constituencies have raised this concern, and governments have taken action to regulate endowments.[4]

Unrealistically high spending for current programs, on the other hand, has its own negative consequences. It can potentially deplete the core of the endowment and jeopardize the capability of the fund to replenish itself to meet future needs. A good spending policy strikes a balance between spending and saving/investment, within the restriction of the donor's intentions and government regulations.

Spending can be measured using a spending/payout rate or a spending dollar amount. The board of a nonprofit must decide how to set up and implement this key policy element of its endowment following the donors' instructions. For example, the board could decide to spend all the investment income (interest and dividends) from the endowment investment while keeping the initial book value of the endowment intact, or it could decide to spend a percentage of the market value of the endowment on a multiyear, moving average basis. Another option would be to keep the purchasing power of the endowment constant and spend the investment returns accordingly. In that case, a portion of the **total returns** from investment, which is the sum of investment income and principal appreciation, would be reinvested to compensate the erosion on principal caused by inflation. For example, the nonprofit financial manager may assume a long-term inflation rate of 2% and an average portfolio return of 7%. To keep the purchasing power of the endowment while providing revenue support for current programs, the nonprofit would adopt a rule to spend 5% of the market value of the endowment averaged over the preceding 3 years.

Many nonprofits, especially larger ones, have adopted the percentage of average asset approach in distributing endowment incomes, wherein a portion of the asset is distributed regardless of the source or amount of the investment returns. This is done because of concerns regarding the disruption of current programs in the context of economic and financial difficulties, some of which would be very difficult and costly to restart or to reconvene. Using the investment assets as the denominator, the variance in the amount to be spent for current programs from year to year, relative to other spending policies, is reduced.

Moreover, income as a component of total return from interest and dividend yields has been declining in recent years. The reduction in the income component of the investment returns is partly a result of low yields from fixed-income securities, caused by the low interest rate environment, and partly a result of low dividend payments for growth-oriented companies. To generate income to support current programming for a nonprofit that adopts an income-based spending policy, the financial manager has to select investment vehicles that focus on generating income, which tend to be suboptimal with regard to total returns. Spending only on income policy therefore interferes with investment decisions, restricting fund managers from making the best investments in terms of total returns.

Potential issues also arise when a nonprofit chooses to spend a portion of the endowment investment assets because this could erode the principal, especially when investment returns are lower than estimated. Rules and adjustments may have to be made under diverse circumstances. For example, if an endowment fund falls below its historic dollar value, it becomes "underwater," and its managers need to follow applicable laws in their states with regard to spending and changes in spending policy. The laws vary from state to state, although most state governments have adopted, to varying degrees, the Uniform Prudent Management of Institutional Funds Act. For example, New York State has rules stating that when a fund is "underwater," the nonprofit may continue to spend the income earned on the fund. "Income" in this context includes dividends, interest, rents, and royalties. New York does not, however, approve the spending of any net appreciation from an underwater fund, except the net appreciation that was appropriated for spending by the governing board before the fund became an underwater fund.[5] Apparently, the New York rules try to balance the two competing objectives of endowments. On one hand, the advice provides legal grounds for continued spending for designated programs for continuity. On the other hand, it limits further deterioration of the endowment fund principal for the perpetuity of the endowment for future generations.

The federal government also has rules governing different kinds of nonprofit organizations with regard to spending and distributions. For instance, educational institutions have a significant degree of latitude in setting their own payout policies, as there are no statutory mandates dictating minimum payout rates. Private foundations, in contrast, have legal requirements concerning their minimum payout rates, currently set at a minimum of 5% of the endowment value. Studies indicate that most foundations are spending at the minimum required level. This has been justified on the grounds that foundations are formed to be perpetual, to serve not only present needs but also the needs of future generations. Some constituencies have leveled claims that foundations are hoarding resources, however. They assert that while people are being disabled and killed by devastating diseases and medical research progresses only slowly, some foundations for health care research have tens of billions of dollars in their endowment funds, investing.[6]

Key Issues in Endowment Investment: Investment Policy

The other key element of overall endowment management is concerned with investment policy. Any spending has to be supported by investment returns. Nonprofit financial managers need to understand the basic concepts and principles of investment and investment strategies, such as modern portfolio theory, to be effective in managing endowment funds.

In the past, the protection of principal was upheld as the first rule in nonprofit endowment fund investment, and fixed-income securities were believed to be the safer investment vehicle relative to stocks and other alternative investment vehicles. As a result, many nonprofits invested their endowments in high-grade, fixed-income securities, and income from their yields was used to measure the success of the investment programs. However, this belief and practice were challenged over time, especially in response to the Great Recession of 2008. The Federal Reserve began purchasing long-term government debt, therefore pushing down long-term interest rates (this is termed quantitative easing). Fixed-income securities, especially bonds in longer maturity, lost their earning power as a tool for new investment. The facility recently provided by the Federal Reserve in purchasing corporate bond ETFs (exchange traded funds), individual company bonds, and even high yield bonds to support the U.S. economy during the Covid-19 pandemic furthered the decline of returns from fixed income. In the longer run, an endowment can lose significant principal when historically low interest rates eventually go up, which is most likely and is expected by most economists.

The central concepts in measuring and managing endowments should be total return and real total return. In long-term investment, safety cannot be achieved merely through investing in the highest-quality fixed-income security, the so-called safe haven. Low risk is associated with low returns, as we discussed earlier, and the current low returns cannot even offset inflation, let alone support a nonprofit's current programs. A financial manager needs to recognize and manage investment risks to achieve the objective of an endowment fund—that is, in most of the cases, to provide income and capital appreciation for current programs and preserve and increase total assets in real terms for future programs/generations.

Total return, as alluded to earlier, is defined as the sum of investment income and capital appreciation over a period of time, wherein investment income includes interest from fixed-income investments and/or distributions or dividends; capital appreciation represents the change in the market price of the securities. Real total return is the total return after adjustment for inflation. Only through increasing real total returns consistently can endowments achieve their purposes of meeting the current spending needs of the nonprofit while growing the endowment to compensate for inflation in the long run.

Many factors affect the total returns of endowment funds. Asset allocation is by far the most significant way to achieve endowment total return goals over time. Historical records show that in the long run equities, such as common stocks of corporations, are associated with higher total returns than are fixed-income securities (see Figure 12.1). Most investment professionals and academicians agree that asset allocation accounts for about 90% of variations in investment fund returns.

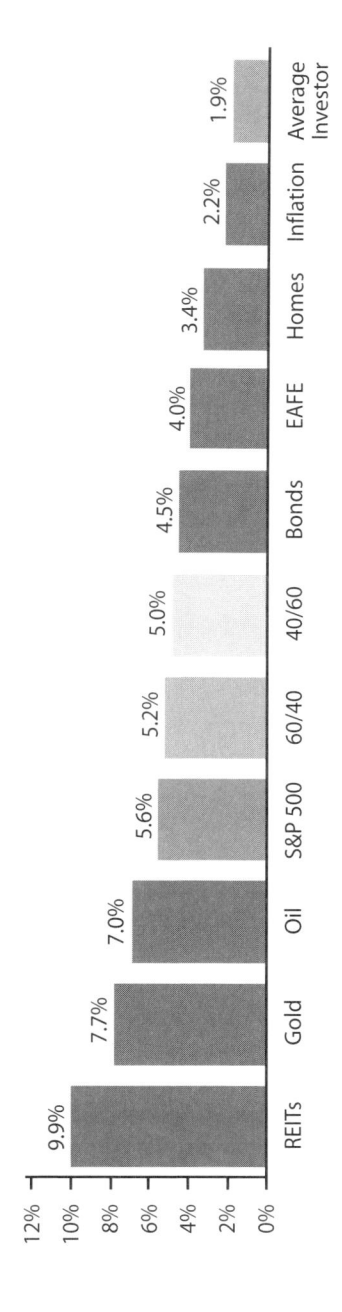

Figure 12.1 Example of average returns by asset class, 1999–2018.

Source: J.P. Morgan Asset Management and Dalbar.

REITs	9.9%
Gold	7.7%
Oil	7.0%
S&P 500	5.6%
60/40	5.2%
40/60	5.0%
Bonds	4.5%
EAFE	4.0%
Homes	3.4%
Inflation	2.2%
Average Investor	1.9%

Three asset allocation compositions, 60/40, 70/30, and 80/20 between stocks and bonds with increasing aggressiveness (higher risks and higher expected returns), are often used in traditional investment portfolios. The expected total return for the portfolio is the weighted average of the expected returns of the two asset classes. The asset allocation of a nonprofit should be clearly defined in its investment policy statement. This reflects the level of risk the nonprofit has decided to tolerate and the level of return the nonprofit expects from the endowment fund.

An example illustrates this problem. Assume that you are the investment manager for a nonprofit and you are in charge of allocating assets for your nonprofit's endowment fund within its investment policy. After investigation, you expect that the inflation rate will be approximately 2% for the next year and that the return rate will be 10% for equity and 2% for bonds. What asset allocation is needed to provide 5% spending for your endowment program if the spending policy allows the nonprofit to spend investment total return only?

You can find the asset allocation you need by solving the following equation, in which X is the percentage of equity and therefore $1 - X$ is the percentage of bonds:

$$10\% \times X + 2\% \times (1 - X) = 5\% + 2\%$$

Solving for X:

$$8\% \times X = 5\%$$

$$X = 5\% / 8\% = 62.5\%$$

$$100\% - X = 100\% - 62.5\% = 37.5\%$$

Therefore, the nonprofit needs to invest approximately 62.5% in equity and 37.5% in fixed-income securities to be able to generate the 7% total return required for the objective of the endowment fund (5% for spending and 2% to compensate inflation).

It should be noted that asset allocation does not guarantee total returns. All future return estimations are expectations and are derived from statistical analysis based on data from the past, which does not represent the future.

Increasingly, nonprofits have turned to alternative investment vehicles, such as venture capital and hedge funds, to achieve the investment objectives of their endowment funds. This is especially true for large public charities and foundations, which have the investment expertise internally or are able to seek advice from prestigious outside investment firms. For instance, in Commonfund's 2016–2017 series of studies of nonprofits, the patterns of asset allocations have moved away markedly from the traditional mixture of equities and fixed-income securities toward more inclusiveness of international equities and alternative investments (see Table 12.1).

Although the positive association between risks and returns is fully recognized, some risk can be reduced through diversification, that is, the use of a combination of diverse investment vehicles that are uncorrelated or, even better, negatively correlated in terms of returns. **Modern portfolio theory (MPT)** is in essence based on this phenomenon. MPT concerns portfolios, rather than individual investment instruments, and addresses the issue of maximization of expected return of a port-

Table 12.1 Asset Allocations of Nonprofit Health Care Organizations by Fiscal Year and Asset Class, 2016–2017

Asset Class	2016	2017
U.S. Equities	19%	21%
Fixed Income	31%	31%
Non-U.S. Equities	19%	20%
Alternative Strategies	26%	25%
Short-Term Securities/Cash/Other	5%	3%
Total	100%	100%

Source: 2016–2017 Commonfund Benchmarks Study® of Healthcare Organizations Report.

folio for a given amount of risk or minimization of risk for a given level of expected return. MPT classifies risks into two broad categories: systematic risks and nonsystematic risks. **Systematic risks** are market risks wherein the prices of all securities decrease or increase simultaneously. Systematic risk is the result of the general ebb and flow of the market as a whole. The early days of the Great Depression in the 1930s, when almost all asset classes fell in value, is an example of systematic risk. Asset prices in a market can decrease because of major economic, political, or military and other unexpected and widely influential events. Systematic risks cannot be eliminated by diversification.

Nonsystematic risk is default risk of a specific corporation or institution. For instance, a company can go bankrupt and investors, having this company's securities, will by and large lose their investments. Nonsystematic risks, by definition, have very little to do with the general ebb and flow of the overall market and therefore, according to MPT, can be reduced or eliminated through diversification, wherein the reduction of value for some securities can be offset by the increase in value of other securities that are negatively correlated with the former.

The implication of MPT is that one can reduce exposure to nonsystematic risk by combining a variety of investments, such as stocks, bonds, and real estate, which are unlikely to move in the same direction over time, into a portfolio. In a large endowment, a well-diversified portfolio may include small cap stocks and large cap stocks, international stocks and U.S. stocks, and corporate bonds and U.S. Treasury bonds, as well as short-, intermediate- and long-term fixed-income investments. Modern portfolio theory shifts investment strategies from risk aversion to risk management, and the theory, among other considerations, has provided the thinking behind the trending practices of investment early in the twenty-first century, including the infusion of individually risky derivatives and private equities. We should emphasize, however, that risky investments should be handled by full-time qualified investment professionals; their services are often beyond the reach, or even the need, of small and midsize nonprofits given the likely small amount of investments involved.

Other Key Investment Practices and Considerations

In planning and implementing long-term investment programs, nonprofits should take many other issues into consideration. We discuss some key concepts below, including growth versus value investment styles, active and passive management of funds, and the selection and management of fund managers, given their significance in endowment management.

Investment style, in terms of growth versus value orientation, can make a major difference in expected returns, second only to asset allocation. Value investors seek to purchase securities at prices below their intrinsic value. Growth investors attempt to purchase securities that have high expected future growth in revenues and earnings. The two styles have been in and out of favor alternately along with economic cycles and stock market movements. For stable investment returns, nonprofit financial managers may employ a neutral strategy by using a combination of the styles in their endowment programs. Similar to asset class diversification to varying degrees, negatively correlated styles can help the nonprofit endowment to weather different economic cycles and financial environments.

Endowment funds can be managed actively or passively, with different costs and, potentially, different performance ramifications. One way to decide between actively or passively managed funds is to calculate the net returns. If the returns of an actively managed fund, net of all fees and expenses, are higher than the returns of similar portfolios with a similar level of risk, then the nonprofit has one reason to consider an active investment style in its endowment fund management. Actively managed funds have the potential to outperform the market but tend to incur the higher costs of security transactions and a higher level of management fees. The higher management fees can be justified to the extent that the actively managed funds consistently outperform passive funds, as indicated by the so-called alpha factor. Alpha is measured by the extra return the fund generates over and above similar portfolios with a similar level of risk—that is, a risk-adjusted measure of the active return on an investment. A nonprofit must be careful to monitor the situation, however, as very few fund managers can outperform the market on a consistent basis.

The implementation of the policy portfolio requires time and skill that may or may not be available to a nonprofit organization. Most nonprofits with large endowment funds hire professional investment managers internally or externally. The selection of suitable investment managers is another important aspect of endowment investment management that deserves adequate attention. The selection process requires time and resources. Often, large nonprofits will use consulting services in the recruitment process. A number of financial consulting companies can provide services in this area.[7] Standard questionnaires are readily available that facilitate the selection of appropriate investment managers.

Even with the support of consulting companies, a nonprofit's board and/or its investment committees need to be diligent in selecting investment managers. Procedures for the selection and management of investment managers should be specified in a nonprofit's investment policy statement. Criteria and benchmarks should be clearly specified in the investment policy and understood by all the parties involved. See Table 12.2 for an example from the University of California.

It is not uncommon for the board of a nonprofit to be dissatisfied with the services of an investment manager. When such dissatisfaction arises, sensible solutions should be sought to resolve any issues in a timely fashion. The financial manager should try to resolve the issues with the investment manager directly. The problem may simply involve a misunderstanding about investment policies or procedures, in which case the selection of a new investment manager will only waste time and resources without solving the problem. If the problem is more fundamental, involving philosophical or major performance issues, then separation should be considered following the procedures specified in the investment policy.

Table 12.2 Benchmarks for Endowment Performance Evaluation, University of California, 2020

Asset Class	Benchmarks
Global Equity	MSCI All Country World Index (ACWI) Investable Market Index (IMI) Tobacco and Fossil Fuel Free—Net Dividends
Fixed Income	Bloomberg Barclays 1–5 Year U.S. Government/Credit Index
Private Equity	Russell 3000 + 3*%
Real Estate	NCREIF Fund Index—Open End Diversified Core Equity (ODCE)
Real Assets	Actual Real Assets Portfolio Return
Private Credit	Actual Private Credit Portfolio Return
Absolute Return	HFRI Fund of Funds Composite
Cash	BofA 3-Month U.S. Treasury Bill Index

Source: University of California General Endowment Pool [UC Endowment] Investment Policy Statement (regents.universityofcalifornia.edu/policies/6102.pdf).

Key Long-Term Investment Vehicles

Institutionalized in its investment policies and guidelines, and based on the current laws and regulations in the jurisdiction, each nonprofit has an implicit or explicit list of allowable investment vehicles. For small and medium-size nonprofits, bonds and stocks are the staples in the investment portfolio. Cash is often held for transition and liquidity purposes, although it is not commonly effective in terms of generating income and growth, which is the objective of endowment funds.

Bonds provide income in yields, and they can also potentially generate price appreciation when the interest rate declines. Bonds are fixed-income investments, as interest is normally paid periodically using a predetermined rate during the investment period. Zero coupon bonds do not pay interest regularly; rather, the interest is already built into the differences between bond prices and par values that the investors receive at maturity.

Stocks can generate returns in terms of dividends and price appreciation. Some stocks, called growth stocks, do not pay dividends. These stocks tend to have higher price appreciation for their growth potential. Other investment vehicles from corporations, such as preferred stocks, warranties, and convertible bonds, are hybrid securities. They combine features of bonds and stocks, providing both income and the potential for price appreciation while curtailing the participation of the investors in corporate governance.

Bonds and stocks from credible companies can provide returns higher than what can be expected from short-term and/or fixed-income investment to meet the long-term investment goals of nonprofit organizations. They are the primary investment vehicles used by nonprofits for endowment, self-insurance, and pension funds. Some level of liquid, safe haven securities, such as treasuries, may be included in the portfolio for diversification (among other things), especially in times of economic crisis, but nonprofits with such investments should be prepared to make regular adjustments/rebalancing as the market situation improves and interest rates change.

Other investment vehicles, such as derivatives, including mortgage-backed securities, collateralized debt obligations, currencies, futures, and options, are also available investment vehicles. They are often lumped together under the label of alternative investment instruments. These vehicles, however, are not recommended for small and medium-size nonprofit organizations, as noted earlier.

A number of large endowment funds, nonetheless, have included and increased selections of alternative securities in their portfolios. The results of these decisions have been mixed and bumpy. The real total returns via alternative investment securities can be brilliant in good times. However, they can turn sour and lose a great deal of the endowment assets when times are bad. For instance, the Harvard Financial Management Fund is one that investment managers envy, as it used alternative investment securities to generate outstanding performance returns for the university. In the 2008–2009 fiscal year, however, it lost almost $11 billion when the market went belly-up during the 2008 financial crisis and the ensuing economic recession. This loss accounted for more than 27% of the total value of the endowment, much more than many other more traditionally managed endowments.[8]

Large nonprofits with sizable endowments may consider alternative investment if they have or can mobilize the professional expertise to take on calculated risks and to take advantage of the potential market inefficiency in long-term investing. The Yale University endowment is another major endowment that uses this strategy to diversify its portfolio extensively and to increase the expected returns (see Table 12.3). Although the endowment lost close to 25% in 2009, which could happen again due to the Covid-19 pandemic, Yale achieved high returns after the 2008 recession with alternative allocations. The moral is that nonprofits need to manage risks, not purely avoid them, in long-term investment, especially with regard to their true endowments, which are established for perpetuity.

Table 12.3 Returns, Spending, and Asset Allocation of Yale University Endowment Funds

Endowment Highlights	Fiscal Year				
	2019	2018	2017	2016	2015
Market Value (in millions)	$30,314.8	$29,351.1	$27,176.1	$25,408.6	$25,572.1
Return	5.7%	12.3%	11.3%	3.4%	11.5%
Spending (in millions)	$1,354.7	$1,281.0	$1,225.8	$1,152.8	$1,082.5
Operating Budget Revenues (in millions)	$4,181.4	$3,874.9	$3,692.2	$3,472.4	$3,297.7
Endowment Percentage	32.4%	33.1%	33.2%	33.2%	32.8%
Asset Allocation (as of June 30)					
Absolute Return	23.2%	26.1%	25.1%	22.1%	20.5%
Domestic Equity	2.7	3.5	3.9	4.0	3.9
Foreign Equity	13.7	15.3	15.2	14.9	14.7
Leveraged Buyouts	15.9	14.1	14.2	14.7	16.2
Natural Resources	4.9	7.0	7.8	7.9	6.7
Real Estate	10.1	10.3	10.9	13.0	14.0
Venture Capital	21.1	19.0	17.1	16.2	16.3
Cash and Fixed Income	8.4	4.7	5.8	7.2	7.7

Source: Yale Investments Office. 2019 The Yale Endowment (investments.yale.edu/reports).

Conclusion

Many nonprofit organizations have temporary surplus cash, and some also have endowment funds. These financial assets should be invested for safety, liquidity, and returns. The board of directors has fiduciary responsibility for a nonprofit's assets, and therefore is charged to oversee the organization's investment programs. The board governs the investment programs by developing investment policies, delegating the management of the investments to an investment committee or a key financial officer/manager, and monitoring performance. The board should review the organization's investment policies and revise them as necessary at least once a year, so that these policies reflect the changing environment and advances in investment management.

Investment can be classified into short term and long term with different objectives and strategies. For short-term investment, the first priority should be safety, followed by liquidity. Yield is less important for operating reserves, for example. Key suitable short-term investment instruments include bank savings accounts, CDs, short-term U.S. Treasury and agency securities, and money market mutual funds. Large nonprofits may consider commercial paper, bankers' acceptances, or repos if their short-term investments are substantial, in the range of millions of dollars.

For endowments and other long-term investments, the rules of engagement change. The balance of the investment objectives moves toward returns and away from liquidity, although safety is still paramount. Safety, however, is no longer achieved through the selection of short-term, safe securities, but through the creation of portfolios with asset allocation aiming at high expected total returns within a deliberately predetermined level of risk tolerance. More investment instruments can be used for long-term investment, including equity and fixed-income vehicles of longer maturity and, for qualified nonprofits and endowments, alternative investment instruments for greater diversification and potential higher returns. Spending policy based on mission consideration and constrained by legal requirements is an important consideration for endowment management, which, in combination with investment policy and new capital development, determines the success of the long term, overall endowment program—that is, with variation and balance of donor intents, providing for current program operations and extending/sustaining the endowment in perpetuity for future programs/generations.

KEY TERMS

default risk
endowment funds
fiduciary
investment policy statement
laddering
market risk

modern portfolio theory (MPT)
nonsystematic risk
operating reserve
systematic risk
total returns

DISCUSSION QUESTIONS

1. Who has fiduciary responsibility for a nonprofit?
2. What are the board's fiduciary responsibilities?
3. What does the board do to fulfill these fiduciary responsibilities?
4. Why should the board create an investment policy statement?
5. What are the three objectives in the selection of investment vehicles?
6. What are short-term investment vehicles?
7. Why do nonprofits create long-term investments?
8. What are the types of endowments funds and how do endowments work?
9. What are the considerations for the spending policy of an endowment?
10. Why is asset allocation key in investment policy?

SUGGESTED READINGS

Commonfund Institute. *Commonfund Benchmarks Studies* (commonfund.org/commonfund-benchmark-studies).

Fry, Robert P., Jr. (1998). *Nonprofit Investment Policies: Practical Steps for Growing Charitable Funds.* New York: John Wiley & Sons.

Kinder, Peter D., Steven D. Lydenberg, and Amy L. Domini (1992). *The Social Investment Almanac: A Comprehensive Guide to Socially Responsible Investing.* New York: Henry Holt.

Linzer, Richard, and Anna Linzer (2007). *The Cash Flow Solution: The Nonprofit Board Member's Guide to Financial Success.* San Francisco: Jossey-Bass.

Zietlow, John, and Alan G. Seidner (2007). *Cash and Investment Management for Nonprofit Organizations.* New York: John Wiley & Sons.

CASE STUDY

THE FINANCIAL MANAGER TAKES STEPS TO MANAGE A NEW ENDOWMENT

You are the financial manager of a midsize nonprofit organization. The nonprofit has been distressed by money shortages in recent years caused by donor fatigue and an economic downturn. You have been informed that an endowment of a substantial amount from a long-term supporter has been just received. The board members are excited because years of effort have gone into seeking this endowment, and they are expecting that the endowment will mean increased financial stability for the nonprofit in the future. They do not, however, know how an endowment should be managed. A couple of members have knowledge of accounting and auditing, but no one on the board is an investment expert, and the nonprofit has no experience in endowment investment, given that this is the first endowment the nonprofit has received.

You, as the financial manager of the nonprofit, have been asked to take on the responsibility of establishing and managing the endowment fund (a situation not uncommon in small and midsize nonprofits). You are very happy with the infusion of capital, but you take on the role of managing the endowment with some trepidation, knowing how unprepared the nonprofit is for this new financial management task. You want to perform well with the endowment for the mission of the nonprofit, but you do not want to take the blame if the endowment does not achieve excellence, despite your best efforts, because of uncontrollable events such as swings in the market and economic fluctuations. What should you take into consideration and what steps should you undertake for this new and significant responsibility?

ASSIGNMENTS

Assignment 12.1. Formulating an Investment Policy

You are the financial manager of a newly established nonprofit. Part of your responsibilities will include evaluating and overseeing short- and long-term investment funds. What should you consider including in the investment policy statement?

Assignment 12.2. Where to Invest Short-Term Cash

What is the most appropriate instrument that you, as financial manager, can use for the short-term investment of your small nonprofit's $20,000 in operating reserve that is not expected to be used in the next 3 months?

Assignment 12.3. Managing Endowment Funds

You are the new executive director of a bio-tech research nonprofit organization. Your nonprofit has a midsize true endowment fund that is managed in-house by a financial manager. The endowment has not been generating consistent returns to support your nonprofit's programs. This was especially true during the Covid-19 pandemic in 2020, when your fund lost a substantial amount of its value initially. An investigation revealed that the endowment is primarily invested in a 60/40 split between stocks and bonds and the investment policy has not been reviewed for years. What will you do to improve the performance of the endowment fund?

Assignment 12.4. Managing Endowment Funds—Measured by Total Real Return

You are the executive director of a bio-tech research nonprofit organization. Your nonprofit has a true endowment fund and you worked with your board to establish a set of investment policies. The fund has been managed well in accordance with federal and state laws and donor intent. During the course of a year, the permanent endowment fund performed so well that the value of the assets increased substantially in real terms. Instead of being praised for the great job you have done, you are criticized by the medical community, and questioned even by some donors, for not investing enough in developing vaccines to combat the new Covid-19 virus. What would you say and do in response? Why?

NOTES

[1] Fry, Robert P., Jr., (1998). *Nonprofit Investment Policies: Practical Steps for Growing Charitable Funds* (p. 3). New York: John Wiley & Sons.

[2] U.S. Department of the Treasury (2020, January 16). Treasury to Issue New 20-Year Bond in First Half of 2020. Press Release (home.treasury.gov/news/press-releases/sm878#:~:text=treasury%20to%20issue%20new%2020-year%20bond%20in%20first,in%20the%20first%20half%20of%20calendar%20year%202020).

[3] Rodriguez, Eddy (2020, April 16). "Harvard, With a $40 Billion Endowment, Will Receive $8.7 Million in Aid." *Newsweek* (newsweek.com/harvard-40-billion-endowment-will-receive-87-million-federal-aid-coronavirus-relief-1498366).
Hess, Abigail (2019, October 28). Harvard's Endowment Is Worth $40 Billion—Here's How It's Spent. CNBC.com (cnbc.com/2019/10/28/harvards-endowment-is-worth-40-billionheres-how-its-spent.html).

[4] Linzer, Richard S., and Anna O. Linzer (2007). *Cash Flow Strategies: Innovation in Nonprofit Financial Management*. Hoboken, NJ: John Wiley & Sons.

[5] We refer interested readers to the following State of New York Department of Law's publication for details: "Advice for Not-for-Profit Corporations on the Appropriation of Endowment Fund Appreciation" (charitiesnys.com/pdfs/endowment.pdf).

[6] Pilar Cowan, Lisa (2020, May 19). Why Philanthropy Can't Keep Hoarding Assets in the Pandemic. The Chronicle of Philanthropy. Opinion (philanthropy.com/article/Why-Philanthropy-Can-t-Keep/248806).

[7] Interested readers can find lists of consulting firms in specialized books such as Zietlow and Seidner's *Cash and Investment Management for Nonprofit Organizations* (2007).

[8] *Harvard Magazine* (2009, October 19). "Harvard's Annual Financial Report Fully Details 2009 Losses" (harvardmagazine.com/2009/10/harvard-financial-report-details-2009-losses).

13

Internal Controls

> As the economy gets worse, you'll find there's more pressure, and people who have the opportunity to commit fraud will find the rationalization to do it.
>
> —Janet Greenlee[1]

LEARNING OBJECTIVES

The learning objectives for this chapter are as follows:
- Defining internal controls and their components
- Setting standards for internal controls
- Setting standards for audits
- Understanding the influence of the Sarbanes–Oxley Act
- Understanding how internal controls can be violated

A nonprofit's executive director may find it difficult to closely watch the ways his staff members are using the organization's finances. When his key people are given credit cards, cell phones, and bank debit cards for business use, the executive director assumes that these individuals are reliable and hardworking—he trusts his staff to be honorable regarding their use and does not require any rules or guidelines. Yet maybe the executive director's idea of honor differs from that of his key staff.

When he discovers that one of them has been charging her cigarettes to the nonprofit's debit card, what is the lesson that the executive director should learn? The executive director should have established a set of written internal controls that includes the proper use of the organization's debit cards.

Defining Internal Controls

The private sector often influences the actions taken in the nonprofit sector. Nonprofits have become increasingly concerned with controlling their financial reporting and ensuring the effectiveness of their programs. Much of what they have learned has come from the Committee of Sponsoring Organizations of the Treadway Commission (COSO), a national organization formed in 1985 to study fraud in financial reporting. "COSO's goal is to provide thought leadership dealing with three interrelated subjects: enterprise risk management, internal control, and fraud deterrence."[2] COSO was formulated as the joint initiative of five major professional associations: American Accounting Association (AAA), American Institute of Certified Public Accountants (AICPA), Financial Executives International (FEI), Institute of Internal Auditors (IIA), and the Association of Accountants and Financial Professionals in Business.

COSO defines **internal controls** in an organization as a process of achieving efficiency and effectiveness of operations, reliability of financial reporting, and compliance with laws and regulations. According to COSO, effective internal controls include five components:

- They control the environment through strong leadership.
- They conduct risk assessments on a regular basis.
- They create an information and communication system that keeps the organization's members informed of internal control standards.
- They create policies and procedures that help to control the organization's activities.
- They create monitoring as a continuous process.

This list is good management 101 and a useful reference for nonprofits.

The Internal Control System

Every nonprofit should create a system of internal controls. Most create and distribute to all staff members electronic or printed manuals listing all internal controls, so that staff are clearly informed of the organization's rules. This type of communication is invaluable. For new staff members, many nonprofits provide a morning of training during which a designee of the executive director walks them through the internal controls manual so that they are thoroughly familiar with it. Nonprofits often have written standards for managing their resources in their manuals. In addition, they usually include sections on assets, personnel and nonpersonnel services, and auditing.

Safeguarding Assets

Nonprofit organizations must provide safeguards for all grant property, whether cash or other assets, and ensure that it is used solely for authorized purposes. What does this mean? Most nonprofits keep logs to track where their assets are secured. Each asset class must be examined on a regular basis to ensure that the assets are being protected. Cash is the first asset; we discuss the guarding of cash below. Marketable securities are short-term bonds, certificates of deposit, and U.S. Treasury bills, which the nonprofit wants as liquid as possible. The executive director must determine where the documentation for these financial instruments is to be kept. For such instruments, most nonprofits use the services of an external financial manager. Copies should be kept in the nonprofit's office. Account receivables also must have the appropriate documentation, whether electronic or paper. Every nonprofit must have a safe place to secure deeds to its fixed assets, such as buildings. Some may keep such deeds in safe deposit boxes or secure them with an attorney.

An Example of Careless Record Keeping. Let me tell you a true story. In a small nonprofit in New York City, a new executive director was reviewing the nonprofit's financial statements with the board's finance committee chair. The executive director asked where the stock certificates for the small amount of stocks recorded on the financial statements were kept. The finance committee chair had no idea, and neither did anyone on the staff. The nonprofit was not associated with any outside investment bank. That night, the executive director searched the files and found the stock certificates tucked away in a file labeled "Wall Street." She called the finance committee chair and asked her if she knew anyone at one of the large investment banks. The chair did, and the executive director suggested that the chair ask her connection if the nonprofit could file its stock certificates with his firm; she did so, and he agreed. Several thousand dollars could have been lost had the executive director not found the stock certificates.

Controlling Cash and Its Equivalents. In this age of credit and debit cards, cash still exists. Although nonprofits rarely receive cash donations in the mail, most do operate petty cash accounts and often accept cash for publications and fees. How can nonprofit staff members protect their organizations against the theft of such cash? Petty cash transactions must be monitored, and the supporting documentation must be present. The person in charge of petty cash should not be implicitly trusted just because he or she has always handled the petty cash. Ideally, the task of taking care of petty cash should be passed on after established time periods; one person should not be in charge for 5 years. Protecting publications revenue and fees is similar. Documentation must be kept, transactions must be monitored, and staff duties need to be shared.

For incoming cash and checks, it is important to issue numbered receipts, so that a written record is created. The nonprofit should keep copies of all such receipts and compare any bank deposits to them, so that the nonprofit is assured that all cash and checks are deposited. As much as possible, two people should open the mail and make a list of all the checks received.

Another serious consideration is the use of credit and debit cards, which has become quite common in the nonprofit world. It is essential that a nonprofit limit the use of its credit and debit cards to only a few people. Not everyone who wants a credit card should get one; the need must be clearly spelled out. If a staff member travels a great deal on the nonprofit's business, he or she might find having a credit card quite handy. However, travel plans can be made at the organization's central office; plane, bus, and train reservations can be made and paid for at the central office. Even hotels can be paid for ahead of time. Dining expenses can be reimbursed. Not everyone needs a credit card.

Separation of Duties. Individuals are much less likely to commit financial fraud against their employers if they are not isolated but, rather, work with others. No one person should be responsible for a financial transaction from beginning to end. The concept of **separation of duties** is the foundation for financial control. In very small organizations, however, separation of duties is not always feasible. There are no easy answers to this. One solution in a small nonprofit may be for the executive director to open the mail and copy any financial dealings, such as checks and grant awards; in that way the executive director has some control before turning the mail over to the accountant. Or, as suggested above, two people should open the mail together.

Reconciliation of Bank Accounts. Most nonprofits create trial balances every month in their accounts. When this reconciliation is done, it should be done by someone other than the person who signs the checks. Often the finance director is responsible for reconciling the bank accounts, and the executive director or deputy is responsible for signing checks. Many nonprofits require two signatures when a check amount is above an agreed upon figure. For example, a nonprofit board and executive director may decide that any check for more than $500 must have two signatures. This is an effective technique to prevent fraud. If the person who writes the checks is the same person who receives the bank statements and reconciles them, that person can easily cover up writing a check for personal use. No one would ever know.

Fidelity Insurance. All nonprofits should carry fidelity insurance, which ensures that if embezzlement occurs, they can recover their loss. Fidelity insurance provides protection against employees' or volunteers' dishonesty and also discourages theft, because employees know that insurance companies are bound to press charges against dishonest employees to regain any monies possible. Carrying fidelity insurance also means that a nonprofit is required to keep good records, which is motivation for its leaders to hold themselves to high standards of internal controls.

Controlling Personnel and Nonpersonnel Services

As we noted in our discussion of budgeting in Chapter 2, the term *personnel services* (PS) refers to the salaries and benefits of nonprofit staff; *nonpersonnel services*

(NPS) refers to such things as supplies, equipment, consultants, and travel. Who signs off on payroll is important—this is a personnel function that cannot be neglected. Many nonprofits, large and small, have either the executive director or the finance officer sign off on the payroll. Others can prepare it, but the sign-off must come from someone high up in the organization. And, just as in other functions, there must be a separation of duties. The person who prepares the payroll cannot be the same person who approves the payroll. It is far too easy for someone to put his or her friends and relatives on the payroll if no one is paying attention.

Controlling Travel and Cell Phones. Nonprofits often allow staff members to use their personal cars for official business and then reimburse them for the use of their cars. If gas prices are high, such practices could become cost prohibitive. Executive directors have choices in limiting the monies that go to travel. They can either curtail travel by staff members or repay them for the use of their cars. In big cities, executive directors can encourage staff to use public transportation, but in smaller cities such alternatives may not be available.

Similarly, cell phone usage is problematic for nonprofits. Many nonprofits buy and pay monthly charges for cell phones for key staff members, but many other organizations cannot afford to do so. Executive directors can certainly tell staff members that cell phones are to be provided only to key staff. Cell phones represent a controllable expense if executive directors choose to curtail their availability to staff.

Controlling Vendors. One of the most common methods of committing financial fraud is to set up dummy vendors (seller of goods) and deliver supplies to them, which the organization pays for. When a staff member orders supplies, some form of purchase order, often electronic, is completed, and the accounting office encumbers the money. The supplies arrive and the person who receives the goods signs the invoice and sends the invoice to the accounting office for payment. Under such a system, what is to keep a person from ordering supplies, having them delivered somewhere else, and then signing the invoice and sending the invoice to the accounting office? Nothing. In a small office, people might notice; in a large office, no one notices. How can such fraud be prevented? Nonprofits should make sure that someone other than the person who ordered the supplies reviews the delivery and approves the invoice.

Setting Audit Standards

The bylaws of most nonprofits require an annual outside audit of their books. The outside auditor's overall task is to verify the financial books. He or she does this by verifying the bank deposits with the deposit slips and copies of checks, verifying expense reimbursements, and reconciling bank accounts. Just as important, the auditor, if asked, will conduct a management audit. He or she will examine the policies and procedures governing the nonprofit's finances and inventory, and make recommendations if weaknesses are revealed. The auditor can be the executive director's best friend.

In addition, the federal government requires audits of funds it has distributed by contract to the organizations spending the funds. The federal Office of Management and Budget established federal regulations in Circular A-133 requiring standards for federal audits of nonprofits. Any nonprofit that spends more than $500,000 a year must have a federal audit. Often, the nonprofits hire independent accounting firms to conduct the audits at the nonprofits' expense. The nonprofits can include the costs of these audits in their budgets when seeking funding from the federal government. The IRS can also audit nonprofits, but this is rare—the IRS is too busy to conduct random audits on the thousands of nonprofits that exist.

Independent Sector and Accountability

Independent Sector is a national membership organization that provides leadership to all in the nonprofit sector. It serves its members by publishing an annual report on the health of nonprofits, fighting for public policies that support the nonprofit sector, facilitating the development of citizen engagement in the sector, supporting the highest level of ethical standards, and promoting community building so that the sector can thrive.[3]

Independent Sector advocates for the highest standards of good governance and ethical practices through a commitment to polices in three areas: code of ethics, conflict of interest, and whistle-blower policy. Its publication, *Principles for Good Governance and Ethical Practice*, which should be required reading for all of a nonprofit's board and key staff members, outlines 33 principles of sound practices related to legal compliance and public disclosure, effective governance, financial oversight, and responsible fundraising.[4] It provides guidelines on how to:

- Develop a culture of accountability and transparency.
- Adopt a statement of values and a code of ethics.
- Adopt a conflict of interest policy.
- Ensure that board members understand their fiduciary responsibility.
- Ensure that the nonprofit has an annual independent financial review.
- Ensure the accuracy of the nonprofit's Form 990.
- Adopt a policy of transparency.
- Establish and support a policy of reporting misconduct.
- Adopt a policy of remaining current with the law.

Every nonprofit would benefit by examining and committing to the recommendations in this list.

The first step for a nonprofit is to develop a culture of accountability and transparency. What this means is that staff and board members need to understand what accountability and transparency mean. It is much harder for a staff member to commit fraud if the nonprofit he or she works for adopts a policy of strict accountability and openness about finances. Each staff and board member needs to be part of conversations about why their nonprofit organization must promote ethical behavior and must be willing to be open about its finances and programs. This is the beginning of quality governance.

The second step is to adopt a statement of values and a code of ethics. A written code of ethics should outline the values of the nonprofit, as well as the practices that all of its members are expected to follow. The code of ethics should include specific policies and procedures that describe how it will be implemented and enforced. Both the board and members of the nonprofit should be involved in developing and applying a code that addresses the needs of the nonprofit and its programs.[5]

The third step is to adopt a policy concerning conflicts of interest for all associated with the nonprofit. This is particularly important for board members, who may have substantial funds at their disposal and wish to use the nonprofit's funds in their own investment ideas. It is imperative that nonprofits use their funds only for their programs and not be linked in any way to board members' individual financial gains. Although it is not illegal for a nonprofit to provide funding to board members who are doing board business, such actions may not pass the "smell" test; that is, would donors or the general public be skeptical of a nonprofit that pays board members for their work? It is a slippery slope, and one that might provide unnecessarily bad publicity for a nonprofit.

The fourth step is to make sure that all board members fulfill their financial responsibilities. In the end, staff members are the hired help. It is the board that has fiduciary responsibility. Board members need to examine and understand the audited financial statements. Often this means that nonprofits' financial managers need to educate board members. It also makes clear the importance of the thoughtful selection of board members and of ensuring that board candidates have the right qualifications to be on the board.

The fifth step is to make sure that the nonprofit has an annual audit, an independent financial review. Board members should ensure that an external financial expert examines the finances at least once a year. The board is responsible for ensuring that the same accounting firm does not prepare the nonprofit's audited financial statements for an extended number of years. Nonprofits should change accounting firms after 3–5 years, to let fresh eyes look at their finances. In addition, accounting firms can conduct management audits; such audits can be incredibly valuable to nonprofits' leadership. A management audit can allow a nonprofit's leaders to say it is time for a change from old methods of doing business to newer and perhaps more useful methods to ensure financial integrity.

The sixth step is to ensure the accuracy of and make public the nonprofit's IRS Form 990. GuideStar, a nonprofit that provides information about nonprofits, has information on more than 1 million nonprofits on its website, including their Form 990s. The IRS Form 990 is a major way that nonprofits share their information with the public. This form ought to be completed by the outside accountant and executive director so that the information is as accurate as possible. The board, or at least a board committee, usually the finance or audit committee, should review the completed form. This focus on accuracy is the best signal that the nonprofit is highly interested in transparency.

Transparency is the seventh step. Independent Sector recommends that every nonprofit include the following on its website:

- Vision and mission statements
- Code of ethics
- Conflict of interest policy
- Form 990
- Audited financial statements
- Program information
- Performance information
- Annual report
- Any accreditations
- List of board members and officers and staff
- List of contributors
- Form 1023 (the original application for nonprofit status)
- Bylaws

The eighth step is to establish and support a policy on the reporting of suspected misconduct. This is important; it is in effect a whistle-blower protection policy. Individual staff members should be confident that they can report illegal practices or questionable behaviors of the nonprofit without fear of retribution. Such a policy is vital because board members are responsible for the financial health of the agency, and if staff members are fearful of coming forward, then board members are at risk.

The ninth step is to always remain current with the law. The executive board is ultimately responsible for overseeing and ensuring that the nonprofit complies with all of its legal obligations. Board members should be familiar with the basic rules and requirements with which they must comply and should secure the necessary legal and financial advice and assistance necessary to structure appropriate oversight and manage assets responsibly.[6]

A nonprofit should comply with all applicable federal and state laws and regulations. On the federal level, part of the Sarbanes–Oxley Act is an attempt to ensure ethical behavior in nonprofit organizations.

Box 13.1 REMEMBER: Transparency

The most important protection a nonprofit can have is transparency in its finances.

As Donna Valente of the Christopher Reeve Foundation has explained, "Nonprofit transparency means that the organization's finances, operations and programs are absolutely ethical and open to inspection."[7]

Openness can prevent fraud and misjudgments.

The Sarbanes–Oxley Act

In 2002, the U.S. Congress passed the Sarbanes–Oxley Act as a reaction to the accounting scandals of Enron, Tyco, and others. Seeking to restore public trust in the corporate world, the **Sarbanes–Oxley Act** requires publicly traded corporations to adhere to governance standards that include a broader role for corporate boards in corporations' finances and auditing procedures. For the most part, the act ignores the nonprofit sector; however, it has two provisions that do apply to nonprofits: one prohibits corporations, including nonprofits, from retaliating against whistle-blowers, and the other prohibits corporations, including nonprofits, from destroying, altering, or concealing documents or impeding investigations.

The Sarbanes–Oxley Act has had a great impact on nonprofits not because of those two provisions, but because of other requirements of the law with which nonprofits do not have to comply. In a jointly authored paper on the implications of the Sarbanes–Oxley Act for nonprofits, BoardSource and Independent Sector argue that nonprofits should adopt several of the law's requirements for corporations even though they are not obligated to do so. These include the following:

- Separate board audit committees. Most nonprofit boards have finance committees; large nonprofits should also have separate audit committees, as some already do.
- Rotate the outside auditor every 5 years. Bringing in a new outside auditor brings a fresh pair of eyes to a nonprofit's finances.
- Require the CEO and CFO to certify financial statements. The CEO and the CFO must certify that the financial statements fairly represent the financial condition of the nonprofit. Such a requirement would certainly force the executive director to pay close attention to the outside audit.
- Prohibit loans to board members and CEOs. Providing private loans to insiders is not a common practice in nonprofits, but it is worthwhile to make the prohibition of such loans a part of policy.
- Publicly disclose financial statements. Since most nonprofits are required to file a Form 990, a picture of a nonprofit's finances is available to the public.[8]

Upon passage of the Sarbanes–Oxley Act, several states instituted laws mandating that nonprofits within their borders meet some of the requirements of the act.

- Connecticut now requires all nonprofits with more than $200,000 in revenues to submit audited financial statements to the state's attorney general's office. Two board members must attest to the accuracy of the information.
- New Hampshire adopted a similar requirement.
- Kansas now requires nonprofits with more than $100,000 in revenues to produce audited financial statements.
- Maine requires audited financial statements for almost all nonprofits in the state.
- In California, nonprofit organizations with annual gross revenues of $2 million or more must make audited financial statements available to the state's attorney general and the public.[9]

Although not all of the provisions in the Sarbanes–Oxley Act are applicable to nonprofits, Mulligan makes the point that small nonprofits cannot possibly afford to meet some of its requirements, and those states that have enacted Sarbanes–Oxley–like rules will not necessarily improve their governance.[10] The requirement of transparency, however, can be helpful and may give those who might abuse their authority pause. Certainly transparency gives donors confidence that the nonprofits they are considering are being open and aboveboard about their financial resources and their mission.

Examples of Fraud

In a study of 959 fraud cases, the Association of Certified Fraud Examiners found that "the median loss for nonprofit organizations that had been victimized by an embezzler was $109,000 . . . the median time to detect a theft was 24 months."[11] Another study that examined 58 nonprofit fraud cases established an interesting profile: "The typical fraud . . . involved a loss of less than $50,000, and the perpetrator was typically a woman who earned less than $50,000 a year and had never before committed a crime. The median age was 41 and the median tenure with the organization was seven years."[12]

Controlling Cash and Its Equivalents and Reconciliation of Bank Accounts

A few days after becoming the chief financial officer (CFO) of the United Way in East Lansing, Michigan, the CFO discovered that dozens of checks were missing from the records. She asked the bank to fax her copies of the missing checks, and she discovered that the checks had been made out to the organization's former vice president of finance, that each check had the forged signatures of two officers to make it appear valid, and that this had gone on over a period of 19 years. In 2004, the former vice president of finance was ordered to repay more than $2 million to the United Way and was sentenced to 4 years in prison. This theft could have been prevented in several ways:

- The auditors should have been far more careful. The United Way sued the auditors for failing to notice the theft.
- If the United Way had had segregated duties within its finance department, the theft would not have happened. Even though the vice president of finance did not have authority to write checks, she had sole responsibility for reconciling the checking account. No one else looked at it.
- The vice president of finance accounted for lost funds by claiming that revenues had a shortfall because donors were not fulfilling their pledges. No one investigated the truth of this statement.
- After the theft was discovered, the United Way called the police and the board of directors. In short order, an accounting firm was hired to conduct

an investigation (i.e., forensic accounting), the chief executive officer resigned, and the board began the process of damage control in the media. As a result of this incident, the United Way had to work for a long time to recover public credibility.

Accessing Cash: Forging Signatures and Controlling Payroll

In Tucson, Arizona, a bookkeeper, who had been working for an art museum for more than 18 years, began stealing from her employer in 2001 because of a gambling problem. She embezzled almost $1 million before she resigned in December 2008. She forged the signatures of the chief financial officer and the museum director and stole cash intended for deposit as well.[13]

This next example is one of money flowing to nonprofits, though not for pursuit of its mission, but for personal gain. In 2010, when a prominent New York City councilman was indicted on federal fraud and money-laundering charges, many people in the city were not surprised. He was not the first councilman who had funneled city funds to nonprofits that "employed" the councilman's relatives and friends, and then overcharged the city for rent and other expenses. Yet such fraud is preventable with the implementation of regulations requiring the city to audit closely any nonprofit involved with an elected official.

Nonprofits as Victims

Another kind of fraud committed in the nonprofit sector involves nonprofit organizations themselves as victims of fraud committed elsewhere. Hundreds of nonprofits have been asked to return donated money in response to government efforts to return "ill-gotten gains from financial frauds, like Ponzi schemes."[14] This is called "clawback." Charities have received these gifts in good faith; it is not their fault that they have been the recipients of, in effect, dirty money. In 2011, the Florida nonprofit Family Central had to return a $25,000 gift received from a South Florida lawyer who had pleaded guilty to running a Ponzi scheme.[15]

Of course, large sums of money can be involved in such cases. In the same Florida case, a children's hospital had to return $800,000 to federal authorities. The hospital took the name of the donor off the emergency room that had borne his name.[16] Vigilance is important, but it is not sufficient to protect nonprofits from such problems; there is little protection against a Ponzi scheme from a respectable member of the community. Nonprofits, however, should investigate potential donors' backgrounds when large gifts are proposed.

Internal Control Issues

Nonprofit organizations continually face new challenges. In 2020, the Covid-19 pandemic and the ensuing shutdown of nonessential services forced many organizations to change their operations and their employees had to work at home. This can, and has in many cases, create challenges with internal controls with regard to, for instance, the lack of timely and sufficient records for reconciliation, difficulties in co-signing documents or co-opening mail, omission of regular counting of inventories, etc. Recognizing the effects of the pandemic requires that new approaches and new technologies are needed to put in place effective internal controls during times of lowered income, depression, and confusion, which is when fraud is more likely to occur.

Conclusion

Board members of nonprofits must be assertive to ensure that adequate internal controls are in place for their organizations. There is no excuse for even the smallest nonprofit not to have an internal control system. The Independent Sector's checklist presented earlier in this chapter is a perfect tool for board members and executive directors to use in reviewing the internal controls that exist in their organizations. Even though the Sarbanes–Oxley Act does not entirely apply to the nonprofit sector, this federal law has forced nonprofits in the United States to embrace internal controls. Even with internal controls in place, however, there is no substitute for vigilance on the part of an organization's leadership team.

Key Terms

internal controls   Sarbanes–Oxley Act   separation of duties

Discussion Questions

1. Why is it important for a nonprofit to develop and maintain an internal control system?
2. What is separation of duties?
3. Why is it important for a nonprofit to develop a culture of accountability and transparency?
4. Why are independent financial reviews necessary in a nonprofit?
5. Why is Form 990 important?
6. What does the Sarbanes–Oxley Act require of nonprofits?
7. How has the Sarbanes–Oxley Act influenced nonprofit governance?

Suggested Readings

BoardSource and Independent Sector (2003, March 1). The Sarbanes–Oxley Act and Implications for Nonprofit Organizations. GuideStar Blog (trust.guidestar.org/the-sarbanes-oxley-act-and-implications-for-nonprofit-organizations).

Gross, Malvern J., Jr., John H. McCarthy, and Nancy E. Shelmon (2005). *Financial and Accounting Guide for Not-for-Profit Organizations* (7th ed.). New York: PricewaterhouseCoopers.

Independent Sector (2015). *Principles for Good Governance and Ethical Practice: A Guide for Charities and Foundations* (2nd ed.). Washington, DC: Independent Sector.

New York State, Office of Attorney General, Charities Bureau (2005, January). *Internal Controls and Financial Accountability for Not-for-Profit Boards* (nyc.gov/html/nonprofit/downloads/pdf/Internal%20Controls%20and%20Financial%20Accountability%20for%20Not-for-Profit%20Board%20OAG.pdf).

Petrovits, Christine, Catherine Shakespeare, and Aimee Shih (2009). *The Causes and Consequences of Internal Control Problems in Nonprofit Organizations* (centerforpbbefr.rutgers.edu/20thFEA/AccountingPapers/Session4/Petrovits,%20Shakespeare,%20and%20Shih.pdf).

ASSIGNMENTS

Assignment 13.1. Crafting Internal Control Policies to Prevent Conflict of Interest

In April 2011, the nonprofit organization Central Asia Institute, founded by Greg Mortenson and author of the book *Three Cups of Tea*, found itself under fire because of the way it had been spending its resources. Although the nonprofit's website showed the schools in Afghanistan and Pakistan that the organization built and sometimes staffed, the nonprofit's financial statements indicated that the majority of the funding went to domestic (American) outreach, namely, paying for speaking engagements and advertisements for Mortenson's books. The three-member board (of whom Mortenson was one, as well as executive director) wanted to reassure the donors that the institute was fulfilling its mission.[17] As of 2012, the Central Asia Institute has survived the scandal; a lawsuit is pending, and no criminal charges have been filed. However, other nonprofits can learn from this unfortunate case. What internal control policies should the nonprofit's board have adopted that would have avoided these problems?

Assignment 13.2. Applying Internal Control Policies to Guard against Theft

A small nonprofit organization, a junior football league, discovered that its treasurer had stolen more than $50,000 from the league over a 2-year period. The treasurer had sole responsibility for writing and depositing checks. What internal control policies should have been in place to prevent such theft?

Assignment 13.3. Using Internal Control Policies to Discourage Fraud

One of the most famous fraud cases involving a nonprofit took place in California, where employees of Goodwill Industries stole merchandise from the organization and sold it. Over more than 20 years, the employees stole more than $25 million in merchandise.[18] The chief executive of the Goodwill branch was involved in the thefts and had opened bank accounts in Switzerland to hide the stolen money. What internal control policies would have prevented such fraud?

Assignment 13.4. Internal Control in Remote Working Environment

During the Covid-19 pandemic, your nonprofit has the majority of staff working at home, including people with signing authorities. What can you do to maintain, or even increase, internal controls under these circumstances? For instance, if your internal control policy specifies that two people are needed to sign certain documents/transactions, how can the nonprofit follow this instruction when people are working at home individually?

Notes

[1] Janet Greenlee, associate professor of accounting, University of Dayton, quoted in Frazier, Eric (2009, May 21). "Fighting Nonprofit Fraud: Charities Need to Tighten Controls against Theft in Tough Economy." *Chronicle of Philanthropy* (philanthropy.com/article/Fighting-Nonprofit-Fraud/57179).

[2] Committee of Sponsoring Organizations of the Treadway Commission (2021). About Us. (coso.org).

[3] Independent Sector. About Us (independentsector.org/about).

[4] Independent Sector. Principles of Good Governance and Ethical Practice (independentsector.org/programs/principles-for-good-governance-and-ethical-practice).

[5] Independent Sector (2015). *Principles for Good Governance and Ethical Practice: A Guide for Charities and Foundations* (2nd ed., p. 12). Washington, DC: Independent Sector.

[6] Ibid., p. 11.

[7] Quoted in Coffman, Suzanne E. (2006, November 1). What Nonprofit Transparency Means to You. GuideStar Blog (guidestar.org/rxa/news/articles/2006/what-nonprofit-transparency-means-to-you.aspx?articleId=1072).

[8] BoardSource and Independent Sector (2003, March 1). The Sarbanes–Oxley Act and Implications for Nonprofit Organizations. GuideStar Blog (trust.guidestar.org/the-sarbanes-oxley-act-and-implications-for-nonprofit-organizations).

[9] Mulligan, Lumen N. (2007). "What's Good for the Goose Is Not Good for the Gander: Sarbanes–Oxley-Style Nonprofit Reforms." *Michigan Law Review*, 105(8): 1981–2009.

[10] Ibid., p. 1982.

[11] Cited in Frazier, "Fighting Nonprofit Fraud."

[12] Ibid.

[13] Kornman, Sheryl (2009, May 5). "Ex-Bookkeeper Accused of Embezzling $970K from Tucson Museum of Art." *Tucson Citizen* (tucsoncitizen.com/morgue/2009/05/05/115796-ex-bookkeeper-accused-of-embezzling-970k-from-tucson-museum-of-art).

[14] Blum, Debra E. (2011, March 6). "When Donors Commit Fraud, Nonprofits Often Pay the Price." *Chronicle of Philanthropy* (philanthropy.com/article/When-Donors-Commit-Fraud/126571).

[15] Ibid.

[16] Ibid.

[17] Chan, Emily, and Gene Takagi (2011, May 5). "Charities Should Drink Deeply of the 'Three Cups of Tea' Scandal's Lessons." *Chronicle of Philanthropy*, 31.

[18] Friedrichs, David O. (2010). *Trusted Criminals: White Collar Crime in Contemporary Society* (4th ed., p. 117). Belmont, CA: Wadsworth Cengage Learning.

Part V

New Directions

14

Adapting to Turbulent Times

> Social entrepreneurs are not content just to give a fish or teach how to fish. They will not rest until they have revolutionized the fishing industry.
>
> —Bill Drayton[1]

LEARNING OBJECTIVES

The learning objectives for this chapter are as follows:
- Understanding the effects of economic crises
- Understanding fiscal risk assessment methods
- Developing fiscal strategies to mitigate risk
- Understanding the growth of capital intermediaries
- Examining the role of government in developing innovation
- Examining the role of foundations in encouraging philanthropy
- Understanding the new fourth sector of social enterprise

*W*hen the economy dips, the financing of nonprofits suffers. When the economy struggles, nonprofits are imperiled. The mission of a nonprofit is something a board of directors and executive director work to achieve for a long time. A severe recession puts the mission in danger. Cutbacks in programs can make it that much harder for a nonprofit to succeed in fulfilling its goals. The global economic crisis of 2008 left nonprofits struggling to make up funding reductions due to losses in government contracts and grants, foundation dollars, and donor support. Nonprofits often operate with little margin of safety because reserve funds are few. As a recession deepens, the financial condition of government institutions worsens, and the financial support they provide for many nonprofits dwindles. The Center on Budget and Policy Priorities has noted, for example, that in the United States, 29 out of 45 states cut funding for health care programs in 2009, and 24 states plus the District of Columbia cut services for elderly and disabled persons.[2] Foundations suffered losses in their stock portfolios, which reduced their ability to fund nonprofits. Assets of all active U.S. foundations fell 17.2%, to $565 billion. All of this had a significant impact on nonprofits.

Another example is the Covid-19 pandemic. After the expiration of the Paycheck Protection Program in July 2020, nonprofits had to let go thousands of workers. Unemployment rose; demands on nonprofits rose as well. But nonprofits were not in a position to increase their capacity; they were losing revenue from contributors, government, and foundations.

Clearly, much of what we have discussed in this book can help nonprofits with fiscal hard times. Coordinating strategic planning with budgeting, conducting regular financial analysis, carefully managing and tracking resources—all of these strategies and methods can help organizations to avoid or cope with a financial crisis. In a serious recession, however, other strategies can be adopted as well.

The Effects of the 2008 Economic Crisis

Due to the 2008 crisis, with grants and donations down, most foundations took steps to improve their financial conditions by cutting staff, travel, and other expenses, making fewer site visits, attending fewer conferences, using electronic media whenever possible, and generally operating more efficiently. The Foundation Center reported that 75,000 grant-making foundations reduced their giving by an estimated 8.4%, to $42.9 billion, in 2009—roughly a $3.9 billion decline from the prior year's record high. This followed a more than 17% drop in foundation assets in 2008. The number of foundations receiving gifts and bequests of at least $5 million decreased from 1,234 to 1,051.[3]

States faced monumental financial issues, which affected nonprofits' finances. California struggled with a $12 billion shortfall; then governor Arnold Schwarzenegger proposed a 2010–2011 budget that would force 200,000 children off lowcost medical insurance, end in-home care for 350,000 seniors, and possibly dismantle the state's welfare-to-work system. On March 11, 2010, the Arizona legislature slashed $1.1 billion from its budget that year, eliminating Medicaid health care coverage for more than 47,000 children and 310,000 low-income adults, shutting down full-day kindergarten, and taking other drastic actions.

Several national organizations conducted surveys of nonprofits to determine their financial conditions during the recession. These surveys found that nonprofits were hard hit by the recession: their cash flow was seriously impaired, the demand for their services increased, and their funding decreased. The Nonprofit Finance Fund (NFF) annual survey of nonprofits showed that, in 2010, 61% of those surveyed had less than 3 months of cash available; 12% had none. Only 18% of the nonprofits surveyed expected to end 2010 above the break-even point; 80% anticipated an increase in demand for services, although only 49% expected to be able to meet the demand level.[4]

The 2010 GuideStar survey of 7,000 nonprofits found similar troubles:

- Some 40% saw declines in contributions in the first 5 months of 2010, while 63% saw an increase in demand for services.
- Many experienced cash-flow issues because of delays in governmental payments.
- Of nonprofits with missions of food, 56% experienced a modest increase in contributions.[5]

The most in-depth assessment of 100 of the largest U.S. nonprofits is conducted by the *NonProfit Times*. As reported in the 2009 analysis, these nonprofits range from $151 million in income to almost $6 billion, with the YMCA of the USA, Catholic Charities USA, United Way, Goodwill Industries, and the American Red Cross having the largest incomes. In 2009:

- Of the 100 nonprofits, 51 reported a deficit.
- Investment income became a proportionally greater source of the nonprofits' revenue, increasing from 0.62% of total revenue in 2008 to 3% in 2009.
- Contributions declined from 52% to 50%.
- Most of the nonprofits suffered cuts from government spending.

By any view of the data, nonprofits suffered large financial losses in the 2008 recession. The strategies developed and implemented by nonprofits to weather this recession show the way to long-term stability and effectiveness for the twenty-first century nonprofit organization.

The Effects of the Covid-19 Pandemic

Although the Covid-19 virus first appeared in Asia in 2019, it hit the United States in 2020 and the effect on the nonprofit world was severe. It will be years before analysts have comprehensive data about the pandemic's effect upon nonprofit finances. A survey from La Piana Consultants shows that 90% of U.S.-based social service nonprofits experienced a reduction in revenue by April 2020. In addition, 18% of the surveyed nonprofits' staff were laid off or furloughed; 83% of the nonprofits' operations were moved from work to home; 69% sought Paycheck Protection Program (PPP) loans as part of the CARES Act, but fewer than half received that funding. Moreover, nonprofits that employed more than 500 employees were not eligible for governmental aid.[6] An NFF survey of U.S.-based organizations showed that

75% were seeing reduced earned revenue, 50% reduced contributions, and 27% reduced government revenue.[7] At the same time, many organizations were seeing increased need—and thus, a greater expense burden.

The Center for Civil Society Studies at Johns Hopkins University estimated that more than 1 in 8 people employed by a nonprofit in the United States in February were not employed as of the end of May. More than 1 million nonprofit workers lost their jobs in 3 months.[8]

Social services nonprofits were hard hit. In Minnesota, more than 9,000 social service nonprofits lost over $1 billion in revenue in April alone; 78% received PPP support. However, 100 nonprofits in the state had more than 500 employees and did not qualify for PPP. Nonprofits, such as Lutheran Social Services, Nexus, People Incorporated, Fraser, and Opportunity Partners, began furloughs and laying off workers in March.[9] Like much of the nonprofit sector, the YMCA found itself in financial jeopardy just as it was needed most. Before the pandemic, YMCA affiliates were typically operating on margins of 3% or less, and during 2020 their revenues were down 30–50% nationwide. Most furloughed 70–95% of their workers, and without help, hundreds of branches may be forced to close. Specifically, the arts and cultural organizations were particularly hard hit. ArtNet reported in July that at least 17 nonprofits had laid off an estimated 1,350 staff members. These included well-known museums such as the San Francisco Museum of Modern Art and the Brooklyn Museum.

Assessing Financial Risks

How should a nonprofit respond to terrible fiscal constraints? The executive director and board members must first assess the risks to develop a clear understanding of the financial threats to the organization. With a frank understanding of the issues, and using the best data available, they must then mitigate the financial risks with efficiencies, creativity, and flexibility. They must conduct complete and careful assessments to identify which revenues will be affected, and thus which programs will be affected. The immediate risk of loss of liquidity is the most important consideration. How many months are covered by cash? What is the nonprofit's working capital? Are there any reserve funds?

The long-term risk of the loss in net assets over time must also be determined. The balanced approach for institutional stability requires that both aspects of risk be addressed. Dennis Young identifies three methods of risk assessment:[10]

- *Market risk* is evaluated through a comparison of the nonprofit's financial changes to the market. The best practice is to benchmark against a subset of organizations similar in finances.
- *Sector risk* can be evaluated through the application of the IRS classifications in which a nonprofit can measure itself against other nonprofits in its industry.
- *Firm risk* can be evaluated through longitudinal analysis, using several years to measure changes in spending and revenues.

Once the risk is assessed, it must be addressed. How can nonprofits increase their liquidity? How can they ensure a more financially secure future in economically harsh times? As nonprofits seek answers to these questions, often they are adopting tools from the business world.

Mitigating Risk: Increasing Revenues

To solve its financial problems, a nonprofit must find efficiencies and must develop creative solutions, seek out and adopt successful strategies implemented by other nonprofits, and look to methods found in the for-profit sector. Indeed, business tools offer a number of strategies that are useful for improving a nonprofit's financial condition. Some strategies have been used by businesses for decades but are now being adopted in increasing size and complexity by nonprofits. Some strategies are newly developed and require creativity and flexibility to be well implemented as financial risk mitigation tools.

Some nonprofits are returning to small donors to increase revenue. The idea is to create a donor base that is an inch deep and a mile wide. If enough donors gave $25 apiece, then a nonprofit would have a powerful revenue stream. Some environmental groups are going door-to-door to solicit credit card donations of $25 a month to address environmental problems that have earned the concern of local citizens.

In another effort to develop more revenue sources, some nonprofits have expanded fundraising to include the vast number of corporate foundations that have developed in the United States. For example, the Boys and Girls Clubs of America raised only $14 million in revenue from the private sector in 1995, but in 2005 it raised more than $100 million from the private sector. It received numerous grants from corporate foundations and corporate-related marketing projects: the Taco Bell Foundation for Teens, Kimberly-Clark Foundation, ConocoPhillips, Morgan Stanley, the Walmart Foundation, the JCPenney Afterschool Fund, the Charles Schwab Foundation, Microsoft, and Best Buy Children's Foundation. Certainly, nonprofits can become creative about raising additional revenues.

Technology has played an increasing role in raising revenue. Nonprofits have developed fundraising tactics that include virtual events, peer-to-peer fundraising and crowdfunding, and utilizing social media to livestream content and promote the goals of the nonprofit. Online campaigns can be assisted by organizations such as GoFundMe as well as by online influencers, or by enrolling contributors to play games such as Jeopardy.

Mitigating Risk: Cutting Costs

A nonprofit can minimize the risk to itself during times of economic crisis not only by seeking new revenue sources but also by examining where it can cut costs within the organization. Cost-cutting measures may include outsourcing and pooling resources with other nonprofits.

A successful cost-cutting strategy for nonprofits seeking to reduce expenses has been to outsource back-office functions such as human resources, information technology, and payroll. By contracting these types of services to specialists, a nonprofit can save money through eliminating personnel costs. Since personnel costs are the largest portion of a nonprofit's budget, cutting back on staff salaries and benefits by eliminating positions can save a great deal of money. The most popular service for outsourcing is payroll processing. For a fee, a for-profit company will process a nonprofit's payroll, pay the payroll taxes, and file returns to the appropriate government office.

Nonprofits have also increasingly been organizing coordinating committees with one another to pool resources and implement the consumer power of collective purchasing to reduce costs and share information and experience. For a small fee, the member nonprofits can hire a staff for the coordinating committee to arrange for common services, including discounts from office supply stores, discounts on payroll processing, and reductions in insurance premiums on the cost side. The coordinating committee also combines resources to develop and disseminate information about government grants and other funding resources. The best known of these coordinating committees is the Nonprofit Coordinating Committee (NPCC) of New York, which, with a staff of six, offers an extensive number of services to more than 1,700 member nonprofits. On the West Coast, the California Association of Nonprofits (CAN) performs the same function, offering its members ways to save money while engaging in advocacy on common issues and providing information and resources. Similar associations have been established in several states.

Mitigating Risk: Collaborations

Some foundations encourage nonprofits to cooperate with one another in ways beyond coordinating committees. For example, Sunset Park Alliance for Youth in Brooklyn, New York, shares space and programs with another nonprofit. The Foundation for the Carolinas raised $5 million for its Community Catalyst Fund to support innovation during the 2008 recession, including collaborations. The Community Foundation for Southern Arizona has awarded grants only to coalitions of groups that work together to solve community problems. After the foundation brought 200 local nonprofit organizations together to discuss its new strategies, the foundation received 29 collaborative grant proposals.[11] These types of collaborations allow nonprofits to end their competition with one another and pool their resources in pursuit of common missions.

One of the most interesting incentives to collaborate comes from a partnership among universities and a foundation. The Arizona-Indiana-Michigan (AIM) Alliance is a collaboration of the Lodestar Center for Philanthropy and Nonprofit Innovation at Arizona State University, the Center on Philanthropy at Indiana University, and the Dorothy A. Johnson Center for Philanthropy and Nonprofit Leadership at Grand Valley State University (Michigan). In 2008, AIM Alliance partnered with the Lodestar Foundation to create a new initiative called the Collaboration Prize. It was designed to inspire cooperation among nonprofit organizations and shine a spotlight on the efficiencies gained from collaborations among nonprofit organizations that would otherwise provide the same or similar programs or services and compete for clients, financial resources, or staff. This strategy of collaboration is being promoted by think tanks within universities and foundations, a powerful combination. Candid, a nonprofit which was a merger of the Foundation Center and GuideStar, created the Collaboration Hub database that provides a comprehensive collection of 650 profiles of four types of collaborations: back office consolidation, joint programming, mergers, and alliances.

Mitigating Risk: Changing the Structure

Another strategy for reducing risk involves actually changing the structure of the nonprofit. Strategies such as becoming a landlord, engaging in a merger, or creating for-profits or social enterprise companies are increasingly common.

Adopting Landlord Status. Nonprofits are finding new revenue streams as landlords. The Boys and Girls Clubs of America bought a new facility and rented out most of the space. Now tenant rental income provides a significant portion of the nonprofit's earned income. This is a strategy rolling across the country. One nonprofit in Richmond, Virginia, was faced with losing its lease and responded by raising the capital funds it needed through borrowing to purchase the building in which it was located. The nonprofit created a limited liability corporation, bought the building, renovated it, and now rents two-thirds of the building's space to income-producing tenants.

Mergers. A traditional for-profit strategy that nonprofits could use to increase efficiency in a difficult economic environment is the merger. When two nonprofits have similar missions in the same geographic area, they might seriously consider merging as a cost-effective method to reduce costs. The Bridgespan Group, a consulting firm for nonprofits and NGOs, describes three rationales for considering a merger: expand a nonprofit's scope, grow economies of scale, or streamline operations. Each of these rationales have their own challenges, so a nonprofit must thoroughly consider its needs and determine the best course of action.

North Carolina focused its mental health funds on large, comprehensive providers. Smaller providers had to change or be left out of the funding. Mergers have been an effective response to this situation. Barium Springs Home for Children doubled its budget in little more than a year through mergers.[12]

Creating For-Profits. A nonprofit may invest in either starting a for-profit or acquiring one, but there are laws governing such investment. For example, the Uniform Prudent Management of Institutional Funds Act (UPMIFA) provides guidance to nonprofits regarding investment decisions and endowment expenditures. It is a uniform law, which means that it has been adopted state by state with their own provisions. Other state laws prohibit self-dealing, private benefit, or excess benefit transactions that enrich an individual at the expense of the nonprofit. There are also rules prohibiting the diversion of assets that do not engage in the nonprofit's mission.[13]

We have found examples of earned-income ventures that do support nonprofits' missions, particularly in the area of job training. Rubicon Bakery, in Richmond, California, employs adults from a wide range of disadvantaged communities to produce premium cakes and tarts that it sells to retailers. Pedal Revolution, in San Francisco, employs homeless youths to repair and sell bicycles. These businesses operate primarily to fulfill the social goal of providing training to the poor; any money they earn in the process is a side benefit that helps them supplement their philanthropic funding.[14]

Of course, there are risks involved. If the newly created for-profit does not make a profit, then a new revenue stream is not realized. If the for-profit is successful, however, the nonprofit enjoys a new revenue stream without the responsibility of running the service.

Social Enterprise Companies. Some nonprofits create **social enterprises** as a solution to their financial problems. A social enterprise company achieves its primary social or environmental mission using business methods.[15] In other words, it is a business with a social mission and can be a nonprofit or for-profit organization. Any surplus revenue is put back into the organization. Nonprofits are turning to the sustainable revenue streams generated from fees and from selling activities related to their social missions.

One famous example of a social enterprise nonprofit is Grameen Bank, which provides credit to the poor in rural Bangladesh without any collateral. It was one of the earliest forms of microfinancing. The initial revenue comes from contributions from foundations and individual donors. Additional examples are Minnesota Diversified Industries (MDI), a nonprofit that serves people with disabilities by developing job opportunities in private businesses, and the for-profit company Ever Green Recycling, a leading recycling and environmental business that seeks out employees with mental health problems.

The Work of the Social Entrepreneur. Closely related to the social enterprise model is the **social entrepreneur** model. Although the concept of entrepreneurship is not new, in the past, it was related primarily to for-profit business. Now it is aimed at social concerns. If a nonprofit model and a business model were placed on a continuum, a social enterprise or social entrepreneur model sits somewhere in between (see Figure 14.1). On one end is the traditional nonprofit financed by mostly philanthropic capital, and on the other end is the conventional business financed by commercial capital. Traditional nonprofits exist throughout the United States, but the numbers of enterprise nonprofits that blur the lines between business and nonprofit are growing.

The Ashoka Foundation defines social entrepreneurs as "individuals with innovative solutions to society's most pressing social problems."[16] The spirit of social entrepreneurship is about using innovative techniques to untangle difficult social problems. It has grown beyond individuals. Foundations also fund nonprofits that they deem organizational social entrepreneurs. For example, New Profit, a foundation based in Boston, funds several traditional nonprofits with the

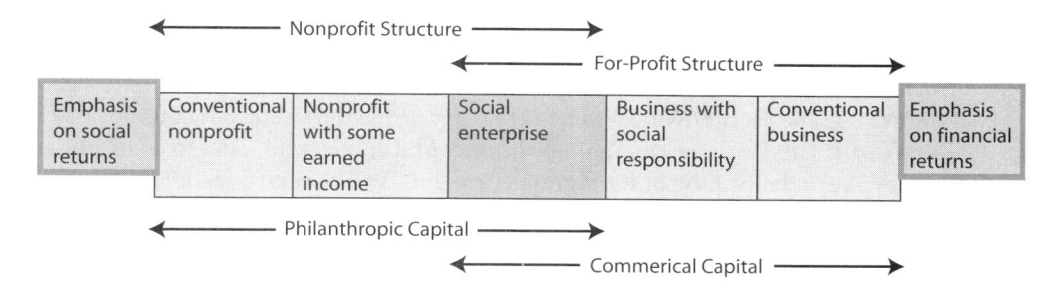

```
         ←———— Nonprofit Structure ————→
                          ←———————— For-Profit Structure ————————→
| Emphasis   | Conventional | Nonprofit  | Social     | Business with   | Conventional | Emphasis     |
| on social  | nonprofit    | with some  | enterprise | social          | business     | on financial |
| returns    |              | earned     |            | responsibility  |              | returns      |
|            |              | income     |            |                 |              |              |
         ←————— Philanthropic Capital —————→
                         ←——————— Commerical Capital ———————→
```

Figure 14.1 Spectrum of social and financial returns.

Source: *Stanford Social Innovation Review* (2008, Spring). See also Kathy O. Brozek (2009). "Exploring the Continuum of Social and Financial Returns: When Does a Nonprofit Become a Social Enterprise?" *Community Development Investment Review, Federal Reserve Bank of San Francisco* (community-wealth.org/sites/clone.community-wealth.org/files/downloads/article-brozek.pdf).

goal of expansion, including Achievement First, which developed Amistad Academy and a network of public charter schools in Connecticut, New York, and Rhode Island. New Profit identifies nonprofits led by ambitious leaders who apply innovative solutions to difficult problems and are committed to measuring their success, which can be expanded to related projects.

Another example is Echoing Green, a foundation that has been identifying, funding, and supporting emerging social entrepreneurs since 1987. Echoing Green has provided seed money for 845 social entrepreneurs and their organizations in 86 countries.[17]

> **Box 14.1**
>
> **REMEMBER: Social Entrepreneurship**
>
> Echoing Green is a nonprofit that promotes social entrepreneurship through fellowships. Its mission: "We discover emerging social entrepreneurs and invest deeply in the growth of their ideas and leadership. Over 30 years, we've built a broad, dynamic ecosystem to support these leaders as they solve the world's biggest problems" (echoinggreen.org).

The Growth of Nonprofit Capital Intermediaries

Social enterprise is growing in part because several groups of intermediaries have sought to provide incentives to nonprofits to change their strategies.[18] These include venture philanthropy and nonprofit loan funds, both of which seek to encourage nonprofits to embrace more entrepreneurial strategies.

Venture Philanthropy

The **venture philanthropy** intermediary arose in the 1990s, when Wall Street was booming. This kind of enterprise applies the tools and techniques of venture capitalism to philanthropic goals. It is characterized by funding on a multiyear basis; a focus on capacity building rather than on programs; high involvement among donors, who often join the boards of the nonprofits in which they invest; a focus on measurable results; and a willingness to try new approaches. A good example is the Robin Hood Foundation, which has targeted reducing poverty in New York City as its goal. "By applying sound investment principles to philanthropy, we've helped the best programs save lives and change fates." The approach is simple:

- Because the Robin Hood Foundation underwrites all administrative expenses, 100% of all contributions go to programs.
- The foundation attacks the root causes of poverty and thus focuses on poverty prevention through programs targeting early childhood, youth, education, jobs, and economic security.
- The foundation leverages its investments with top-notch management and technical assistance. It has in-house management experts to help nonprofits funded by Robin Hood with strategic and financial planning, with recruiting and legal concerns, and with organizational issues and capital needs.
- The foundation also emphasizes evaluation and has created metrics to compare the relative poverty-fighting success of similar programs and even the effectiveness of dissimilar programs.

Although such an approach is quite invasive of a nonprofit's internal structure and processes, it can be life changing to a nonprofit as capital and expertise pour in once it is accepted as a grantee. Other organizations practicing venture philanthropy are similar in their approaches.

Nonprofit Loan Funds

Organizations offering nonprofit loan funds provide below market rate financing to nonprofits. Organized in 1980, the Nonprofit Finance Fund (NFF) is one of the nation's leading community development financial institutions (CDFIs). It lends millions of dollars to nonprofits and advocates for fundamental improvement in how money is given to and used in the sector. Congress created CDFIs in 1994 through the Riegle Community Development and Regulatory Improvement Act to promote economic revitalization and community development of underserved populations and communities in the United States. A pioneer CDFI, the NFF manages over $371 million. Since 1980, NFF has provided $988 million in financing and access to additional capital in support of over $3 billion in projects for thousands of organizations nationwide.[19]

The Role of Government in Promoting Innovation

The U.S. government and some state and city governments have made commitments to work with the nonprofit sector.

The Federal Level

The role the federal government plays in the nonprofit sector varies, not only from administration to administration, but also as a result of the focus of legislation passed in Congress. Here we provide recent, and stark, examples.

The Social Innovation Fund was established in April 2009 by the Edward M. Kennedy Serve America Act. The objective of the fund was to expand innovative programs and support successful programs, as well as to attract private capital and foundation support to promote their expansion. It was also designed to invest in the development of new models of partnership among government, private capital, social entrepreneurs, and foundations. In 2010, the fund awarded $50 million in grants to 11 nonprofits. These grantees selected community-based organizations to replicate their programs. Examples include Jobs for the Future, which is a national job training program; Foundation for a Healthy Kentucky, which has a unique program aimed at helping citizens to access health services; and New Profit, which seeks to help young people make the transition from high school to college.

In December 2009, President Barack Obama created the Office of Social Innovation and Civic Participation within the White House, and appointed Sonal Shah as director. This office was "focused on doing business differently by promoting service as a solution and a way to develop community leadership, increasing investment in innovative community solutions that demonstrate results, and developing new models of partnership."[20] It received funding from 2010–2016.

During his administration, President Trump paid no attention to the nonprofit sector. The aggressive approach adopted by the Obama administration became dependent upon the impact of the "hands off" approach of the Trump administration. The Social Innovation Fund did not receive funding during this period, and no new grants have been given out since the Obama administration. Before Trump, the federal government had turned to the nonprofit sector, sought out the best of nonprofit programs, and worked to replicate them within the nonprofit sector.

State Governments

State governments are also involved in increasing collaboration and innovation with nonprofits. Throughout American history, state governments have succeeded in creating innovative solutions to pressing social problems. States are increasingly turning to collaboration among government, private capital, and nonprofits to solve pressing human needs. Andrew Wolk and Colleen Gross Ebinger have published a report on social innovation in which they document the developing coordination between nonprofits and state governments.[21] They describe several models of cooperation:

- In New York, Governor Mario Cuomo established the Interagency Coordinator for Nonprofit Organizations position within the governor's office.
- Governor Steve Beshear of Kentucky created the Commission on Philanthropy to better align Kentucky's public and private financial resources for work on social issues. The commission's first area of focus was early childhood education and health.

- Lieutenant Governor Mitch Landrieu founded the Louisiana Office of Social Entrepreneurship to advance social innovation through innovative, measurable, and sustainable solutions to social problems.
- The Massachusetts Executive Office of Education partnered with New Profit and Root Cause to launch the Dropout Prevention Initiative. School districts established partnerships with community-based programs, which then could apply for state innovation grants.
- Governor Deval Patrick of Massachusetts signed a Social Innovation Compact to bring the nonprofit, business, and government sectors together in order to maximize the state's resources.
- In Ohio, the Governor's Office of Faith-Based and Community Initiatives launched the Ohio Social Entrepreneurship Initiative to expand social entrepreneurship.

Local Governments

As on the federal and state levels, local governments have also found it constructive to enter into relationships with nonprofits. Several large local governments have focused on the nonprofit sector in some form of partnership:

- New Urban Mechanics was formed in Boston in 2010 to focus on innovations in local government.
- The Denver Office of Strategic Partnerships, created in 2004, serves as a liaison between the city of Denver and the nonprofit sector.
- In Fairfax County, Virginia, the Department of Economic Initiatives, established in 2008, encourages public-private partnerships.
- The Los Angeles Office of Strategic Partnerships works as a liaison between the city and the nonprofit community.

Another focus on local government came from former Mayor Michael Bloomberg. His foundation, Bloomberg Philanthropies, focuses on several areas. One is government innovation in which his foundation staff work closely with city leaders to support those leaders' efforts to take on the toughest challenges. The foundation funds numerous projects on the local level, such as improving care for frontline caregivers and early childhood learning programs, that are then replicated in other cities. Often these projects provide close working relationships between city government and nonprofits. An interesting project is Harvard's Innovations in American Government Awards Program, where local governments often receive grant funding that ties government programs with nonprofits.

Although all three levels of government have long contracted with nonprofits to provide social services, the innovations described here are different. Governments seek to maximize their resources, and in so doing they turn to the concept of innovation and collaboration among all those interested in solving pressing human needs. The same motivation—insufficient resources to meet all citizens' needs—exists in many countries.

Universities

Universities have joined in the quest to solve difficult social issues through innovation. Several universities have set up degree programs in social entrepreneurship:

- Founded by J. Gregory Dees, the Center for the Advancement of Social Entrepreneurship at Duke University's Fuqua School of Business seeks to promote the entrepreneurial pursuit of social impact through the use of business expertise.
- Carnegie Mellon University's Institute for Social Innovation seeks to advance entrepreneurship and innovation to solve social problems.
- The Wharton School at the University of Pennsylvania has established the Wharton Social Entrepreneurship program, which is a global field research program that examines the use of social impact business models to address societal changes.
- Baruch College School of Business has created a social entrepreneurship category within its annual business planning competition.

Other universities, such as Harvard and Yale, have established similar programs. Of course, a cynic would say that universities have simply discovered another source of tuition—students interested in doing good. However, these students will enroll to learn how to create businesses that help people. At the same time, these universities are creating a cadre of young people who are highly trained and exposed to the most recent business methods available, and their intent is to meet social needs through their efforts.

The Role of Foundations in Promoting Social Enterprise

Foundations are nonprofits that provide funds to nonprofits. The Internal Revenue Service Code lists two types of foundations: private and community. Private foundations are funded by individuals, families, or corporations, while public foundations, also known as community foundations, raise their money from public sources. As of 2015, there are over 86,000 entities in the United States that exist for the sole purpose of funding other nonprofits.[22] Private foundations, subject to a 2% excise tax, have more restrictions and fewer tax benefits than public foundations.

The federal government has shaped the growth of foundations. The Revenue Act of 1913 established tax exemption for foundations and other nonprofits that operate exclusively for religious, charitable, scientific, or education purposes. In 1917 Congress allowed tax deductions for contributions to such organizations. The Revenue Act of 1943 required foundations to file an annual return with the IRS listing income and expenses. The Tax Reform Act of 1969 taxed private foundations for the first time (4% excise tax on the net investment income, which was later reduced to 2%), making community foundations more attractive repositories for charitable funds, along with the higher annual deduction limit for individual gifts to community foundations. The Tax Reform Act of 1969 also required foundations to distribute their investment income within one year or award at least 6% (later reduced to 5%) of their assets in grants, whichever was greater. Because of these tax laws, billions of dollars were awarded to many nonprofits during the twentieth century. In 2017, Congress made major changes in the U.S. tax code in the Tax Cuts and Jobs Act (TCJA). Although charitable giving remained deductible, many taxpayers received a double tax deduction and thus would be less likely to itemize their deductions. Overall, the TCJA reduced the marginal tax benefit of giving to charity by more than 30% in 2018, raising the after-tax cost of donating by about 7%.[23] In 2020, Congress modified the excise tax on private foundations from 2% down to 1.39%.

The technological revolution of the late twentieth century fueled enormous growth of foundations, the result of vast assets amassed by the very wealthy, such as Bill Gates, David Packard, William Hewlett, and Gordon Moore. With this increase came experimentation in ways to fund nonprofits through an emphasis on social enterprises to solve pressing social problems.

The Fourth Sector of Social Enterprise

This emphasis on social enterprise has driven the development of a fourth sector. In our introduction to this book, we discussed three sectors: business, government, and nonprofits. A critical mass of organizations within business, government, and nonprofits is evolving into a fundamentally "new organizational landscape that integrates social purposes with business methods."[24] Many nonprofit organizations are altering into a hybrid of market-driven methods that transcends the traditional three sectors; they no longer fit in a particular category. The movement toward market-driven solutions can be found in both social enterprises and social entrepreneurs.

- The Greyston Bakery in Yonkers, New York, is a nonprofit that operates a social enterprise that employs the homeless and makes a profit.
- Grameen Danone Foods is a joint venture between the French dairy company Group Danone and the Grameen Group of social enterprises. This company sells yogurt in Bangladesh with the goal of ensuring better health for millions.
- Cafédirect, based in the United Kingdom, is one of the largest fair trade hot drinks companies in the world. It was started by an unusual partnership of four organizations: the government-created Twin Trading, the worker cooperative Equal Exchange, the charity Oxfam, and the foundation-owned Traidcraft.
- Interface, Inc., is one of a new breed of investor-owned for-profit companies dedicated to becoming fully sustainable and eliminating any negative impact on the environment.[25]

This model is championed by one of the world's richest global capitalist philanthropists, Bill Gates, who has stated, "We need a creative capitalism where business and non-governmental organizations work together to create a market system that eases the world inequities."[26]

The Fourth Sector Group, which promotes this growing sector, is combining market-based approaches with the social and environmental goals of the nonprofit sector to deal with pressing issues. The initiatives that they have undertaken are quite diverse, and all promote for-benefit businesses. For example, there is a major initiative in 22 countries of Latin America and the Iberian Peninsula to develop a new ecosystem. There is a Buy For-Benefit Coalition that seeks to transition profit-centered business models to for-benefit alternatives. Oxfam has committed to using for-benefit businesses in their supply chains.

The *Financial Times* in the United Kingdom published an article praising the fourth sector: "The establishment of social enterprise as a distinct, flourishing sector faces many challenges, but history is encouraging. Concerns over income inequality, environmental degradation and social justice have prompted people to search for an experiment with new ways to do business."[27] Indeed, that is happening. The debate that exists is to what extent this is any different from traditional nonprofits that have sought private funding, as well as other revenues, to meet their missions while operating in a very businesslike fashion. However, some advocates say that most nonprofits are not run in a businesslike fashion. The fourth sector is still developing, so it is hard to say how different this growing sector will be.

The Yunus Centre

One of the best-known examples of social enterprise is the Yunus Centre, the focal point of activity for all the philanthropic work of Nobel Peace Prize winner Muhammad Yunus. Most people know Yunus's name because he founded the Grameen Bank, which provides loans to poor people to establish businesses; they may be unaware that he has gone on to lead the world in expanding social enterprises. According to Yunus,

> A social enterprise is a cause-driven business. In a social business, the investor/owner can recoup the money invested, but he cannot take any dividend beyond that point. Purpose of the investment is purely to achieve one or more social objectives through the operation of the company, no personal gain is desired the investors. The company must cover all costs and make a profit [to pay back investors], at the same time achieve the social objective, such as, health care for the poor, housing for the poor, financial services for the poor, . . . etc., in a business way.[28]

Yunus has encouraged thousands of people to build cause-driven businesses in which investors provide support but do not benefit from any profits. There are other related models.

Program-Related Investments and the New L3Cs

Program-related investments (PRIs) are loans; they are investments made by private foundations to for-profit ventures to support charitable activities. The Tax

Reform Act of 1969 first authorized the creation of PRIs to allow foundations to invest in for-profit projects that, while furthering the foundations' missions, would also give nominal returns to the foundations. However, most foundations never used PRIs because of their regulatory complexity and the punitive fines that could be incurred for noncompliance with complicated IRS record keeping and form-filing requirements. Some examples of PRIs include:

- The John D. and Catherine T. MacArthur Foundation gave $10 million as a PRI to the Local Initiatives Support Corporation to create the Preservation Compact Loan Facility, an initiative to preserve affordable rental homes in Cook County, Illinois.
- The MacArthur Foundation gave $15 million as a PRI to the Shore Bank Corporation for the Rescue Loan and Prevention Program in Chicago.
- The McKnight Foundation gave $5 million as a PRI to the Family Housing Fund to revitalize neighborhoods and expand housing opportunities in Minnesota.

With the active participation of many in the nonprofit world, and a new legal structure that allows foundations to take advantage of its benefits, the PRI is becoming a vehicle of major investment change for nonprofits. A new organizational model has been created: the L3C. This model came out of a 2006 meeting convened by the Aspen Institute's Nonprofit Sector and Philanthropy Program. Three people gathered together after the meeting: Robert Lang, president of the Mary Elizabeth & Gordon B. Mannweiler Foundation; Marcus Owens, a partner with the Washington, DC law firm of Caplin & Drysdale and former director of the Exempt Organizations Division of the Internal Revenue Service; and Arthur Wood, director of Social Financial Services for Ashoka Foundation, an international organization that promotes social entrepreneurship. The Mannweiler Foundation hired Owens to create a business model that would deal with the tax laws to link capitalism with nonprofits.

The result, the **low-profit limited liability company (L3C)**, which can bridge the gap between for-profit and nonprofit organizations. It is a method to legalize a structure that will protect its members and yet retain flexibility. This new legal entity, the L3C, is a limited liability corporation and as such is a pass-through in which taxes pass through the corporation to the members. The members have the liability protection of a corporation and the flexibility of a partnership. The innovation of the L3C is that this entity facilitates investments in socially beneficial, for-profit ventures while complying with IRS rules concerning program-related investments. What does this mean? Public-spirited L3Cs receive seed money from large nonprofit foundations. An L3C runs like a business and can be profitable. The primary business of an L3C, however, is not to make a profit but to achieve a socially beneficial objective. The L3C model now exists in 10 states, three tribes, and Puerto Rico.

One of the major purposes of the L3C is to bring more money into the nonprofit sector. An L3C must fulfill three requirements in order to qualify as a recipient of PRIs:

- The L3C must significantly further the accomplishment of one or more charitable or educational purposes.
- The L3C, while it may make a profit, cannot make the pursuit of income its primary objective.
- The L3C must not be organized to achieve a political purpose.

Although it is legally possible for an L3C to have a hundred investors, each with an arrangement with the L3C, efficiency indicates that three levels of investors are the most efficient. First is the equity level, which foundations buy into and which has the highest risk and lowest return. Second is the mezzanine level, in which individuals, banks under the Community Reinvestment Act, and corporations have less risk and more return. Third is the senior level, in which pension funds would invest at very low risk.

The L3C can leverage a foundation's program-related investments to access millions of dollars of market-driven capital intent on major social impact. A foundation can retain ownership rights to an L3C, recover its investment, and realize a capital gain that increases the amount of funds available for the foundation's charitable purposes. Or, to put it another way, L3Cs can bring together foundation funds, corporate profits, and pension funds that are not otherwise available for socially beneficial investments. On April 30, 2008, Vermont became the first state to recognize the L3C as an official legal structure. As of 2020, it is now a legal structure in 10 states. Examples of current L3Cs include: a motorcycle safety school, farmer's markets, and a research organization to make pediatric X-rays and CT scans safer for kids.

The exciting possibilities of L3C formation reside in the opportunity to access major capital funds, such as pension funds, that offer billions to be used in socially beneficial investments. This kind of legal structure for financial investment is the future if the nonprofit world wishes to see a substantial increase in this sector's impact on world social issues. The L3C entity encourages foundations to make program-related investments, rather than grants, so funds are leveraged from a variety of profit-making organizations to further the missions of foundations.

The Rise of the B Corporation

The **benefit corporation (B corporation)** is another structure in the evolving fourth sector sitting between the for-profit and the nonprofit. It seeks to have a positive impact on society and the environment, redefines fiduciary responsibility to include nonfinancial interests when making decisions, and utilizes the B Impact Assessment to measure its impacts on its workers, community, environment, and customers. In essence, a B corporation is a responsible corporation. There are over 3,900 B corporations that participate in 150 industries found in 74 countries. B corporation certification is the only certification process that measures a company's entire social and environmental performance. It is also a long-term commitment by the company to adhere to particular standards regarding its supply chain, charitable giving, and employee benefits that are built into its legal structure.[29] The best known B corporations are Ben & Jerry's, Eileen Fisher, Patagonia, and Stonyfield Organic.

In effect, B corporations are capitalist corporations that get protection from shareholder lawsuits for doing the "right" thing. B corporations can effectively consider social and environmental impacts in their decision making without being sued by shareholders who only wish to make a profit.

Conclusion

The numerous strategies discussed in this chapter indicate several trends. First, there may be fewer nonprofits in the future as nonprofits merge or close because of financial difficulties triggered by large-scale crises, such as the 2008 recession and the 2020 pandemic. Philanthropy, however, is experimenting with different ways of giving and certainly has the potential to expand and grow in new and challenging ways.

Second, the face of philanthropy is changing as newer generations embrace a more activist stance in which donors seek places at the decision-making table. No longer are philanthropists satisfied with writing checks; they wish to sit on the boards and play active roles in policy making.

Third, capitalism has entered the nonprofit world in a new way. The market-driven economy has entered into the thinking of board members and executive directors. How can the nonprofit leadership take advantage of the tools of a market-driven economy? How can the nonprofit leadership embrace capitalism, not as a result of philanthropy, but as a means to expand its resources? Social enterprise has been around for a very long time. The YMCA and Goodwill Industries, for example, both in the top 10 of revenue-producing nonprofits, have always earned the vast percentage of their revenues through sales. To that extent, social enterprise is not new. Something is different now, however. The change encompasses the aggressive capitalism of the new philanthropy and the range and innovation of the market economy's financial tools being used by modern nonprofits.

Finally, the infrastructure of the nonprofit world is changing. A fourth sector is emerging, the social enterprise sector, distinguished from the traditional nonprofit by its diversity of revenue allocation. The fourth sector is a merger of business and nonprofits offering enormous potential to capture very large revenue streams for social missions. Whether a corporation becomes an L3C or a B corporation is not as important as the fact that these new legal structures exist and are spreading across the country.

Of all these trends, the market-driven enterprise as a nonprofit may be the most challenging to the nonprofit sector. Adopting business methods as a major operating strategy is not generally accepted throughout the nonprofit world. Many board members do not wish to become overly involved in a nonprofit's operations, and many executive directors do not welcome social investors who push performance indicators that are difficult and time-consuming to track. Skeptics challenge the value of the new market-driven strategies compared with the time proven, well understood old strategies of revenue generation. The issue concerns more than just the size and scope of nonprofits; the issue is that enthusiasm may shift major funding from foundations and major donors away from traditional nonprofits and toward the most recent eye-catching nonprofits. Nevertheless, business methods will be part of the nonprofit methodology. The question remains whether this will amount to the moderate incorporation of methods into traditional forms or the wholesale establishment of a fourth sector of for-profit businesses with established social missions. It may become the rise of "conscious capitalism."

KEY TERMS

benefit corporation (B corporation)
low-profit limited liability company (L3C)
program-related investments (PRIs)
social enterprise
social entrepreneur
venture philanthropy

DISCUSSION QUESTIONS

1. What effects did the 2008 recession and the 2020 pandemic have on the nonprofit world?
2. What is financial risk assessment in the nonprofit context?
3. What are some of the strategies nonprofits use to respond to difficult economic times?
4. What is a social enterprise? Give some examples.
5. What is social entrepreneurship? Give some examples.
6. What is the difference between social enterprise and social entrepreneurship?
7. What is the emerging fourth sector? What are the other three sectors?
8. What new legal structure has been created to encourage social enterprise?
9. What do you think are the possibilities of success of a fourth sector?
10. Why is a market-driven economy seen as a way to help nonprofits?

SUGGESTED READINGS

Certified B Corporations. www.bcorporation.net.
Cohen, Richard J., and Tine Hansen-Turton (2009, October). "The Birth of a Fourth Sector." *Philadelphia Social Innovations Journal* (philasocialinnovations.org/site/index.php?Itemid=31&catid=20:what-works-and-what-doesnt&id=32:the-birth-of-a-fourth-sector&option=com_content&view=article).
Fourth Sector Network. The Emerging Fourth Sector (fourthsector.net/the-emerging-fourth-sector).
Sabeti, Heerad (2009). *The Emerging Fourth Sector: A New Sector of Organizations at the Intersection of the Public, Private and Social Sectors* (Executive Summary). Washington, DC: Aspen Institute (aspeninstitute.org/publications/emerging-fourth-sector-executive-summary).

Assignment

Assignment 14.1. Exploring Social Entrepreneurship

If you could be a social entrepreneur, what form would your enterprise take? How would you proceed to make your dream a reality? With whom would you consult and collaborate? What would you need to learn? Write 3–5 pages describing your dream and how you would bring it to fruition.

Notes

[1] PBS. The New Heroes: What Is Social Entrepreneurship? (pbs.org/now/enterprisingideas/what-is.html).

[2] Johnson, Nicholas, Phil Oliff, and Erica Williams (2010, March 8). *An Update on State Budget Cuts.* Washington, DC: Center on Budget and Policy Priorities (cbpp.org/cms/?fa=view&id=1214).

[3] Foundation Center (2010, October). Highlights of Foundation Yearbook. Foundations Today Series (foundationcenter.org/gainknowledge/research/pdf/fy2010_highlights.pdf).

[4] Nonprofit Finance Fund. 2011 State of the Sector Survey (nonprofitfinancefund.org/state-of-the-sector-surveys).

[5] GuideStar (2010, June). *The Effect of the Economy on the Nonprofit Sector.* Washington, DC: GuideStar.

[6] La Piana Consulting (2020, May). The Continuing Impact of Covid-19 on the Social Sector (lapiana.org/wp-content/uploads/2020/07/R2-COVID-Data-Share-Final.pdf?ver=2020-05-07-094644-193).

[7] Harold, Jacob (2020, July 15). Candid (blog.candid.org/post/how-many-nonprofits-will-shut-their-doors).

[8] Salamon, Lester M., and Chelsea L. Newhouse (2020, June). *2020 Nonprofit Employment Report* (Nonprofit Economic Data Bulletin No. 48). Baltimore, MD: Johns Hopkins Center for Civil Society Studies (ccss.jhu.edu/wp-content/uploads/downloads/2020/06/2020-Nonprofit-Employment-Report_FINAL_6.2020.pdf).

[9] Smith, Kelly (2020, July 3). "Large Minnesota Nonprofits Caught in Stimulus Aid Gap, Face Cost-Cutting." *Star Tribune* (startribune.com/large-minnesota-nonprofits-caught-in-stimulus-aid-gap-face-cost-cutting/571622902).

[10] Young, Dennis R. (2009, April). How Nonprofit Organizations Manage Risk. AIEL Series in Labour Economics 4:33–46. doi: 10.1007/978-3-7908-2137-6_3

[11] Wallace, Nicole (2011, January). "A Grant Maker Requires Grantees to Collaborate." *Chronicle of Philanthropy* (philanthropy.com/article/A-Foundation-Requires-Grantees/159271).

[12] Wallace, Nicole (2011, January 9). "A N.C. Charity Finds Mergers Help It Expand Services." *Chronicle of Philanthropy* (philanthropy.com/article/Mergers-Help-a-NC-Charity).

[13] NEO Law Group (2019, June 22). Can a Nonprofit Own a For-Profit? Nonprofit Law Blog (nonprofitlawblog.com/can-a-nonprofit-own-a-for-profit-can-a-for-profit-own-a-nonprofit).

[14] Foster, William, and Jeffrey L. Bradach (2005, February). "Should Nonprofits Seek Profits?" *Harvard Business Review* (hbr.org/2005/02/should-nonprofits-seek-profits).

[15] See the Social Enterprise Alliance website (socialenterprise.us).

[16] Ashoka Foundation. Social Entrepreneurship (ashoka.org/en-us/focus/social-entrepreneurship).

[17] Echoing Green (2020, December 18). Annual Report 2020 (echoinggreen.org/news/annual-report-2020).

[18] Brozek, Kathy O. (2009). "Exploring the Continuum of Social and Financial Returns: When Does a Nonprofit Become a Social Enterprise?" *Community Development Investment Review*, 5(2): 7–17 (frbsf.org/publications/community/review/vol5_issue2/brozek.pdf).

[19] Nonprofit Finance Fund (2021, March 22). Financing (nff.org/financing).

[20] Office of Social Innovation and Civic Participation. About SICP—The Community Solutions Agenda (whitehouse.gov/administration/eop/sicp/about).

[21] Wolk, Andrew, and Colleen Gross Ebinger (2010, Summer). "Government and Social Innovations: Current State and Local Models." *Innovations: Technology, Governance, Globalization*, 5(3):135–157.

[22] Foundation Center (2021, March 23). Foundation Stats 2015 (data.foundationcenter.org).
[23] Tax Policy Center, Urban Institute, and Brookings Institution (2020). Briefing Book. Key Elements of the U.S. Tax System (taxpolicycenter.org/briefing-book/how-did-tcja-affect-incentives-charitable-giving).
[24] Sabeti, Heerad (2009). *The Emerging Fourth Sector: A New Sector of Organizations at the Intersection of the Public, Private and Social Sectors.* Washington, DC: Aspen Institute (aspeninstitute.org).
[25] Ibid.
[26] Quoted in Sabeti, Heerad (2010, March 9). Fourth Sector Solutions for the Fourth Estate. Presentation: How Will Journalism Survive the Internet Age? (ftc.gov/sites/default/files/documents/public_events/how-will-journalism-survive-internet-age/sabeti.pdf).
[27] Feiss, Chris (2009, June 15). "Social Enterprise—The Fledging Fourth Sector." *Financial Times* (ft.com/intl/cms/s/0/6e8285f2-5944-11de-80b3-00144feabdc0.html#axzz1ewo6sl2z).
[28] Yunus Centre. Social Business (muhammadyunus.org/post/2113/social-business).
[29] B Lab. B Corporations (bcorporation.net).

Appendix A

IRS Form 990, Return of Organization Exempt From Income Tax

Appendix A

Form 990

Return of Organization Exempt From Income Tax

Under section 501(c), 527, or 4947(a)(1) of the Internal Revenue Code (except private foundations)

▶ Do not enter social security numbers on this form as it may be made public.
▶ Go to *www.irs.gov/Form990* for instructions and the latest information.

OMB No. 1545-0047

2020

Department of the Treasury
Internal Revenue Service

Open to Public Inspection

A For the 2020 calendar year, or tax year beginning _____, 2020, and ending _____, 20 ___

B Check if applicable:
☐ Address change
☐ Name change
☐ Initial return
☐ Final return/terminated
☐ Amended return
☐ Application pending

C Name of organization _____

Doing business as _____

Number and street (or P.O. box if mail is not delivered to street address) | Room/suite

City or town, state or province, country, and ZIP or foreign postal code

F Name and address of principal officer: _____

D Employer identification number

E Telephone number

G Gross receipts $ _____

H(a) Is this a group return for subordinates? ☐ Yes ☐ No
H(b) Are all subordinates included? ☐ Yes ☐ No
   If "No," attach a list. See instructions

I Tax-exempt status: ☐ 501(c)(3) ☐ 501(c) ( ) ◀ (insert no.) ☐ 4947(a)(1) or ☐ 527

J Website: ▶ _____

H(c) Group exemption number ▶ _____

K Form of organization: ☐ Corporation ☐ Trust ☐ Association ☐ Other ▶ **L** Year of formation: **M** State of legal domicile:

Part I Summary

		Activity	
Activities & Governance	1	Briefly describe the organization's mission or most significant activities: _____	
	2	Check this box ▶ ☐ if the organization discontinued its operations or disposed of more than 25% of its net assets.	
	3	Number of voting members of the governing body (Part VI, line 1a)	3
	4	Number of independent voting members of the governing body (Part VI, line 1b)	4
	5	Total number of individuals employed in calendar year 2020 (Part V, line 2a)	5
	6	Total number of volunteers (estimate if necessary)	6
	7a	Total unrelated business revenue from Part VIII, column (C), line 12	7a
	b	Net unrelated business taxable income from Form 990-T, Part I, line 11	7b

			Prior Year	Current Year
Revenue	8	Contributions and grants (Part VIII, line 1h)		
	9	Program service revenue (Part VIII, line 2g)		
	10	Investment income (Part VIII, column (A), lines 3, 4, and 7d)		
	11	Other revenue (Part VIII, column (A), lines 5, 6d, 8c, 9c, 10c, and 11e) . . .		
	12	Total revenue—add lines 8 through 11 (must equal Part VIII, column (A), line 12)		
Expenses	13	Grants and similar amounts paid (Part IX, column (A), lines 1–3)		
	14	Benefits paid to or for members (Part IX, column (A), line 4)		
	15	Salaries, other compensation, employee benefits (Part IX, column (A), lines 5–10)		
	16a	Professional fundraising fees (Part IX, column (A), line 11e)		
	b	Total fundraising expenses (Part IX, column (D), line 25) ▶ _____		
	17	Other expenses (Part IX, column (A), lines 11a–11d, 11f–24e)		
	18	Total expenses. Add lines 13–17 (must equal Part IX, column (A), line 25) .		
	19	Revenue less expenses. Subtract line 18 from line 12		

			Beginning of Current Year	End of Year
Net Assets or Fund Balances	20	Total assets (Part X, line 16)		
	21	Total liabilities (Part X, line 26)		
	22	Net assets or fund balances. Subtract line 21 from line 20		

Part II Signature Block

Under penalties of perjury, I declare that I have examined this return, including accompanying schedules and statements, and to the best of my knowledge and belief, it is true, correct, and complete. Declaration of preparer (other than officer) is based on all information of which preparer has any knowledge.

Sign Here
▶ Signature of officer   Date
▶ Type or print name and title

Paid Preparer Use Only
Print/Type preparer's name	Preparer's signature	Date	Check ☐ if self-employed	PTIN
Firm's name ▶			Firm's EIN ▶	
Firm's address ▶			Phone no.	

May the IRS discuss this return with the preparer shown above? See instructions . . . . ☐ Yes ☐ No

For Paperwork Reduction Act Notice, see the separate instructions.   Cat. No. 11282Y   Form **990** (2020)

IRS Form 990, Return of Organization Exempt From Income Tax

Form 990 (2020)   Page **2**

Part III   Statement of Program Service Accomplishments
        Check if Schedule O contains a response or note to any line in this Part III . . . . ☐

1   Briefly describe the organization's mission:
_____
_____
_____

2   Did the organization undertake any significant program services during the year which were not listed on the prior Form 990 or 990-EZ? . . . . ☐ Yes   ☐ No
      If "Yes," describe these new services on Schedule O.

3   Did the organization cease conducting, or make significant changes in how it conducts, any program services? . . . . ☐ Yes   ☐ No
      If "Yes," describe these changes on Schedule O.

4   Describe the organization's program service accomplishments for each of its three largest program services, as measured by expenses. Section 501(c)(3) and 501(c)(4) organizations are required to report the amount of grants and allocations to others, the total expenses, and revenue, if any, for each program service reported.

4a   (Code: _____) (Expenses $ _____ including grants of $ _____) (Revenue $ _____)
_____
_____
_____
_____
_____
_____
_____
_____
_____
_____

4b   (Code: _____) (Expenses $ _____ including grants of $ _____) (Revenue $ _____)
_____
_____
_____
_____
_____
_____
_____
_____
_____
_____

4c   (Code: _____) (Expenses $ _____ including grants of $ _____) (Revenue $ _____)
_____
_____
_____
_____
_____
_____
_____
_____
_____
_____

4d   Other program services (Describe on Schedule O.)
      (Expenses $ _____ including grants of $ _____) (Revenue $ _____)

4e   Total program service expenses ▶

Form **990** (2020)

294 Appendix A

Form 990 (2020) Page **3**

Part IV Checklist of Required Schedules

			Yes	No
1	Is the organization described in section 501(c)(3) or 4947(a)(1) (other than a private foundation)? *If "Yes," complete Schedule A* . .	**1**		
2	Is the organization required to complete *Schedule B, Schedule of Contributors* See instructions?	**2**		
3	Did the organization engage in direct or indirect political campaign activities on behalf of or in opposition to candidates for public office? *If "Yes," complete Schedule C, Part I*	**3**		
4	**Section 501(c)(3) organizations.** Did the organization engage in lobbying activities, or have a section 501(h) election in effect during the tax year? *If "Yes," complete Schedule C, Part II*	**4**		
5	Is the organization a section 501(c)(4), 501(c)(5), or 501(c)(6) organization that receives membership dues, assessments, or similar amounts as defined in Revenue Procedure 98-19? *If "Yes," complete Schedule C, Part III*	**5**		
6	Did the organization maintain any donor advised funds or any similar funds or accounts for which donors have the right to provide advice on the distribution or investment of amounts in such funds or accounts? *If "Yes," complete Schedule D, Part I*	**6**		
7	Did the organization receive or hold a conservation easement, including easements to preserve open space, the environment, historic land areas, or historic structures? *If "Yes," complete Schedule D, Part II* . . .	**7**		
8	Did the organization maintain collections of works of art, historical treasures, or other similar assets? *If "Yes," complete Schedule D, Part III*	**8**		
9	Did the organization report an amount in Part X, line 21, for escrow or custodial account liability, serve as a custodian for amounts not listed in Part X; or provide credit counseling, debt management, credit repair, or debt negotiation services? *If "Yes," complete Schedule D, Part IV*	**9**		
10	Did the organization, directly or through a related organization, hold assets in donor-restricted endowments or in quasi endowments? *If "Yes," complete Schedule D, Part V*	**10**		
11	If the organization's answer to any of the following questions is "Yes," then complete Schedule D, Parts VI, VII, VIII, IX, or X as applicable.			
a	Did the organization report an amount for land, buildings, and equipment in Part X, line 10? *If "Yes," complete Schedule D, Part VI*	**11a**		
b	Did the organization report an amount for investments—other securities in Part X, line 12, that is 5% or more of its total assets reported in Part X, line 16? *If "Yes," complete Schedule D, Part VII*	**11b**		
c	Did the organization report an amount for investments—program related in Part X, line 13, that is 5% or more of its total assets reported in Part X, line 16? *If "Yes," complete Schedule D, Part VIII*	**11c**		
d	Did the organization report an amount for other assets in Part X, line 15, that is 5% or more of its total assets reported in Part X, line 16? *If "Yes," complete Schedule D, Part IX*	**11d**		
e	Did the organization report an amount for other liabilities in Part X, line 25? *If "Yes," complete Schedule D, Part X*	**11e**		
f	Did the organization's separate or consolidated financial statements for the tax year include a footnote that addresses the organization's liability for uncertain tax positions under FIN 48 (ASC 740)? *If "Yes," complete Schedule D, Part X*	**11f**		
12a	Did the organization obtain separate, independent audited financial statements for the tax year? *If "Yes," complete Schedule D, Parts XI and XII*	**12a**		
b	Was the organization included in consolidated, independent audited financial statements for the tax year? *If "Yes," and if the organization answered "No" to line 12a, then completing Schedule D, Parts XI and XII is optional*	**12b**		
13	Is the organization a school described in section 170(b)(1)(A)(ii)? *If "Yes," complete Schedule E*	**13**		
14a	Did the organization maintain an office, employees, or agents outside of the United States?	**14a**		
b	Did the organization have aggregate revenues or expenses of more than $10,000 from grantmaking, fundraising, business, investment, and program service activities outside the United States, or aggregate foreign investments valued at $100,000 or more? *If "Yes," complete Schedule F, Parts I and IV.*	**14b**		
15	Did the organization report on Part IX, column (A), line 3, more than $5,000 of grants or other assistance to or for any foreign organization? *If "Yes," complete Schedule F, Parts II and IV*	**15**		
16	Did the organization report on Part IX, column (A), line 3, more than $5,000 of aggregate grants or other assistance to or for foreign individuals? *If "Yes," complete Schedule F, Parts III and IV.*	**16**		
17	Did the organization report a total of more than $15,000 of expenses for professional fundraising services on Part IX, column (A), lines 6 and 11e? *If "Yes," complete Schedule G, Part I* See instructions	**17**		
18	Did the organization report more than $15,000 total of fundraising event gross income and contributions on Part VIII, lines 1c and 8a? *If "Yes," complete Schedule G, Part II*	**18**		
19	Did the organization report more than $15,000 of gross income from gaming activities on Part VIII, line 9a? *If "Yes," complete Schedule G, Part III*	**19**		
20a	Did the organization operate one or more hospital facilities? *If "Yes," complete Schedule H*	**20a**		
b	If "Yes" to line 20a, did the organization attach a copy of its audited financial statements to this return? .	**20b**		
21	Did the organization report more than $5,000 of grants or other assistance to any domestic organization or domestic government on Part IX, column (A), line 1? *If "Yes," complete Schedule I, Parts I and II*	**21**		

Form **990** (2020)

IRS Form 990, Return of Organization Exempt From Income Tax

Form 990 (2020) Page **4**

Part IV Checklist of Required Schedules *(continued)*

			Yes	No
22	Did the organization report more than $5,000 of grants or other assistance to or for domestic individuals on Part IX, column (A), line 2? *If "Yes," complete Schedule I, Parts I and III*	22		
23	Did the organization answer "Yes" to Part VII, Section A, line 3, 4, or 5 about compensation of the organization's current and former officers, directors, trustees, key employees, and highest compensated employees? *If "Yes," complete Schedule J*	23		
24a	Did the organization have a tax-exempt bond issue with an outstanding principal amount of more than $100,000 as of the last day of the year, that was issued after December 31, 2002? *If "Yes," answer lines 24b through 24d and complete Schedule K. If "No," go to line 25a*	24a		
b	Did the organization invest any proceeds of tax-exempt bonds beyond a temporary period exception?	24b		
c	Did the organization maintain an escrow account other than a refunding escrow at any time during the year to defease any tax-exempt bonds?	24c		
d	Did the organization act as an "on behalf of" issuer for bonds outstanding at any time during the year?	24d		
25a	**Section 501(c)(3), 501(c)(4), and 501(c)(29) organizations.** Did the organization engage in an excess benefit transaction with a disqualified person during the year? *If "Yes," complete Schedule L, Part I*	25a		
b	Is the organization aware that it engaged in an excess benefit transaction with a disqualified person in a prior year, and that the transaction has not been reported on any of the organization's prior Forms 990 or 990-EZ? *If "Yes," complete Schedule L, Part I*	25b		
26	Did the organization report any amount on Part X, line 5 or 22, for receivables from or payables to any current or former officer, director, trustee, key employee, creator or founder, substantial contributor, or 35% controlled entity or family member of any of these persons? *If "Yes," complete Schedule L, Part II*	26		
27	Did the organization provide a grant or other assistance to any current or former officer, director, trustee, key employee, creator or founder, substantial contributor or employee thereof, a grant selection committee member, or to a 35% controlled entity (including an employee thereof) or family member of any of these persons? *If "Yes," complete Schedule L, Part III*	27		
28	Was the organization a party to a business transaction with one of the following parties (see Schedule L, Part IV instructions, for applicable filing thresholds, conditions, and exceptions):			
a	A current or former officer, director, trustee, key employee, creator or founder, or substantial contributor? *If "Yes," complete Schedule L, Part IV*	28a		
b	A family member of any individual described in line 28a? *If "Yes," complete Schedule L, Part IV*	28b		
c	A 35% controlled entity of one or more individuals and/or organizations described in lines 28a or 28b? *If "Yes," complete Schedule L, Part IV*	28c		
29	Did the organization receive more than $25,000 in non-cash contributions? *If "Yes," complete Schedule M*	29		
30	Did the organization receive contributions of art, historical treasures, or other similar assets, or qualified conservation contributions? *If "Yes," complete Schedule M*	30		
31	Did the organization liquidate, terminate, or dissolve and cease operations? *If "Yes," complete Schedule N, Part I*	31		
32	Did the organization sell, exchange, dispose of, or transfer more than 25% of its net assets? *If "Yes," complete Schedule N, Part II*	32		
33	Did the organization own 100% of an entity disregarded as separate from the organization under Regulations sections 301.7701-2 and 301.7701-3? *If "Yes," complete Schedule R, Part I*	33		
34	Was the organization related to any tax-exempt or taxable entity? *If "Yes," complete Schedule R, Part II, III, or IV, and Part V, line 1*	34		
35a	Did the organization have a controlled entity within the meaning of section 512(b)(13)?	35a		
b	If "Yes" to line 35a, did the organization receive any payment from or engage in any transaction with a controlled entity within the meaning of section 512(b)(13)? *If "Yes," complete Schedule R, Part V, line 2*	35b		
36	**Section 501(c)(3) organizations.** Did the organization make any transfers to an exempt non-charitable related organization? *If "Yes," complete Schedule R, Part V, line 2*	36		
37	Did the organization conduct more than 5% of its activities through an entity that is not a related organization and that is treated as a partnership for federal income tax purposes? *If "Yes," complete Schedule R, Part VI*	37		
38	Did the organization complete Schedule O and provide explanations in Schedule O for Part VI, lines 11b and 19? **Note:** All Form 990 filers are required to complete Schedule O.	38		

Part V Statements Regarding Other IRS Filings and Tax Compliance

Check if Schedule O contains a response or note to any line in this Part V . . . . ☐

			Yes	No
1a	Enter the number reported in Box 3 of Form 1096. Enter -0- if not applicable	1a		
b	Enter the number of Forms W-2G included in line 1a. Enter -0- if not applicable	1b		
c	Did the organization comply with backup withholding rules for reportable payments to vendors and reportable gaming (gambling) winnings to prize winners?	1c		

Form **990** (2020)

Appendix A

Form 990 (2020) Page **5**

Part V Statements Regarding Other IRS Filings and Tax Compliance *(continued)*

		Yes	No
2a	Enter the number of employees reported on Form W-3, Transmittal of Wage and Tax Statements, filed for the calendar year ending with or within the year covered by this return [2a]		
b	If at least one is reported on line 2a, did the organization file all required federal employment tax returns? **2b**		
	Note: If the sum of lines 1a and 2a is greater than 250, you may be required to *e-file* (see instructions)		
3a	Did the organization have unrelated business gross income of $1,000 or more during the year? **3a**		
b	If "Yes," has it filed a Form 990-T for this year? *If "No" to line 3b, provide an explanation on Schedule O* **3b**		
4a	At any time during the calendar year, did the organization have an interest in, or a signature or other authority over, a financial account in a foreign country (such as a bank account, securities account, or other financial account)? **4a**		
b	If "Yes," enter the name of the foreign country ▶ _____		
	See instructions for filing requirements for FinCEN Form 114, Report of Foreign Bank and Financial Accounts (FBAR).		
5a	Was the organization a party to a prohibited tax shelter transaction at any time during the tax year? **5a**		
b	Did any taxable party notify the organization that it was or is a party to a prohibited tax shelter transaction? **5b**		
c	If "Yes" to line 5a or 5b, did the organization file Form 8886-T? **5c**		
6a	Does the organization have annual gross receipts that are normally greater than $100,000, and did the organization solicit any contributions that were not tax deductible as charitable contributions? **6a**		
b	If "Yes," did the organization include with every solicitation an express statement that such contributions or gifts were not tax deductible? **6b**		
7	**Organizations that may receive deductible contributions under section 170(c).**		
a	Did the organization receive a payment in excess of $75 made partly as a contribution and partly for goods and services provided to the payor? **7a**		
b	If "Yes," did the organization notify the donor of the value of the goods or services provided? **7b**		
c	Did the organization sell, exchange, or otherwise dispose of tangible personal property for which it was required to file Form 8282? **7c**		
d	If "Yes," indicate the number of Forms 8282 filed during the year [7d]		
e	Did the organization receive any funds, directly or indirectly, to pay premiums on a personal benefit contract? **7e**		
f	Did the organization, during the year, pay premiums, directly or indirectly, on a personal benefit contract? **7f**		
g	If the organization received a contribution of qualified intellectual property, did the organization file Form 8899 as required? **7g**		
h	If the organization received a contribution of cars, boats, airplanes, or other vehicles, did the organization file a Form 1098-C? **7h**		
8	**Sponsoring organizations maintaining donor advised funds.** Did a donor advised fund maintained by the sponsoring organization have excess business holdings at any time during the year? **8**		
9	**Sponsoring organizations maintaining donor advised funds.**		
a	Did the sponsoring organization make any taxable distributions under section 4966? **9a**		
b	Did the sponsoring organization make a distribution to a donor, donor advisor, or related person? **9b**		
10	**Section 501(c)(7) organizations.** Enter:		
a	Initiation fees and capital contributions included on Part VIII, line 12 [10a]		
b	Gross receipts, included on Form 990, Part VIII, line 12, for public use of club facilities [10b]		
11	**Section 501(c)(12) organizations.** Enter:		
a	Gross income from members or shareholders [11a]		
b	Gross income from other sources (Do not net amounts due or paid to other sources against amounts due or received from them.) [11b]		
12a	**Section 4947(a)(1) non-exempt charitable trusts.** Is the organization filing Form 990 in lieu of Form 1041? **12a**		
b	If "Yes," enter the amount of tax-exempt interest received or accrued during the year [12b]		
13	**Section 501(c)(29) qualified nonprofit health insurance issuers.**		
a	Is the organization licensed to issue qualified health plans in more than one state? **13a**		
	Note: See the instructions for additional information the organization must report on Schedule O.		
b	Enter the amount of reserves the organization is required to maintain by the states in which the organization is licensed to issue qualified health plans [13b]		
c	Enter the amount of reserves on hand [13c]		
14a	Did the organization receive any payments for indoor tanning services during the tax year? **14a**		
b	If "Yes," has it filed a Form 720 to report these payments? *If "No," provide an explanation on Schedule O* **14b**		
15	Is the organization subject to the section 4960 tax on payment(s) of more than $1,000,000 in remuneration or excess parachute payment(s) during the year? **15**		
	If "Yes," see instructions and file Form 4720, Schedule N.		
16	Is the organization an educational institution subject to the section 4968 excise tax on net investment income? **16**		
	If "Yes," complete Form 4720, Schedule O.		

Form **990** (2020)

IRS Form 990, Return of Organization Exempt From Income Tax

Form 990 (2020) Page **6**

Part VI Governance, Management, and Disclosure
For each "Yes" response to lines 2 through 7b below, and for a "No" response to line 8a, 8b, or 10b below, describe the circumstances, processes, or changes on Schedule O. See instructions.

Check if Schedule O contains a response or note to any line in this Part VI . . . . ☐

Section A. Governing Body and Management

			Yes	No
1a	Enter the number of voting members of the governing body at the end of the tax year . . **1a**			
	If there are material differences in voting rights among members of the governing body, or if the governing body delegated broad authority to an executive committee or similar committee, explain on Schedule O.			
b	Enter the number of voting members included on line 1a, above, who are independent . **1b**			
2	Did any officer, director, trustee, or key employee have a family relationship or a business relationship with any other officer, director, trustee, or key employee?	**2**		
3	Did the organization delegate control over management duties customarily performed by or under the direct supervision of officers, directors, trustees, or key employees to a management company or other person? .	**3**		
4	Did the organization make any significant changes to its governing documents since the prior Form 990 was filed?	**4**		
5	Did the organization become aware during the year of a significant diversion of the organization's assets? .	**5**		
6	Did the organization have members or stockholders?	**6**		
7a	Did the organization have members, stockholders, or other persons who had the power to elect or appoint one or more members of the governing body?	**7a**		
b	Are any governance decisions of the organization reserved to (or subject to approval by) members, stockholders, or persons other than the governing body?	**7b**		
8	Did the organization contemporaneously document the meetings held or written actions undertaken during the year by the following:			
a	The governing body?	**8a**		
b	Each committee with authority to act on behalf of the governing body?	**8b**		
9	Is there any officer, director, trustee, or key employee listed in Part VII, Section A, who cannot be reached at the organization's mailing address? *If "Yes," provide the names and addresses on Schedule O*	**9**		

Section B. Policies *(This Section B requests information about policies not required by the Internal Revenue Code.)*

			Yes	No
10a	Did the organization have local chapters, branches, or affiliates?	**10a**		
b	If "Yes," did the organization have written policies and procedures governing the activities of such chapters, affiliates, and branches to ensure their operations are consistent with the organization's exempt purposes?	**10b**		
11a	Has the organization provided a complete copy of this Form 990 to all members of its governing body before filing the form?	**11a**		
b	Describe in Schedule O the process, if any, used by the organization to review this Form 990.			
12a	Did the organization have a written conflict of interest policy? *If "No," go to line 13*	**12a**		
b	Were officers, directors, or trustees, and key employees required to disclose annually interests that could give rise to conflicts?	**12b**		
c	Did the organization regularly and consistently monitor and enforce compliance with the policy? *If "Yes," describe in Schedule O how this was done*	**12c**		
13	Did the organization have a written whistleblower policy?	**13**		
14	Did the organization have a written document retention and destruction policy?	**14**		
15	Did the process for determining compensation of the following persons include a review and approval by independent persons, comparability data, and contemporaneous substantiation of the deliberation and decision?			
a	The organization's CEO, Executive Director, or top management official	**15a**		
b	Other officers or key employees of the organization	**15b**		
	If "Yes" to line 15a or 15b, describe the process in Schedule O (see instructions).			
16a	Did the organization invest in, contribute assets to, or participate in a joint venture or similar arrangement with a taxable entity during the year?	**16a**		
b	If "Yes," did the organization follow a written policy or procedure requiring the organization to evaluate its participation in joint venture arrangements under applicable federal tax law, and take steps to safeguard the organization's exempt status with respect to such arrangements?	**16b**		

Section C. Disclosure

17 List the states with which a copy of this Form 990 is required to be filed ▶ _____

18 Section 6104 requires an organization to make its Forms 1023 (1024 or 1024-A, if applicable), 990, and 990-T (Section 501(c)(3)s only) available for public inspection. Indicate how you made these available. Check all that apply.
☐ Own website   ☐ Another's website   ☐ Upon request   ☐ Other *(explain on Schedule O)*

19 Describe on Schedule O whether (and if so, how) the organization made its governing documents, conflict of interest policy, and financial statements available to the public during the tax year.

20 State the name, address, and telephone number of the person who possesses the organization's books and records ▶

Form **990** (2020)

Appendix A

Form 990 (2020) Page **7**

Part VII **Compensation of Officers, Directors, Trustees, Key Employees, Highest Compensated Employees, and Independent Contractors**

Check if Schedule O contains a response or note to any line in this Part VII . . . . ☐

Section A. Officers, Directors, Trustees, Key Employees, and Highest Compensated Employees

1a Complete this table for all persons required to be listed. Report compensation for the calendar year ending with or within the organization's tax year.

- List all of the organization's **current** officers, directors, trustees (whether individuals or organizations), regardless of amount of compensation. Enter -0- in columns (D), (E), and (F) if no compensation was paid.
- List all of the organization's **current** key employees, if any. See instructions for definition of "key employee."
- List the organization's five **current** highest compensated employees (other than an officer, director, trustee, or key employee) who received reportable compensation (Box 5 of Form W-2 and/or Box 7 of Form 1099-MISC) of more than $100,000 from the organization and any related organizations.
- List all of the organization's **former** officers, key employees, and highest compensated employees who received more than $100,000 of reportable compensation from the organization and any related organizations.
- List all of the organization's **former directors or trustees** that received, in the capacity as a former director or trustee of the organization, more than $10,000 of reportable compensation from the organization and any related organizations.

See instructions for the order in which to list the persons above.

☐ Check this box if neither the organization nor any related organization compensated any current officer, director, or trustee.

(A) Name and title	(B) Average hours per week (list any hours for related organizations below dotted line)	(C) Position (do not check more than one box, unless person is both an officer and a director/trustee)						(D) Reportable compensation from the organization (W-2/1099-MISC)	(E) Reportable compensation from related organizations (W-2/1099-MISC)	(F) Estimated amount of other compensation from the organization and related organizations
		Individual trustee or director	Institutional trustee	Officer	Key employee	Highest compensated employee	Former			
(1)										
(2)										
(3)										
(4)										
(5)										
(6)										
(7)										
(8)										
(9)										
(10)										
(11)										
(12)										
(13)										
(14)										

Form **990** (2020)

IRS Form 990, Return of Organization Exempt From Income Tax   299

Form 990 (2020) Page **8**

Part VII Section A. Officers, Directors, Trustees, Key Employees, and Highest Compensated Employees *(continued)*

(A) Name and title	(B) Average hours per week (list any hours for related organizations below dotted line)	(C) Position (do not check more than one box, unless person is both an officer and a director/trustee) — Individual trustee or director / Institutional trustee / Officer / Key employee / Highest compensated employee / Former	(D) Reportable compensation from the organization (W-2/1099-MISC)	(E) Reportable compensation from related organizations (W-2/1099-MISC)	(F) Estimated amount of other compensation from the organization and related organizations
(15)					
(16)					
(17)					
(18)					
(19)					
(20)					
(21)					
(22)					
(23)					
(24)					
(25)					

  1b Subtotal . . . . ▶

    c Total from continuation sheets to Part VII, Section A . . . . . . ▶

    d Total (add lines 1b and 1c) . . . . ▶

  2 Total number of individuals (including but not limited to those listed above) who received more than $100,000 of reportable compensation from the organization ▶

		Yes	No
3	Did the organization list any **former** officer, director, trustee, key employee, or highest compensated employee on line 1a? *If "Yes," complete Schedule J for such individual*	**3**	
4	For any individual listed on line 1a, is the sum of reportable compensation and other compensation from the organization and related organizations greater than $150,000? *If "Yes," complete Schedule J for such individual*	**4**	
5	Did any person listed on line 1a receive or accrue compensation from any unrelated organization or individual for services rendered to the organization? *If "Yes," complete Schedule J for such person*	**5**	

Section B. Independent Contractors

  1 Complete this table for your five highest compensated independent contractors that received more than $100,000 of compensation from the organization. Report compensation for the calendar year ending with or within the organization's tax year.

(A) Name and business address	(B) Description of services	(C) Compensation

  2 Total number of independent contractors (including but not limited to those listed above) who received more than $100,000 of compensation from the organization ▶

Form **990** (2020)

Appendix A

Form 990 (2020) Page **9**

Part VIII Statement of Revenue

Check if Schedule O contains a response or note to any line in this Part VIII . . . . ☐

			(A) Total revenue	(B) Related or exempt function revenue	(C) Unrelated business revenue	(D) Revenue excluded from tax under sections 512–514
Contributions, Gifts, Grants and Other Similar Amounts	1a	Federated campaigns 1a				
	b	Membership dues 1b				
	c	Fundraising events 1c				
	d	Related organizations 1d				
	e	Government grants (contributions) 1e				
	f	All other contributions, gifts, grants, and similar amounts not included above 1f				
	g	Noncash contributions included in lines 1a–1f . . . . 1g $				
	h	**Total.** Add lines 1a–1f . . . . ▶				
Program Service Revenue			Business Code			
	2a	_____				
	b	_____				
	c	_____				
	d	_____				
	e					
	f	All other program service revenue . .				
	g	**Total.** Add lines 2a–2f . . . . ▶				
Other Revenue	3	Investment income (including dividends, interest, and other similar amounts) . . . . ▶				
	4	Income from investment of tax-exempt bond proceeds ▶				
	5	Royalties . . . . ▶				
			(i) Real	(ii) Personal		
	6a	Gross rents . . . 6a				
	b	Less: rental expenses 6b				
	c	Rental income or (loss) 6c				
	d	Net rental income or (loss) . . . . ▶				
			(i) Securities	(ii) Other		
	7a	Gross amount from sales of assets other than inventory 7a				
	b	Less: cost or other basis and sales expenses . 7b				
	c	Gain or (loss) . . 7c				
	d	Net gain or (loss) . . . . ▶				
	8a	Gross income from fundraising events (not including $ _____ of contributions reported on line 1c). See Part IV, line 18 . . . 8a				
	b	Less: direct expenses 8b				
	c	Net income or (loss) from fundraising events . . ▶				
	9a	Gross income from gaming activities. See Part IV, line 19 . 9a				
	b	Less: direct expenses 9b				
	c	Net income or (loss) from gaming activities . . . ▶				
	10a	Gross sales of inventory, less returns and allowances . . 10a				
	b	Less: cost of goods sold . . . 10b				
	c	Net income or (loss) from sales of inventory . . . ▶				
Miscellaneous Revenue			Business Code			
	11a	_____				
	b	_____				
	c	_____				
	d	All other revenue				
	e	**Total.** Add lines 11a–11d . . . . ▶				
	12	**Total revenue.** See instructions . . . . . . ▶				

Form **990** (2020)

IRS Form 990, Return of Organization Exempt From Income Tax 301

Form 990 (2020) Page **10**

Part IX **Statement of Functional Expenses**

Section 501(c)(3) and 501(c)(4) organizations must complete all columns. All other organizations must complete column (A).

Check if Schedule O contains a response or note to any line in this Part IX . . . . ☐

	Do not include amounts reported on lines 6b, 7b, 8b, 9b, and 10b of Part VIII.	(A) Total expenses	(B) Program service expenses	(C) Management and general expenses	(D) Fundraising expenses
1	Grants and other assistance to domestic organizations and domestic governments. See Part IV, line 21 .				
2	Grants and other assistance to domestic individuals. See Part IV, line 22				
3	Grants and other assistance to foreign organizations, foreign governments, and foreign individuals. See Part IV, lines 15 and 16				
4	Benefits paid to or for members				
5	Compensation of current officers, directors, trustees, and key employees				
6	Compensation not included above to disqualified persons (as defined under section 4958(f)(1)) and persons described in section 4958(c)(3)(B) . .				
7	Other salaries and wages				
8	Pension plan accruals and contributions (include section 401(k) and 403(b) employer contributions)				
9	Other employee benefits				
10	Payroll taxes				
11	Fees for services (nonemployees):				
a	Management				
b	Legal				
c	Accounting				
d	Lobbying				
e	Professional fundraising services. See Part IV, line 17				
f	Investment management fees				
g	Other. (If line 11g amount exceeds 10% of line 25, column (A) amount, list line 11g expenses on Schedule O.) .				
12	Advertising and promotion				
13	Office expenses				
14	Information technology				
15	Royalties				
16	Occupancy				
17	Travel				
18	Payments of travel or entertainment expenses for any federal, state, or local public officials				
19	Conferences, conventions, and meetings .				
20	Interest				
21	Payments to affiliates				
22	Depreciation, depletion, and amortization .				
23	Insurance				
24	Other expenses. Itemize expenses not covered above (List miscellaneous expenses on line 24e. If line 24e amount exceeds 10% of line 25, column (A) amount, list line 24e expenses on Schedule O.)				
a	--				
b	--				
c	--				
d	--				
e	All other expenses ----------------------------				
25	**Total functional expenses.** Add lines 1 through 24e				
26	**Joint costs.** Complete this line only if the organization reported in column (B) joint costs from a combined educational campaign and fundraising solicitation. Check here ▶ ☐ if following SOP 98-2 (ASC 958-720) . . .				

Form **990** (2020)

Appendix A

Form 990 (2020)   Page **11**

Part X   Balance Sheet

Check if Schedule O contains a response or note to any line in this Part X . . . . ☐

			(A) Beginning of year		(B) End of year
Assets	1	Cash—non-interest-bearing		1	
	2	Savings and temporary cash investments		2	
	3	Pledges and grants receivable, net		3	
	4	Accounts receivable, net		4	
	5	Loans and other receivables from any current or former officer, director, trustee, key employee, creator or founder, substantial contributor, or 35% controlled entity or family member of any of these persons		5	
	6	Loans and other receivables from other disqualified persons (as defined under section 4958(f)(1)), and persons described in section 4958(c)(3)(B)		6	
	7	Notes and loans receivable, net		7	
	8	Inventories for sale or use		8	
	9	Prepaid expenses and deferred charges		9	
	10a	Land, buildings, and equipment: cost or other basis. Complete Part VI of Schedule D . . . **10a**			
	b	Less: accumulated depreciation **10b**		10c	
	11	Investments—publicly traded securities		11	
	12	Investments—other securities. See Part IV, line 11		12	
	13	Investments—program-related. See Part IV, line 11		13	
	14	Intangible assets		14	
	15	Other assets. See Part IV, line 11		15	
	16	**Total assets.** Add lines 1 through 15 (must equal line 33)		16	
Liabilities	17	Accounts payable and accrued expenses		17	
	18	Grants payable		18	
	19	Deferred revenue		19	
	20	Tax-exempt bond liabilities		20	
	21	Escrow or custodial account liability. Complete Part IV of Schedule D		21	
	22	Loans and other payables to any current or former officer, director, trustee, key employee, creator or founder, substantial contributor, or 35% controlled entity or family member of any of these persons		22	
	23	Secured mortgages and notes payable to unrelated third parties		23	
	24	Unsecured notes and loans payable to unrelated third parties		24	
	25	Other liabilities (including federal income tax, payables to related third parties, and other liabilities not included on lines 17–24). Complete Part X of Schedule D		25	
	26	**Total liabilities.** Add lines 17 through 25		26	
Net Assets or Fund Balances		**Organizations that follow FASB ASC 958, check here ▶ ☐ and complete lines 27, 28, 32, and 33.**			
	27	Net assets without donor restrictions		27	
	28	Net assets with donor restrictions		28	
		Organizations that do not follow FASB ASC 958, check here ▶ ☐ and complete lines 29 through 33.			
	29	Capital stock or trust principal, or current funds		29	
	30	Paid-in or capital surplus, or land, building, or equipment fund		30	
	31	Retained earnings, endowment, accumulated income, or other funds		31	
	32	Total net assets or fund balances		32	
	33	Total liabilities and net assets/fund balances		33	

Form **990** (2020)

Form 990 (2020) Page **12**

Part XI — Reconciliation of Net Assets

Check if Schedule O contains a response or note to any line in this Part XI . . . . ☐

1	Total revenue (must equal Part VIII, column (A), line 12)	1
2	Total expenses (must equal Part IX, column (A), line 25)	2
3	Revenue less expenses. Subtract line 2 from line 1	3
4	Net assets or fund balances at beginning of year (must equal Part X, line 32, column (A)) . . .	4
5	Net unrealized gains (losses) on investments	5
6	Donated services and use of facilities	6
7	Investment expenses	7
8	Prior period adjustments	8
9	Other changes in net assets or fund balances (explain on Schedule O)	9
10	Net assets or fund balances at end of year. Combine lines 3 through 9 (must equal Part X, line 32, column (B))	10

Part XII — Financial Statements and Reporting

Check if Schedule O contains a response or note to any line in this Part XII . . . . ☐

		Yes	No
1	Accounting method used to prepare the Form 990: ☐ Cash ☐ Accrual ☐ Other _____ If the organization changed its method of accounting from a prior year or checked "Other," explain in Schedule O.		
2a	Were the organization's financial statements compiled or reviewed by an independent accountant? . . . If "Yes," check a box below to indicate whether the financial statements for the year were compiled or reviewed on a separate basis, consolidated basis, or both: ☐ Separate basis ☐ Consolidated basis ☐ Both consolidated and separate basis	2a	
b	Were the organization's financial statements audited by an independent accountant? . . . . If "Yes," check a box below to indicate whether the financial statements for the year were audited on a separate basis, consolidated basis, or both: ☐ Separate basis ☐ Consolidated basis ☐ Both consolidated and separate basis	2b	
c	If "Yes" to line 2a or 2b, does the organization have a committee that assumes responsibility for oversight of the audit, review, or compilation of its financial statements and selection of an independent accountant? . If the organization changed either its oversight process or selection process during the tax year, explain on Schedule O.	2c	
3a	As a result of a federal award, was the organization required to undergo an audit or audits as set forth in the Single Audit Act and OMB Circular A-133?	3a	
b	If "Yes," did the organization undergo the required audit or audits? If the organization did not undergo the required audit or audits, explain why on Schedule O and describe any steps taken to undergo such audits .	3b	

Form **990** (2020)

Appendix B
Debits and Credits

This appendix draws on information discussed in Chapter 6 and is for students who wish to learn more about accounting language and its methods. The language of accounting can be somewhat confusing. When transactions occur, they are added and/or subtracted from asset or liability categories. This is referred to as adding and subtracting debits and credits. All the word *debits* means is that these transactions go in the left-hand column of a ledger, and all the word *credits* means is that these transactions go in the right-hand column. This can be confusing because it is common to think of a debit as something that subtracts and a credit as something that increases. In accounting those definitions do not apply, however. In accounting, when cash is debited, it is increased, and when we cash is credited, it is decreased.

Figure B.1 presents a picture of what is happening. In all asset categories, increases are recorded by debits and decreases are recorded by credits. In all liability categories, the opposite occurs, increases are recorded by credits and decreases are recorded by debits. In net assets or the fund balance, there are both—expenses are recorded like the assets and revenues are recorded like the liabilities.

Now let us return to the first transactions of the Access to Learning corporation, as discussed in Chapter 6. We said:

1. On January 2, the nonprofit used $1,000 in cash to pay down accounts payable. The transaction is listed as a decrease in cash and a decrease in accounts payable. Because this transaction is recorded on both sides of the equation, the balance sheet remains balanced.

How would we apply credits and debits? We credit cash $1,000 and we debit accounts payable $1,000.

2. On January 5, the nonprofit receives $50,000 in revenue from a foundation. The transaction is recorded as $50,000 in cash and $50,000 in revenue (listed under net assets). Because this transaction is recorded on both sides of the equation, the balance sheet remains balanced.

306   Appendix B

| | Assets | = | Liabilities | + | Net Assets (Fund Balance) |

Cash

Debit	Credit
+	−

Accounts Payable

Debit	Credit
−	+

Expenses

Debit	Credit
+	−

Accounts Receivable

Debit	Credit
+	−

Revenues

Debit	Credit
−	+

Figure B.1 Debits and credits.

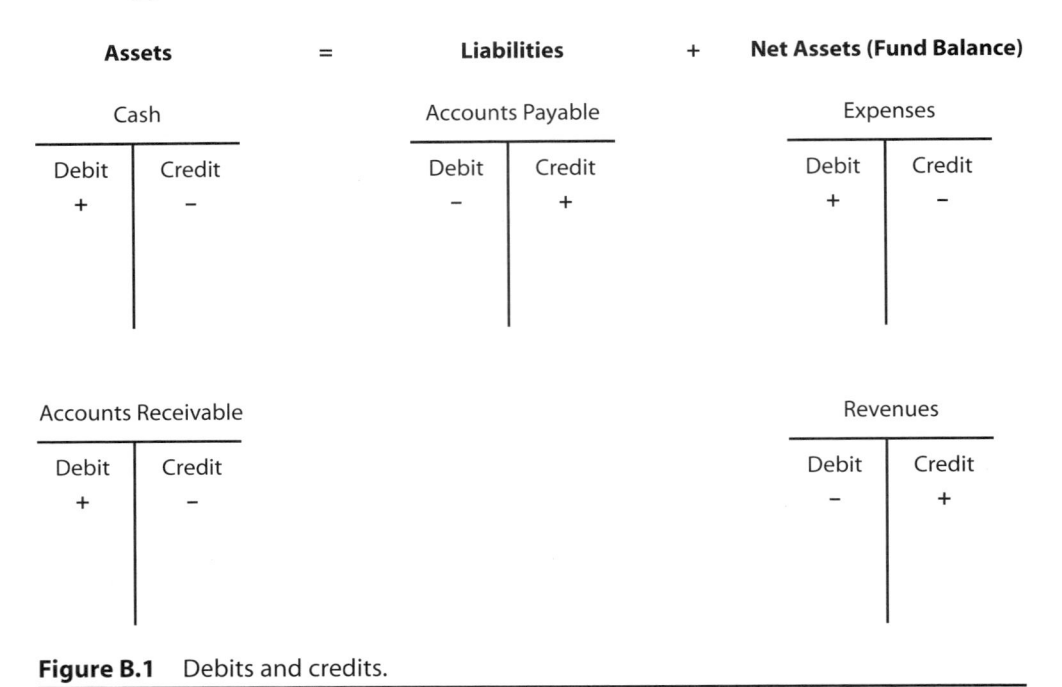

How would we apply credits and debits? We debit cash $50,000 and credit revenue $50,000.

Now please take the time to go through each transaction listed for January in Chapter 6 and apply credits and debits to each example.

The trial balance is a list and totals of all the debits and credits in a given period, usually after a month or year. The trial balance is listed in the form of two columns, one for debits and one for credits. This is a method for ensuring that debits equal credits. Table B.1 provides an example of the trial balance for the Access to Learning nonprofit after January.

At the end of the fiscal year, the trial balance is used to prepare the income statement or statement of activities. The statement of activities adds up all the revenue and expenses to determine the surplus or deficit for the year. The amount of the surplus or deficit is added to the unrestricted net assets in the statement of financial position.

Closing Out the Year

If the nonprofit is using accrual accounting, then the financial books need to be adjusted. At the end of the accounting period, whether it is a monthly trial balance or a fiscal year trial balance, adjusting entries must be done Adjusting entries are

Table B.1 Trial Balance for January, Access to Learning Nonprofit Corporation

	Debits	Credits
Cash	$ 57,000	
Net Assets (January 1)		$ 201,800
Marketable Securities	1,000	
Accounts Receivable	85,000	
Pledges Receivable	12,000	
Prepaid Expenses	1,000	
Equipment	6,800	
Investments	121,000	
Building	100,000	
Accounts Payable		15,000
Salaries Payable		2,000
Mortgage Payable		5,000
Deferred Revenue		10,000
Mortgage Loan		25,000
Revenues		145,000
Expenses	20,000	— —
Total Trial Balance	$ 403,800	$ 403,800

changes made to revenues and expenses to place them in the accounting periods in which they actually occurred. There are two types of adjusting entries: accrual and deferred. Accrual adjusting entries are for those revenues and expenses that are matched to dates before the transaction has been recorded. Common accrual adjusting entries are accrued salaries and unbilled revenue. An example of an accrual adjusting entry is accrued expenses, usually salaries. If a nonprofit pays weekly salaries and the accounting period ends midweek, the nonprofit has accrued salary expenses that have not been paid. Let's say that amount is $2,000. Therefore, the adjusting entry to reflect the unpaid salaries is to debit $2,000 to salary expenses and credit $2,000 to salaries payable.

Deferred adjusting entries are for those revenues and expenses that are matched to dates after the transaction has been recorded. Common deferred adjusting entries are depreciation and prepaid expenses. A good example is depreciation expense. At the end of the fiscal year, an adjusting entry is made for all depreciation expenses. Let's say that the nonprofit has a depreciation schedule that calls for depreciating $5,000 worth of depreciating expenses each year throughout the life of a car. The adjusting entry would be to debit depreciation expense $5,000 and credit $5,000 to accumulated depreciation (car). Remember, the idea behind adjusting entries is to record revenues and expenses in the accounting periods in which they occurred.

Appendix C

A Sample Investment Policy Statement

When it comes to risk tolerance, adopting an investment policy is a sound way to develop an approach to investing in assets that will meet the objectives of the nonprofit. The following is a sample investment policy statement for a nonprofit operating in New York State that was created by the New York Council of Nonprofits.

ABC, Inc.
Policy Number: _____
Investment Policy
Date of Board Resolution: _____

Purpose

This policy establishes investment objectives, policies, guidelines and eligible securities related to all assets held by ABC, INC., and/or any of our subsidiary corporations, primarily for investment purposes ("institutional funds"). In doing so the policy:

- clarifies the delegation of duties and responsibilities concerning the management of institutional funds.
- identifies the criteria against which the investment performance of the organization's investments will be measured.
- communicates the objectives to the Board, staff, investment managers, brokers, donors, and funding sources that may have involvement.
- confirms policies and procedures relative to the expenditure of institutional funds.
- serves as a review document to guide the ongoing oversight of the management of the organization's investments.

Appendix C

Delegation of Responsibilities

The Board of Directors has a direct oversight role regarding all decisions that impact ABC, INC.'s institutional funds. The Board has delegated supervisory responsibility for the management of our institutional funds to the (Oversight Committee Name). Specific responsibilities of the various bodies and individuals responsible for the management of our institutional funds are set forth below:

Responsibilities of the Board. The Board shall ensure that its fiduciary responsibilities concerning the proper management of ABC, INC.'s institutional funds are fulfilled through appropriate investment structure, internal and external management, and portfolio performance consistent with all policies and procedures. Based on the advice and recommendations of the (Oversight Committee Name), the Board shall:

- select, appoint, and remove members of the Committee.
- approve investment policies and objectives that reflect the long-term investment-risk orientation of the endowment.

Responsibilities of the (Oversight Committee Name). Members of the (Oversight Committee Name) are not held accountable for less than desirable outcomes, rather for adherence to procedural prudence, or the process by which decisions are made in respect to endowment assets. In consideration of the foregoing, the Committee is responsible for the development, recommendation, implementation, and maintenance of all policies relative to ABC, INC.'s institutional funds and shall:

- develop and/or propose policy recommendations to the Board with regard to the management of all institutional funds.
- recommend long-term and short-term investment policies and objectives for our institutional funds, including the study and selection of asset classes, determining asset allocation ranges, and setting performance objectives.
- determine that institutional funds are prudently and effectively managed with the assistance of management and any necessary investment consultants and/or other outside professionals, if any.
- monitor and evaluate the performance of all those responsible for the management of institutional funds.
- recommend the retention and/or dismissal of investment consultants and/or other outside professionals.
- receive and review reports from management, investment consultants, and/or other outside professionals, if any.
- periodically meet with management, investment consultants, and/or other outside professionals management, investment consultants, and/or other outside professionals.
- convene regularly to evaluate whether this policy, investment activities, risk management controls, and processes continue to be consistent with meeting the goals and objectives set for the management of institutional funds.

Responsibilities of Management. Management shall be responsible for the day-to-day administration and implementation of policies established by the Board and/or the (Oversight Committee Name) concerning the management of institutional funds. Management shall also be the primary liaison between any investment consultants and/or other outside professionals that may be retained to assist in the management of such funds. Specifically, management shall:

- oversee the day-to-day operational investment activities of all institutional funds subject to policies established by the Board and/or the (Oversight Committee Name).
- contract with any necessary outside service providers, such as: investment consultants, investment managers, banks, and/or trust companies and/or any other necessary outside professionals.
- ensure that the service providers adhere to the terms and conditions of their contracts; have no material conflicts of interests with the interests of ABC, INC.; and performance monitoring systems are sufficient to provide the (Oversight Committee Name) with timely, accurate, and useful information.
- regularly meet with any outside service providers to evaluate and assess compliance with investment guidelines, performance, outlook and investment strategies; monitor asset allocation and rebalance assets, as directed by the (Oversight Committee Name) and in accordance with approved asset allocation policies, among asset classes and investment styles; and tend to all other matters deemed to be consistent with due diligence with respect to prudent management of institutional funds.
- comply with official accounting and auditing guidelines regarding due diligence and ongoing monitoring of investments, especially alternative investments. Prepare and issue periodic status reports to the Board and the (Oversight Committee Name).

Investment Considerations

In accordance with ABC, INC.'s understanding of NYPMIFA, the (Oversight Committee Name) must consider the purposes of both ABC, INC. and our assets in managing and investing institutional funds. All individuals responsible for managing and investing ABC, INC.'s institutional funds must do so in good faith and with the care that an ordinarily prudent person in a like position would exercise under similar circumstances. In making any decision relative to the expenditure of institutional funds, each of the following factors must be considered, and properly documented, in the minutes or other records of the applicable decision-making body:

1. general economic conditions;
2. possible effect of inflation or deflation;
3. expected tax consequences, if any, of investment decisions or strategies;
4. the role that each investment or course of action plays within the overall investment portfolio of the fund;

5. expected total return from the income and appreciation of investments;
6. other resources of the organization;
7. the needs of the organization and the fund to make distributions and preserve capital; and
8. an asset's special relationship or special value, if any, to the organization's purposes.

Guidelines for Investing

The investment goal of the total return fund is to achieve a total return (income and appreciation) of 5% after inflation, over a full market cycle (3–5 years). The following guidelines apply to the three main investment asset classes:

Money Market Funds: Allowable range: Minimum 5%; Maximum 45% of total assets. A quality money market fund will be utilized for the liquidity needs of the portfolio whose objective is to seek as high a current income as is consistent with liquidity and stability of principal. The fund will invest in "money market" instruments with remaining maturates of one year or less, that have been rated by at least one nationally recognized rating agency in the highest category for short-term debt securities. If non-rated, the securities must be of comparable quality.

Equities: Allowable Range: Minimum 20%; Maximum 60% of total assets.
The equity component of the portfolio will consist of high-quality equity securities traded on the New York, NASDAQ, or American Stock exchanges. The securities must be screened for above average financial characteristics such as price-to-earnings, return-on-equity, debt-to-capital ratios, etc.

No more than 5% of the equity portion of the account will be invested in any one issuer. As well, not more than 20% of the equity portion of the account will be invested in stocks contained within the same industry.

It is acceptable to invest in an equity mutual fund(s) adhering to the investment characteristics identified above, as long as it is a no-load fund, without 12(b)(1) charges, which maintains an expense ratio consistent with those other funds of similar investment styles as measured by the Lipper and/or Morningstar rating services.

Prohibited equity investments include: initial public offerings, restricted securities, private placements, derivatives, options, futures, and margined transactions.

Exceptions to the prohibited investment policy may be made only when assets are invested in a Mutual Fund(s) that periodically utilizes prohibited strategies to mitigate risk and enhance return.

Fixed Income: Allowable Range: Minimum 35%; Maximum 75% of total assets.
Bond investments will consist solely of taxable, fixed income securities that have an investment-grade rating (BBB or higher by Standard & Poor's and Baa or higher by Moody's) that possess a liquid secondary market. If the average credit quality rating disagrees among the two rating agencies, then use the lower of the two as a guideline.

No more that 5% of the fixed income portfolio will be invested in corporate bonds of the same issuer. As well, not more than 20% of the fixed income portfolio will be invested in bonds of issuers in the same industry.

The maximum **average maturity** of the fixed income portfolio will be 10 years, with not more than 25% of the bond portfolio maturing in more than 10 years.

Prohibited securities include: private placements, derivatives (other than floating-rate coupon bonds), margined transactions, and foreign denominated bonds.

Exceptions to the prohibited investment policy may be made only when assets are invested in a Mutual Fund(s) that periodically utilizes prohibited strategies to mitigate risk and enhance return.

Performance Measurements Standards

The benchmarks to be used in evaluating the performance of the two main asset classes will be:

- **Equities**: *S&P 500 Index*—Goal: exceed the average annual return of the index over a full market cycle (3–5 years)
- **Fixed Income**: *Lehman Brothers Government/Corporate Index*—Goal: exceed the average annual return of the index over a full market cycle (3–5 years).

It will be the responsibility of the (Oversight Committee Name) of the Board of Directors to regularly review the performance of the investment account and investment policy guidelines, and report to the Board of Directors at least quarterly with updates and recommendations as needed.

Expenditure Considerations

The Board of Directors and the (Oversight Committee Name) are responsible for the establishment of a balanced reserve fund spending policy to: (a) ensure that over the medium-to-long term, sufficient investment return shall be retained to preserve and grow its economic value as a first priority; and (b) to provide funds for the annual operating budget in an amount which is not subject to large fluctuations from year-to-year to the extent possible.

Expenditure of Institutional Funds

All decisions relative to the expenditure of institutional funds must assess the uses, benefits, purposes, and duration for which the institutional fund was established, and, if relevant, consider the factors:

1. the duration and preservation of the institutional fund;
2. purposes of ABC, INC. and the fund;
3. general economic conditions;
4. possible effect of inflation or deflation;
5. expected total return from income and appreciation of investments;
6. other organizational resources;

7. all applicable investment policies; and
8. where appropriate, alternatives to spending from the institutional fund and the possible effects of those alternatives.

For each decision to appropriate institutional funds for expenditure, an appropriate contemporaneous record should be kept and maintained describing the nature and extent of the consideration that the appropriate body gave to each of the stipulated factors.

Donor Restrictions. In all instances, donor intent shall be respected when decisions are rendered concerning the investment or expenditure of donor restricted funds. If a donor, in the gift instrument, has directed that appreciation not be spent, ABC, INC. shall comply with that directive and consider it when making decisions regarding the management and investment of the fund. Any attempt to lift restrictions on any fund shall be conducted in full compliance with the law.

Reserve Fund Expenditures. Each year, the nonprofit is authorized to withdraw **up to 5%** of the total market value of the insurance premium reserve investment account (market value to be determined as of the last business day of the preceding year) for the organization's operating purposes. That spending percentage is applied to the three year average of the December market value. Using a three-year market value average will help to even out any fluctuations that may occur in the value of the account. The dollar amount and timing of any distribution(s) from the investment account will be left up to the discretion of the Chief Executive Officer and the Treasurer.

Glossary

Accounting cost: The amount of money needed to buy, do, or make something.
Accounting equation: Equation that defines the relationship between assets, liabilities, and net assets: assets = liabilities + net assets. It is the foundation of double-entry bookkeeping.
Accounting principles: Basic accounting guidelines that serve as general rules for the accounting system.
Accounts receivable: Money that other organizations or individuals owe the nonprofit.
Accrual accounting: Accounting system that recognizes income when it is earned and expenses when they are incurred in the same reporting period, rather than when income is received or expenses are paid.
Accrued salary expenses: Money the nonprofit owes at the end of an accounting period.
Adopted budget: A budget that the nonprofit's board of directors has approved.
Allocation: A designation of funds for a particular purpose.
Annuity: A fixed sum of money distributed on a regular basis, whether monthly, quarterly, yearly, or at some other regular interval.
Assets: Those things that have value, can be measured, and are owned or controlled by the nonprofit.
Audit: Procedure in which a nonprofit's financial accounts are verified by a professional accountant.
Average cost: The total cost of all items divided by the number of items.

Balance sheet: A statement of financial position that summarizes an organization's financial situation at one point in time.
Benefit corporation (B corporation): A corporation that seeks to have a positive impact on society and the environment. B corporations redefine fiduciary responsibility to include nonfinancial interests when making decisions and report their impacts on society and the environment using third-party standards.

Benefit-cost ratio (BCR): A measure of program efficiency; the ratio of the benefits of a project relative to its costs, all expressed in monetary terms. Also known as *cost-benefit ratio*.

Benefits theory: This theory classifies the benefits that nonprofit organizations generate into four broad categories based on the goods and services they provide: private benefits, group benefits, public benefits, and trade benefits. It posits that nonprofits should seek support from the beneficiaries and/or those who value the benefits.

Bonds: Debt securities that are essentially long-term contracts between issuers (the borrowers) and investors (the lenders) wherein the principal of the borrowed money, plus an agreed upon amount of interest, is paid back within a certain period of time.

Break-even analysis: A method of determining at what point total costs equal total revenue.

Capital assets: Long-lasting and big-ticket items of value held by a nonprofit, typically including land, facilities, and equipment.

Capital budget: Budgets that allocate financial resources for the acquisition or maintenance of capital/fixed assets such as land, buildings, and equipment. It is normally built on pieces of assets, not departments, as commonly found in operating budgets.

Capital budgeting: Planning process used for the purchase of fixed assets, such as purchasing or renovating a building.

Cash accounting: Accounting system that records financial transactions only when cash has been received or expended.

Cash budget: A month-by-month management plan for the most important part of the fiscal health of a nonprofit—the expected revenues and expenses and the difference for each month of the fiscal year.

Cash flow: Cash receipts and cash disbursements over a given period.

Cash-flow budget: A projection of cash receipts and cash disbursements over a given period. Also known as *cash-flow forecast*.

Cash-flow gaps: Periods when cash outflows exceed cash inflows.

Cash-flow management: The process of forecasting, monitoring, analyzing, and adjusting cash flows so that an organization stays within a liquidity range.

Cash-flow management report: An internal document created to inform a nonprofit's leadership about times the nonprofit may run short of cash even with a balanced annual budget. Also known as *cash management report*.

Cost: The amount paid or required for something, often referred to as *cost objective*.

Cost-benefit analysis (CBA): A method of determining whether or not a certain project should be done. CBA involves finding and quantifying all the positive factors (benefits) and all the negative factors (costs) of a proposed action and determining the difference between them (the net) to decide whether or not the action is advisable.

Coupon rate: Annual interest rate payable to a bondholder as printed on the bond.

Current assets: Those assets that are cash or can be turned into cash within a short period of time.

Current liabilities: Debts to be paid within a short period of time. Also known as *payables*.

Default risk: The risk that investors may lose part or all of their security-invested principal and interest because of a lack of financial soundness on the part of the security or the company that issued the security.

Depreciation: The assigning of a value to the useful life of a capitalized fixed asset and then expending those assets over its economic life.

Direct costs: Costs that can be tracked to a product, a program, or a cost center.

Discount rate: The interest rate used to discount future cash flows to determine the present value of an investment.

Diversification: The balancing of revenue sources across entities with the aim of achieving greater financial security.

Effectiveness: Achievement of a program's or a nonprofit's long-term targets/outcomes.

Efficiency: The ratio of useful output to the total input used to create the output.

Encumbrances: Amounts of money put aside for specific items, such as computers or other equipment.

Endowment funds: Restricted funds in which the principal is invested in perpetuity and its income is used to support the operation of the nonprofit or its designated programs.

Expense budget: A budget that tells how much will be spent for a given period, usually a fiscal year.

Fiduciary: An individual or organization holding assets for another party.

Financial accounting: The preparation of financial statements of an organization's past revenues and expenses. These financial statements are used primarily by parties outside the organization who might have a particular interest in the organization.

Financial Accounting Standards Board (FASB): The designated organization in the private sector for establishing the financial accounting standards that govern the preparation of financial reports by nongovernmental entities.

Financial statements: Written reports of an organization's financial activities. Nonprofits typically produce four financial statements: statement of financial position, statement of activities, statement of cash flow, and statement of functional expenses.

Fiscal year (FY): Any period of 12 months chosen by an organization as its budget year; the period within which revenues and expenses are estimated and tracked.

Fixed costs: Expenses that do not vary with volume.

Form 990: A form that most nonprofits must file annually with the Internal Revenue Service. The information in Form 990, generally available to the public, allows easy comparison of one nonprofit to another.

Fund accounting: Accounting system used by nonprofits that emphasizes accountability rather than profit. Fund accounting allows nonprofits to keep separate sets of funds, both revenue and expense, for particular programs.

Future value: The value of cash or another type of asset at a future date that is equivalent in value to a specified sum now.

General obligation (GO) bonds: Debt instrument issued by a state or local government to finance projects for the general public's benefit, such as libraries and schools. GO bonds are secured by the "full faith and credit" of the issuing government.

Generally accepted accounting principles (GAAP): A widely accepted set of rules and procedures for the recording and reporting of financial information; created by the Financial Accounting Standards Board.

GuideStar: An organization that provides information about and evaluates the financial management of nonprofits. GuideStar merged with the Foundation Center and is now known as Candid.

Indirect cost: Expenses for the nonprofit as an organization that cannot be directly attributable to particular programs.

Input: The resources used in a performance measuring system, such as staffing, supplies, and money.

Interest rate: The percentage rate at which interest is charged on a loan for a period.

Intergenerational equity: A value concept based on the belief that future generations have rights to resources that the current generation must respect.

Internal controls: Rules put in place within an organization to achieve efficiency and effectiveness of operations, reliability of financial reporting, and compliance with laws and regulations.

Internal rate of return (IRR): A measurement of the return on an investment. The IRR is the discount rate at which a project's net present value equals zero.

Investment policy statement: An agreement usually between the board/investment committee and the investment manager, internal or external, documenting investment policies for expectations, consistency, and potential evaluation of investment programs/managers.

Laddering: A method of structuring security terms so that a certain proportion of the investment matures every year over a few years. Laddering can reduce market risk, if used properly.

Leverage: The degree to which an organization is using debt to finance its activities.

Liabilities: Sources of capital used to finance assets. Liabilities are debts the organization owes to third parties and must be paid.

Life-cycle costing (LCC): A method of determining all the costs of an asset over its lifetime.

Line-item budget: A budget that lists individual costs of all budgeted items, such as personnel, supplies, and equipment.

Liquidity: The extent to which an asset can be converted into cash without incurring extraordinary costs.
Long-term assets: Assets such as property, buildings, and equipment that cannot easily be changed into cash in a short period of time.
Long-term liabilities: Debts, such as mortgages, that are to be paid off over multiple years.
Low-profit limited liability company (L3C): A legal entity that facilitates investments in socially beneficial, for-profit ventures while complying with IRS rules concerning program-related investments.

Management accounting: A method of accounting that focuses on using an organization's internal financial data to think through how the organization can be more efficient in its delivery of services or more effective in its accomplishment of program outcomes.
Marginal costs: Additional costs incurred to add one more unit of service or produce one more unit of goods.
Market risk: The risk that investors may lose part or all of their market-invested principal and interest because of changes in the marketplace in general, rather than problems with individual instruments or the organizations that issue them. Also known as *interest risk*.
Marketable securities: Monies invested on a short-term basis (less than 1 year), such as certificates of deposit and stocks.
Mission: The purpose for which a nonprofit is formed.
Modern portfolio theory (MPT): Investment theory that provides the foundation for assets selection in a portfolio; the aim is to maximize expected return for a given amount of portfolio risk or to minimize risk for a given level of expected return.
Municipal bonds: Bonds issued by a city or state government or its agency to finance capital projects. Also known as *munis*.

Net assets: The difference between the assets and liabilities of an organization; the accumulation of the difference between the cumulative revenues and cumulative expenses over the life of an organization.
Net present value (NPV): The difference between cash inflows and cash outflows, both discounted to their present values.
Nonprofit corporation: A legal entity incorporated in one of the 50 U.S. states and operating for educational, charitable, social, religious, or civic purposes. Unlike a for-profit organization, a nonprofit corporation has a board of directors and officers but no shareholders.
Nonsystematic risk: The default risk of a specific corporation or institution.

Operating budget: An organization's adopted budget for the fiscal year that can be amended and lists both revenue and expenses.
Operating reserve: A fund for unexpected events. Often known as a *rainy-day fund*.

Opportunity cost: The potential gain that could have been obtained from the best alternative when one alternative is chosen.

Outcome: The results or effects of an action and/or actions, such as policy, program, project, etc.

Output: The result or product of the program activities in the nonprofit.

Pay-as-you-go financing: Cash financing; that is, the saving up of funds to purchase particular assets.

Pledges: Promises made by donors to give cash, property, or other assets to an organization in the future.

Prepaid expenses: Currents assets that have been paid by the nonprofit before they are incurred.

Present value: The value of cash or another type of asset on a given date of a future payment or series of future payments; discounted to reflect the time value of money.

Private foundation: Nonprofit corporations that make grants mostly to nonprofits and usually raise those revenues from a single source.

Private goods: Goods and services of a private nature that are rival and excludable. For instance, day care service is a private good, benefiting the child and the child's family.

Program budget: A budget in which revenues and expenses are categorized by programs.

Program-related investments (PRIs): Investments made by private foundations in for-profit ventures to support charitable activities.

Proposed budget: A budget that has been drafted but has not yet been adopted by an organization's board of directors.

Prudent investor rule: A revision to the prudent man rule (see below) that enlarges trustees' immunity for the loss of investments to include the entire portfolio.

Prudent man rule: Legal principle that holds that the trustees or board of directors of an organization cannot be held responsible for a loss of investments by the organization as long as they were prudent in their decision making.

Public charities: Nonprofit corporations, classified as 501(c)(3)s, that raise revenue from many sources to provide education, scientific, or social services.

Public goods: Goods and services that are characterized by a lack of rivalry and excludability and are provided without profit to all members of society.

Restricted net assets: Revenues given by donors that are not to be spent but are to be invested in long-term stocks, bonds, and other instruments that will produce interest and dividends.

Revenue bonds: Debt securities issued for facilities that generate revenue by which the bondholders will be repaid, such as airports and toll roads.

Revenue budget: Budget that tells how much revenue will be raised to support particular programs or nonprofits.

Revenues: The monies collected by a nonprofit. Revenues come from many different sources, including contributions (gifts), grants and contracts, fees, interest income and dividends, investment gains, donated services, donated materials, and securities.

Sarbanes–Oxley Act of 2002: A federal law that requires publicly traded corporations to adhere to governance standards that include a broad role for corporate boards in corporations' finances and auditing procedures.

Separation of duties: A fraud prevention measure that involves requiring more than one person to complete a given financial task within an organization.

Serial bonds: Bonds of issues that feature maturities every year over a period of years.

Social enterprises: Organizations or ventures that achieve their primary social or environmental missions using business methods.

Social entrepreneurs: Individuals or organizations that pursue innovative solutions to society's most pressing social problems.

Solvency: The state of having enough assets to cover all debts.

Spending baseline: An estimate of how much it will cost to continue the current year's programs with the same labor and materials next year with next year's costs.

Step costs: Costs that are constant for a given level of activity but increase or decrease, often significantly, once a threshold is crossed.

Systematic risks: Market risks wherein the prices of all securities decrease or increase simultaneously. Systematic risk is the result of the general ebb and flow of the market as a whole.

Term bonds: Bonds of an issue that features a large block of bonds maturing in a single year.

Third sector: The nonprofit sector. The economy in general can be divided into three sectors: government, business, and nonprofits.

Time value of money: The concept that money available now is worth more than the same amount in the future because of its potential earning capacity. This core principle of finance holds that, provided money can earn interest, any amount of money is worth more the sooner it is received.

Total return: A measure of investment performance over a given period. Total return is divided into two categories: income and capital appreciation. Income includes interest paid by fixed-income investments and dividends by equity securities. Capital appreciation represents the increase in the market price of the equity investment.

Unrestricted net assets: Revenues that are not restricted in their use; these include gifts received in a fiscal year for use in that fiscal year.

Variable costs: Expenses that change in proportion to volume.

Variance report: Regular reports, monthly or weekly, that list revenue and expense budgets and actual expenses to date. Such reports allow nonprofit executive directors to understand which revenues are slow to come in and whether or not any particular line items are overspent or underspent.

Venture philanthropy: Venture capitalism used for philanthropic goals. Such philanthropy is characterized by funding on a multiyear basis; a focus on capacity building rather than on programs; high involvement by donors, who often join the boards of the nonprofits in which they invest; a focus on measurable results; and a willingness to try new approaches.

Working capital: Funds of a nonprofit used in day-to-day activities.
Working capital = current assets – current liabilities.

Index

Accountability
  answerability/justification and, 13
  compliance and, 14
  core components of, 13–14
  enforcement/sanctions and, 14
  external monitors, 14
  financial audits and, 44
  financial data records and, 96
  program performance and, 33
  standards for, 14
  transparency and, 13, 112, 258
Accounting costs, 85–86
Accounting cycle, 108–109
Accounting equation, 105
Accounting principles, 97
  constraints, 97, 98
  economic entities and, 98
  fraudulent practices and, 113–114
  generally accepted accounting principles and, 44
  key assumptions and, 97, 98
  reporting requirements and, 109–111
  uniformity of information and, 100
Accounting systems
  accounting standards structure and, 85
  checkbook accounting, 101
  financial accounting and, 96
  financial statements and, 96
  inventories, 121
  management accounting and, 96
  privately vs. publicly held companies and, 97
Accounts payable, 42, 123, 129, 150
Accounts receivable, 42, 63, 120
Accrual accounting, 101
  advantages of, 97
  matching principle and, 99
  trial balances and, 306
  true-to-life financial record and, 101
Accrued salary expenses, 123
Achievement First, 277
Allocations, 22, 244, 248
Alpha factor, 246
American Accounting Association (AAA), 254
American Institute of Certified Public Accountants (AICPA), 96, 254
American Law Institute, 6

American Red Cross, 8, 22, 25, 271
Amistad Academy, 277
Amortization, 98, 224, 226
Annuities, 197, 200, 202
Answerability, 13
Arbitrage, 222
Arizona–Indiana–Michigan (AIM) Alliance, 274
Articles of incorporation, 8, 9
Ashoka Foundation, 276, 284
Aspen Institute Nonprofit Sector and Philanthropy Program, 284
Assets
  accounts receivable, 68, 120
  allocation and investment, 232, 233, 242, 244, 246, 249, 250, 311
  capital, 206, 214, 215, 216
  capitalization and, 122
  cash, 60
  current, 68, 120, 141, 142
  debits/credits and, 105, 305–307
  depreciation and, 98, 106, 122–123
  fund balance and, 118, 124, 305
  inventories, 121
  liquidity and, 59, 60
  long-term, 120, 121–123

marketable securities, 120
net, 59, 103–104
pledges receivable, 120, 121
prepaid expenses and, 120, 121
property/equipment, 122
restricted net, 103–104, 110, 125
return on, 146, 147
safeguarding, 255–256
unrestricted net, 103, 110, 125
Association of Accountants and Financial Professionals in Business, 254
Association of Certified Fraud Examiners, 262
Audits
committee, 10, 23, 109, 110, 259, 261
disclosure principle and, 99
external auditors and, 23
federal/state, 44, 113, 258
finance committees and, 10, 17, 23, 38, 45, 112
financial, 44, 112
fraudulent practices and, 113
generally accepted accounting principles and, 44, 97, 109
management, 44, 257, 259
Sarbanes–Oxley Act and, 109–110, 261–262
standards for, 110

Balance sheet, 106, 107, 119, 302
assets and, 114–115
current assets, 120
current liabilities, 118, 123–124
liabilities, 118
long-term assets, 119, 120
long-term liabilities, 119
net assets, 118, 132
Balanced budget process, 42, 50, 60
Balanced scorecard system, 184–185

Bank credit, 66
Bank investment offerings, 236
Bankruptcy, 58, 235
Barium Springs Home for Children, 275
Beneficiary brokers, 167, 170
Beneficiary builders, 167, 168, 169
Benefit corporation (B corporation), 285–286
Benefits theory, 160–162
concept of exchange, 162
diversification, 148, 171
earned revenues, 162, 166–167
existing sources of revenue, 162–167
funding models, 167–168
government grants and fees, 166
group benefits and, 161
private benefits and, 161
public benefits and, 161
public goods and, 160, 166
trade benefits and, 161
See also Revenues
Beshear, S., 279
Best Buy Children's Foundation, 273
Better Business Bureau (BBB), 14, 27, 150
Big bettors, 167, 169
Big Brothers Big Sisters of America, 170
Board of directors
accountability and, 17
budget approval stage and, 38
budget oversight and, 310
budget preparation stage and, 38
budget reviews/revisions and, 44
cutback budgeting and, 46
day-to-day management duties and, 24, 103
executive director, conflict with, 259
fiduciary responsibilities of, 96, 114, 232

finance committee membership and, 17, 38
investment policies of, 232
planning/budgeting process and, 39
policy making role of, 24
prudent man rule and, 6
strategic planning and, 25, 38
Board of trustees, 5, 10
BoardSource, 261
Bond rating agencies, 96
Bonds
corporate, 222, 242, 245, 313
coupon rates and, 221
earning power of, 242
fair market value and, 98
general obligation, 222
issuance process for, 220–223
municipal, 211, 219, 222, 223, 228
payable, 230
pooled issuance of, 222
public offerings of, 221
returns on, 242
revenue, 222
serial, 223
structure of maturity and, 223
tax-exempt status of, 221
term, 223
zero-coupon, 247
Boys and Girls Clubs of America, 273, 275
Break-even analysis, 87–88
Break-even point, 87, 90, 271
Bridgespan Group, 275
Budget
adopted, 22
approval stage, 38–39
auditing stage, 43–44
balanced budget process, 42
capital, 22, 28–30
cutbacks, 34, 46–47
encumbrances, 22
execution stage, 39–43
expense, 22
formatting, 30–34

Index **325**

instructions, 36
line-item, 30–31
operating, 22, 28
performance, 30, 32
preparation stage, 35
process, as a cycle, 34–45
program, 30–32
proposed, 22
reporting stage, 43–44
revenue, 22
reviews and revisions, periodic, 44–45
spending baseline, 22
Budget year. *See* Fiscal year (FY)
Budgeting
 as a communications tool, 27
 cutback, 34, 46–47
 encumbrances and, 22
 inputs and, 32
 as a management tool, 26–27
 performance-based, 32
 as a planning tool, 24–26
 results-based, 32
 strategic planning and, 36
 See also Capital budgeting
Businesses
 financial records, falsification of, 100
 payment protocols, 70
 private economic marketplaces and, 7
 revenue sources for, 160
Bylaws/rules, 8, 10, 257, 260

Cafédirect, 282
California Association of Nonprofits (CAN), 274
Candid, 275
Capacity building, 215, 216, 278
Capital assets
 acceptance vs. rejection of, 215–216
 types of, 214
Capital budgeting
 bank loans and, 220–223
 bond issuance and, 220–223

capital improvement plans, 216, 226
capital needs, 214
capital projects and, 214, 215, 220, 222, 226
debt financing and, 220–223
donated capital assets, acceptance/rejection of, 215–216
level debt service payments, 223–224
level principal payments, 224–226
life-cycle costing and, 216
pay-as-you-go financing and, 220–221
payment schedules and, 223–226
process of, 216–219
Capital budgets
 and operating budgets, relationship between, 22
 policy, and debt policy, 226–228
Capital improvement plan (CIP), 216, 226
Capital intermediaries, nonprofit, 277–278
Capital reserves, 65, 68
Cash, 120
Cash accounting, 101. *See also* Accrual accounting
Cash budget, 60. *See* Cash-flow budgets
Cash conversion cycle, 59
Cash flow
 actual, 65
 analysis, 63–64
 inflows and, 60
 investing, 69
 net present value and, 194, 195
 operating, 106, 132
 outflows, 59, 60
 patterns and, 63
 pay-as-you-go financing and, 219–220
 solvency and, 138
 statements of, 132–133

strategies, 66–71
 See also Financial statements; Liquidity
Cash-flow budgeting, 59, 64, 65–66
Cash-flow budgets, 65
Cash-flow forecasts, 66
Cash-flow gaps, 65
Cash-flow management
 bank credit and, 66
 and cash, 60
 cash reserves and, 60
 cash shortages and, 60
 examples of, 60–63
 feasibility assessments and, 63
 financial manager role and, 63–64
 short-term borrowing, 68–69
 short-term investments and, 68, 69–70
 short-term surpluses and, 70
 trade discount incentives and, 70–71
 working capital and, 68
Cash-flow management report, 42
Cash-flow statement, 132–133
Catholic Charities USA, 271
Center for Civil Society Studies, 272
Center for the Advancement of Social Entrepreneurship, 281
Center for What Works, 183
Center on Budget and Policy Priorities, 270
Center on Philanthropy, 274
Certificate of deposit (CD), 236
Certified public accountant (CPA), 43, 108
Charities. *See* Public charities
Charity Navigator, 14, 27, 151
Charles Schwab Foundation, 273
Chart of accounts, 127, 128
Christiansen, B., 167

Index

Christopher Reeve Foundation, 260
Circular A-133, 258
City of Sunnyvale, California, 32, 33
Clawback, 263
Collaborations, 274–275, 279, 280
Collateralized debt obligations (CDOs), 235, 248
Commercial paper, 238, 249
Commission on Philanthropy, 279
Commission on Private Philanthropy and Public Needs, 7
Committee of Sponsoring Organizations of the Treadway Commission (COSO), 254
Commonfund, 244
Community Catalyst Fund, 274
Community development financial institutions (CDFIs), 278
Community Foundation for Southern Arizona, 274
Community foundations, 164, 281
Community Reinvestment Act, 285
ConocoPhillips, 273
Conservative principle, 139
Consistency constraint, 98, 99
Contributions
  bequests and, 8, 9
  corporate giving, 164
  individual, 104
  private foundation, 4
  strategic alliances and, 164–165
Cost accounting, 76, 78, 81, 85, 86
Cost principle, 98
Cost-benefit analysis (CBA)
  benefit-cost ratio (BCR) and, 207
  conceptual framework of, 204–205

decision making in, 195, 202
discount rates, 207
ex ante analysis, 205
ex post analysis, 205
internal rate of return (IRR) and, 207
material program impacts, identification/assessment of, 206
net present value and, 202–204
sensitivity analysis, performance of, 208
standing, determination of, 205–206
See also Costs; Time value of money (TVM)
Costing services, 78–81
Costs
  accounting, 85–86
  administrative, 80
  allocating, 78–81
  average, 83–84
  base/criterion, 78, 87
  basic categories of, 78
  common, 77
  cost management and, 81
  cost objective/object, 76, 86
  direct, 76–78
  direct method of allocation and, 78–79
  economic decision making and, 85
  estimation of, 77–78
  fixed, 81–82
  full, 76
  fundraising, 80–81
  indirect, 76–78
  joint, 78
  marginal, 83–84
  opportunity, 85
  pool, 76–77
  program, 86
  step, 81–82
  variable, 81–82
Council on Foundations, 4, 5
Coupon rate, 221

Covid-19 pandemic, 7, 15, 16, 86, 90, 163, 166, 173, 221, 237, 242, 248, 263, 270, 271–272
Credit default swap (CDS), 235
Currency, stable, 98
Current liabilities, 119, 123–124
Cutback budgeting
  equity vs. efficiency considerations and, 46
  governing cutbacks, strategies for, 46

Dartmouth College Board of Trustees, 5
Debt financing strategies
  bank loans and, 220–223
  bond issuance and, 221–223
  capital budgeting policy/debt policy and, 226–228
  collateralized debt obligations and, 248
  pay-as-you-go financing, 219–220
Debt policy, 226–228
Debt securities. *See* Bonds
Dees, J. G., 281
Denver Office of Strategic Partnerships, 280
Department of Economic Initiatives, 280
Department of Family and Children Services (DFCS), 187
Depreciation, straight-line, 122
Derivatives, 70, 245, 248, 312, 313
Development director, 31, 38
Direct costs, 76–78
Direct financing sources, 221
Disclosure, 97, 99, 109, 110
Discount incentives, 70
Discount rates, 207, 208
Diversification
  contributions ratio and, 149
  current size ratio and, 148

program services expense ratio and, 150
ratio analysis of, 140
risk management and, 171
Donations. *See* Contributions
Donors
　charitable donations, tax implications of, 6, 163
　contributions/gifts, 126
　pledges and, 127
　venture philanthropy and, 277–278
　voluntary giving, third sector and, 7
　watchdog organizations, nonprofit evaluations and, 13–15
Dorothy A. Johnson Center for Philanthropy and Nonprofit Leadership, 275
Double-entry bookkeeping, 104–105, 132
Dropout Prevention Initiative, 280

Echoing Green, 277
Economic crisis
　collaboration among nonprofits and, 270
　cost-cutting measures and, 273–274
　creative capitalism and, 282–283
　cutback budgeting and, 46–47
　effects of, 270–271
　financial risks, assessment of, 272
　fundraising, expansion of, 277
　mergers, cost-effectiveness and, 275
　outsourcing services and, 273–274
　pooling of resources and, 273
　revenue-increasing strategies and, 271
　risk mitigation strategies and, 273

Edward M. Kennedy Serve America Act, 279
Effectiveness
　external monitoring and, 14, 15
　government interest in, 34
　performance reports and, 42–43
　performance-based budgeting and, 34
　watchdog organizations and, 13–15
Efficiency
　asset management ratios and, 143–144
　asset turnover ratio and, 144
　cutback budgeting and, 46–47
　days receivable ratio and, 144–146
　nonprofit accountability, watchdog organizations and, 151
　ratio analysis of, 140–141
　unit costs, efficiency measures and, 32
EMBRACE, 187, 188
Encumbrances, 22
Endowment(s),
　quasi-endowments, 239
　term, 104, 239
　true, 239
Endowment fund
　active vs. passive management of, 246
　alpha factor and, 246
　alternative securities and, 248
　creation of, 239
　investment manager, selection of, 246
　investment policy and, 242
　low risk/low returns and, 242
　management, spending policy and, 239–241
　percentage of average asset approach and, 240
　policy portfolios and, 246

principal, erosion of, 240
real total returns and, 242, 248
risk management and, 171
total returns and, 241
Enron Corporation, 100, 261
e-Postcard, 7
Equal Exchange, 282
Equities, 236, 242, 244, 245, 312, 313
Ever Green Recycling, 276
Ex ante analysis, 205
Ex post analysis, 205
Executive director
　audit committee and, 23
　board, conflict with, 10
　cash-flow management reports and, 42
　cash-flow projection, creation of, 42
　day-to-day management duties and, 24
　finance committee membership of, 23
　performance reports and, 42–43
　strategic planning and, 43
　variance reports and, 40
Expense budget
　prepaid expenses and, 121
　proposed budgets and, 22, 36–39
　See also Budgeting; Budgets
Expenses
　disclosure principle and, 99
　in-kind services and, 29–30
　nonpersonnel services and, 29
　personnel services and, 29
　prepaid, 121
　reporting of, 98
　travel, 31
　variance reports and, 40

Fair market value, 98
Family Housing Fund, 284
Fannie Mae, 238
Federal Deposit Insurance Corporation (FDIC), 236
Federal Reserve System, 238

Index

Fees, 8, 26, 46, 126, 127, 162, 166, 167
Fidelity insurance, 256
Fiduciary, 72, 209, 232
Fiduciary responsibilities, 10, 96, 112, 114, 232, 233, 249, 258, 259, 285, 310
Filer, J. H., 7
Filer Commission, 7
Finance committee, 10, 17, 23, 38, 45, 255
Financial accounting, 14, 16, 96, 112, 118
Financial Accounting Foundation, 96
Financial Accounting Standards Board (FASB)
  accounting standards, 96, 103
  reporting requirements and, 109
Financial analysis
  efficiency and, 139
  financial resources and, 138
  overcapitalization and, 138
  profitability and, 139
  rating agencies, 151
  revenue diversification and, 140
Financial Executives International (FEI), 254
Financial statements
  annual filing of, 10
  audited, 44, 96
  certification of, 285
  connections among, 107
  foundation use of, 96
  government use of, 96
  matching principle and, 99
  reporting problems in, 102
  reporting requirements, 109–111
  transparency in, 99, 109
  uniformity of information and, 100
  users of, 100
  year-end, 42
First sector, 7
First-in/first-out (FIFO) flow assumption, 121

Fiscal year (FY), 35–36
Fitch, 235
501(c), 4, 5
501(c)3, 4, 6
Fixed-income securities, 236, 241, 242, 244
For-profit corporations
  fund accounting and, 102–103
  mergers and, 275
  public goods and, 160
  Sarbanes–Oxley Act and, 109–110, 261–262
Forensic accounting, 263
Form 990, 7, 10, 12, 14, 44, 76, 110, 111, 163, 166, 258, 260, 261, 292–303
Form 990-EZ, 111, 163
Form 990-N, 7, 110
Foster, W. L., 167
Foundation Center, 14, 164, 270, 275
Foundation for a Healthy Kentucky, 279
Foundation for the Carolinas, 274
Foundations. See Private foundations
Fourth sector, 282–283, 285, 286, 287
Fraud
  accounting practices and, 96
  examples of, 262–264
  separation of duties and, 256
  See also Audits; Internal controls
Freddie Mac, 238
Fund accounting
  accounting standards and, 103
  multiservice nonprofits and, 140
  restricted net assets and, 103–104
  unrestricted net assets and, 103
Fund balance, 118, 124–125
Fundraising, 80, 133, 273

Funds
  board-designated, 103
  fixed asset, 103, 121, 122
  hedge, 70, 244
  money market mutual, 238–239
  municipal, 222–223
  nonprofit loan, 277, 278
  pension, 239, 248, 285
  rainy-day, 28, 40, 45, 63, 233, 234
  restricted, 9
  underwater, 241
  unrestricted, 9
Future value
  compound interest rate method, 195
  simple interest rate method, 195
Futures, 248, 312

Gates, B., 282
Generally accepted accounting principles (GAAP), 44, 97, 109, 286. See also Accounting principles
Going concern, 98, 108, 139, 146, 236
Goodwill Industries, 265, 271, 286
Government Accountability Office (GAO), 207
Government Accounting Standards Board, 97
Governor's Office of Faith-Based and Community Initiatives, 280
Grameen Bank, 276, 283
Grameen Danone Foods, 282
Grants
  corporate, 164
  foundation, 28, 34, 44, 110
  government, 28, 166
Great Depression, 6, 49, 245
Great Society period, 166
Greater Boston Food Bank, 170
Greyston Bakery, 282
Group benefits, 161, 169, 170, 171

GuideStar, 14, 27, 58, 259, 275

Harvard College v. Amory (1830), 6
Harvard Financial Management Fund, 248
Head Start program, 181, 182
Heartfelt connectors, 167, 168
Hedging, 235, 236
HELP USA, 169
HighScope Perry Preschool Project, 181, 182

Income statement, 106, 125–126, 306
Independent Sector, 12, 258, 260, 261, 264
Industrial Revolution, 166
Inflation, 69, 121, 147, 150, 194, 240, 242, 244
In-kind services, 28, 29–30, 104
Innovation promotion
　federal government role in, 279
　local government role in, 280
　state government role in, 279–280
　university involvement in, 281
Inputs, 32, 179, 180, 206
Insider transactions, 110
Institute for Social Innovation, 281
Institute of Internal Auditors (IIA), 254
Interest rates
　calculation of, 71
　compound, 195
　coupon rate and, 221
　diminishing earning power and, 242
　discount rate and, 207–208
　interest hedging, 235
　simple, 195
　tax-exempt bonds and, 223, 238
　trade discount incentives and, 70–71

Interest swaps, 235
Interface, Inc., 282
Intergenerational equity, 139, 150
Internal controls
　accountability, 258–260
　audit standards, 257–258
　cash/cash equivalents, 255
　code of ethics, 258–259
　components of, 254
　definition of, 254
　embezzlement, 256, 262
　fidelity insurance, 256
　fraud, 262–264
　payroll, 257
　personnel/nonpersonnel services, 256–257
　record keeping, 255
　safeguarding assets and, 255
　Sarbanes–Oxley Act, 261–262
　separation of duties and, 256
　system of, 254–258
　transparency, 258
Internal rate of return (IRR), 207
Internal Revenue Service (IRS)
　audits and, 4
　charitable donations and, 163
　Form 990 and, 10, 12, 76, 110, 111, 259, 291–303
　income tax, imposition of, 6–7
　nonprofit corporation, designation of, 4
　reporting requirements and, 110–111
　tax-exempt status and, 9
Inventories, 121
Investment strategies
　active vs. passive style, 246
　agency securities, 238
　alternative investments, 242, 244, 248
　asset allocation, 232, 233, 242, 244

　bank offerings, 236–237
　board of directors, responsibilities of, 232–233
　cash-flow forecasting system and, 234
　certificates of deposit (CDs), 236
　commercial paper, 238
　default risk, 234–235
　endowment investment, 239–245
　equities and, 236, 242, 244, 245
　fixed-income securities and, 236, 242, 244
　growth vs. value style, 246
　inflation and, 240, 242
　interest risk, 235
　liquidity, 234
　long-term, 239–249
　long-term investment vehicles and, 247–249
　management objectives and, 232, 239–240
　policies and guidelines, 232–233
　policy statement, 233
　repurchase agreements/repos, 238
　risk level, 233
　safety and, 234
　short-term, 236–239
　short-term investment vehicles and, 233–239
　spending policy and, 239–241
　style neutral strategy and, 246
　total returns, 240
　U.S. Treasury securities, 237
　yield, 234
　See also Modern portfolio theory (MPT)
Investments
　capital gains/losses, reporting of, 104
　fair market value and, 98
　gains as unrestricted income, 123

Index **329**

Index

premature liquidation of, 235
program-related, 283–286
regulation of, 233
Iowa Student Loan Liquidity Corporation, 170

JCPenney Afterschool Fund, 273
Jobs for the Future, 279
John D. and Catherine T. MacArthur Foundation, 284
Justification, 13, 14, 214

Kaplan, R. S., 184
Kim, P., 167
Kimberly-Clark Foundation, 273

Laddering, 235
Landrieu, M., 280
Lang, R., 284
Last-in/first-out (LIFO) flow assumption, 121
Level debt payments, 223–226
Level principal payments, 224–226
Leverage, 138, 142, 143
Levine, C. H., 46
Liabilities
  accounts payable, 123
  accrued salary expenses, 123–124
  bonds/notes payable, 124
  current, 123–124
  debits/credits and, 124
  deferred revenue, 124
  long-term, 124
  mortgage loans, 124
  mortgage payable, 124
Life-cycle costing (LCC), 216–219
Lilly Endowment, 183
Liquidity
  cash conversion cycle and, 59
  current ratio and, 141–142
  financial analysis and, 138
  investment strategy and, 233–234
  management and actual cash flow, 59
  reserve/cash balance and, 59
  restricted funds and, 59
  short-term investments and, 58
  targets, 59
  working capital ratio and, 142
  See also Cash flow; Cash-flow management
Lobbying activities, 4, 10
Local nationalizers, 167–168, 170–171
Lodestar Center for Philanthropy and Nonprofit Innovation (Arizona State University), 274
Lodestar Foundation, 274
Los Angeles Office of Strategic Partnerships, 280
Louisiana Office of Social Entrepreneurship, 280
Low-profit limited liability (L3C) company, 284

Madoff, B., 100, 232
Managerial accounting, 12, 96
Marginal analysis, 84, 87
Marginal cost, 83–84
Market failure, 160
Market makers, 167, 170
Market risk
  evaluation of, 234–235
  hedging and, 235–236
  laddering and, 235
  prudent man rule and, 6
  systematic risks and, 245
Marketable securities, 120
Marshall, J., 5, 6
Mary Elizabeth & Gordon B. Mannweiler Foundation, 284
Massachusetts Executive Office of Education, 280
Matching principle, 99, 139
Materiality constraint, 98, 99
McKnight Foundation, 284
Member motivators, 167, 169

Metis Associates, 187, 188
Microsoft, 273
Minnesota Diversified Industries (MDI), 276
Mission
  financial policies and, 11–12
  sustainability interests and, 13
Modern portfolio theory (MPT)
  diverse investment vehicles, reduced risk and, 244
  maximized returns/minimized risk and, 245
  nonsystematic risk and, 245
  risk aversion vs. risk management and, 245
  systematic risk and, 245
Modified accrual accounting method, 102
Monetary unit, 98
Money market mutual funds, 238, 249
Moody's, 235, 312
Morgan Stanley, 273
Mortgage-backed securities, 248

NAACP, 25
National Audubon Society, 25
National Center for Charitable Statistics (NCCS), 7
National Conference of Commissioners on Uniform State Laws, 6
National Council of Nonprofits, 24
National Wild Turkey Federation, 169
Net assets
  balance sheet and, 118–119
  debits/credits and, 105
  restricted, 103–104
  statements of financial position and, 107
  unrestricted, 103
Net present value (NPV), 194, 202–203

New Profit, 276, 277, 279, 280
New Urban Mechanics, 280
Noncharitable nonprofits, 5
Nonpersonnel services (NPS), 28, 29, 256–257
Nonprofit Coordinating Committee (NPCC) of New York, 274
Nonprofit corporations
 accountability, 151
 definition of, 3
 differences between business and, 10–11
 economic crisis/government cutbacks and, 270
 financial policies of, 11–12
 financial statements, 12
 mission and money link, 12–13
 modern nonprofit structure, 5–6
 multiservice, 140
 origins/growth of, 5–7
 public charities and, 4–5
 Revenue Act of 1950, 6
 structure of, 5–6
 Tax Reform Act of 1969, 7, 281, 284
 tax status of, 9–10
 as the third sector, 6–7
Nonprofit Finance Fund (NFF), 271, 278
Nonprofit Integrity Act of 2004 (California), 110
Nonprofit Sector and Philanthropy Program, 284
NonProfit Times, 271
Norton, D. P., 184
Notes payable, 124

Obama, B. H., 279
Objectivity constraint, 99
Office of Management and Budget (OMB), 207, 258
Office of Social Innovation and Civic Participation, 279
Ohio Social Entrepreneurship Initiative, 280

Operating budget
 accrual basis of, 65
 capital budgets and, 22, 28, 30, 65, 214–215
 cash-flow budgeting, practice of, 60–61
 operating cash flows, 60–61
 unrestricted fund and, 215–216
 working capital reserves and, 65
 See also Cash-flow management
Operating reserves, 65, 226, 233, 234, 239
Options, 248, 312
Outcomes, 180, 181, 185
Output, 32, 179, 180, 181, 183
Owens, M., 284
Oxfam, 282, 283

Pacioli, L., 104
Patrick, D., 280
Payables. *See* Current liabilities
Pay-as-you-go financing, 215, 219–220
Performance measurement
 application of, 182
 budgets and, 179
 components of, 179–182
 data collection, 186–188
 development of, 182–186
 efficiency, 180
 efficiency compared to effectiveness, 181
 inputs and, 179
 measures/indicators, selecting, 185–186
 mission success and, 178
 outcomes compared to outputs, 181
 outcomes/effectiveness, 179–180
 process and, 179
 purpose of, 178–179
 relationship between program evaluation and, 186–187

return on investment (ROI) model and, 187–188
 Urban Institute and, 183–184
Performance reporting, 42–43
Personnel services (PS), 28–29
Petty cash, 255
Pledges, 121, 127
Policy innovators, 169–170
Ponzi schemes, 232, 263
Portfolios. *See* Modern portfolio theory (MPT)
Preferred stocks, 248
Present value, 194, 197–204
Preservation Compact Loan Facility, 284
Principles for Good Governance and Ethical Practice Resource Center, 12, 258
Private foundations
 contributions from, 4–5
 direct investment in nonprofits and, 283–284
 Tax Reform Act and, 7
Private goods, 167
Proctor, A. J., 13, 59
Profit margin ratio, 146
Profitability, ratios and, 146–147
Program centers, 78, 79, 80
Program evaluation, 186–188. *See also* Performance measurement
Program services expense ratio, 150
Program-related investments (PRIs), L3C model and, 283–286
Progressive Era, 30
Property and equipment, 106, 121, 122
Proposal writing. *See* Grant writing
Prudence, 98, 99–100
Prudent investor rule, 6, 10
Prudent man rule, 6
Public benefits, 161, 162, 168, 171

Index

Public charities
  donations to, 166
  earned revenues and, 162
  municipal bonds, issuance of, 222
  Revenue Act and, 281
  state interference with, 5–6
  Tax Reform Act and, 6–7, 281
  types of, 4–5
Public goods, 160, 166
Public Law 110-199, 189
Public providers, 167, 169
Putnam, S., 6

Quick ratio, 141, 142

Rainy-day funds, 28, 40, 45, 63, 233, 234
Rating agencies, 96, 151, 235
Ratio analysis, conducting, 140–147
Ratios
  asset management, 143–144
  asset turnover, 144
  benefit-cost ratio (BCR), 207
  common size, 148–149
  contributions, 149
  current, 141–142
  days receivable, 144
  debt-to-asset, 143
  debt-to-equity, 143
  efficiency, 143–146
  leverage, 143
  liquidity and, 138
  matching principle and, 139
  profitability, 139
  rating agencies and, 151
  revenue diversification and, 140
  solvency, 142–143
  working capital, 151
Real estate, 70, 98, 151, 245
Real total returns, 242, 248
Receivables, 65, 68, 120, 121, 139, 148
Recession, 16, 23, 24, 46, 50, 138, 149, 236, 248, 270
Red flags, 138, 159
Religious organizations, 5, 163, 165
Reporting requirements
  consolidated financial statements and, 109
  disclosure principle and, 109, 110
  FASB and, 109, 110
  Form 990 and, 111
  national-level requirements, 109–111
  Sarbanes–Oxley Act and, 109–110
  state-level requirements, 111
  transparency and, 109
Repurchase agreements/repos, 238
Request for proposal (RFP), 63
Rescue Loan and Prevention Program, 284
Resource recyclers, 167, 170
Return on investment (ROI), 187, 208
Revenue
  collection of, 11
  contracts, 28, 126
  cutback budgeting and, 46–47
  direct, 171
  earned, 166–167
  endowment draw and, 126
  existing sources of, 162–167
  fees and, 127
  general support, 103
  in-kind services and, 29–30
  operating budgets and, 28–29
  pledges and, 127
  private foundation contributions and, 281–282
  proposed budgets and, 22
  receivables and, 120
  resources, 8
  surplus/deficit and, 28
  variable, 81
  variance reports and, 40
Revenue Act of 1913, 281
Revenue Act of 1943, 281
Revenue Act of 1950, 5
Revenue strategies
  diversification, risk management and, 171
  funding models and, 167–171
  funding sources, advantages/disadvantages, 171–173
Riegle Community Development and Regulatory Improvement Act, 278
Risk
  aversion vs. management, 171
  default, 234–236
  diverse investment vehicles and, 244
  firm, 272
  interest, 235
  low risk/low returns and, 242
  market, 272
  mitigation strategies, 273
  nonsystematic, 245
  revenue diversification and, 140
  sector, 272
  systematic, 245
Robert Wood Johnson Foundation, 183
Robin Hood Foundation, 278
Rockefeller, J. D., III, 7
Root Cause, 278, 280

Safe havens, 242, 248
Salaries payable, 123, 124
Sanctions, 14
Sarbanes–Oxley Act of 2002, 109–110, 261–262
Second Chance Act of 2007, 189
Second sector, 7
Securities and Exchange Commission (SEC), 96
Securities Exchange Act of 1934, 96
Security rating agencies, 235

Index

Separation of duties, 256
Shore Bank Corporation, 284
Simulation, 208
Social enterprise
   B corporations and, 285–286
   creative capitalism and, 282
   definition of, 276
   foundation promotion of, 281–282
   fourth sector of, 282–283
   L3C model and, 283–286
Social entrepreneurs, 276–277, 280, 281
Social Financial Services for Ashoka Foundation, 284
Social Innovation Compact, 280
Social Innovation Fund, 279
Social service programs, 4
Society for the Relief of Poor Widows with Small Children, 5
Solvency
   debt-to-asset ratio and, 143
   debt-to-equity ratio and, 143
   leverage and, 138
Spending baseline, 22
Spending policy, 239–241
Standard & Poor's, 235
Stanley Medical Research Institute, 169
State governments
   audit requirements and, 44
   B corporations and, 285–286
   contract payments, delay in, 65
   cutback budgeting and, 46
   financial statements, use of, 23, 96
   Form 990 filing requirement and, 10, 110–111
   funding for nonprofits and, 166
   innovation, promotion of, 279
   nonprofit accountability and, 14
   nonprofits, regulation of, 6
   performance-based budgeting and, 32
   tax filing and, 9
Statement of activities
   chart of accounts and, 127, 128
   contributions/gifts and, 126
   expenses and, 127
   fees/business income and, 127
   fiscal year comparisons within, 120, 125
   grants/contracts and, 127
   in-kind services and, 29–30
   pledges and, 121, 127
   revenues and, 126–127
   transference of funds and, 125
Statement of financial position, 105–106. *See also* Balance sheet
Statement of functional expenses, 107–108
Statement of purpose, 9
Statute of Charitable Uses of 1602, 5
Step-down allocation method, 79
Stocks
   debt financing and, 58
   diversified holdings and, 245
   fair market value and, 98
   growth, 246
   marketable securities, 120
   preferred, 248
   prudent investor rule and, 6, 10
   See also Investment strategies; Investments
Strategic planning, 25, 36, 38, 43, 178, 181, 185, 216, 226
Success for All Foundation, 169
Sunset Park Alliance for Youth, 274
Supplies, 29, 40, 76, 86, 99, 101, 120, 121, 182, 257
Support centers, 78, 79
Susan G. Komen organization, 168

Taco Bell Foundation for Teens, 273
Tax Reform Act of 1969, 7, 281
Tax-exempt status, 9, 221
Third sector, 6–7, 16
Time value of money (TVM)
   annuities and, 195
   future monies, uncertainty and, 194
   future value and, 195–197
   inflation and, 194
   interest/interest rates and, 194
   life-cycle costing and, 216–219
   long-term financial planning and, 193, 194, 202
   net present value and, 202
   opportunity cost and, 206
   periods and, 195
   present value, 197
   See also Cost-benefit analysis (CBA)
Total returns, 240–244
Trade associations, 5
Trade benefits, 161
Trade discount incentives, 70–71
Traidcraft, 282
Transparency, 13, 14, 99, 109, 258, 260, 262
Trial balances, 105, 108, 132, 256, 306–307
Trustees
   board of, 10
   prudent investor rule and, 6, 10
   prudent man rule and, 6
Twin Trading, 282

Uniform Prudent Investor Act (UPIA), 6
Uniform Prudent Management of Institutional Funds Act, 241, 275

United Way of America, 183
United Way of Southeastern New England, 185
Unrestricted net assets
 board-designated funds, 103
 expenses, reporting of, 103
 FASB update (2016), 103
 fixed asset funds, 103
 gains on investments and, 126
 reporting requirements, 110
 See also Fund accounting
Urban Institute, performance measurement, 183–184
U.S. Constitution, Article 1, Section 10, 5

U.S. Supreme Court, 5, 6
U.S. Treasury bills, 120, 132, 236, 237, 255

Variance reports, 40, 45
Venture capitalism/philanthropy, 244, 277
Volunteer services, 127

Walmart Foundation, 273
Warranties, 248
Watchdog organizations, 13–15
Webster, D., 5
Weikart, D., 181
Whistle-blower, policies/protection, 110, 111, 258, 260, 261

Wise Giving Alliance, 14, 150, 152
W. K. Kellogg Foundation, 183
Wolk, A., 279
Wood, A., 284
Working capital
 management, 68
 reserves, 142

Yale University endowment funds, 248–249
YMCA of the USA, 8, 271, 272, 286
Young, D., 160, 272
Yunus Centre, 283